A NEW LOOK
AT THE LUTHERAN CONFESSIONS
(1529 — 1537)

A NEW LOOK
AT THE
LUTHERAN CONFESSIONS
(1529 – 1537)

By Holsten Fagerberg

Translated by Gene J. Lund

Concordia Publishing House
St. Louis

Concordia Publishing House, St. Louis, Missouri

Copyright © 1972 Concordia Publishing House
Library of Congress Catalog Card No. 71-179376
ISBN 0-570-03223-7

Aus dem schwedischen Manuskript übersetzt mit
Genehmigung des Verlages Vandenhoeck & Ruprecht,
Göttingen.

Translated from the Swedish original with the permission
of Vandenhoeck & Ruprecht, Göttingen.

5 6 7 8 9 10 11 12 13 14 WP 89 88 87 86 85 84 83 82 81 80

Contents

Abbreviations

AC — The Augsburg Confession
Ap — The Apology of the Augsburg Confession
ARG — *Archiv für Reformationsgeschichte*
AUU — *Acta universitatis Upsaliensis*
CR — *Corpus reformatorum*
CSEL — *Corpus scriptorum ecclesiasticorum latinorum*
Decr. Grat. — *Decretum Magistri Gratiani*
Denz. — H. Denzinger, *Enchiridion Symbolorum*
De sp. et litt. — St. Augustine's *De spiritu et littera*
EKL — *Evangelisches Kirchenlexikon*
Ep — The Epitome of the Formula of Concord
FC — The Formula of Concord
GF — *Glaube und Forschung*
GW — *Gesamt Wiegendrucke* (incunabula)
KuD — *Kerygma und Dogma*
LC — The Large Catechism
LW — *Luther's Works*, American Edition, St. Louis and Philadelphia
MPL — Migne's *Patrologiae cursus completus . . . series Latina*
NA — German translation of an early Latin edition of the Augsburg Confession
NKT — Ny kyrklig tidskrift
NTU — *Nordisk teologisk uppslagsbok*
RGG — *Religion in Geschichte und Gegenwart* (3d ed.)
RThom — *Revue Thomiste*
SA — The Smalcald Articles
SC — The Small Catechism
SD — The Solid Declaration of the Formula of Concord
ST — *Studia theologica*
STh — Thomas of Aquinas' *Summa theologiae*
STK — *Svensk teologisk Kvartalskrift*
SvK — *Svensk Kyrkotidning*
TB — *Traubüchlein* (The Order of Marriage)
ThLZ — *Theologische Literaturzeitung*
ThStK — *Theologische Studien und Kritiken*
Tr — Treatise on the Power and Primacy of the Pope
WA — The Weimar Edition of Luther's Works
WATi — The Weimar Edition of Luther's "Table Talk"
ZKT — *Zeitschrift für katholische Theologie*
ZRG — *Zeitschrift für Religions- und Geistesgeschichte*
ZST — *Zeitschrift für systematische Theologie*
ZTK — *Zeitschrift für Theologie und Kirche*

Introduction

The purpose of the volume is to describe the theology of the confessional statements written by Luther and Melanchthon between 1529 and 1537. Luther published both the Small and the Large Catechisms (SC and LC) in 1529; in 1537 he completed the Smalcald Articles (SA), and Melanchthon published his *De potestate et primatu papae* (Tr) in the same year. The Augsburg Confession, which became the basic confessional statement of the Lutheran Church, appeared in 1530, while the Apology (Ap) was published one year later. Both of these documents originated with Melanchthon, but he used publications prepared by Luther, and he was in constant contact with Luther while writing the Augsburg Confession.[1] Ap, originally a private document, was officially recognized at Smalcald in 1537, and Luther privately endorsed it as well.[2] All of these documents appeared in both German and Latin. The translations were done as a rule by someone other than the author, and in many cases this work was done so freely that they ought to be looked upon as paraphrases rather than translations. Behind AC, Ap, SA, and Tr we find either the representatives of public life or private theologians. The confessional writings appeared therefore as the work of many hands, and with the claim to be the expression of the original common Lutheran point of view.

If it is asked whether or not all of these documents can be harmonized, only the following presentation can supply the answer. As contemporary Luther research has shown, Luther and Melanchthon had their differences. But the external harmony provided by the appearance of the oldest confessional statements is sufficient justification for treating them as a unit. The Formula of Concord (FC), which was published nearly a half century after AC, reflects its own problems

---

[1] W. E. Nagel (1930), p. 172: Von einem direkten Anteil Luthers am fertigen Bekenntnis kann man in keiner Weise reden. Indirekt steht aber das Bekenntnis unter seinem stärksten Einfluss, so dass man ihm einen umfassenden geistigen, inhaltlichen Anteil zusprechen muss. — A more restrictive judgment can be found in H. Pleijel (1941), pp. 23—46.

[2] WA 50, 470:17: Und wundert mich seer, wie man doch kan mir zu messen, das ich das gesetze oder zehen gebot solte verwerffen, so doch alda vorhanden so viel, und nicht einerley, meiner auslegung der zehen geboten, die man auch teglich predigt und ubet inn unsern Kirchen, ich schweige der Confession und Apologia und andern unsern bucher, dazu auch zeyerley weise gesungen werden . . . (*Wider die Antinomer*, 1539).

and demands separate consideration. Hence it is that this volume will
be limited to those writings which appeared between 1529 and 1537
and which gradually received the rank and dignity of official ecclesiastical documents.

The theology of the Lutheran Confessions has been the object of
intense study.[3] The fact that this stream of literature never dries up
is a sign reflecting not only upon the perpetual pertinence of these
writings, but also upon the urgency of the problems they discuss. One
remembers, for example, the extensive theological discussion concerning the doctrine of justification in Ap which was elicited by F. Loof's
article in ThStK (1884), or the discussion which is still in progress
concerning the Confessions' view of Scripture, the Law, the church,
and the ministry.

In the oldest presentations of the theology of the Confessions,
scholars undertook an analysis of each separate document, going
through them article by article. A good example of this method can be
found in J. B. Carpzov's *Isagoge in libros ecclesiarum lutheranum
symbolicos* (1665, 1675). In this work Carpzov, known as "the father
of symbolics," went through the three ancient creeds, AC and Ap,
SA, SC and LC, and finally the entire FC in a rigidly schematic
manner. With the development of the scholastic conceptual apparatus,
the presentations continued to appear in perpetual confrontation with
the Tridentine decrees and other Roman Catholic theology. The
method of treating each document individually continued on into the
19th century,[4] but an interesting alteration can be observed. Under
the influence of romanticism and Hegel, scholars began to discern
certain internal relationships which were developed within the various
confessional statements. An idea merely hinted at in AC was thought
to have reached its ultimate development in the FC.[5] G. J. Planck
marked a turning point with his *Abriss einer historischen und vergleichenden Darstellung der dogmatischen Systeme unserer verschiedenen*

[3] An extensive listing of the literature produced during the first century of the
Reformation can be found in J. G. Feuerlin, *Bibliotheca symbolica evangelica lutherana*, J. B. Riederer, ed. (1768), pp. 17 ff. A pertinent survey of the literature
is included in *Die Bekenntnisschriften der evangelisch-lutherischen Kirche* (1959),
pp. XX f., and in E. Schlink (1961), pp. 318 ff. — Reference is also made below
to other works which I consulted. Certain of the older works are listed by way
of illustrating an approach to the theology of the Confessions. But the listing is
by no means complete.

[4] E. g., E. Köllner, *Symbolik aller christlichen Konfessionen*, I (1837).

[5] See, e. g., G. Billing (1878), pp. 111 ff., 197, 214, 235, 274, etc. Billing
was greatly dependent upon such German confessional theologians as A. Vilmar,
F. J. Stahl, and the Erlangen theologians A. Harless and G. Thomasius.

christlichen Hauptparteien nach ihren Grundbegriffen, ihren daraus abgeleiteten Unterscheidungslehren und praktischen Folgen (1796, 3d ed. 1822). This book merely marks a beginning, to be sure, but it is important inasmuch as it sets forth a holistic point of view. Dogmas form a system, and the religious community is understood on the basis of the fundamental concepts or principles which form the framework of the system. Preceded by Ph. Marheinecke [6] and G. B. Winer, [7] J. A. Möhler took up the thread in his influential work *Symbolik oder Darstellung der dogmatischen Gegensatze der Katoliken und Protestanten* (1832; critical edition, 1958—61). [8] This is a methodical presentation, resulting from the fact that the author based it upon "the official Confessions of the respective churches" (p. 6), in reality upon the entire Book of Concord (pp. 18—22). M. Schneckenburger followed in Möhler's footsteps, but with an entirely different purpose in mind. As one can tell from the title of his book, *Vergleichende Darstellung des lutherischen und reformirten Lehrbegriffs,* I and II (1855), Schneckenburger dealt with an intramural Protestant problem, intending to facilitate a harmony of the Confessions (pp. 5 and 16). In his systematic presentation, however, he did not limit himself to the official documents. He made reference to later orthodox material as well.

Foremost among the books in this area written in the 20th century is Edmund Schlink's *Theologie der Lutherischen Bekenntnisschriften* (1940, 3d ed. 1948; trans. Paul F. Koehneke and Herbert J. A. Bouman, *Theology of the Lutheran Confessions,* 1961), well known for demanding a more precise presentation. This volume is without polemics, purely systematic in character, and it treats the Book of Concord as a unit. This does not mean that Schlink fails to recognize the tensions included therein. The last systematic contribution here was made by F. Brunstäd, *Theologie der lutherischen Bekenntnisschriften* (1951), which unquestionably conceives of the entire Book of Concord "as a unity of one and the same doctrine." (P. 16)

The present volume is also intended to provide a summary of the theology of the Lutheran Confessions, but it differs from the Schlink and Brunstäd presentations on three essential points.

First of all — as already noted — the material is limited to the early

---

[6] Ph. Marheinecke, *Christliche Symbolik oder historischkritische und dogmatischkomparative Darstellung des katholischen, lutherischen, reformierten und socinianischen Lehrbegriffs,* I—III (1810—13, 1897). This ambitious project did not get beyond a description of the Catholic position.

[7] G. B. Winer, *Comparative Darstellung des Lehrbegriffs der verschiedenen christlichen Kirchenparteien* (1824, 1882).

[8] Chief among the many books written in opposition to Möhler's work is the

documents written by Luther and Melanchthon. This decision was made in the interest of throwing the light of a systematic approach upon Reformation theology as it appeared during the era of consolidation in the 1530s. However different these documents may be internally, they have this in common, that they were written either in controversy with contemporary theology within the Catholic Church and on the left wing of the Reformation, or with the intention of strengthening the life of their own congregations. They appeared within a limited period of time, written by men who were personally near to one another, and they claimed to represent the church and not merely private theologians.[9] Inasmuch as they bear the stamp of their authors, factual differences must be noted, but above all their common ideas must be recognized. Apart from these, the Lutheran Church could not have come into being.

In the second place, our presentation has a more distinctive historical orientation than the two which preceded it. AC, Ap, SA, and Tr appeared in controversy with advanced Catholic theology. Between the appearance of AC and Ap came the Catholic Confutation, *Confutatio Augustanae Confessionis,* and certain of Ap's assertions are hard to understand if not actually unintelligible apart from Roman Catholic polemics. Moreover, the Lutheran Confessions frequently argue on the basis of quotations derived from the early church fathers, and many technical terms are used whose meanings are now difficult to comprehend. Thanks to the extremely helpful tool we possess in the critical edition of *Die Bekenntnisschriften der evangelisch-lutherischen Kirche* (1930, 5th ed. 1963), it is possible for us to conceive of the Confessions' historical background. It seemed to be natural and necessary to observe the historical context to the extent that this can contribute to our understanding of their theology.

Finally, an extensive corpus of scholarly literature has developed in the field of Reformation theology. Most of this deals with the individual reformers, but some of it also touches upon the Confessions. To be in a position to write about the material satisfactorily, it seemed necessary to take this previous scholarly literature into consideration. A continuing discussion with material already published will therefore be carried on in this work.

one by K. Hase, *Handbuch der protestantischen Polemik gegen die römisch-katholische Kirche* (1862, 1878).

[9] Both E. Schlink (1961), pp. xvi ff., and F. Brunstäd (1951), pp. 13 f., point out the difference between the writings of individual theologians and those of the church.

The Confessions often claim to represent a Biblical theology in harmony with the earliest church fathers. Characteristic of their point of view is the more definite distinction between Law and Gospel. Our first three chapters seek to clarify their attitude toward the Scriptures and tradition, as well as to determine what the frequently used but often unclear expressions "Law" and "Gospel" really mean. The goal here is to establish, if possible, the content of these concepts, in order thereby to lay the foundation for our analysis of the theology of the Lutheran fathers. Our approach does not claim, any more than do the Confessions themselves, to be an epitome of dogmatics and ethics, but it does raise questions of significance to their theology. Chapter Four discusses the doctrine of the Trinity, which was of great importance to Reformation theology, Chapter Five, anthropology, and Chapter Six, justification. The next three chapters, which all relate to the very heart of Reformation theology, the proclamation of salvation by faith, deal with the sacraments, penitence, and the ministry. The consequences of justification for the church are set forth in Chapter Ten, and for the Christian life in Chapter Eleven. The final chapter provides an eschatological vision and summarizes the foregoing presentation.

Chapter One:

The Basis of the Confessions

1. The Bible

The Confessions of the Reformation rest upon a Biblical foundation. They claim to be derived from the Bible, and they want to be built upon it. In the introduction of AC it is said that the Reformation faith is maintained "on the basis of the Holy Scriptures and God's pure Word" (Introduction 8), and in the conclusion its signers declare themselves prepared, if necessary, to speak more precisely on Scriptural ground (Conclusion 7). This more detailed expression is provided in Ap, which also claims to be based on the Scriptures.[1] In the course of his presentation in Ap Melanchthon·makes detailed references to the Bible, and he justifies his most important doctrinal assertions by careful exegetical analyses, in perpetual discussion with his theological opponents. When the Confessions were written, the authority of the Bible was not a problem; its authority was recognized on both sides of the confessional line of demarcation. Since the entire Bible is God's Word, an argument can be based on an Old Testament text as well as on one in the New. Even the apocryphal books of the Old Testament, as found in the Vulgate, came into play.

What has been said here about AC and Ap holds true for the rest of the Confessions as well. The catechisms are based on the Bible, summarizing its content, and the purpose of catechism instruction is to lead those who study it deeper into the Scriptures (LC New Introduction 18). In SA Luther quotes the Bible against all other authorities, such as the popes and the church fathers. God's Word alone can serve as the basis for articles of faith; the opinions of a church father, however well known, do not suffice.[2] If a doctrine is to secure a foothold in the church, it must be firmly grounded in the Scriptures.[3] When FC, 50 years after AC, asserted that the Old and New Testaments form the one true source and norm by which all teachings and teachers are to be tested,[4] it was not saying anything new. By that time the Council

[1] Ap Introduction 9 and Conclusion 27.

[2] 421:23 ff. (SA II II 15). Luther here reflects Gal. 1:18.

[3] Cf. 435:7 (SA III I 10).

[4] 834:16-22 (SD Von dem summ. Begr. 3).

of Trent had already formulated its principle of authority: the truth received from the apostles, as preserved in the Scriptures and in the unbroken oral tradition within the church.[5] In that situation the Evangelicals made more precise their concept of the Scriptures as the highest authority, which they derived from the reformers. It is possible that they did this also for the purpose of repulsing long-standing traditionalist tendencies within their own groups.[6] But they never questioned the Scripture principle. If the Bible had not been the self-evident point of departure, the reformers would not have taken such pains to uphold their position on the basis of Scripture, where they sought support for all articles of significance. Firm adherence to the teaching of the apostles was a concern of the first rank to all the reformers. The most decisive thing that could be said in opposition to a doctrinal interpretation was that it was set forth *sine auctoritate Scripturae* (Ap XII 119). Men were told not to obey bishops who taught something at variance with the Scriptures, and Melanchthon maintains that this principle held true even in the practice of the early church. (AC XXVIII 28)

In order to see the central position of the entire Bible even more clearly, it is necessary to investigate in more detail the manner in which the authority of Scripture was applied. The Confessions do not provide us with an analysis of this, but on numerous occasions they employ other expressions for the authority on which their doctrines were based. Do these expressions tell us anything about the place of the Scriptures in Reformation theology?

One of the most common expressions used side by side with "the Holy Scriptures" is "God's Word." The Confessions use the concept "God's Word" to refer either to the Bible [7] or to a certain word in the Holy Scriptures.[8] Even the Apostles' Creed, as a summary of the Bible, is conceived of and referred to as God's Word (LC I 89). God's Word can denote the words of absolution in confession (LC Confession 22), it can have the impact of a word of promise (Ap XXI 17), or of a

---

[5] Denz.,783. J. R. Geiselmann in H. Bracht, *Die mündliche Überlieferung* (1957), pp. 123—206. Ibid. (1962), pp. 91—165.

[6] See H. Pleijel (1936), pp. 192 ff., and R. Josefson (1953), pp. 10 f.

[7] 333:38 — causas nostrae sententiae sumptas ex verbo Dei, and 334:8 — from the Holy Scripture (Ap XXIII 4); 643:39 — dass man sein Wort nicht verachte, sondern lerne, gerne höre, heilig halte und ehre (LC I Conclusion 326); 277:48 — detorquentes verbum Dei (Ap XII 123).

[8] 692:18 f. — Here the Word points to the words of institution for Baptism in Matt. 28:19 and Mark 16:16 (LC IV 7); 320:7 — verbum Dei, ex quo certo sciamus (Ap XXI 17).

command.[9] It can be used as a synonym for the Gospel.[10] "God's Word" is very commonly used to denote the oral Word or sermon,[11] but in such cases the reference is not so much to what the Word is in itself as it is to its function; for one must be able to distinguish, in connection with the oral Word, the difference between God's Word and that of false preachers.[12] Regardless of how many other definitions can be and indeed have been applied to the expression "God's Word," its relationship to the Bible must be considered of fundamental significance to Reformation theology. Before we take a somewhat longer look at how the "Word" is used and how it functions in the church, we must direct our attention to its content and its relationship to the Scriptures. It goes without saying that the highly diversified use of the term "God's Word" can create complications and make it hard to state clearly what is meant in one case or another. But an attempt to be as precise as possible must be made.

As a starting point, we can refer to LC I 30 ff.,[13] where Luther comments upon Ex. 20:5 ff., which tells us how God will duly reward those who keep His commandments, and punish unto the fourth generation those who do not. Here, clearly, Luther finds a word of God, including both threats and promises, whose truth stands firm—even if things seem to go well for those who despise God and ill for those who fear Him. Luther obviously recognized a connection between the expression "God's Word" and Scripture. He is here referring not to the entire Bible, and even less to a distinct meaning, but to a concrete Bible word whose author is God. "God's Word" in this passage in LC signifies a distinct word out of God's mouth, contained and preserved in the Bible. Inasmuch as God does not speak falsely, His Word must be true, a fact which LC claims to find confirmed in the Bible's report concerning Saul and David, for example, as well as in our daily experience. The conclusive thing for Luther was not that the Word possessed a certain quality—e. g., that it could be described as Gospel—but that it is found to be a clear, divine statement in the Bible. When the reformers wish to know what God has said or what He wills, they refer to the Scriptures, apart from which no one can

---

[9] 694:9 — God's Word or command (LC IV 16).

[10] 714:10 — the entire Gospel or the Word of God (LC V 32).

[11] 454:20 — the Scriptures or the oral Word of the apostles (SA III VIII 4).

[12] 573:27 — wenn falsche Prediger aufstehen und ihren Lügenstand für Gottes Wort dargeben (LC I 54).

[13] 567:26 ff.

know the will of God.[14] God's Word, as preserved there, possesses an authority which, in contrast to the word of man, is free from groping uncertainty; [15] it rests upon solid ground and is true. In the church this Word is the highest authority and stands over both pastors and bishops (Tr 11). Adherence to God's Word gives life a sure sense of direction, for it frees the conscience from false ideas and heavy burdens both by what it commands and by what it gives.

The Fourth Commandment is an example of such a word. Because it expresses God's will, it is of value to those who obey it.[16] In such a context "God's Word" is identified with His will, as an expression of His command. Most decisive, however, is the fact that this Word of God is found in the Scriptures. Here you have "a sure text and a divine testimony" by which God has commanded you to live in your calling and not to abandon it for a life in the cloister.[17] Promises of grace and decrees without Biblical support cannot qualify as God's Word, but God's clear Word in the Scriptures is binding both as promise and as command. Other distinct statements in Scripture are also reckoned as God's Word, whether spoken by God to a prophet, by Jesus Himself, or by an apostle. The intimate relationship between "God's Word" and Scripture is so well certified in the Confessions that it is almost superfluous to mention it. In certain contexts in SA Luther uses the expression "God's Word" almost constantly when referring to Bible words in his polemic against abuses in the Catholic Church.[18]

God's Word and the Scriptures sometimes become virtual equivalents. The Confessions do make the distinction, however, that "Scripture" refers to the entire collection of canonical books, while "God's Word" frequently denotes a certain passage therein. The manner in which "God's Word" and the Scriptures came to be used interchangeably is illustrated in both SA and Ap. In SA Luther rejects the doctrine of purgatory because it lacks the Scriptural support without which no article of faith can be formulated.[19] In Ap, correspondingly, both

---

[14] 299:45 — Quomodo de voluntate Dei certos reddet homines, sine mandato et verbo Dei? (Ap XV 14).

[15] 550:2 (LC New Preface 11).

[16] 589:26—590:19 (LC I 114 ff.)

[17] 591:21 (LC I 120).

[18] 422:10—424:9 (SA II II 18 ff.)

[19] 420:13—421:25 (SA II II 13 ff.)

expressions, "God's Word" and "the Scriptures," are used interchangeably.[20]

The formula "God's Word" always has some connection with the
Bible, either as another expression for it or as a designation for a
certain passage therein, e. g., the words of institution for the Lord's
Supper or the admonition to repentance in Matt. 4:17.[21] In many
cases it is hard to say exactly what the expression "God's Word"
refers to, not least of all because it often points to something not
specifically included in the Bible, although closely associated with it.
When Luther speaks about "God's Word" in his explanation of the
Third Commandment, he has in mind the Ten Commandments, the
Creed, and the Lord's Prayer.[22] That the Creed is also referred to here
as "God's Word" depends, of course, on the fact that it is considered
a good summary of the content of the Scriptures.[23]

The varied use of the expression "God's Word" reveals, as in a
flash, two things. First of all, the Confessions never lend their support
to an uncritical Biblicism; that belongs to another time and another
context. Secondly, neither do they allow any emancipation from the
Bible. Whenever "God's Word" is mentioned, it stands in one relationship or another to the Bible. Apart from this relationship, one would
have to decide for oneself between what goes back to God Himself
and what originates in the mouth of man. The words of the Bible are
clear (Ap XXVII 60) and can be understood. There is no suggestion
here that these words can be interpreted in fundamentally different
ways and be given variant meanings. The fact that the words of the
Bible have been interpreted differently, both in the Reformation
period and later, is another matter, which is not discussed in the
Confessions. They look upon "God's Word" as revealed truth, found
in the Bible.[24] Inasmuch as it alone can impart true knowledge about
God's will, Scripture, individual words in the Bible, or other words
closely related thereto are called *God's* Word.

Scripture becomes the highest authority in questions concerning
faith and doctrine,[25] and the Confessions accordingly cite it as such.
Apart from the support of the Bible the reformers could never have

---

20 149:28 and 43 (Ap II 11 f.); 257:1—258:12 (Ap XII 28 ff.)
21 708:16 (LC V 3); 280:32 (Ap XII 134).
22 582:42—583:15 (LC I 89 f.); 547:37—548:12 (LC New Preface 15).
23 557:5-26 (LC Preface 15). Cf. Meyer (1929), 256 ff.
24 434:9 — der Schrift Offenbarung (SA III I 3).
25 83c:15 and 83d:1 (AC Conclusion 2); 276:41 (Ap XII 119).

fought in defense of their opinions, and accusations of subjectivism would have confronted them ceaselessly.

Also other expressions that refer to the doctrinal authority of the Lutheran Symbols can be traced back to the Scriptures as the highest authority. We have already noted that "God's Word" points toward a God who wills. The combination of "God's Word and will" [26] appears in the Confessions and casts further light upon the reformers' consistent return to the words of Scripture. Intellectual interests are not dominant here. The Confessions use the Word in such a way that men can be made certain of their salvation and their conscience given peace. A purely theoretical knowledge of God lies beyond the Confessions' sphere of interest; the reality of God is never questioned but looked upon as self-evident. Anyone at all, even the devil and the evil spirits, must believe in God's existence. But this is a dead faith, with no significance for man's salvation. Salvation involves the need to know God's will, which at bottom is a good and saving will, accessible to us in the Holy Scriptures. Apart from God's own Word one cannot say anything certain about His will. [27]

Another expression of God's active will which frequently appears in the Symbols is the Biblical term *mandatum Dei*, God's command. It is uncontestable that *mandatum* too stands in a very close relationship to the words of Holy Scripture. Melanchthon asks how anyone can be certain of God's will "without the command and Word of God," *sine mandato et verbo Dei* (Ap XV 14). Is it more than accidental that Melanchthon here brings together these three important concepts, God's Word, God's will, and God's command?

This question has become pertinent as a result of the publication of W. Maurer's book *Pfarrerrecht und Bekenntnis* (1957). Maurer too certifies the significant connection between *mandatum* and God's active, creative will. But he does not look upon *mandatum* simply as a clear New Testament command. One cannot determine what *mandatum* is simply by applying the formula which holds that such a word of command is to be found in the Scriptures, Maurer maintains, but *mandatum* must possess the quality of a word of promise and stand in an absolute relationship to justification. "The divine *mandatum* is always a word of promise." [28]

---

[26] 590:14 (LC I 116); 602:31 (LC I 164).

[27] 300:12 — so kein Mensch Gottes Willen anders erfahren oder wissen kann denn allein durch sein Wort (Ap XV 17); 212:1-2 (Ap IV 262). Ap here deviates radically from Luther's interpretation, according to A. Siirala (1956), pp. 75 ff.

[28] W. Maurer (1957), p. 97.

Does Maurer's thesis find support in the sources? The question is worth looking into. The Confessions make a clear distinction between *mandatum* and promise, *promissio*. It is of the greatest importance not to confuse these two concepts, not least of all in the interest of comprehending the Confessions' view of the sacraments. Ap XIII 3 defines a sacrament as a divine action, commanded by God, *habent mandatum Dei,* to which is added a promise of grace. According to Melanchthon, each of these criteria serves its own independent purpose. Certain Old Testament ceremonies were commanded by God too, but because they lacked the promise of grace, they cannot be called sacraments. Other sacred rites, such as confirmation and extreme unction, were not commanded by God, so neither can they be called sacraments (Ap XIII 6). For anything to qualify as promise, it must be traced back to God's will as expressed in Scripture, but promise and command are not therefore identical. Marriage is commanded by God, but because it lacks the promise of justification and grace, it is not a sacrament.[29]

The Biblical *mandatum* (Matt. 15:9; 28:20; John 13:34) can be used as a technical term in reference to the Ten Commandments, although they are usually called *praecepta Dei. Mandatum* most often designates a word in Scripture which includes a command from God. The first time the expression appears in the Confessions is in AC VI, in the form of a participle of the verb *mando:* "giving a command." Only those deeds which God has commanded are to be performed. As a noun, we find *mandatum* many times in the latter part of AC, in the so-called abuse articles. There it always appears to have a direct or an indirect connection with a specific Biblical saying. AC XXII discusses the Lord's Supper under both the bread and the wine. Reference is made to Matt. 26:27, and this passage is called "the Lord's command," *mandatum Domini.* A custom which has come into use in contradiction to God's commands, *contra mandata Dei,* cannot be accepted.[30] Clerical celibacy is thus opposed with reference to precise Bible passages (1 Cor. 7:2 and 9; Matt. 19:11; Gen. 1:27). "God's command," *mandatum,* and God's rule, *ordinatio,* cannot be

[29] See further 320:6—321:4 (Ap XXI 17 ff.), where Melanchthon clearly distinguishes between *promissio* and *mandatum.*

[30] 85:2-7 (AC XXII 1); 86:1 — consuetudo contra mandata Dei introducta non sit probanda (AC XXII 9). In setting forth this opinion Melanchthon intended to make a direct connection with canonical law, *Decr. Grat.* I, d.8, c.4. See also Maurer (1957), p. 94.

nullified by any human laws or vows.[31] Arguments in opposition to monastic vows were also based on certain Bible passages (1 Cor. 7:2; Gen. 2:18) which were understood to be clear commands from God, *mandata Dei*.[32] That which God has commanded in His Word — by which the Confessions always mean a concrete Bible passage — is opposed by what Matt. 15:9 refers to as invalid "precepts of men," *mandata hominum*.[33] In the same way AC XXVIII alludes to definite Bible passages to prove the responsibilities and duties of the church's bishops (John 20:21-23; Mark 16:15). Every time *mandatum* is used, there is a direct or indirect connection with a specific Biblical statement. Inasmuch as the Bible opposes work-righteousness, *mandatum* does also. But the promise does not cause a Bible passage to be designated as *mandatum;* it is rather the result of God's command expressed in the Bible. Therefore *mandatum* need not contain a promise; what is decisive for a *mandatum* is its direct or indirect connection with the Bible.[34]

In principle, God's commands can be divided into different categories. One such has reference to the activities which the Christian man carries on as a result of his faith. In the struggle against work-righteousness, the alternative was not between works or no works at all, but good works versus the false. Only those works which God commands in His Word can be considered, and they include the many everyday tasks implicit in the Christian calling. Community and family life are commanded by God, but not monasticism or life in the cloister.[35]

A second category of commands touches upon all that is connected with worship services and ecclesiastical usage. The confessional writers based their critique of penance and purgatory upon the commands given by Christ in the Scriptures.[36] Limiting the number of

---

[31] 87:7-23 (AC XXIII 3 ff.); 90:40 — nulla lex humana potest mandatum Dei tollere (AC XXIII 24).

[32] 113:17—114:5 (AC XXVII 18 ff.).

[33] 417:28 — Hominum vero inventiones tuto omittere possumus, ut Christus testatur Matthaei 15: Frusta colunt me mandatis hominum (SA II II 2). Matt. 15:9 is frequently cited in the Confessions.

[34] 289:34 — Those works which "are not based on the Scriptures or the Gospel" need not be carried out.

[35] 60:4 — bona opera mandata a Deo (AC VI 1); 102:9 — mandata Dei iuxta vocationem (AC XXVI 10); 310:17-36 (Ap XVI 13). Cf. 583:46—584:5 (LC I 92).

[36] 280:24—282:2 (Ap XII 133 ff.); 422:10 f. (SA II II 18); 423:4 (SA II II 21).

sacraments, demanding that the Lord's Supper be celebrated under both the bread and the wine, and criticizing certain fasts and holy days [37] are further examples of commands of this kind. The Confessions provide no detailed instructions regarding the worship service, but they do insist on the rejection of all the alien material smuggled in under the guise of work-piety but without God's command. Every form of worship that serves such piety is false, for it lacks support in the commands given by God in Scripture.[38]

This coincides with the fact that Scripture consistently rejects such piety. God exhorts us to have faith in His gracious will toward us; He commands us to believe that He, for Christ's sake, forgives us our sins.[39] In such contexts *mandatum* appears to be virtually identical with Gospel; God's command to believe in the forgiveness of sin for Christ's sake is the true meaning of the Gospel.[40]

But *mandatum* also has a third connotation, and this is of the utmost importance. God's command is the same as His gracious command; God's will is His mercy as revealed in Christ (Ap IV 345). The Gospel and *mandatum* are very closely related here. It might seem plausible to combine them and give them the same meaning. But this would be done in defiance of the Confessions' explicit statements upholding the tripartite usage of *mandatum*.

It is not hard to understand why the Symbols find it so easy to combine *mandatum* and Gospel. These writings came into being in a situation in which work-righteousness was the most serious bone of contention, the overshadowing problem. Inasmuch as this teaching openly disputes the New Testament message of salvation through faith in Christ, all of the commands based upon the Bible serve to free the conscience from human efforts and ecclesiastical decrees. In opposition to the pope's claim to be a lawgiver, the Confessions point to God's own commands, to His *mandata* in Scripture. These are known by the fact that they free the conscience; they do not enslave it.[41] Since God's will is a gracious one, there is a close connection between

---

[37] 245:50—246:1 (Ap VII 45).

[38] 377:1 — Interim omnes, qui vere credunt evangelio, debent improbare illos impios cultus excogitatos contra mandatum Dei ad obscurandam gloriam Christi et iustitiam fidei (Ap XXIV 98).

[39] 226:47 — Nam evangelium proprie hoc mandatum est, quod praecepit, ut credamus Deum nobis propitium esse propter Christum (Ap IV 345).

[40] 270:10 — Mandatum Dei esse et ipsum evangelium, ut certo statuant propter Christum gratis remitti peccata (Ap XII 88).

[41] 472:7-17 (Tr 6).

command and Gospel – but they are not identical and should therefore not be placed on an equal footing.

The problem suggested here concerning the different connotations of *mandatum* and its relationship to the Bible is also inherent in the concept "Gospel," which plays such an important role in the Confessions. This concept is frequently used to designate the Bible or God's Word. The conflict concerning the meaning of the Gospel arose early. FC attempts to settle this through an analysis of its content. "Gospel" is used in a wider and in a narrower sense – in the former case referring to Jesus' entire proclamation about penitence and the forgiveness of sin in the New Testament, in the latter case pointing only to the grace of God.[42] FC's clarification is important; we shall return to a more detailed explanation of the content of the Gospel in Chapter Three. To decide what is meant by "Gospel" in case after case, the New Testament as a whole or the message of forgiveness contained in the New Testament, can be very difficult. Nevertheless, it is completely clear that "Gospel" sometimes refers to the New Testament. In Ap Melanchthon discusses satisfaction in the sacrament of penance and rejects it since "the Gospel does not command" it. "If the Gospel commanded *(si evangelium iuberet)* . . . such works, then they would certainly be obligatory." But since in reality this is not the case, they must be rejected.[43]

The expression "according to the Gospel," *iuxta* or *secundum evangelium,* which goes back to an older linguistic usage,[44] is also clearly associated with the view of the Gospel here set forth. By referring to the Gospel, i. e., the four gospels of the New Testament, AC desires to limit the duty of bishops to the administration of the sacraments and the control of the keys which bind and loose.[45] When the Confessions employ the formulae "the Gospel teaches," *evangelium docet,* and "the Gospel requires," *evangelium tribuit*[46] – in which *evangelium* is the subject – it is also used as a substitute for the entire New Testament. The dividing line between the New Testament

[42] 952:18—954:8 (SD V 3 ff.).

[43] 289:27—290:2 (Ap XII 172 f.).

[44] In canonical law and in the Confutation "the Gospel" quite simply refers to the New Testament. *Decr. Grat.,* I, d.1; CR 27, 111 — contra evangelium; 113 — contra expressum evangelium; 162 — praeter evangelium; 176 — secundum evangelium (Confutation). W. Maurer (1957), p. 94.

[45] 121:12 (AC XXVIII 5); 400:2 and 7 (Ap XXVIII 12 f.). Cf. W. Kahl in *Festgabe für O. Gierke,* I (1910), 315.

[46] 298:17 (Ap XV 5); 489:32 (Tr 60).

and the Gospel is not always as sharp as many may be inclined to believe.[47]

It was chiefly in regard to questions of church order that the Gospel, in this sense, was cited as authority. One explanation of this can be found in the fact that the Confessions adopted a fixed linguistic pattern then in use. Another cause was that the ceremonial law of the Old Testament was abolished and therefore no longer applied to the church. In questions concerning church order, it was felt that Christians were bound to the will of Jesus or the apostles as expressed in the Gospel—i. e., in the New Testament. In the Confessions, therefore, the Gospel became a critical authority in questions of church order, used in opposition to all that disputed the New Testament and its central meaning. The *critical* function of the Gospel became predominant in this area. There is no statement in the Confessions to the effect that the Gospel has nothing to do with questions of church order. The Gospel does not provide us with instructions related to civil life, but it does contain directions concerning, e. g., the work of priest and bishop.

That the Gospel understood as New Testament Scripture has a critical function is also made clear by the expression "divine right," *ius divinum,* which is frequently used as a substitute for Gospel or *mandatum.*[48] This concept originated in canon law,[49] but the reformers gave it a new meaning. If one asks what this "new meaning" is, however, he will find that opinions have been seriously divided.[50] This, in turn, is related to the fact that the Confessions themselves do not explain what they mean by "divine right." Neither does Kahl, who has published a basic research study of *ius divinum.* Rather than attempt a summary definition, he contents himself with formulations which can give rise to different interpretations, depending on how one defines such terms as *mandatum,* God's Word, and Gospel. *Ius divinum* is the authority "which has the command of God," *quod habet mandatum Dei* (Kahl, p. 348). The authority of God's Word must stand behind the *ius divinum,* which is based directly on the

[47] See 277:22-46 (Ap XII 122).

[48] 124:1 — Secundum evangelium seu, ut loquuntur, de iure divino (AC XXVIII 21); 429:9 (SA II IV 7). W. Kahl (1910), 348 ff., has found more than 100 references to this concept in AC, Ap, and SA.

[49] *Decr. Grat.,* d.1-14; J. B. Sägmüller, I:2 (1926), 151—54 (Litt.).

[50] See W. Kahl (1910), p. 308; W. Maurer (1957), pp. 104—10; J. Heckel, Lex charitatis (1953); H. Thielicke in *Festschrift für K. D. Schmidt* (1956), pp. 162—75.

unchangeable divine will, as revealed in the Gospel. It is not a legal concept in a technical sense; in general it means the same as *ordinatio* or *mandatum Dei*.[51] In general there is no reason to object to Kahl's analysis, but it is so vague that it doesn't really explain the entire problem related to *evangelium* and *mandatum Dei*. The same confusion is to be found in Maurer. He combines *ius divinum* with the creative word of command. That which is necessary to salvation is also *iure divino*, according to his interpretation.[52] He holds that what is decisive of a "word of command" is not its agreement with Scripture but its intrinsic authority. Absolution, e. g., is *iure divino* (Ap XII 12), says Maurer, not because it is commanded and announced in Scripture but because it is an "efficacious word of grace."[53]

The Confessions often point out that inasmuch as absolution is "commanded by God," it is also *iure divino* (Ap XII 11). On the contrary, the canonical demand that all sins be enumerated in confession is not *iure divino*, i. e., it is "not commanded by God" (Ap XII 104 and 116). In Ap XI 6 f., where this trend of thought is developed further, the German text clarifies what is meant when it is said that something has not been commanded by God: it lacks support in the Holy Scriptures. Absolution, on the contrary, which is nothing other than the promise of the forgiveness of sins (Ap XII 61), is something the Confessions find throughout the Bible. Therefore it is *iure divino*. Marriage too is *iure divino*, for it is based on the clear Word of Scripture (Ap XXIII 3 and 6 ff.). But hierarchical distinctions of rank among the clergy lack such support and are therefore not divine law. On the contrary, divine law asserts that all the servants of the church are equals (Tr 10-11). The pope cannot base his claim of primacy on divine law, i. e., on God's will as confirmed in Scripture.[54]

Ius divinum as an expression of God's will as revealed in Scripture forms a critical authority in opposition to the ecclesiastical practices and dogmas introduced by the papal church without Biblical legitimation. The same type of argument can be found in Luther's thinking. In his debate with Eck at Leipzig in 1519 Luther, pressed to define what he meant by *ius divinum*, replied by referring to Scripture. A clear

---

[51] W. Kahl (1910), p. 350.

[52] W. Maurer (1957), p. 100: Heilsnotwendigkeit, d. h. für das Bekenntnis — quid sit necessarium iure divino.

[53] Maurer (1957), p. 98.

[54] 427:7 — Dass der Bapst nicht sei iure divino oder aus Gottes Wort das Haupt der ganzen Christenheit . . . (SA II IV 1); 472:30 — Ostendamus ex evangelio, quod Romanos episcopus non sit jure divino supra alios episcopos (Tr 7).

word from an apostle takes precedence over anything found in the church fathers.[55] If no properly certified new revelation has been forthcoming, one cannot oppose or go beyond Scripture, *which in the true sense of the term is ius divinum.*[56] The Confessions take the same attitude toward the question of authority; they look upon God's will as confirmed in Scripture to be *ius divinum.* As a result, the confessional writers felt that they were freed from many decrees, ordinances, and prescriptions which lacked Biblical and therefore divine support. They discerned a connection between the Bible and *ius divinum. Ius divinum* cannot be in conflict with God's will as revealed in the Bible, and it thereby became a critical authority in opposition to the dogmas set forth by the papal church without a Biblical basis.

The problem of the reformers, then, was to understand and properly explain the relationship between *ius divinum* and the words of the Bible. Although Scripture formed the basis of their pronouncements in matters relating to faith and church order, it could not be used without difficulty in other areas. Ethics, which also derived guidance from the Bible, never became a corpus of fixed rules. God's will, expressed in *mandatum* or *ius divinum,* stands in relation to the words of the Bible, but its formulations were not repeated in a literal way. Without sacrificing the continuity and consistency of God's will, the reformers left room for the uniqueness of actual situations. Their dealing with Scripture therefore gives rise to new questions concerning the use, application, and interpretation of the Bible.

2. The Function of the Bible

One need not read long in the Confessions or other Reformation literature before he discovers the important role played therein by the *oral* Word. In SA, e. g., Luther asserts in a characteristic manner that it is not God's will to speak to us men except by the oral Word and the

[55] WA 2, 278:3 — Quod si etiam Augustinus et omnes patres Petrum intellexerunt per petram, resistam eis ego unus per auctoritate apostoli, id est iure divino, qui scribit (references follow to 1 Cor. 3:11 and 1 Peter 2:4 ff.). (*Disputatio I. Eccii et M. Lutheri Lipsiae habita,* 1519).

[56] WA 2, 279:23 — Nec potest fidelis Christianus cogi ultra sacram scripturam, que est proprie ius divinum, nisi accesserit nova et probata revelatio. Luther felt that he was supported in this by Augustine and Gerson. Cf. also WA 6, 586:11—587:3 (*Von den neuen Eckischen Bullen und Lügen,* 1520); WA 8, 419: 21—420:7 (*De abroganda missa privata,* 1521), and A. Ebneter in ZKT (1962), pp. 18 ff.

sacraments.[1] The Gospel reaches us in various ways, above all in the oral Word, in which the forgiveness of sins is proclaimed.[2] According to a constant theme in LC, the Word must be set forth in preaching. No one can come to Christ and be brought into the fellowship of the church apart from the preaching of the Word.[3] What LC says here ties in with the fact that the Holy Spirit is given to us through preaching and the administration of the sacraments (AC V). "Where Christ is not preached, there is no Holy Spirit to create, call, and gather the Christian church, and outside it no one can come to the Lord Christ." (LC II 45)

There can be no doubt about the origins of this strong emphasis upon the oral Word. The Word is a means whereby God the Holy Spirit actively intervenes and works among us. When the Word of God as given in the Bible is set forth in preaching and in the administration of the sacraments, individuals and the church are born spiritually. When the Word, as Luther says in his catechism, is "in full swing," *im Schwang,*[4] it becomes living and active. (LC I 100 f.)

The confessional writers found support for this view of God's Word as a living, active power in the entire Bible. One can think first and foremost of what Paul wrote in Rom. 1:16 about the Gospel as "the power of God for salvation to every one who has faith." The Confessions combine this Bible verse with the assurance given in Is. 55:11 that God's Word "shall not return to Me empty."[5] God now works through His Word; He has no other way of coming to us. The preaching of the Word in the church is simply a continuation of the activity which has always been carried on, and of which the Bible also speaks. When Paul says in Rom. 10:17 that "faith comes from what is heard," *fides est ex auditu,* this, according to the Confessions, is another way of saying the same thing: God's Word must be preached in order to be received in faith.[6] The Word and faith are related in the most intimate manner, for faith is born of the preached Word (as just noted in Rom.

---

[1] 456:1-7 and 456:23 — quod Deus non velit nobiscum aliter agere nisi per vocale verbum et sacramenta (SA III VIII 10).

[2] 449:8 — through the oral Word (SA III 4).

[3] 654:22-42 (LC II 38); 655:11 (LC II 43 ff.); 657:33-38 (LC II 51 f.).

[4] 583:6 and 584:29 (LC I 89 and 94).

[5] 293:44—294:1 (Ap XIII 11); 586:10-22 (LC I 101).

[6] 173:24 — At cum Deo non potest agi, Deus non potest apprehendi nisi per verbum. Ideo iustificatio fit per verbum, sicut Paulus inquit: Evangelium est potentia Dei ad salutem omni credenti (Rom. 1:16). Item: Fides est ex auditu (Rom. 10:17).

10:17). In contributing to this renaissance of the spoken Word, the reformers recognized that they were sharing in an activity which had gone on uninterruptedly down through the years. "Even to Moses God wished to appear first through the burning bush and the spoken word, and no prophet, whether Elijah or Elisha, received the Spirit without the Ten Commandments.[7] John the Baptist was not conceived without the preceding word of Gabriel, nor did he leap in his mother's womb until Mary spoke." [8] This quote from SA is of great significance, inasmuch as it reveals Luther's interest in the spoken Word so clearly and shows his conviction that this Word bears the power of the Holy Spirit, or, to be more exact, that the Holy Spirit's power is activated through the Word. The Word is a Word of promise, which is valid now and is addressed to us through a personal assurance of God's grace and the forgiveness of sins. As we well know, Luther and the Confessions attached an unusual amount of importance to the oral assurance of forgiveness provided in the absolution.

With this overwhelming evidence before us, it goes without saying that Luther research has taken note of the significance of the spoken Word. Von Loewenich says that when Luther spoke of the Gospel, he had the spoken and not the written Word in mind. Von Loewenich refers to an early expression of Luther's: "I do not speak about the written but about the spoken Gospel," *non de evangelio scripto sed vocali loquor,* in which Luther alludes to Matt. 4:4 – "Man shall not live by bread alone, but by every word that proceeds from the mouth of God." [9] Those who have expounded the theology of the Lutheran Confessions can also testify to the great weight attributed to the proclaimed Word. Schlink points out that the Gospel in the Confessions "is essentially proclaimed doctrine," and that the song of praise to the Word in LC's exposition of the Third Commandment is directed not to the Bible in book form but to the Word which is made alive in proclamation.[10] If possible, the importance of the preached Word is even more pronounced in Josefson, who goes so far as to say that when Luther and the Confessions refer to the Word it is *most often* the proclaimed and not the written Word which they have in mind, and

---

[7] The Ten Commandments are mentioned here as an example of the speaking, living Word.

[8] 456:5-11 (SA III VIII 11 f.).

[9] W. von Loewenich (1959), p. 203; WA 7, 721:15 (*Ad librum . . . Ambrosii Catharini . . . responsio,* 1521); Ragnar Bring in *En bok om bibeln* (1947), p. 256, and Regin Prenter in *Biblical Authority for Today* (1951), pp. 98—111.

[10] E. Schlink (1961), pp. 7—8.

that the written apostolic message in the Bible was resorted to only out of necessity. Josefson also maintains that we misunderstand Luther and the Confessions if we identify the saving Word of God exclusively with the Scriptures. The Bible is not, in and of itself, a means of grace, but it becomes such only in connection with its proclamation.[11]

Does the emphasis on the preached Word in the Lutheran Confessions imply a limitation of Biblical authority, so that the spoken Word could somehow be played off against the written? No Lutheran theologian would agree to that, but many are inclined to find in it a contradiction of the later orthodox verbal inspiration theory and of a "legalistic" or "formal" Biblicism.[12] The criticism therefore is directed not against Scriptural authority as such, but against an "anti-Reformational" identification of the Bible with God's Word. As has been well known for a long time, the Lutheran Confessions include no doctrine of inspiration, and they say nothing about the size or scope of the Biblical canon. Their silence on these matters "must be taken seriously as a theological decision," says Schlink, and understood to be the expression of a conscious repudiation of a Biblicistic interpretation. According to Schlink the authority of the Bible is not found in the written but the spoken Word, the Gospel, as addressed and preached to men.[13] Bring follows the same line of thought when he asserts that the *Bible in function,* and not the book as such, possesses authority. The Bible is not God's Word, but it is "the bearer of God's word." "The word" means "the Bible in function," and the authority of the Bible rests in the function. Here the spoken Word becomes "primary" not only in the historical but also in the fundamental sense.[14] Against this background, we have reason to investigate what the confessional writings say about the spoken Word.

It is unfortunate that the Lutheran Symbols did not analyze the relationship between the written and the spoken Word; neither, therefore, did they touch directly upon the entire problem which is undeniably inherent in this relationship. But judging on the basis of what

---

[11] R. Josefson (1953), pp. 31 and 34; same author, "Christus und die heilige Schrift" in *Lutherforschung heute* (1958), p. 58.

[12] R. Bring in *En bok om bibeln* (1947), pp. 267 f. and 272 ff.; same author (1958), pp. 9, 11, and 37; W. Maurer (1957), pp. 98 f. — Legalistic Biblicism is characterized by Bring (1958) as an effort to "comply with every precept in the Bible," p. 37.

[13] E. Schlink (1961), 5—6. Cf. R. Bring (1947), p. 267, and R. Josefson (1953), p. 30.

[14] R. Bring (1947), p. 257 — "The word . . . is, so to speak, superior to the Bible as a book. The word is found in the Bible, and it works through the Bible."

can be seen, they do not interpret the content of the spoken Word as anything other than the Word of *Scripture*. While they do not demand a literal repetition of the written Word, the content of the preached Word is not to deviate from the Scriptures. So when the Confessions mention "the Word," they refer to the written Word as often as to the proclaimed Word. Melanchthon writes in Ap XXIII 28 that the marriage of believers "is pure because it has been sanctified by the Word of God." If the functional view of the Bible were correct, "the Word" here ought to refer to the spoken Word. But Melanchthon rather has in mind certain concrete Bible passages in which Christ and the apostles express their approval of marriage (Matt. 19:6; 1 Cor. 7:14; 1 Tim. 2:15; 4:5). As hallowed by God's Word, marriage is "something which the Word of God permits and approves, as the Scriptures abundantly testify." [15]

That the proclamation of the church must be identical with the preaching of the prophets and the apostles is one of Melanchthon's basic ideas.[16] The heart of this proclamation is the promise of the forgiveness of sins for Christ's sake. Justification by faith is completely dependent on the divine promise, for faith and promise are inextricably related. Melanchthon finds the promise repeated time after time, from the protevangel of Gen. 3:15 on up to his own time. Where is the promise confirmed? Melanchthon answers: in the Scriptures. The promise of the grace given in Christ "is repeated continually throughout Scripture; first it was given to Adam, later to the patriarchs, then illumined by the prophets, and finally proclaimed and revealed by Christ among the Jews, and spread by the apostles throughout the world." [17] The Confessions therefore emphasize that the preaching of the Reformation does not deviate at any point from the doctrines of the early church, which a comparison with Scripture and the apostolic fathers should bear out.[18] The promise must be given by God, and its guarantee, say the Confessions, is found in the Scriptures.[19]

Since faith, as the Confessions point out so often, comes by hearing (Rom. 10:17), the Bible with its promises must be brought to life by preaching and the administration of the sacraments. This, naturally,

[15] 339:18-30 (Ap XXIII 28).

[16] P. Fraenkel, *Testimonia patrum* (1961), pp. 61—64 and 173—78.

[17] 261:50-56 (Ap XII 53).

[18] 316:29-31 (Ap XX 14); 368:41-44 (Ap XXIV 67); 376:12 — Vobiscum litigamus, qui haeresin manifeste pugnantem cum prophetis, apostolis et sanctis patribus sceleste defenditis (Ap XXIV 96).

[19] 320:6-46 (Ap XXI 17 ff.).

does not imply any displacement of the words written in the Bible, for they form the very basis of God the Holy Spirit's activity in the present. The fundamental importance of the written Word needs no special emphasis, therefore, but it is mentioned now and then: "Faith in the Word should continually be strengthened through hearing sermons, through reading(!), through the use of the sacraments" (Ap XII 42 German). One can have contact with God's Word in a variety of ways; it can be "taught, preached, heard, read(!), or pondered" (LC I 92). God's Word is made alive for us in a special way in the assurance of forgiveness received through absolution.

Because of this, the Confessions energetically defend absolution, or the Word of promise. Melanchthon does not hesitate to call it a sacrament. Luther doesn't go that far, since absolution does not fulfill the formal requirements of a sacrament, but he does call it God's Word.[20] God Himself speaks in absolution (LC Confession 22), and Melanchthon tells us that when we listen to the Word of promise in absolution, we hear "a voice from heaven" (Ap XI 2 German). "It is not the voice or word of the man who speaks it, but it is the Word of God, who forgives sin" (AC XXV 3 f.). Because absolution is pronounced on the basis of God's authority, it is *iure divino*.[21] When the penitent receives the forgiveness of sin, he hears the voice of Christ Himself (according to Luke 10:16 — "He who hears you hears Me . . .").

The Bible passage just cited occupies a central position in the Reformation concept of the ministry. The Lutheran Confessions represent a functional view of the ministry. The pastors and bishops of the church have but one responsibility: to proclaim the Word of Christ as preserved in Scripture. It is through the Word that God now works among men. The church cannot set forth any new words; its sole task is to proclaim Christ's living Word. The word of absolution, which "is not our word but the voice and word of Jesus Christ, our Saviour" (Ap XII 2 German), fulfills these conditions. A distinct limitation is placed upon the mission entrusted to pastors and bishops. If they deviate from the Scriptures, men should deny them their ears and their obedience.[22]

Christ's own voice is heard in absolution, for Jesus Himself commanded it in Scripture and with the command combined a promise of

---

[20] 733:13 — God's Word or absolution (LC "Confession" 34).

[21] 255:11 (Ap XII 13); 272:44 (Ap XII 99).

[22] 401:30 — testimonium datum apostolis, ut eis de alieno verbo, non de proprio, credamus (Ap XXVIII 18); 402:34 — Darum wenn sie unchristlich und wider die Schrift lehren, soll man sie nicht hören (Ap XXVIII 21).

the forgiveness of sins. Absolution too brings us back to the Scriptures. The promise of forgiveness contained in the Scriptures is the prerequisite of absolution's assurance, "Your sins are forgiven." The Confessions recognize no new revelation on the same level with Scripture; instead, they insist that God the Holy Spirit is living and active among us when the words of Scripture come alive in preaching, absolution, and the administration of the sacraments. The spoken Word does not become a critical authority to be used in opposition to the Bible, but it is God's active Word in the present, precisely because it bases itself on Holy Scripture. The words of Scripture brought to life in preaching and in the administration of the sacraments are the means by which God acts. The accuracy of this thesis can be confirmed even better through an investigation of the Word as *mandatum*.

The Confessions make the observation that according to the testimony of Scripture God's Word is a creative Word. When God expresses His will in the Word, something always happens. The confessional writers discovered a paradigm of this mode of operation in the Biblical account of creation. When God said (Gen. 1:11) that the earth should "put forth vegetation, plants yielding seed," His words not only had immediate consequences, but as a further result fields bear their harvests and trees their fruit every year. So also with human fertility, which is based on the *mandatum* of Gen. 1:28 and is permanently manifested in the attraction of the sexes to each other. What God commanded once upon a time in the moment of creation continues to be realized in the sexual instincts of men and women, in the *appetitus* which is the natural prerequisite of marriage.[23]

These examples of God's powerful, creative Word form a paradigm for the spoken Word and constitute the foundation of our view of Baptism, the Lord's Supper, absolution, and the ministry as well. Baptism and the Lord's Supper are sacred acts in which God Himself is active through His servant (Ap XXIV 17). "To be baptized in God's name is to be baptized not by men but by God Himself. Although it is performed by men's hands, it is nevertheless truly God's own act" (LC IV 10). In *Vom Abendmahl Christi* (1528) Luther explains what occurs in the Lord's Supper by referring to the account of creation in Gen. 1. The words of institution are "words of authority which produce what they say." [24] Whenever the pastor pronounces the forgiveness of sin to the penitent in absolution, he speaks the Word of God which effects the healing of forgiveness. In the same way

23 334:50—335:31 (Ap XXIII 7 f.).

24 WA 26, 283:4 (*Vom Abendmahl Christi Bekenntnis*, 1528).

God's own voice is to be heard and His will done in all the functions of the ministry.[25] But how can anyone be sure of God's will, and how can one know what God commands, without the support of God's own Word (Ap XV 14)? According to Luke 10:16 God permits His will to be expressed through the acts of the church. But a boundary, which must not be overstepped, has been established: Pastors are in error when they "teach or command something contrary to the divine Holy Scriptures" (AC XXVIII 28). Maurer[26] has introduced the term "creative *mandatum*" as a designation for the creative character of God's Word. But *mandatum* does not stand in opposition to Scripture, or superior to it. In principle, it is nothing other than God's Word as preserved in the Bible. And it is the task of the church to carry this farther and farther through preaching, absolution, and the administration of the sacraments. The divine Word possesses the creative, active qualities which enable it to act as a serviceable channel for God's will.

3. The Interpretation of the Bible

Inasmuch as the words of the Bible must function in preaching, instruction, and the administration of the sacraments, it is natural that the spoken Word cannot simply be identified with the written, if the spoken Word is not to be reduced to a sheer recitation of the Bible. It is obvious that the question concerning the interpretation of the Bible under such conditions must be confronted and the whole problem of the development of doctrine and churchly tradition opened up.

By way of introduction, we might recall to mind that Evangelical theology, even though the Confessions are silent about it, was confronted with this problem early in its development.[1] Luther was well aware of the problems involved in interpreting Scripture, not least of all because of his familiarity with the fourfold exegetical method used in the medieval period, the roots of which went back before the time of Augustine.[2] He had further reason to think this through as a result

[25] 294:3 — Dass Gott durch Menschen und diejenigen, so von Menschen gewählt sind, predigen und wirken will (Ap XIII 12).

[26] W. Maurer (1957), pp. 84 ff. and 98.

[1] See, e.g., Ansbacher Ratschlag in *Die fränkischen Bekenntnisse* (1930), 221 ff.; Schmidt's introduction, pp. 13 ff., 74 ff., 107 ff.; and E. Schlink (1961), pp. 1—2, n. 1.

[2] WA 3, 11:20 ff. (*Dictata super Psalterium*, 1513—16). K. Holl (1923), pp. 544—82; F. Hahn in ZST (1934/35), pp. 165—218; G. Ebeling (1942), pp. 511 ff., and the same author in ZTK (1951), pp. 172 ff.; H. Rückert in *Lutherforschung heute* (1958), p. 114.

of his confrontation with the so-called "enthusiasts" in the mid-1520s.[3]

Without further discussion, the Lutheran Confessions attempt to prove on the one hand that Scripture is authority, while emphasizing on the other hand that its Word must be set forth in vivid preaching and instruction. As a necessary consequence of these two principles, the Confessions actually proceed to the interpretation of Scripture, but without directly telling us which principle is being employed in the process.

At the same time, however, seemingly good reasons can be adduced to the effect that the Confessions have provided us with a key to the interpretation of Scripture by their distinction between Law and Gospel.[4] The entire Bible, both the Old Testament and the New, can be studied from the point of view of Law and Gospel (Ap IV 5). Justification is the article which "alone opens the door to the entire Bible" (Ap IV 2 German). Schlink, who here represents a large number of theologians, has seized upon these and other similar expressions and has concluded that Law and Gospel are not only the keys which open the door to the secrets of Scripture, but also that the Gospel is that which is normative in Scripture; Scripture is the norm for the sake of the Gospel.[5] Against this background, we have reason to review what the Confessions say about the importance of Law and Gospel in the interpretation of Scripture.

The question is touched upon for the first time in the fourth article of Ap, in which justification is discussed: "All Scripture should be divided into these two chief doctrines, the law and the promises. In some places it presents the law. In others it presents the promise of Christ; this it does either when it promises that the Messiah will come and promises forgiveness of sins, justification, and eternal life for his sake, or when, in the New Testament, the Christ who came promises forgiveness of sins, justification, and eternal life." (Ap IV 5)[6]

---

[3] See, e. g., WA 18, 62—214 (*Wider die himmlischen Propheten, von den Bildern und Sakrament,* 1525).

[4] Cf. Josefson (1960), p. 53 — "[Law and Gospel] cannot and must not be looked upon as one form of interpretation alongside of the others. They rather constitute the basic presupposition of the Biblical and theological work of the reformation."

[5] E. Schlink (1961), p. 6 — "This intense concern with the Gospel suggests that the Gospel is the norm in Scripture and Scripture is the norm for the sake of the Gospel."

[6] 159:30 — Universa scriptura in hos duos locos praecipuos distribui debet: in legem et promissiones. Alias enim legem tradit, alias tradit promissionem de

It is entirely clear why Melanchthon's principal statement about
the Bible precedes the article on justification. He did not intend to
provide a fundamental explanation of the interpretation of Scripture.
His goal was more limited. He wanted to provide a background for the
chief doctrine of the Reformation—that the man who is oppressed by
the Law receives forgiveness of sin through faith (Ap IV 1). In order
to understand this doctrine one must, according to Ap, clearly have in
mind that it is taught throughout the entire Bible. In the Old Testament
as in the New (= Gospel), mention is made of God's demands, the
Law, as well as of His will to save (= Promise). The "Gospel" denotes
the New Testament; the "promise" is found both there and in the
Old Testament.

Melanchthon returns to the same theme later on in the fourth
article of Ap (IV 183 ff.) and also in Ap XII 53, where he discusses
the Evangelical doctrine of penitence. In these sections he is not
talking about the authority of Scripture, and neither is he referring
in the first place to the interpretation of Scripture in general; what he
does have in mind is the Reformation's major doctrine, justification by
faith alone, *sola fide* (Ap IV 73). The validity of this doctrine is under
discussion in articles IV and XII of Ap. Melanchthon therefore sets
up two aims for himself. He wants to demonstrate, first, that the
Reformation doctrine of justification is Scriptural, and, second, that
it is consistent with the many seemingly contradictory statements in
the Scriptures concerning the place of good works in the Christian life.
Both of these views of the doctrine of justification go together naturally; justification is important because of its basis in Scripture, and it
makes good sense of what Scripture says about salvation. But this
doctrine is not a general key to the Scriptures. Instead of being the
sole principle for the interpretation of the Scriptures, it provides the
basic rule which clarifies the Scriptural view concerning the relation
between faith and good works.[7]

Christo, videlicet cum aut promittit Christum venturum esse, et pollicetur propter
eum remissionem peccatorum, iustificationem et vitam aeternam, aut in evangelio
Christus, postquam apparuit, promittit remissionem peccatorum, iustificationem et
vitam aeternam (Ap IV 5).

[7] 230:27 — Ex hoc canone diximus supra iudicari posse omnes locos de
operibus (Ap IV 372). One must interpret Luther's familiar promotion theses
regarding faith in the same way; see WA 39 I, 47:19 — Quod si adversarii scripturam urserint contra Christum, urgemus Christum contra scripturam (*Thesen de
fide*, 1535). As is clear from the context, the question of justification by faith
is applicable here too. Luther does not therefore question the authority of Scripture, but rather the interpretation of Scripture which denies the teaching of justification by faith and supports work-righteousness. Et Scriptura est, non contra,

More will be said about the Biblical basis of the doctrine of justification in another context. According to the Confessions the entire Bible deals with salvation through Christ.[8] Justification occupies a central position in the Bible and illumines its statements regarding faith and good works. The related rule concerning Law and Gospel reveals "how a man becomes just before God" (Ap IV 87 German), and it also interprets all that the Bible says about "law and works" (Ap IV 185). Apart from Christ, the Law could not be fulfilled as God intended. "In commending works, therefore, we must add that faith is necessary, and that they are commended because of faith as its fruit or testimony." (Ap IV 184)

Melanchthon's commentary on the Scriptures (Ap IV 183-400) provides a number of examples of how this rule on faith and works is to be applied. We must be satisfied here with a few test samples — the first an interpretation of a passage from the apocryphal Book of Tobit: "Alms free from every sin and from death" (Tobit 4:11). What is said here, clearly, is that a good work — giving alms — provides forgiveness of sin and deliverance from death. This would seem to contradict the Reformation doctrine of justification. This same passage was quoted as an argument in their favor by the authors of the Confutation.[9] Ap did not reply with a reminder that this statement was derived from an Old Testament apocryphal source and could therefore mean something contrary to the New Testament (which, according to our contemporary historical point of view, would be entirely possible). Ap rather chose, at this point, to refer to the distinction between Law and Gospel. "We must come back to the rule that without Christ the teaching of the law has no value. Thus God is pleased by that almsgiving which follows justification or reconciliation, not by that which precedes" (Ap IV 277 f.). This interpretation reveals, first of all, that the whole of Scripture is looked upon as a uniform divine Word,[10] and second, that the distinction between Law and Gos-

sed pro Christo intelligenda, ideo vel ad eum referenda, vel pro vera Scriptura non habenda (WA 39 I, 47:3). In contrast to the interpretation of Luther's statements set forth here, R. Josefson (1958) has sought to demonstrate that according to Luther "die Heilige Schrift in gewissem Fall nicht wahr ist," pp. 60 f. But the following theses, 57—60, make Josefson's position untenable. S. von Engeström provides a correct interpretation of Luther's theses.

[8] 177:18-34 (Ap IV 83); 264:49—265:22 (Ap XII 65 ff.); 313:35-38 (Ap XX 2).

[9] CR 27, 122 (commentary on AC XX). Tobit 4:11 is quoted from the Vulgate: quoniam eleemosyna ab omni peccato, et a morte liberat.

[10] Cf. von Engeström (1933), pp. 45 f., and Fraenkel (1961), pp. 62 and 162 ff.

pel is designed to assist the reader in understanding that good works
are the fruit of faith.

The exposition of 1 Cor. 13:2; 13:13; Matt. 22:37; Col. 3:14,[11]
and other Bible passages dealing with love and good works, proceeds
in the same spirit. Love to God and our fellowmen is by all means the
foremost virtue (Ap IV 226), but it does not bring justification. Paul
rather suggests that the justified man performs deeds of love. The
opponents corrupt the sense of the Bible when they interpret these
and other passages in the Bible in support of a doctrine of work-
righteousness (Ap IV 224). James 2:24 is interpreted after the same
pattern: "You see that a man is justified by works and not by faith
alone." The words of the apostle refer to the works which follow faith.
(Ap IV 244 ff.)

The Confessions never question the validity of the Decalog, but
they are convinced that only the man made righteous by faith can
fulfill it (Ap IV 269 ff.). Their intention is faithfully to reproduce
Paul's view. When Paul in Eph. 6:2 promised a reward to those who
kept the Fourth Commandment, he was referring to those already
justified. (Ap IV 197)

Numerous other examples of the application of the rule concerning
Law and Gospel could be given. The rule was never applied as an
obtrusive hermeneutic principle, and least of all set over the Scriptures as an authority. Rather, Melanchthon looked upon it as a means
of guidance for Bible readers in those sometimes confusing areas
where statements are made about good works, and to give all of these
passages a uniform meaning.

If Law and Gospel had provided a general rule of interpretation,
the Confessions should have limited the questions they put to the Scriptures, confining them to matters directly concerned with this rule. But
such is not the case. Nothing daunted, they go on to ask what the Bible
says about the Lord's Supper, about the ministry and its various ranks
and responsibilities, about marriage and clerical celibacy, about good
works. One can find no basic limitation to questions directly connected
with the distinction between Law and Gospel.

This unfettered view of the Bible is related to another principle of
interpretation, one which can be formulated thus, that the church and
the individual Christian are bound by God's commands, i. e., by the
Bible's *mandata Dei*. What cannot be traced back to God's will as expressed in the Bible is pure invention and is not binding.[12] By virtue

[11] 201:36 ff. (Ap IV 218 ff.)

[12] 416:20 (SA II II 2); 373:40 — mandatum ex scripturis (Ap XXIV 89).

of God's expressed *mandatum,* the Lord's Supper must be celebrated under both bread and wine [13] and the number of sacraments reduced from seven to three (Ap XIII). The sacrifice of the Mass must be suspended for the same reason. Nowhere in Scripture can it be found that God commanded purgatory, pilgrimages, the worship of saints, relics and indulgences.[14] Looked at positively, this *mandatum* rule of interpretation implies that the good works which God has commanded must be carried out. This is, as a matter of fact, a most important facet of Lutheran theology, constituting as it does a defense against those works which lack divine sanction, as well as against antinomianism. God demands of Christian men those works which He has commanded.[15] As a consequence, the Confessions hold that it is legitimate to seek guidance for Christian conduct in the Bible. What form one's good deeds should take in actual practice is a complicated question (we shall take note of this in Chapter Eleven on the New Life). It can be said in a preliminary way that the Symbols look upon the Decalog as a framework within which good deeds can be done.[16] But even though God has commanded them, they have no justifying quality – they are the fruit of faith.

Closely associated with the *mandatum* rule of interpretation is the important principle of the Christian calling or vocation, *vocatio.* Properly speaking, the latter is a consequence of the former, but it occupies such an important place in the confessional writers' interpretation of the Bible that it must be listed as a special rule. The connection between command and calling is revealed in the fact that these two concepts are frequently combined.[17] Community and family life, which the Symbols include in the Christian calling, are commanded by God in opposition to celibacy, monasticism, and cloister piety.[18] The fact that the principle of the calling is based on the Bible has herme-

[13] 85:1 ff. (AC XXII); 328:39 ff. (Ap XXII); 451:3-9 (SA III VI 3); 709: 23-26 (LC IV 8).

[14] 416:8—427:20 (SA II II 1 ff.)

[15] 197:45 — Sunt enim facienda opera propter mandatum Dei (Ap IV 189); 290:9 — qui sint boni fructus docent mandata (Ap XII 174); 393:4 (Ap XXVII 54).

[16] 164:39 — propter mandatum Dei necessario sint facienda honesta opera, quae Decalogus praecepit (Ap IV 22); 290:9 — was rechte gute Werk sein, lehren die zehen Gebot (XII 174).

[17] 102:9 — mandata Dei iuxta vocationem (AC XXVI 10); 309:18 (Ap XXVII 41).

[18] 310:16-36 (Ap XVI 13); 639:11 ff. (LC I 311 ff.); 583:47 ff. (LC I 92); 609:41—610:30 (LC I 195 ff.)

neutic consequences which can be illustrated by the following example. The statement in Matt. 19:29, "And every one who has left houses or brothers or sisters . . . for My name's sake, will receive a hundredfold, and inherit eternal life," was looked upon by the authors of the Confutation as referring to the monkish life of poverty, obedience, and chastity.[19] According to the Lutheran Confessions this cannot be the case, inasmuch as God has commanded us to live, not in cloisters but in our everyday calling. As a result, there are two kinds of leave-taking. The one takes place "without a call, without a command of God," and is not approved by Christ. The other occurs when a man suffers persecution and separates himself from his relatives for the sake of the Gospel. It is of this that Jesus spoke in the passage quoted above.[20]

The principle that it is God's command to live in one's vocation has far-reaching implications. The reformers found that there was much in contemporary life of which they could approve in a positive Christian sense. What the First Commandment signified in the Decalog's First Table (according to Luther's exposition) was signified by the Fourth Commandment in the Second Table (LC I 116). This commandment sanctions one's daily vocation and forms a barrier against the self-chosen cloister piety.[21]

The above-named rules, which are relatively unambiguous, are nevertheless broken at certain points by others, which make the reformers' interpretation of the Bible both more difficult and more diversified. Together with *mandatum Dei,* the New Testament also includes instructions which, in both essence and meaning, are conditioned by the time in which they were written. "Even the apostles ordained many things that were changed by time, and they did not set them down as though they could not be changed." [22] Consequently, not all Biblical commands are binding.

This rule was formulated to oppose both an uncritical Biblicistic attitude and the claim of the Catholic Church to have the right to interpret Scripture and issue new decrees through its clergy. According to the Catholic conception, the apostolic guidelines for ruling the church set down in Acts 15:20 were based upon the authority given to the apostles by Christ to function in His stead.[23] The Confessions ob-

---

[19] CR 27, 172.

[20] 389:53—390:44 (Ap XXVII 40 ff.)

[21] 588:35 ff. (LC I 112 ff.)

[22] 401:7 — pleraque ordinaverunt ipsi apostoli, quae tempore mutata sunt. Neque ita tradiderunt, ut mutare non liceret (Ap XXVIII 16).

[23] Cf. CR 27, 177—83.

jected to this reasoning by saying that even the apostles were bound by the Word which they had been called to administer. Their authority, therefore, was limited (Ap XXVIII 18). Inasmuch as they accepted the words of Peter in Acts 15:10 ("Why do you make trial of God by putting a yoke upon the neck of the disciples . . . ?"), the regulations of Acts 15 and other similar passages in the New Testament must by their very nature be time-conditioned. Such decrees are never referred to as *mandata;* from the very outset, therefore, they bear the imprint of the time in which they were written. The apostles "did not contradict their own writings, in which they worked hard to free the church from the idea that human rites are necessary acts of worship." (Ap XXVIII 16)

Closely related to the above-named rule of interpretation is another, which also precludes a mechanical treatment of Scripture and presupposes a clear-cut theological judgment. The Old Testament law has three divisions, the moral, the civil, and the ceremonial (Ap IV 6). Of these three, only the Moral Law (or the Decalog) is applicable to the church. The reason for this is the same as before: Scripture itself provides the principle of interpretation. By setting aside the commandment concerning the seventh day as a day of rest, it has once and for all declared that the ceremonial law is no longer binding upon the church.[24]

That the Confessions find it useful to apply certain rules to the interpretation of the Bible is based upon certain important presuppositions. In principle, the meaning of Scripture is clear, and what it intends to say can be formulated in comprehensible statements. When there is some doubt about the meaning of a given passage, such a passage must be understood in the light of those whose meaning is clear. In interpreting the Bible, one must hold to the clear Word of the apostles, and not simply refer to their example.[25]

Other rules governing the interpretation of Scripture could be set forth,[26] but we shall now summarize the most important ones in the following 10 points.

---

[24] 130:13 — Scriptura abrogavit sabbatum (AC XXVIII 59).

[25] 244:30 — Itaque voluntas et consilium apostolorum ex scriptis eorum quaeri debet, non est satis allegare exemplum (Ap VII 40); 394:37 (Ap XXVII 60). Concerning the young Luther's view of the clarity of Scripture see, e. g., WA 8, 83:3-5, and S. von Engeström (1933), p. 143, plus E. Thestrup Pedersen (1959), pp. 193 and 343 f.

[26] An important principle here is that the Scriptures are completely opposed to the *opus operatum* concept (Ap XXIV 94 f.).

1. Scripture is the highest authority in questions related to faith and doctrine. The Confessions do not state the extent of the canon of Scripture, but they use both the canonical and the apocryphal books of the Old Testament, together with the New Testament canon.

2. The meaning of Scripture is unambiguous, and its message is everywhere the same. There is nothing to hinder the quotation of an Old Testament saying alongside one taken from the New Testament.

3. Unclear Scriptural passages must be interpreted by those whose meaning is obvious.

4. Christ is the Center of the entire Bible. All of the prophets bear witness to Him.

5. Only the words of the apostles, and not their examples, can be cited in the interpretation of Scripture.

6. The principle of Law and Gospel provides the proper understanding of what Scripture says about justification, faith, and good works.

7. Of the three sections of the Mosaic law, only the Moral Law or the Decalog is binding on Christians.

8. The Biblical *mandatum* contains positive instructions concerning God's will.

9. Those Biblical injunctions which cannot be identified as *mandata* lack significance for the Christian.

10. The Christian's vocation in this world has God's special *mandatum*.

The Confessions contend that these 10 rules are derived from the Bible itself. This does not mean, however, that the words of Scripture must be repeated literally; these rules do permit the expositor a certain amount of freedom. An example of a purely literal attitude toward the Bible can be found in the *Ansbacher Ratschlag,* a forerunner of AC. In this work the difference between God's Word and man's is pointed out with great emphasis and it is stated that one must interpret "Scripture by Scripture, and a text from the Bible through or with another." [27] The young Luther set down similar points of view; in writing against Latomos he took exception to the *homoousios* principle because it is not found in the Bible.[28] But he later changed his mind. In his contro-

---

[27] *Die fränkischen Bekenntnisse* (1930), p. 223. See also the commentary in W. F. Schmidt (1930), pp. 13 ff.

[28] WA 8, 117:14—118:9 (*Rationis Latomianae confutatio,* 1521). The rejection of the *homoousios* concept did not, however, imply a denial of the *fact,* as J. Eck claimed in his 82 theses (W. Gussmann [1930], p. 113). L. Grane (1959), 17 f.

versy with the radical "enthusiasts" he came to realize where a purely Biblicistic view of Scripture could lead. In his *Wider die himmlischen Propheten* (1525) he used the word "sacrament" without hesitation, even though it is not found in the Bible.[29] He gave as his reason that God had not forbidden it.[30] Luther also listed a number of rules for interpreting the Bible. These were designed to safeguard, as far as possible, the literal wording of Scripture [31] but at the same time to leave room for a suitable interpretation of the Bible.[32]

The Lutheran Symbols follow similar principles. Their authors adhere to the Nicene Creed (AC I; Ap I and III) and no longer feel bound by the Bible's literal formulations. The Reformation's central affirmation, *sola fide*, is not found in Scripture in those precise words, but it is defended anyway, for according to the Symbols it clearly reflects the sense of Scripture in regard to the question of salvation (Ap IV 73 f.). On the basis of the Seventh Commandment the Symbols derived the general rule that it is legitimate for Christians to own private property. If the right of ownership was not permitted by God, it would have been meaningless to distinguish between one's own property and another's as this commandment does. From the same source they derived the idea that Christians can accept the laws and ordinances of society without scruples of conscience and seek protection for their lawful claims within them (Ap XVI 9-12). The Symbols derived their doctrine of vocation from the Fourth Commandment (LC I 112 ff.), and in their exposition of the Fifth Commandment they distinguished between the divine rules for the individual on the one hand and for the government on the other (LC I 180 f.). Summing up, it can be said that Reformation theology in its entirety is an expression of a distinct interpretation of Scripture. What this actually means can be clarified only by studying the various confessional statements.

---

[29] *Sacramentum* in Eph. 5:32 and 1 Tim. 3:16 (Vulgate) does not have the connotation intended here. For the history of this concept see J. de Ghellink, *Pour l'histoire du mot sacramentum*, I (1924); Ch. Mohrmann in *The Harvard Theological Review*, 1954, pp. 141—52; P.-Th. Camelot in RThom, 1957, pp. 429 ff.

[30] WA 18, 139:28 ff. (*Wider die himmlischen Propheten*, 1525).

[31] Carlstadt was criticized for wanting to draw up articles of faith "concerning the Scriptures" (WA 18, 146:30 ff.; *Wider die himmlischen Propheten*, 1525).

[32] Here are some of Luther's hermeneutical principles used at this time: the words of Scripture which, in context, cannot be interpreted literally, must be explained in agreement with the articles of faith (18, 147:23-35). The law of Moses is valid only to the extent that it is in harmony with natural law (18, 81:4-17). One must take note of who it is that a given passage of Scripture is directed to (16, 428:31—430:32. *Predigten über das 2. Buch Mose*, 1524—27).

The Symbols give few direct answers to the question of who is responsible for the interpretation of Scripture. Some guidance can be found in the signatures appended to the separate confessional documents, AC, SA, and Tr. We find here two groups of signers: some are theologians, others are secular authorities, although only theologians were the authors of these documents. We have at least an indication here that the teachings of the church were understood to be a matter for the entire church, for laymen as well as for theologians and pastors. In LC III 37 it is said that preaching itself is the task of the church, and in Tr 56 reference is made to the fact that synods were held in ancient times to make decisions in questions of faith, using God's Word as the basis for so doing. The interpretation of the Bible would seem therefore to be one of the tasks which, in the final analysis, rest upon the church as a whole.

Chapter Two:

Scripture and Tradition

1. The Importance of Tradition

When the Confessions assert that they are based on the Bible and have grown up on its ground, they are following one of the basic Reformation principles, which can be traced straight through the theological writings of both Luther and Melanchthon. But alongside of the Bible, and also occupying a major place in the Confessions, is ecclesiastical tradition—as this can be seen above all in the church's oldest doctrinal formulations. This appears both in programmatic expressions and in actual procedures. Von Loewenich, who is by no means inclined to overemphasize the "catholic" element in Luther's works, reminds us of the reformers' efforts to preserve a genuine continuity with the ancient church. Luther reveals the same tendency in his attitude toward the iconoclasts, the liturgy, and the dogmas of the early church.[1] In his rejection of the early Christian heretics,[2] his acceptance of infant baptism, and his defense of private confession we see a clear indication of the Reformation tendency to preserve and restore. The aim of the Reformation was not to launch a radical new beginning but to link up with the heritage of the ancient church. Luther had a feeling for continuity.[3]

This attitude toward the early church is seen to be even stronger in Melanchthon and in the confessional documents he wrote. Since Fraenkel published his major work on the role of the patristic element in Melanchthon's theology—from the first writings to the last—we can better understand why AC and Ap adhere so closely to the doctrinal formulations of the early church. Fraenkel demonstrates that Melanchthon's interest in the traditions of the early church remained unchanged throughout his career as an author in the field of theology.[4] Against

[1] W. von Loewenich (1959), p. 243; W. Elert, I (1930), pp. 183 f.; J. Koopmans (1955), pp. 24—27; F. W. Kantzenbach (1957), pp. 32—41.

[2] See, e. g., WA 26, 500:30 ff. (*Vom Abendmahl Christi Bekenntnis,* 1528); E. Kinder in KuD (1955), pp. 182—84.

[3] P. Fraenkel (1961), p. 24, n. 69, and WA 30 II, 219. A critical evaluation of Luthers attitude toward the fathers is to be found in P. Polman (1932), pp. 9—31.

[4] P. Fraenkel (1961), p. 29.

this background we can see all the more clearly the earnestness of
AC's declaration: "Nothing has been received among us, in doctrine
or in ceremonies, that is contrary to Scripture or to the church catholic,
contra Scripturam aut ecclesiam catholicam. For it is manifest that
we have guarded diligently against the introduction into our churches
of any new ungodly doctrines." [5] In order to evaluate the statements of
the Lutheran Confessions in controversial theological questions, it is
important that their orientation in the direction of the older formulations, especially those of the early church, be kept in view. In the
contest of opposing theological tendencies which marked their era,
the reformers supported historical continuity and refuted doctrines
they judged to be novel, without support in either the Bible or the
fathers of the early church. It was their desire to link up with the traditions of the Western Church—after these had been freed of later additions and excrescences.

This view of the Reformation's achievement has long prevailed
within Lutheranism itself, and it is reflected not only in FC and in
Lutheran orthodoxy but also in the confessional theologians of the
19th century, who sought in a creative and independent manner to
carry the Lutheran heritage even further. They conceived of the history
of dogma as an organic and dialectical development, which was inter-
rupted during the Middle Ages and led into false channels—only to
have the reformers return it to its origins and continue its development in accordance with the laws of growth. Thomasius therefore concluded that the Reformation did in fact link up with the doctrinal
formulations of the early church and that it continued this doctrinal
development.[6] AC and FC were two of the new steps in this organic
development of doctrine.[7] The same point of view was expressed by
Vilmar in *Die Augsburgische Confession* (1870) and by the Swedish
bishop G. Billing. In their Symbols the Lutherans wished to "confess
that they had no desire to separate themselves from the universal
church, neither to build a new church, but rather to be the faithful
children of the church." [8]

---

[5] 134:18-23 (AC Conclusion 5). Cf. E. Schlink (1961), pp. 17 ff.

[6] G. Thomasius, II (1876), 202.

[7] Thomasius, I, 11, and II, 211, 237, and 326.

[8] G. Billing, "Vilken uppfattning av traditionen är utmärkande för det lu-
terska reformationsverket?" ("What Concept of Tradition Is Characteristic of the
Lutheran Reformation?"), in *Bihang till Linköpings stiftstidningar, Supplement to
the Bulletin of the Linköping Diocese* (1871). Our quotation is taken from the
same author, *Lutherska kyrkans bekännelse, The Confessions of the Lutheran
Church* (1876—78), p. 123. Cf. H. Fagerberg in STK, 1953, pp. 239—44.

Nevertheless, a completely different view of the relationship of the Lutheran Symbols to doctrinal formulations in previous church history has been set forth. According to Pleijel and Josefson, the fact that the ancient creeds were included in the Book of Concord was due exclusively to the influence of Melanchthon, who, deviating from Luther, accepted these creeds and defended the ecclesiastical traditions. At bottom, Melanchthon's fondness for the old dogma depended on his — in contrast to Luther's — "intellectual" outlook. Pleijel means that Melanchthon transformed Luther's religious view of the Gospel as a "message of joy" into a corpus of distinct doctrinal truths.[9] In addition to Melanchthon's influence, says Pleijel, church politics also played a decisive role in the inclusion of the ancient creeds in the official documents of the Reformation. Ever since the Edict of Theodosius the Great (A.D. 380) the Nicene Creed had been the judicial basis for religious liberty in the German-Roman empire. Therefore any church group which wished to enjoy religious liberty in 16th-century Germany had to recognize the Nicene Creed. According to Pleijel's interpretation, the inclusion of the Nicene Creed had political overtones and cannot be used as an argument for the Reformers' positive attitude toward the older dogmas. It does appear, generally speaking, that Luther had a distinctly freer view of the older dogmas than did Melanchthon.[10]

Pleijel and Josefson give expression to a trend of thought which had been suggested earlier by researchers in the field of the history of dogma. The theory which points to Melanchthon as the progenitor of a traditionalist tendency within Lutheranism was supported with vigor by O. Ritschl[11] in his famous and influential book on the history of dogma. While Luther maintained a consistent Biblicism throughout his life, Melanchthon surrendered this by degrees, finally ending up with a traditionalism not much different in principle from that of the Council of Trent (O. Ritschl, I, 338). The idea that AC established a connection with the Nicene Creed for political reasons originated with

[9] H. Pleijel (1936), pp. 192 ff.; same author in *Ein Buch von der Kirche* (1951), p. 229; R. Josefson (1953), pp. 10 f.

[10] H. Pleijel (1941), pp. 28—30 and 47—58.

[11] O. Ritschl, I (1908), pp. 268 ff. and 276—340. Ritschl's theology has been very influential and has been adopted among others by R. Seeberg, *Dogmengeschichte*, IV, 2 (1920), 424 ff., and H. E. Weber, I, 1 (1937), 170 ff. For a critique of this position see P. Fraenkel (1961), 24—28, and E. Schlink (1961), pp. 62 ff.

A. Ritschl.[12] Neither of these two assertions, however, is in complete agreement with the actual facts.

There are good reasons for assuming that political motivations were involved in the drafting of AC. The Western Church was not yet officially divided at that time, and since the Evangelicals at the Diet of Augsburg attempted to avoid the charge of heresy, it was natural for them to use irenic formulations.[13] Nevertheless, the purely political explanation is not satisfactory. When Melanchthon supported the Evangelical position with arguments derived from the early church fathers, this was in harmony with his considered opinion concerning the Reformation as a continuation of the doctrinal formation of the early church. A study of those parts of the confessional writings for which Melanchthon was responsible reveals that the formal statements in the introduction and conclusion of AC were not simply there for tactical-political reasons; they rather reflect a well-thought-out and distinctive point of view. The frequently repeated quotations from the church fathers speak very clearly as the expression of the theological method upon which the confessions are patterned. Reference is made first of all to the Bible, which must clearly support a doctrinal opinion, and secondly to the writings of the fathers. In connection with the controversial doctrine of original sin, Melanchthon asserted that there was nothing novel about it. We teach, he insisted, nothing concerning original sin which is in opposition to the Scriptures or the universal church; we have simply set forth the chief ideas of the Bible and the fathers.[14] The same reasoning was applied to the doctrine of justification, which has support not only in the Bible but also in many of the church fathers, of whom Augustine, with his anti-Pelagian views, was cited first and foremost.[15] Ambrose and Cyprian were also included.

---

[12] A. Ritschl, I (2d ed. 1882), 146 f.

[13] W. Elert, I (1962), 274 f.; F. W. Kantzenbach (1957), p. 44; H.-W. von Gensichen (1955), pp. 68 f.

[14] 153:24-27 (Ap II 32). Cf. CR 21, 669 (*Loci theologici,* 1543), and P. Fraenkel (1961), p. 38.

[15] 165:32-36 (Ap IV 29). For further references to the fathers see Ap IV 49 ff., and 77:17-30 (AC XX 12 ff.: Augustine and Ambrose); 181:28—182:38 (Ap IV 103—106: Ambrose and Augustine); 194:15 ff. (Ap IV 166 ff.: tota scriptura, tota ecclesia, Augustine); 200:45 ff. (Ap IV 211: Antony, Bernard, Dominic, Francis); 222:10 ff. (Ap IV 322 f.: tota ecclesia, Augustine, Cyprian, clarissima testimonia in scriptura et ecclesiasticis patribus); 314:10 ff. (Ap XX 5: infinita hoc loco testimonia ex scriptura, ex patribus citare possemus); 316:25 ff. (Ap XX 14: Augustine); 368:41 ff. (Ap XXIV 67: Dicemus et nos de usu sacramenti ea, quae certum est consentanea esse patribus et scripturae); 376:13 (Ap XXIV 96: cum prophetis, apostolis et sanctis patribus).

Melanchthon frequently referred to the fathers of the Eastern Church.[16] Ideas which Melanchthon derived from Gratian are also given some space.[17] Among the latter was the proposition that any custom which entered the church *contra mandata Dei* ought not be accepted or approved.[18]

One finds the same attitude in Luther, generally speaking, although his critical eye was sharper. In those portions of the Confessions which he wrote quotations from the church fathers are relatively scarce and much further in the background. Luther makes direct references to the fathers only on a few occasions. Augustine is given a special place. Among the older fathers Luther also mentions Jerome, whom he quotes in support of his view concerning the equality of popes and bishops.[19] Among the younger theologians he pays close attention to Bernard, Gerson, and Hus, which shows his unconventional attitude to ecclesiastical tradition.[20]

Two other factors are of even greater importance. First of all, Luther rejected the radical, anti-Trinitarian reform movement, whose supporters were known as "enthusiasts." There can be no doubt that this choice was made deliberately. In a letter concerning rebaptism Luther took a stand against Balthaser Hubmaier[21] and wrote as follows:

> It is our confession that in the papacy there are the right Holy Scriptures, the right Baptism, the right Sacrament of the Altar, the right keys for forgiveness of sins, the right preaching office, the right catechism,

[16] Fraenkel (1961), pp. 19 and 21. Also see Benz (1952), pp. 17—20. Melanchthon even went so far as to translate AC into Greek in the hope that it would be favorably received by the Greek patriarch. E. Benz (1949), pp. 94—128, and F. K. Schumann in *Die Evangelische Christenheit in Deutschland* (1958), pp. 131 f.

[17] See the index in *Die Bekenntnisschriften* (1963), 1148. The index is not complete, however. Luther quoted Gratian in SA II IV 9 and 11. He is referred to most frequently in Tr, where a number of the propositions in the Decretals are discussed.

[18] 86:1-3 (AC XXII 9). Cf. 36:1-5 (Melanchthon's outline of the preface of AC). The reference concerns *Decr. Grat.,* I, d.8; c.5 ff., where, however, the expression *mandata Dei* is not to be found. 126:3-7 (AC XXVIII 34, with reference to *Decr. Grat.,* I, d.9, c.1 ff.). Cf. WA 50, 524:12-24 (*Von den Konziliis und Kirchen,* 1539).

[19] 430:10 and 458:13 (SA II IV 9 and III X 3).

[20] 701:7 (LC IV 50). Concerning Luther's attitude toward those here named see W. Köhler, I:1 (1900), 162—236, 301—33, and 342—63. Cf. Althaus (1962), p. 17 — Luthers ganze theologische Arbeit setzt die Autorität der Schrift und die abgeleitete der rechten Tradition der Kirchen voraus.

[21] Concerning this individual see T. Bergsten (1961).

such as the Lord's Prayer, the Ten Commandments, the Creed . . . .
Now if Christianity exists under the pope, it must be Christ's true body
and members. If it is His body, then it has the right Spirit, Gospel,
Creed, Baptism, Sacrament, keys, preaching office, prayer, Holy
Scriptures, and everything that Christianity should have. Therefore
we do not rave like the "enthusiasts" that we reject everything in the
papacy.[22]

Second, Luther attached himself positively to the dogmatic formulations of the early church. In his introduction to SA he pointed to the
doctrines on which both of the opposing parties agreed, and in so doing
he made a direct connection with both the Nicene and Athanasian
Creeds.[23]

These and similar expressions by Luther and Melanchthon clearly
reveal the tradition to which they intended to adhere. Such utterances
provide us with a preliminary intimation concerning the Reformation's
Sitz im Leben. Any interpretation of Reformation theology that
disregards the historical continuity of which Luther and Melanchthon were conscious has lost something of vital importance. On
the other hand, this point should not be emphasized to such an extent that what is new in the Reformation is lost sight of. It should be
remembered that even Calvin, who was considerably more radical,
was also concerned about maintaining the connection with the early
church (though to a lesser degree).[24] This underlining of continuity
was "naturally in the air," so to speak; it was a prominent argument in
theological controversy. But pointing to the alleged relationship is
one thing; it is even more important to ask if the actual nexus was
effected. The answer to this question must be a trifle different.

One problem which makes a correct judgment difficult has to do
with the way isolated quotations are cited in the Confessions. These
are often used out of context, and their meaning can be distorted as a
result.[25] In their understanding of sin, it cannot be said that the Confessions have fully grasped Augustine's position. This is partly because
they attribute different connotations to the term *concupiscentia,* and

[22] WA 26, 147:15—148:7 (*Von der Wiedertaufe,* 1528). Cf. F. W. Kantzenbach (1957), p. 38.

[23] 414:10—415:3 (SA I 1-4). Luther here holds to his *Bekenntnis* of 1528,
where he took the same position toward the dogmatic formulations of the early
church (409:20 f.; SA Introduction 3).

[24] J. Koopmans (1955), pp. 32—48, and P. Polman (1932), pp. 65—94.

[25] Cf., e. g., a quotation from Ambrose in Ap II 19 (150:46—151:1). For
more on this see Chapter Five below.

partly because of a different opinion concerning the conditions which determine whether or not something is sinful.[26] In regard to justification by faith, the chief doctrine of the Reformation, precise agreement with Augustine is also lacking, primarily because of differing concepts of grace. Like Augustine in *De spiritu et littera,* Luther expresses the conviction that righteousness is a gift of God and not a human accomplishment.[27] Denifle [28] has presented material which shows that Luther's understanding of *iustitia Dei* (Rom. 1:17) and of justification was not unknown to Bible exegetes in the Western medieval tradition. But the results of Denifle's efforts are evaluated in a completely different manner by Bornkamm, who holds that Luther arrived at his insights through an independent study of the Bible which resulted from his controversy with scholastic theology. In other words, he was not the heir of residual vestiges of Augustine's exegesis.[29] Using their refined methods, researchers in the field of the history of dogma have shown that, generally speaking, Luther and Augustine employed disparate presuppositions and different points of departure.[30]

Apart from the question marks which can be placed alongside their citations of ecclesiastical tradition, it must be said that the reformers, unlike the theologians of the 19th century, did not think of church history as a continuous development. Together with their appreciation of tradition, the Confessions also include sharp criticism of the church fathers, plus a negative attitude toward everything referred to as tradition. This makes the picture more complicated, and more light is needed to illumine it on all sides.

2. The Nature of Tradition

To say that tradition occupies a prominent place alongside of the Bible in the Lutheran Confessions may seem bewildering at first, inasmuch as they are highly critical of tradition at many points and, as Skydsgaard has observed, generally give the term "tradition" a negative connotation.[1]

[26] See below, Chapter Five.

[27] WA 54, 186:16-20 (Foreword to Luther's collected works in Latin).

[28] H. Denifle, *Die abendländischen Schriftausleger bis Luther,* Rom. 1:17 (1905).

[29] H. Bornkamm (1942), p. 26.

[30] Anders Nygren, *Eros and Agape,* II (1937); same author, "Simul justus et peccator According to Augustine and Luther" in *Filiosofi och motivforskning, Philosophy and Motif-Research* (1940), pp. 136—56, and W. von Loewenich (1959), pp. 75—87.

[1] K. E. Skydsgaard (1952) in *Kristen gemenskap,* 1952, p. 160; same author in KuD (1955), pp. 168 ff.

If one looks up the term in the index of *Die Bekenntnisschriften
der evangelisch-lutherischen Kirche* (1963), one finds that at times it
is used only in the plural form, *traditiones,* and at other times with
reference to the German word *Menschensatzungen.* Tradition and
human effort are here identical; tradition denotes all of the usages and
customs which the church had accepted without Biblical support and
which were observed in the hope that salvation could thereby be
attained.[2] The injunction that all sins should be enumerated in confession and made good for through the imposed satisfactions is said
to be a tradition of this kind.[3] Traditions are human inventions, and
because they lack Biblical support they are called *traditiones humanae*
(in conjunction with Mark 7:8 and Col. 2:8).[4] They are related to the
ceremonial laws of Moses, inasmuch as they, like them, require justifying deeds.[5] The polemics directed at tradition were combined with a
militant defense of God's will and command, of Scripture and the
Gospel.[6] Tradition's changeable and temporary *ius humanum* is in
opposition to the unchangeable *ius divinum* found in Scripture. There
is an irreconcilable contrast between tradition and God's command.
Human invention *(Menschentand, Menschenfundlein, hominum
inventiones, figmenta humana)* is opposed to God's Word.[7] Both
Luther and Melanchthon set God's Word and human regulation in
opposition to one another, on the basis of Jesus' statement in Matt.
15:9: "In vain do they worship Me, teaching as doctrines the precepts
of men." [8]

Although the Confessions frequently point up areas of agreement
with the early church fathers, they also include a variety of criticisms.
Their attitude is that the church fathers cannot be accepted *en bloc.*
They were not infallible; as men they could make mistakes; their
opinions often revealed a serious lack of harmony.[9] Since many of the

[2] 461:16—462:2 (SA III XV 1).

[3] 250:55—251:39 (Ap XI 6 ff.); 282:51—283:27 (Ap XII 143—145); 255:
2-8 (Ap XII 11).

[4] A. Sperl in *Das Wort Gottes in Geschichte und Gegenwart* (1957), p. 149.

[5] 298:52—299:2 (Ap XV 10).

[6] 402:10-19 (Ap XXVIII 20).

[7] 423:3 and 14 (SA II II 21); 417:2 and 28 (SA II II 2).

[8] 104:13 ff. (AC XXVI 22); 116:2 (AC XXVII 36); 282:55 (Ap XII 143);
298:25 (Ap XV 5); 384:35-42 (Ap XXVII 23); 396:24 (Ap XXVII 69); 417:3
(SA II II 2); cf. 128:13-17 (AC XXVIII 47 f.).

[9] 375:49 — Et patrum magna dissimilitudo est. Homines erant et labi ac
decipi poterant (Ap XXIV 95). Cf. E. Schlink (1961), 3, and F. Brunstäd
(1951), 19.

fathers built with "hay and straw" on the true foundation, Christ, their work cannot endure (Ap VII, 20 f.). No church father is infallible, not even the best of them all, Augustine; he too is criticized when he expresses opinions contrary to God's Word.[10]

These and similar observations presuppose minds capable of historical criticism, and the reformers had this capacity. With regard to the sacrament of penance and the preaching office they discovered an obvious development, which they looked upon as a deviation. They maintained that the word "confession" had lost its original meaning and significance.[11] Episcopal duties had increased over the centuries,[12] and the number of sacraments was gradually fixed at seven.[13] Luther and Melanchthon agreed with the humanists Erasmus and Lorenzo Valla in claiming that Dionysius the Areopagite was a pseudonym used by a man much more recent than the one mentioned in Acts 17:34. They also criticized other authors of whom it was erroneously said that they had written books which they could not in fact have produced.[14]

There is also an obvious effort at classification to be seen in what the Confessions say about the doctrinal development of the early church. Some of the fathers are appreciated more than others. In general, the testimony of those who lived closest to the time of Christ is accepted in preference to those who lived later. The risk of error increased with the passing of time. The scholastic theologians were criticized with particular sharpness for their blending of theology and Aristotelian philosophy. Ap XXI 41 says of this: "We ourselves have heard excellent theologians ask for limitations upon scholastic doctrine because it leads to philosophical disputes rather than to piety. The earlier scholastics are usually closer to Scripture than the more recent ones, so their theology has steadily degenerated." [15] One can also observe, in a number of concrete instances, how the confessional writers play off the early fathers against the scholastic theologians, including, most prominently, Thomas, Duns Scotus, and Gabriel

[10] 421:17-25 (SA II II 15); cf. WA 50, 524, 19-24 (*Von den Konziliis und Kirchen*, 1539).

[11] 274:21-25 and 274:51—275:12 (Ap XII 109 and 112).

[12] 491:42—492:5 (Tr 70 f.)

[13] 292:7-8 Ap XIII 2).

[14] 492:5-7 (Tr. 71). See especially *Die Bekenntnisschriften* (1963), 492, notes 2—4.

[15] 326:24-31 (Ap XXI 41). Cf. 265:50 — Dieselbigen Scribenten haben nicht anders denn Philosophie gelehret, und von Christo und Gottes Werk nicht gewusst (Ap XII 68 f.).

Biel.[16] With regard to the doctrines of original sin, penance, and the Lord's Supper the Lutheran Confessions seek support from the early fathers, inasmuch as their position was different from that taken by the scholastics.[17] A number of individual theologians from the high and late Middle Ages also provided support for the Reformation teaching, at least at certain points. Among these, Bernard of Clairvoux and John Gerson were mentioned most frequently.[18]

As a result of Fraenkel's investigation into the function of the patristic element in Melanchthon's theology, we can better understand why the confessional writings express themselves in such seemingly contradictory terms concerning the older tradition, appreciation alternating with severe criticism. Melanchthon wanted to preserve the historical continuity between the Lutheran Reformation and the older forms of Christianity, and he also wanted to eliminate irregularities within the church. These were the basic guidelines which he derived from his study of church history.

According to Melanchthon, the Lutheran Reformation was not an interruption of church history but a continuation.[19] As he saw it, church history proceeds according to a definite pattern and is characterized by both apostasy and reformation.[20] The divine truth concerning man's salvation is one and the same from the beginning of the world to the present. This truth has been stifled and threatened with destruction time after time, only to be brought back into the light through a reforming movement. The church has always existed, sometimes strong, sometimes enfeebled. During periods of decay the true church lives on as a minority church.

In the earliest years of Christian history this pattern involved the revelation of the divine truth through Jesus and the apostles, whom Melanchthon considered to be reformers. Decay set in after the apostolic age, which reached its culmination in Origen and called forth

---

[16] 265:44 (Ap XII 68); 182:5 — Nam alii vocantur angelici, alii subtiles, alii irrefragabiles (Ap IV 105). Melanchthon here alludes to Thomas, Scotus, and Alexander of Hales. 383:40 (Ap XXVII 20); 301:52 (Ap XV 24); 450:2 (SA III V 2); 461:14 (SA III XIV 3); 330:32 (Ap XXII 9).

[17] 150:20 ff. (Ap II 15); 265:43—266:49 (Ap XII 68 ff.); 295:49—296:3 (Ap XIII 23).

[18] See the Index of *Die Bekenntnisschriften* (1963), 1147 and 1150. The influence of Gerson has been pointed out by A. Sperl (1957), p. 149.

[19] P. Fraenkel (1961), p. 109.

[20] Fraenkel, pp. 71—75. Fraenkel here speaks of four "laws of history: (1) the general corruption of mankind, (2) the law of the minority, (3) the law of Reformation, (4) the law of eschatology or of relativity."

a reformation via Augustine. After the Augustinian purge the same course of events recurred anew: decay throughout the entire medieval period, which elicited the Lutheran Reformation.[21] But during the entire process, characterized by renewal-decay-renewal, the truth was always preserved by a minority. The truth can be stifled, but it can never be completely destroyed. Melanchthon could see a dogmatic doctrinal continuity running throughout the centuries of church history and the periods of decay,[22] and it was to this that the Reformation wanted to attach itself. The Reformation was not designed to introduce novelties but to revive the ancient truths which had been forgotten or obscured as a result of the church's decay.

This view of history is to be found in the Lutheran Symbols, and it throws light on both positive and negative expressions concerning the church's doctrinal development. Augustine is accorded the highest rating. He was the only church father lectured upon regularly in Wittenberg.[23] It also explains the generally negative attitude the Symbols take toward the post-Augustinian epoch, in which Pope Gregory the Great was thought to have brought about a trend leading in the wrong direction.[24] It also makes clear why certain medieval theologians could be consulted on particular questions: the light was never completely put out, and the truth never totally obscured. How this pattern functioned in practice can be shown by using an illustration.

In Ap XII 65 the idea that faith plays a major role in penitence is defended on the basis of Acts 10:43. According to the Law and Gospel principle, the penitent man receives forgiveness of sin through faith in Christ. The opposition disputed the truth of this doctrine, and they were able to quote many theologians in support of their position:

> They have on their side some theologians of great reputation, like Duns Scotus, Gabriel Biel, and the like in addition to patristic statements which the decrees quote in garbled form. Certainly, if we were to count authorities, they would be right; for there is a great crowd of worthless commentators on the *Sentences* who as though by a con-

[21] CR 5, 691—93 (*Praefatio*, 1545); P. Fraenkel (1961), pp. 82—83.

[22] P. Fraenkel (1961), pp. 41, 133—34, and 251. With regard to Melanchthon's view of the various traditions see P. Fraenkel in ST (1959), p. 120.

[23] See P. Fraenkel (1961), p. 94, n. 217, where Luther's attitude is also presented, and pp. 299—303. Cf. WA 18, 640:8-9 (*De servo arbitrio*, 1525), and 50, 526:2-7 (*Von den Konziliis und Kirchen*, 1539).

[24] 95:4 (AC XXIV 35); 317:13 (Ap XXI 3); 351:1 — veteres scriptores ante Gregorium (Ap XXIV 6); 375:48 (Ap XXIV 94). Cf. P. Fraenkel (1961), pp. 96—100.

spiracy defend the false notions we have been discussing . . . . Lest
anyone be moved by this large number of quotations, it must be kept in
mind that no great authority attaches to the statements of later theologians who did not produce their own books but only compiled them
from earlier ones and transferred these opinions from one book to another. (Ap XII 68-69)

It is clear from this quotation (1) that the Confessions distinguish
between older and newer traditions, (2) that the testimony of the older
tradition is preferred to the newer, (3) that later writers frequently
cited older ones in a distorted form, and (4) that the sheer number of
quotations is not as important as their agreement with revealed truth.
The decisive factor in Melanchthon's reasoning here is found in Acts
10:43, where Peter says that "every one who believes in Him [Christ]
receives forgiveness of sins through His name." To this Ap adds the
following commentary: "Surely the consensus of the prophets should
be interpreted as the consensus of the universal church." [25] (5) It can
be said, finally, that the Confessions also sought to find support for
their position from certain of the more recent theologians, in this case
Bernard of Clairvaux. (Ap XII 73 f.)

The confessional writers' view of history also resulted in a critical
attitude toward the fathers. All of the fathers were recognized as being
human and therefore capable of falling into error (Ap XXIV 95). This
critical attitude led to the rejection of a number of theologians whose
teachings were not in harmony with the revealed truth of Scripture.
What is really of interest here is that this critical edge could be directed
even against such a recognized authority as Augustine. Fraenkel has
discovered a statement made by Melanchthon in 1543 in which he
said that Ambrose and Augustine support the Evangelical position
without any doubt, but that they do not always express themselves
with sufficient clarity.[26] Similar cautious statements can be found in
SA and some of Luther's other writings.[27] The purpose of this his-
torical-critical method was to draw out the original truth found in the
early fathers. The emphasis was placed upon *doctrinal* continuity,

---

[25] 265:20 — Profecto consensus prophetarum iudicandus est universalis ecclesiae consensus esse (Ap XII 66).

[26] CR 5, 234 — De scriptoribus Ambrosio et Augustino non dubium est eos
nobiscum sentire, sed non semper satis commode loquuntur ("Letter to Chancellor
Brück," 1543). P. Fraenkel (1961), pp. 269—72, 300 f., and CR 2, 502 ("Letter
to Brenz," 1531).

[27] 421:14-25 (SA II II 14 f.); WA 50, 525:3-30 (*Von den Konziliis und
Kirchen,* 1539).

which existed in all centuries, independent of the church's external, historical continuity via the bishops and the apostolic succession.

Although the role of Scripture and tradition was not fixed precisely before the Council of Trent, it will be of value to compare the Lutheran Symbols' concept of tradition with the Catholic concept. Here contrasting opinions were asserted, of course, but a number of common touches also appear. The polemical theologian John Driedo recognized as a firm fact that Scripture contains all that is necessary to salvation, but he also insisted that this had to be read and interpreted in agreement with the church, *secundum traditionem universalis ecclesiae aut secundum antiquam Christianorum scholam.*[28] As a consequence references to the fathers played a very positive role. The Catholic theologians purported to demonstrate that Catholic doctrine was in harmony with the fathers and that it formed an unbroken continuity.[29] A few individual Catholic theologians were able to recognize the presence of decay in church history and to demand a return to the doctrinal position of the early church (according to Vincent of Lerins' well-known *consensus antiquitatis*), but even in such cases the testimony of all the fathers was preferred to that of the 16th-century critics, because the fathers lived nearer to the sources, and above all because they were not involved in the controversies then raging.[30] But the chief line of demarcation ran elsewhere. For while the Lutherans judged the earlier tradition with a critical eye and accepted it only at certain points, the Catholic theologians purported to find an unbroken and undifferentiated doctrinal continuity throughout the entire history of the church.[31] Their assertion was closely related to the idea that the church is under the guidance and protection of the Holy Spirit.[32]

In the 19th century an organic view of tradition developed, which was used on both sides of the confessional line of demarcation. Tradition was looked upon from a developmental point of view, as growth resulting from an increase of religious understanding. That this view of

---

[28] J. R. Geiselmann (1962), pp. 180—83. Cf. the same author (1957), p. 159, and J. L. Murphy (1959), pp. 273—80.

[29] This point of view dominates Herborn's Enchiridion (1529), 49 — Unus est ecclesiae communis sensus, quatenus ad fidem attinet, quem Spiritus sanctus iis suggerit, qui in unitate ecclesiae catholicae consistunt.

[30] W. Trusen (1957), pp. 40—43.

[31] Herborn, *Enchiridion,* 90:28 ff., and Chapters Eight and Ten.

[32] P. Fraenkel (1961), p. 174.

tradition was current back in the 16th century is scarcely probable.[33]
As far as the Lutheran Confessions are concerned, tradition definitely
did not have this function. The truth was given and established once
and for all time. Those fathers whose work was acceptable had not
formulated any new doctrines; they had restored the original ones and
freed them from irrelevant additions.[34] The Confessions sought to
return to those fathers who had preserved the pure doctrines, without
falsification. But to attempt such a critical sifting of the church fathers'
statements demanded the use of a higher norm, and the Lutherans
found it in Scripture. This makes the question of the relationship between Scripture and tradition pertinent.

3. Scripture and Tradition

As one would expect, the Lutheran Symbols view tradition in
relation to their concept of the church's living proclamation. The
church has God's revealed Word, which is also a living Word. What the
church proclaims cannot be altered; its content must remain the same
from age to age. The Symbols place the greatest emphasis on the
church's living proclamation. Doctrine and preaching are very closely
connected to one another in the Confessions — not in such a way that
preaching should lack doctrinal content and that *doctrina* could be
translated as *preached* Word, but so that God's revelation and salvation may be told and taught and brought to life anew in every generation. This is expressed most clearly in the words of absolution and in
the words of institution of both Baptism and the Lord's Supper, where
no additions may be made; only God's own voice is to be heard. As a
result, the only function or duty of the clergy is to cause the voice of
Christ to be heard. Put another way, the church must give voice to
Christ's Word. In preaching, in absolution, and in the administration
of the means of grace we are to hear Christ's own voice (in accordance
with Luke 10:16). The Confessions energetically oppose the idea that
the clergy have the authority to add new words themselves, either in
the doctrinal sphere or with regard to church discipline. It is above
all in this connection that they express themselves in opposition to

[33] This is intimated in P. Fraenkel (1961), pp. 63 and 176. It was J. A.
Möhler and John Henry Newman who developed the Catholic concept of organic
tradition. There is more on this, e. g., in J. R. Geiselmann's book *J. A. Möhler,
Die Einheit in der Kirche oder das Prinzip des Katholizismus* (1957), pp. 589 f.,
and by H. Fries in Bracht (1957), 100 ff., and Chadwick (1957). In the evangelical context this has been used within confessional Lutheran theology by
Holsten Fagerberg (1952) and by Kantzenbach.

[34] Cf. P. Fraenkel (1961), pp. 176—78.

tradition: "Certainly the statement, 'He who hears you hears me' (Luke 10:16), is not referring to traditions but is rather directed against traditions. It is not what they call a 'commandment with unlimited authority,' but rather a 'caution about something prescribed,' about a special commandment. It is a testimony given to the apostles so that we may believe them on the basis of another's Word rather than on the basis of their own" (Ap XXVIII 18). It is on the basis of special divine authority that the power of the keys imparts the forgiveness of sin. (Ap XII 99)

One of the major points made by the Reformation has to do with the permanent identity of the church's proclamation. The church has *one and the same* message to proclaim, from the promise of the *protevangelium* (in Gen. 3:15) forward to the present time. The promise of salvation given to Adam was repeated to the patriarchs and the prophets; it was renewed by Christ, and preached by the apostles as being valid for all men in all ages (Ap XII 53).[1] It is into this context that legitimate ecclesiastical tradition must be placed. The symbols of the early church, certain of the church fathers, and a number of later theologians are included in the long list of witnesses. Melanchthon — and Luther too — was profoundly convinced of the church's doctrinal continuity.[2] The Confessions located the source and norm of the divine message in the Bible; as a result, the Bible occupies such a central position in Reformation theology. The apostolic Word is found preserved in Scripture, and all statements must be verified by Scripture. As Fraenkel has pointed out, the primacy of Scripture was axiomatic.[3]

The fact that Scripture was accorded such significance did not mean, however, that its words had to be repeated in a literal way. As a result of the application of the Scripture principle there were circles within the Reformation where this demand was no stranger — but in the Confessions it is completely unknown. What is said in the Bible is also to be found in certain of the early church fathers and has been codified in the ancient creeds of the church. It is certainly true that they sometimes use other words and different modes of expression, but they nevertheless preserve the meaning of Scripture. Luther considered the Apostles' Creed to be a revealed Word of God, faithfully

---

[1] For more, see 262:1-10 (Ap XII 54 German).

[2] P. Fraenkel (1961), pp. 142—47. Melanchthon was of the opinion that continuity is manifested in a "repetition of statements."

[3] Fraenkel, pp. 34 f., 41 f., 44, 61.

preserving and summarizing Scripture's Gospel.[4] In SA Luther associated himself unreservedly with "the sublime articles of the divine majesty," as these are formulated in the three oldest creeds.[5] Both Luther and Melanchthon identified themselves in this manner with the doctrines of the early church because they considered these doctrines to be in harmony with the Scriptures. There was no difference of opinion between the two reformers on this point (as O. Ritschl purportedly discovered). On the contrary, they both found a secure basis for the church's doctrine and proclamation in the creeds of the early church.[6] Inasmuch as the creeds were looked upon as an interpretation of Scripture, the Bible became both the source and the norm for judging the legitimate ecclesiastical tradition. That which harmonized with Scripture was accepted; that which did not was discarded. According to the Lutheran Confessions the real basis of all legitimate tradition is nothing other than *the ecclesiastical exposition of the Bible.*

That which can be accepted as genuine ecclesiastical tradition must be capable of verification by Scripture. Tradition may not include theses which lack Biblical support. It is this principle which gave rise to the saying, "The Word of God shall establish articles of faith" (SA II II 15)[7] and which explains the critical rejection of certain points in the older doctrinal development. One of the Bible passages used most frequently in this connection was Acts 10:43, which says that forgiveness of sins for Christ's sake is given to all who believe in Him. This unanimous *consensus prophetarum* is the same as the church's consentient opinion, and it carries more weight than all of the contrary teachings of the later theologians.[8] Negatively, it implies a critique of individuals as well as of opinions. The conventional distinction made in the doctrine of penance between two kinds of repentance, *contritio* and *attritio,* as well as the doctrines of satisfac-

---

[4] 557:19-26 (LC Preface 18); 660:18-47 (LC II 63); J. Meyer (1929), pp. 259—63.

[5] 414:10—415:3 (SA I); cf. WA 26, 500:26 ff. (*Vom Abendmahl Christi Bekenntnis,* 1526).

[6] E. Kinder in KuD (1955), pp. 182 f. (lit.); R. Prenter (1946), pp. 182 ff. and 245 ff.

[7] See also 124:26 — Nec catholicis episcopis consentiendum est, sicubi forte falluntur aut contra canonicas Dei scripturas aliquid sentiunt (AC XXVIII 28). Cf. P. Meinhold (1962), pp. 123 f.

[8] 177:31 — consensum omnium prophetarum. Hoc vere est allegare ecclesiae auctoritatem (Ap IV 83); 214:37 (Ap IV 273); 265:20-22 (Ap XII 66); 313: 35-41 (Ap XX 2).

tion,[9] purgatory,[10] and *opus operatum*,[11] are contrary to Scripture. But this appeal to Scripture in no way includes a demand to reiterate Scriptural formulations in a literal way.[12] The Confessions, too, use terms that cannot be found in the Bible but are in harmony with its meaning. The same is true of the formulations employed in the ancient creeds of the church. Using Scripture as their point of departure, the Symbols recognize the need to criticize certain aspects of the medieval tradition based upon Peter Lombard's *Sentences*.[13] For the same reason they can accept at least a number of isolated statements found in the medieval tradition. The dominant viewpoint is always the same: The proclamation of the church must remain identical with itself, forever unchanged. That which has been preached about God's grace and salvation through Christ *from the beginning of the world* is always valid.[14]

The conviction concerning the identity of the church's proclamation also gives tradition a certain importance for the exposition of the Bible. Scripture therefore does not have a merely critical function to fulfill over against tradition; the latter also has a degree of importance as a guide for the church in its own exposition of Scripture. To support the argument that the Confessions did not introduce any novelties, it was important to be able to refer to patristic utterances. There is, in other words, a line which runs from the Scriptures to the later tradition; but also in the reverse: Beginning with tradition, one can also find the road which leads back to Scripture. During the 16th-century theological confrontations the ancient creeds served as guides to the Scriptures. Luther and Melanchthon approved of Biblical interpretations which affirmed the dogma of the Trinity, while those which did not were rejected as mistaken.

That Luther deliberately chose a line running counter to the radical

[9] 291:42 — Sie werden auch sehen, dass die Widersacher viel aus eigenem Hirn erdichten von Verdienst der Attrition, von der Erzählung der Sunde, von Gnugtuung, welchs alles in der Schrift ungegründet (Ap XII 178).

[10] 421:3 (SA II II 13).

[11] 374:5-15 (Ap XXIV 89).

[12] Cf. what was said above on this, together with Luther's statements in WA 8, 419:28 (*De abroganda Missa privata*, 1521), plus the critique thereof in CR 27, 91.

[13] 266:6 — Non igitur hanc Petri vocem (Acts 10:43) non dubitemus opponere quamlibet multis legionibus Sententiariorum, quae allegat consensum prophetarum (Ap XII 70).

[14] 266:20 — Et hanc sententiam sciant a principio mundi in ecclesia extitisse apud sanctos (Ap XII 73).

tendencies within the Reformation can be seen in his letter on rebaptism written in 1528. He traced all heresy back to the denial of the
Second Article of the Creed, which sets Christ forth as true man and
true God.[15] Melanchthon also upheld the idea that the ancient creeds
can be used as guides back to Scripture.[16] But the connecting line is
not unbroken, not even in the first five centuries of the church's
existence. Rather, the truth is to be found in isolated points, elucidated
by individual theologians, with Scripture serving at all times as the
supreme norm. The authenticity of what the church says today depends
on its factual agreement with what the church has said in all ages,
through those who have understood the true meaning of Scripture.
Finally, it becomes a question of the most valid interpretation of the
Bible, but references to the fathers serve to remind us of the continuity
in the church's proclamation.

Article VII of the Augsburg Confession is also properly explained
from this point of view. It begins with the confession that "one holy
Christian church will be and remain forever," and at the conclusion
Melanchthon refers to Eph. 4:4-6. It is no secret that Melanchthon attached great importance to Eph. 4, as supporting the claim that the
church shall never be destroyed.[17] And when he quoted the same
chapter from Ephesians in AC VII, we have in this a direct expression
of the Reformation's twofold intention: to let the Word of God reign,
but in the light of the tradition whose roots go back all the way to the
protevangelium of the Old Testament, and which has been preached
to successive generations with varying degrees of success and power
ever since. Against this background the Lutheran Reformation developed its special character of preserving and reforming at one and the
same time.

[15] WA 50, 267:14 — 268:20 (*Die drei Symbole oder Bekenntnis des Glaubens
Christi,* 1538). Cf. John 1:22 f. and 4:2 f.

[16] P. Fraenkel (1961), p. 180.

[17] CR 5, 691 (*Praefatio,* 1545); P. Fraenkel (1961), pp. 153—62.

Chapter Three:

Law and Gospel

1. The Law

As we have seen, the distinction between Law and Gospel plays a most important role in Reformation theology. To be able to distinguish properly between these two was looked upon as the most difficult art in the field of theology. In LC, Luther drew a sharp contrast between commandment and faith. The former deals with what we must do vis-à-vis God, the latter with what God does for us (LC II 67).[1] Melanchthon introduces his lengthy presentation on justification in Ap IV with a reminder of how important the distinction between Law and Gospel (or, as he usually says, Law and Promise) is *to an understanding of the doctrine of justification by faith.* [2]

But, as we can also show, the confessional statements on Law and Gospel do not contain any general orientation for the interpretation of the Bible; Law and Promise serve a different, clearly limited purpose. They are designed to assist the Bible reader and the preacher in understanding what the Bible says—often in seemingly contradictory passages—about faith and works, justification by grace, and a life of holiness. Melanchthon introduced his discussion of justification by faith with the important distinction between Law and Gospel in order to clarify the premises on which the doctrine of justification rests. The distinction between Law and Gospel enabled him to establish a uniform interpretation of what the Bible says about good works. In his controversy with Roman Catholic theology Melanchthon made it clear that the Bible speaks of the necessity of good works in many places. But as he understood them, these statements must be placed in their proper context. When the Bible speaks of works, it always presupposes justification by faith. Works in the Bible are always the fruits of justification, not the cause. By using the concept of Law and Promise as a lens through which to view the Scriptural statements concerning good

[1] 661:21-25. Cf. 646:3-12 (LC II 1), and 642:10-11 (LC Conclusion).

[2] 159:14-20 (Ap IV 4). Ap does not here provide principles for the interpretation of the Bible, but instead sets forth the Biblical background for the teaching of justification by faith, and therefore for the questions involved in how the Biblical statements about faith and works should be understood. See above, Chapter One, part 3.

works, contradictions can be eliminated. Then the Biblical expressions
become uniform. Law and Gospel are not therefore master keys to the
Bible, but only to the significant question concerning man's justification before God. The principle, *regula,* of Law and Promise gives
meaning to all Scriptural statements on good works (Ap IV 185). But
if Law and Gospel do not constitute a general principle to which even
clear and obvious Bible passages must conform, they are important
enough when related to that problem which the reformers considered
the weightiest of all theological problems, viz., how can man be freed
from sin and become righteous before God? As a result, it is all the
more urgent to find out what the Symbols mean by Law and Gospel.
A closer look at these concepts reveals that their content is highly
complicated.

There is no definition of Law in the Lutheran Confessions. The
word appears in different contexts, and its meaning varies. It may
point to clearly defined statements, such as the Ten Commandments,
e. g., or to their corresponding substance, wherever this may appear in
the Bible. But in other contexts Law has a purely functional meaning
and points to a word which the reader understands to be a demand or a
judgment. Used positively, Law can serve as a norm and guide, but
negatively it appears as an accusing power which can be overcome only
by the promise of the Gospel. In this way, both cooperation and tension are found to exist between Law and Gospel.

In the midst of these numerous and seemingly antithetical statements on the Law there is, nevertheless, an important and dominant
point of view. The Law is, above all, God's eternal will. The divine
will includes directions concerning one's mode of living and relations
to God, and is directed against human unrighteousness and sin.[3] This
double function of the divine will explains why the Law can appear
both as a guide and as an accuser. It is inevitable, however, that certain questions which demand more definitive answers will arise. What
is the Law? Where does it appear? How does it work, and how is it
fulfilled?

What the Law Is

In his *Loci theologici* Melanchthon distinguishes between natural,
divine, and human law *(lex naturae, lex divina, lex humana).* When
thinking of *lex divina,* he has in mind the divine law as revealed in
Scripture, which confronts us in both the Old and New Testaments,
and whose chief and universally applicable facet is the Moral Law or

---

[3] Cf. CR 21, 388 (*Loci theologici,* 1535), and Althaus (1962), p. 219.

the Decalog.[4] *Lex naturae* is the knowledge of the Moral Law or Decalog imbedded in human nature.[5] *Lex humana* is the summary of the law-making function of society. In contrast to *lex divina,* it is temporary and demands only external obedience.

The same concepts of the Law are to be found in the Confessions, although they are not so systematized. The Confessions distinguish between civil [6] (human), natural, and divine law. The latter two of these, and their relationship to each other, are of the greatest interest to us here.

In consonance with all Reformation theology, the Lutheran Confessions recognize *natural law.* Man's natural knowledge of God was certainly reduced a good deal after the Fall, but it has not been completely lost. With regard to its content, natural law coincides in a general way with the Decalog, which was thought to have been written on all men's hearts. "The Ten Commandments . . . are inscribed in the hearts of all men" (LC II 67). Ap says: "To some extent human reason naturally understands the law since it has the same judgment naturally written in the mind" (IV 7). Through his powers of reason, man has the ability to understand what God has commanded in the Second Table of the Decalog, though only to a limited extent.[7] When forced to make a concrete decision, man has a congenital power of judgment, *iudicium,* which enables him to distinguish between right and wrong. He can obey parents and superiors, refrain from murder, adultery, and theft. In addition to this, he possesses knowledge of God, and he can worship Him in an external manner.[8]

The view of natural law in Ap harmonizes well with what Luther says in LC and other writings.[9] There are two questions, however,

[4] CR 21, 116 and 390 (*Loci,* 1521 and 1535). Siirala (1956) is of the opinion that this division is not typical of Luther, in spite of the fact that Luther made use of it as, e. g., in WA 39 I, 478, 4 f. (*Die zweite Disputation gegen die Antinomer,* 1538). Cf. 160:1-5 (Ap IV 6).

[5] CR 21, 398 — Lex naturae est notitia legis divinae, naturae hominis indita. CR 21, 390 relates *lex divina* and *lex moralis,* which are summarized in the Decalog.

[6] 70:8 (AC XVI 1); 122:27 (AC XXVIII 13); 307:36 f. (Ap XVI 1).

[7] 160:11 — humana ratio naturaliter intelligit aliquo modo legem (habet enim idem iudicium scriptum divinitus in mente) (Ap IV 7); 311:33 — reliqua sit in natura hominis ratio et iudicium de rebus sensui subiectis (Ap XVIII 4). With regard to an analysis of *iudicium,* reference can be made to L. Haikola, *Studien* (1958), 31—37. Haikola, however, exaggerates the demands of the situation at the expense of that which is constant in the will of God.

[8] 311:26-39 (Ap XVIII 4 f.)

[9] In addition to 661:25-26 (LC II 67), see WA 18, 80, 15—81, 3 (*Wider*

that demand a closer look at this point. (1) Does natural law provide knowledge concerning the existence of God? (2) How is natural law related to the Ten Commandments? Josefson deals with both of these problems in his book *Den naturliga teologins Problem hos Luther (The Problem of Natural Theology in Luther)*.[10]

(1) What does it mean to have a God, and what is God? LC raises such questions,[11] and Josefson responds by asking whether our natural knowledge of God includes the certainty of His existence. He both affirms and denies this. Knowledge of God manifests itself in man's ineradicable need of something or someone to depend upon. According to the genuine Lutheran point of view, the lives of all men assume a religious form or shape, i. e., all men act as if they had a relationship to a god. Such gods need not be conceived in supranatural terms, however; they can be created things, which are to be found right within the world around us. (Josefson, pp. 53 – 60)

Luther, however, distinguished between a *general* knowledge of God and a *true* knowledge of Him. Man possesses the latter only because of the revelation of Christ, but all men have knowledge of His existence and of His upholding power.[12] Natural law includes actual though obscure knowledge of the fact that God is, but only Christ provides us with true knowledge of Him.[13] The same point of view

die himmlischen Propheten, 1525); WA 39 I, 374, 2-5 (*Die erste Disputation gegen die Antinomer*, 1537); 540:8—541:1 (*Die dritte Disputation gegen die Antinomer*, 1538). Additional and detailed verification can be found in H. Olsson, *Grundproblemet i Luthers social-etik*, I (1934), which is the basic work within Swedish theology concerning the concept of creation and the Law. Cf. L. Haikola, *Usus legis* (1958), p. 95, which, however, overlooks the fact that the Decalog is written on the human heart, and on the other hand emphasizes the new demands of each actual situation.

[10] R. Josefson (1943), pp. 23 ff. Josefson also deals with this same problem in writing about the authority of the Bible (1953).

[11] 560:9 — Was heisst ein Gott haben oder was ist Gott? (LC I 1); Josefson (1943), p. 48.

[12] WA 40 I, 607:28 — Duplex est cognitio Dei, generalis et propria. Generalem habent omnes homines, scilicet, quod Deus sit, quod creaverit coelum et terram. . . . Sed qui Deus de nobis cogitet, quid dare et facere velit, ut a peccatis et morte liberemur et salvi fiamus (quae propria et vera est cognitio Dei) homines non noverunt. (*In epistolam S. Pauli ad Galatas commentarius*, 1535); WA 46, 669:19-32 (*Auslegung des ersten und zweiten Kapitels Johannis*, 1537—38). Cf. Althaus (1962), pp. 27 ff.

[13] WA 16, 372:1 — hae quaedam leges datae omnibus gentibus, ut quod unus deus sit (*Predigten über das 2. Buch Mose*, 1524—27), and WA 40 I, 607:19 — omnes homines naturaliter habent illam generalem cognitionem, quod sit Deus (*In epistolam S. Pauli ad Galatas commentarius*, 1535). For further details consult H. Olsson (1934), pp. 37 f., and L. Haikola, *Usus legis* (1958), p. 96, n. 39.

appears in the Confessions. The heathen, the Turks, and the Jews know that God is, but they do not know what He is really like in the essence of His being.[14] The Confessions emphasize the *defectiveness* of the natural knowledge of God; it provides a false picture of God and therefore promotes work-righteousness. They do not so much stress the lack of natural knowledge about God as they do its falseness. The natural knowledge of God sets forth a distorted picture of Him. It is incapable of showing us the God who justifies and saves from sin.

As Josefson has shown, Luther presented a different point of view in his exposition of the First Commandment in LC. But this difference can be explained by the fact that he was not in that instance discussing the problem of our natural knowledge of God; he was rather dealing with the matter of true faith or false faith, whereby a man has either God or an idol as his Lord. In LC's discussion of the First Commandment it is pointed out that "the purpose of this commandment . . . is to require true faith." [15] Since questions completely different from the one concerning the existence of God are treated in the exposition of the First Commandment, it does not offer us a suitable basis on which to discuss the problem of our natural knowledge of God. Even there it is said, however, that God is merciful to those who fear Him, and wrathful toward those who meet Him with contempt. And this presupposes that God is. But true knowledge of Him comes to man in no way other than through Christ's revelation.[16]

(2) The second question concerns the relationship between natural law and the Ten Commandments. Luther's lofty evaluation of the Decalog is well known. He gives expression to this in the catechisms, where these very commandments form the frame for Christian morality. It will suffice to quote what LC says in the conclusion to the exposition of the Ten Commandments: "Here, then, we have the Ten Commandments, a summary of divine teaching on what we are to do to make our whole life pleasing to God. They are the true fountain from which all good works must spring, the true channel through which all good works must flow. Apart from these Ten Commandments no deed,

---

[14] 661:7-15 (LC II 66). The corresponding Latin text reads thus: quamquam unum tantum et verum Deum esse credant et invocent, neque tamen certum habent, quo erga eos animatus sit animo. Cf. WA 28, 611:26-38 (*Predigten über das 5. Buch Mose,* 1529).

[15] 560:30-31 (LC I 4). Cf. WA 30 I, 28:6-7 (*Katechismuspredigten,* 1528).

[16] Cf. on this problem Schlink (1961), pp. 48—57, as well as Brunstäd (1951), pp. 32—34. Schlink downgrades the natural knowledge of God in the Confessions.

no conduct can be good or pleasing to God, no matter how great or precious it may be in the eyes of the world." [17]

But in opposition to this seemingly unreserved adherence to the Decalog are other statements, much more temperate, nearly negative in tone. Most of these appeared before 1528. The law of Moses, which, according to Luther, also included the Decalog, was intended only for the Jews. It is "der Juden Sachsenspiegel" [18] and is valid for Christians only to the extent that it agrees with natural law. "Therefore I keep the commandments which Moses gave, not because Moses gave them but because they have been implanted in me by nature and Moses here agrees with nature." [19]

Without touching upon Luther's various statements on the Decalog before and after 1528, Josefson [20] emphasizes the following in discussing the relationship between the Decalog and natural law, *lex naturae:* (a) *Lex naturae* is the critical principle as far as the law of Moses is concerned. Only those commandments which correspond to natural law are binding. (b) Natural law does not in any precise way go beyond the command to love one's neighbor. It is given meaning and content within a concrete social context.[21] (c) In a given situation man can use his powers of reason to decide what the law (i. e., love) demands of him (whether or not he thinks of himself as a Christian does not matter). One certainly cannot comprehend God through reason, but one can nevertheless sense his responsibility to his neighbor in accordance with God's will. (d) It is therefore to a certain extent unnecessary to speak of a unique Christian ethic. In an external sense, the Christian behaves in the same way as the non-Christian.[22]

Of basic significance in this line of reasoning is the idea that *lex naturae,* as a superior principle, is a critical authority vis-à-vis the

[17] 639:11-19 (LC I 311); 164:39-41 (Ap IV 22).

[18] WA 18, 81:14 (*Wider die himmlischen Propheten,* 1525).

[19] WA 16, 380:23 (*Predigten über das 2. Buch Mose,* 1524—27). Concerning this mode of thought in Luther see, e. g., Meyer (1929), pp. 155—57 (lit.), and Olsson (1934), pp. 32—35, plus Josefson (1943), pp. 84—93.

[20] R. Josefson (1943), pp. 84 ff.

[21] Josefson, pp. 93 ff. Cf. the same trend of thought in Olsson (1934), pp. 19 and 62; in Haikola, *Usus legis* (1958), p. 95; and the same author in *Studien* (1958), pp. 31—35. These ideas have played a prominent role in the discussion of social matters.

[22] In his later work, *Bibelns auktoritet* (1953), pp. 177—83, Josefson has revised his earlier view at several points. The situation-ethic concept has been modified, and greater emphasis has been given to the Decalog.

Decalog. Does this hold up in the presence of Luther sources and the Confessions?

One must point out here, in the first place, that natural law has a far more definitive content than one might derive from what was said above. When Luther says in LC that the Ten Commandments are written on the hearts of all men,[23] this is — generally speaking — characteristic of the Reformation point of view. Every time Luther speaks of the *lex naturae*, he has in mind that its meaning corresponds to the Decalog. He points to both a general (although distorted) knowledge of God and to a rational insight into our responsibility toward our neighbor.[24] To Luther, Paul's statements as recorded in Romans 1:19 ff. and 2:14 were binding proof of the natural law.[25] A similar view of natural law can be found in those parts of the confessional writings for which Melanchthon was responsible.[26]

In the second place, Luther's statements critical of the Decalog are related to his opposition to Andreas Carlstadt and the Biblical interpretation of the radical wing of the Reformation (WA 18, 16:12 ff.). In opposing their adherence to the Old Testament ban on pictures (Ex. 20:4) and their demands for a radical alteration of the Mass, Luther emphasized that the Decalog is not a law applicable to Christians. They are bound to it only to the extent that it corresponds to natural law.[27]

Thomas Aquinas had expressed the idea that natural law is a critical authority vis-à-vis the law of Moses, inasmuch as the latter also includes ceremonial law and judicial law, but he never questioned the Decalog. The Decalog is a summary of the Moral Law, which in turn reflects the meaning of *lex naturae*.[28]

---

[23] 661:25-26 (LC II 67).

[24] WA 16, 372:6 — Wie wol die Heyden auch etlich gesetz haben gemeyn mit den Juden, Als: das ein Got sey, des man niemant beleydige, das man nicht ehebreche, todtschlahe, stele etc. das yhnen natürlich yns hertz geschrieben (*Predigten über das 2. Buch Mose*, 1524—27); WA 18, 80:15-35 (*Wider die himmlischen Propheten*, 1525); WA 39 I, 454:4 — a condito mundo decalogus fuit inscriptus omnium hominum mentibus (*Die zweite Disputation gegen die Antinomer*, 1538), and 374:2-5 (*Die erste Disputation gegen die Antinomer*, 1537). Cf. Althaus (1962), pp. 218 ff.

[25] WA 16, 379:14 ff. (*Predigten über das zweite Buch Mose*, 1524—27); WA 18, 80:19 and 30 (*Wider die himmlischen Propheten*, 1525), Cf. A. Hamel, II (1935), 39 f., and Augustine, *De sp. et litt.*, 26, 43 (CSEL 60, 196).

[26] 166:27-29 (Ap IV 34); 311:26-39 (Ap XVIII 4). Cf. CR 21, 398—405.

[27] WA 16, 373:14 ff. (*Predigten über das 2. Buch Mose*, 1524—27), and 18, 81:4—82:6 (*Wider die himmlischen Propheten*, 1525).

[28] STh 1, II, q. 98, a. 5, and q. 100, a. 1 and 3.

Luther's basic downgrading of the Decalog therefore brought him one step further than Thomas, but the idea of a connection between it and natural law is considerably older than Luther. Since natural law contains nothing about the picture ban or about instructions concerning the Sabbath rest on a certain day of the week (i. e., the seventh day, Saturday), these provisions in the Decalog can be set aside. A day of rest is observed not because Moses prescribed it but because nature teaches us about our need for a day of rest. This can be done on any day at all (WA 18, 81:18 ff.). One perceives immediately that if *lex naturae* is to be able to function in this way as a critical authority superior to the Decalog, it must have a fairly clear meaning.

But there are no traces of this point of view in the Confessions. To be sure, they are still critical of the literal interpretation of the Third Commandment,[29] but the reason for abolishing it is something else. Christians are not bound by those Mosaic regulations which the New Testament has abrogated.[30]

As time passed, the reformers began to emphasize the Decalog more and more and to give it precedence over natural law. One reason for this came out of experiences incident to the church visitations, beginning in 1527. The moral conditions thus exposed caused Luther and Melanchthon to recognize the need for instruction in the Ten Commandments also.[31] The knowledge of God's will provided by natural law was not sufficient; formal instruction in the Ten Commandments was seen to be required. A complete parallel to this development in the preaching of the Law can be found in the Reformation attitude toward confession. Originally confession and absolution were synonymous, but as time went on the former developed into an instrument for church discipline and for determining the extent of Christian knowledge.[32]

Pedagogical justification for a stronger emphasis on the Decalog was strengthened by theological reasoning at this point. Our insights

[29] 580:40-41 (LC I 82). Cf. 633:38-40 (LC I 293), and Meyer (1929), pp. 15 f.

[30] 130:13 (AC XXVIII 59). Cf. WA 16, 374:14 ff. and 424:28 (*Predigten über das 2. Buch Mose,* 1524—27). The Sabbath commandment had been a problem for a long time. There was agreement that Christians were not bound by the literal interpretation thereof. See *De sp. et litt.,* 14, 23 (CSEL 60, 177), and STh 1, II, q. 100, a. 3, ad 2, and 2, II, q. 122, a. 4.

[31] Meyer (1914), pp. 21 f.; same author in NKZ (1915), p. 552; Von Loewenich (1959), pp. 279 ff.; WA 26, 203:5 ff. (*Unterricht der Visitatoren,* 1528), and 50, 470:18-34 (*Wider die Antinomer,* 1539).

[32] K. Aland (1960), pp. 452—519, especially 462 ff.

into natural law, it was said, have been greatly obscured by sin.[33] As a result, the elucidation of natural law by the Decalog is necessary. This more reserved attitude toward natural law is to be found in the confessional writings. There is nothing in them to indicate that the Ten Commandments have been forced aside by natural law. On the contrary, man's natural knowledge of God is thought to be seriously defective. Contrary to Thomas, man's reason is not sufficient to enable him to comprehend the intrinsic order of things, and even less can he bring his will into harmony therewith. Man has an incomplete knowledge of God's law [34] and knows it only *aliquo modo,* "in bits and pieces" (Ap IV 7). Consequently, the Ten Commandments were accorded great significance.

So if one asks what the Confessions mean by "Law," the answer finally comes down to the Ten Commandments. "By 'law' in this discussion we mean the commandments of the Decalogue, wherever they appear in the Scriptures" (Ap IV 6). The Ten Commandments are certainly related to natural law, which man can understand in part by the use of reason. But inasmuch as man's knowledge of God has been obscured by sin, the Symbols select the Moral Law of Scripture, the Decalog, as the truest expression of the Law. Since the Confessions clearly define their concept of Law by telling us that they have the Moral Law in view when they speak of Law, we must take their explanation seriously — for there are very few definitions in the Symbols. It will not do to replace the Law with something else — such as man's situation-conditioned understanding of the divine will of love — and claim at the same time that one is reflecting the Reformation position as found in the Symbols. When Luther and Melanchthon there write of Law, they have in mind the definitive expression of God's will as seen in the Ten Commandments. They agree with Augustine in this concentration on the Decalog, for the latter (as in *De spiritu er littera)* always referred to the Decalog when he spoke of the Law.[35]

But the Confessions make this significant additional statement concerning the Ten Commandments: "wherever these may be read in Scripture." This means that the will of God as expressed in the Decalog is to be found in all of Scripture. The admonitions recorded

[33] Luther set forth this point of view as early as in his *Predigten über das 2. Buch Mose,* 1524—27 (WA 16, 447:20-25), and in WATi 3, 484:10 (1537). Cf. CR 21, 140 *(Loci,* 1521).

[34] Cf. E. Schlink (1951), 247 f., and H. Olsson in STK (1950), 371 ff.

[35] *De sp. et litt.,* 13, 21—14, 23 (CSEL 60, 173 ff.).

in Romans 12 are an expression of this uniform, divine will.[36] The
Confessions do not, therefore, restrict the Law to the two chapters in
the Old Testament which include the Decalog (Exodus 20 and Deu-
teronomy 5). On the other hand, the spirit of the Moral Law is reflected
in the entire Bible, in the teaching of Jesus and the apostles, and in
specific events referred to throughout Scripture. This rather unfettered
view of the Law is related to what the Confessions consider one of the
fundamental facts, viz., that the Law is not a collection of statements
which must be strictly applied; it is an expression of the will of God.
The content of this will is by all means clear and distinct, particularly
as summarized in the Ten Commandments. But its application takes
place in concrete situations.

If one therefore bears in mind that "law" in the Confessions refers
to the Decalog or to that which corresponds to it (i. e., the Moral Law),
it may seem strange that the authors also appear at times to speak of
law as having a purely functional meaning. In some statements it
seems as though the Law is not identified with the Decalog. On the
other hand, it is said to be a divine activity, an expression of God's
active will. The emphasis clearly shifts from content to activity, to
God's action through the Law. It appears that the Law is identified
with this activity.

Does this imply a completely new concept of law, one at variance
with the Moral Law? The question is important, for a consistently
functional interpretation of law is frequently found in contemporary
Lutheran theology. According to this modern concept, the Law and
the Decalog are not the same thing. Mention of the word "law" evokes
the question of how the word "operates," and not the idea of a static
meaning.[37]

In order to be able to take a position vis-à-vis this significant problem, we must take a look at the most important sources. As we already
know, the Lutheran Symbols introduce their presentation of justification by distinguishing between Law and Gospel. In this connection
Melanchthon expressly states that when he speaks of law he means
the Moral Law, which is contained and summarized in the Decalog
(Ap IV 5 f. and IV 183-188). But here it must be observed that the

---

[36] Cf. CR 21, 390 — Et quia decalogus continet summam talium praeceptorum; ideo appellatione decalogi plerumque solemus intelligere moralia praecepta, ubicunque in scripturis extant, quae praecipiunt aliquid de virtutum officiis;
cuiusmodi sunt praecepta Rom. 12 et alibi (*Loci,* 1535).

[37] A. Gyllenkrok in NKT (1953), p. 77. Cf. G. Wingren (1955), pp. 257 ff.,
G. Ebeling in ThLZ (1950), pp. 243 f., plus the critique in H. Ivarsson (1956),
pp. 79 f., and E. Schlink (1961), pp. 135 f.

Confessions can, in quite the same way, speak of the Law in the sense of a divine activity. In connection with a statement in Is. 28:21 [38] they distinguish between God's proper work and His alien work, between *opus proprium* and *opus alienum,* and these concepts are placed in juxtaposition with the distinction between Law and Gospel. The Law is God's alien work, the Gospel His proper work. The idea is summarized thus: "These are the two chief works of God in men, to terrify and to justify and quicken the terrified. One or the other of these works is spoken of throughout Scripture. One part is the law, which reveals, denounces, and condemns sin. The other part is the Gospel, that is, the promise of grace granted in Christ. This promise is repeated continually throughout Scripture." (Ap XII 53) [39]

These sentences are found in a section on penitence in which Melanchthon insists that repentance and faith are its two components.[40] The whole of Scripture tells us how God deals with man in a twofold manner. He frightens him and reveals to him the serious consequences of sin, and He frees him from agony of conscience. He kills and makes alive; he brings down into the realm of the dead and back up again (1 Sam. 2:6; Ap XII 50). A report of this appears in the very first pages of the Bible, when Adam, after the fall into sin, was confronted not only by the consequences of his actions but also by the promise of a coming Savior (Gen. 3:15; Ap XII 55). The same process continues at all times. God works repentance and faith in man, and the means He uses are the Law and the Promise. Just as the Word of God must be brought to life in preaching, so must the Law be presented in an existential manner. For the Confessions, then, there is no thought of a law other than the Moral Law; it is through the latter that man is confronted by judgment and that he senses the awfulness of sin in his conscience. When the Confessions speak of the Law as God's alien work, *opus Dei alienum,* they therefore refer not to a new law but to the function of the Decalog when God judges men for their sins.

In the same way one must understand another expression which could also give rise to a purely functional interpretation of the Law:

[38] This passage reads as follows in the Vulgate: . . . irascetur: ut faciat opus suum, alienum opus eius: ut operetur opus suum.

[39] 261:43 — Haec enim sunt duo praecipua opera Dei in hominibus, perterrefacere, et iustificare ac vivificare perterrefactos. In haec duo opera distributa est universa scriptura. Altera pars lex est, quae ostendit, arguit et condemnat peccata. Altera pars evangelium, hoc est, promissio gratiae in Christo donatae, et haec promissio subinde repetitur in tota scriptura (Ap XII 53).

[40] 260:20 — hae partes praecipuae nominantur: contritio et fides (Ap XII 45).

The Law is that Word which convicts of sin and judges sin.[41] Inasmuch as this statement is to be found in that same section on penitence which we are here analyzing, there is no reason to interpret it in any other way. In order to give expression to God's activity in the present, the Confessions speak of the Law as *opus Dei alienum*. Speaking of the Law in this functional manner is very common in connection with penitence. In SA Luther proceeds in a characteristic fashion from the Law to human remorse, which is a consequence of the functional interpretation of the Law. The Law is coordinated with God's wrath over sin. Preaching the Law is identical with preaching repentance and amendment of life.[42]

This functional view of the Law is based on Luther's exegesis of the Bible [43] and is related to the vital content which he had found in the Biblical concepts. In the Bible righteousness, wisdom, and power are the result of God's activity in man. So too with the Law. God has not only announced His will in the Decalog; He is also active in it. He works repentance and alarms man's conscience, as expressions of His power to judge. Repentance is man's response to the work of the Law. That the Law operates thus is related to the fact that—in its First Table—it demands a spiritual righteousness which lies beyond man's ability.

Since the Law requires man to do certain things, it can also be compared in some ways to salvation by works. According to this way of looking at things, to teach the Law is the same as saying that good works merit the forgiveness of sins.[44] The Law appears to serve here as an indication of man's efforts to win grace and righteousness before God by means of good works. But neither does this point of view presuppose a new concept of the Law, for here too the Law is understood on the basis of how it operates. The Law is indeed designed to elicit good works (cf. LC II 1). On the other hand, referring to a *doc-*

[41] 260:56 — Lex est verbum, quod arguit et condemnat peccata (Ap XII 48). Cf. WA 39 I, 535:2 ff. (*Die dritte Disputation gegen die Antinomer*, 1538), and 50, 471:23-26 (*Wider die Antinomer*, 1539), plus R. Hermann, *Zum Streit um die Überwindung des Gesetzes* (1958), pp. 19 f.; H. Ivarsson (1956), pp. 77 f.

[42] 436:16 ff. (SA III III 1 ff.); 260:53—261:42 (Ap XII 48 ff.). Cf. WA 26, 202:34 f., with the characteristic comparison of "Busse" and "Gesetz" (*Unterricht der Visitatoren*, 1528).

[43] A. Hamel, I (1934), 129 ff.; G. Ebeling in ZTK (1951), pp. 212 ff. and 227 ff.; A. Gyllenkrok (1952), pp. 31 ff.; WA 3, 9-11, and 465:33-35 (*Dictata super psalterium*, 1513—15).

[44] 267:3 — adversarii dicunt . . . per hunc actum meretur accipere remissionem peccatorum. Hoc nihil est nisi legem docere (Ap XII 75); 174:12-14 (Ap IV 70); cf. R. Josefson (1943), p. 90.

trinal assertion as Law, in contrast to the message, the kerygma, which would then be the Gospel, is unknown.[45] Such a contrast, based on modern ideas, is not to be found in the Confessions.

The confessional concept of the Law is uniform. Law refers in part to natural law, but above all to the Moral Law. The divine will as given there stands forth as an active power.

How the Law Functions

The Law is an expression of God's will. What God wants and says is made clearest in the Ten Commandments. If one recognizes the positive nature of God's will, and presupposes its constancy, the Law operates as a *norm* for men's actions and interpersonal relationships. But if one looks upon the Law as a Word of judgment, it becomes an *accusing power*. Both of these aspects of the Law in operation are to be found in Luther's theology,[46] as well as in the Confessions. With regard to the concept of the Law as norm, the Confessions direct their attention to the positive aspect of the Law in function. With regard to the concept of the Law as accuser, they turn their attention to the negative function of the Law. Therefore their view of the Law in operation is characterized by a dialectic which is one of the distinctive features of Reformation theology. On the one hand, the Law is a power for good, and on the other hand something the Christian can overcome only through Christ. Neither side of its function can be ignored without losing something essential in the Reformation concept of the Law.

A. THE LAW AS ACCUSER

Reformation theology is distinctive for the importance it attaches to the judging and accusing function of the Law. Luther's frequent references to the Law as a power to be overcome are well known.[47] According to Melanchthon, the primary task of the Law is "to reveal

[45] Ragnar Bring in *En bok om Bibeln* (1947), pp. 258 and 261; same author (1961), p. 34. This concept is analyzed and criticized by R. Holte in *Kyrka, folk, auktoritet* (1960), pp. 99 ff.

[46] W. Joest (1951), pp. 51—82, and L. Haikola, *Usus legis* (1958), p. 31. Haikola shares the idea set forth by a number of Luther scholars that the positive will of God manifests itself in the deeds associated with a man's calling.

[47] R. Bring (1929), pp. 154 ff., 174, 207—27; A. Gyllenkrok (1952), pp. 109 f. — Gewöhnlich hat ja das Wort lex in der Theologie Luthers den Nebenton von etwas Falschem, durch den Christenmenschen zu Überwindendem und aus dem Wege zu Räumendem.

sin, accuse, frighten, and judge the conscience." [48] This concept of the
Law's function is not found in Thomas,[49] but it is found in Augustine,[50]
who strongly emphasized that the Law demands much more than we
are capable of. But the idea of the Law as an accuser of the conscience
is even more pronounced in Luther and Melanchthon.

In order to be in a position to understand the confessional interpretation of the Law we must keep in mind the decisive distinction between the First and Second Tables of the Law. The Symbols draw this
distinction [51] on the basis of the New Testament (Matt. 22:36-40) and
ecclesiastical exposition from the early period of Christian history.[52]
In the First Table God demands faith and trust in Him; in the Second,
love to one's neighbor. On the strength of his own powers, natural
man can fulfill the Second Table in a limited fashion, but not the First.
Inasmuch as the commands to love one's neighbor are written in the
heart of all men, it is also possible to fulfill their requirements to a certain degree, i. e., in an external manner. Man can comprehend with his
reason, *ratio,* what God demands, and he is able to live a respectable
life in the external sense.[53]

But a hallmark of Reformation theology is its stronger emphasis on
what man cannot do than on what he can do. Fulfillment of the natural
law is not a basis for justification before God, and besides, such attempts are highly defective. So strong is the power of sin, and so great
is man's inability, that only a few live up to the demands of the Second
Table of the Law. In general, men follow their evil desires rather than
the light of knowledge which they possess by virtue of their congenital
power of judgment, *iudicium.* When even philosophers fail to live
according to their knowledge — men who theoretically possess certain
insights into the right way — we must expect natural righteousness,
iustitia civilis, to be rare.[54]

---

[48] CR 21, 405 — ostendere peccata, accusare, perterrefacere et damnare conscientias (*Loci,* 1535). Cf. CR 21, 149 ff. (*Loci,* 1521), and CR 15, 633 (*Com.
in epist. Pauli ad Romanos,* 1532).

[49] STh 1, II, q.92, a.2; q.98, a.6; q.99, a.2; q.100, a.12.

[50] *De sp. et litt.,* 5, 8 f. (CSEL 60, 160 f.). This facet of the function of the
Law is strongly emphasized in this book.

[51] 150:15 (Ap II 14). This matter is frequently touched upon in the Confessions, e.g., 160:19-27 (Ap IV 7 f.) and 643:8 (LC I 324—27).

[52] Augustine, *Contra Faus. Manich.,* 15,4 (MPL 42, 306 f.). STh 1, II, q.100,
a.4; G. Biel, *Sent.* II, d.30, q.2, a.l; J. Meyer (1929), pp. 101 f.

[53] 73:2 — Man, to some extent, has the ability "äusserlich ehrbar zu leben
und zu wählen unter den Dingen, so die Vernunft begreift" (AC XVIII 1).

[54] 311:40-49 (Ap XVIII 5).

It is even less possible to fulfill the demands of the First Table of the Law. The greatest demands of the Law are set forth in the First Table's three commandments concerning love to God and trust in God. As has been noted many times before, LC summarizes all of the commandments in the First. "The entire Scriptures have proclaimed and presented this commandment everywhere, emphasizing these two things, fear of God and trust in God." [55] If one is properly adjusted to the First Commandment, fulfilling the others will follow as a matter of course.[56] The First Commandment is the bond which holds everything together, the common denominator of all Ten Commandments. It can be compared to a spring of water which flows through all of the other commandments and gives them life.[57]

But by himself no man can fulfill what God demands in the First Commandment. This commandment is, in itself, good, but because it demands the impossible, and subjects man to judgment, accusation, and ruin, it becomes the very opposite. No man can progress to the point where he is able to keep any of the commandments as God desires.[58] God is not content with external obedience. He expects the commandments to be observed as the result of the kind of unconditioned confidence and obedience that no man is capable of. Man lacks the ability to keep the commandments according to the standard of spiritual righteousness. He cannot fulfill the demand of complete and undivided trust in God. "For who loves or fears God enough? Who endures patiently enough the afflictions that God sends? Who does not often wonder whether history is governed by God's counsels or by chance? Who does not often doubt whether God hears him? Who does not often complain because the wicked have better luck than the devout . . . ? Who is not tempted by lust? . . . And David says . . . 'Therefore let every one who is godly offer prayer to thee' (Ps. 32:6). Here he shows that even the godly must pray for the forgiveness of sins." [59]

Ap can likewise refer God's demand to the entire First Table. "But the Decalogue does not only require external works that reason can somehow perform. It also requires other works far beyond the reach

[55] 643:8-10 (LC I 324). Cf. A. Siirala (1956), pp. 24 ff.

[56] 572:12 — wo das Herz wohl mit Gott dran ist und dies Gepot gehalten wird, so gehen die andern alle hernach (LC I 47).

[57] 644:17-22 (LC I 328); 643:24-30 (LC I 326).

[58] 640:39 — kein mensch so weit bringen kann, dass er eins von den zehen Gepoten halte, wie es zu halten ist (LC I 315).

[59] 194:31 (Ap IV 167 f.). Cf. 155:33-43 (Ap II 42 f.) and 282:41 — nemo tantum facit, quantum lex requirit (Ap XII 142).

of reason, like true fear of God, true love for God, true prayer to God, true conviction that God hears prayer, and the expectation of God's help in death and all afflictions." [60]

In Ap IV 131 Melanchthon refers to the "eternal law," *lex aeterna,* by which he means God's demands in the First Table of the Law.[61] Theology is distinct from philosophy because it requires faith in God and is not content with good works alone. In the theological sense, the Law demands much more than good works; it is directed toward human desires, toward the emotions and the affections of the heart.[62] Equipped with the proper affections, man's inner life is filled with faith, love, and obedience toward God. In this way he fulfills what the Law, in a theological sense, requires (i. e., he fulfills the First Table of the Law). Evil affections, on the other hand, are called into being by faithlessness, lack of love for God and trust in Him, ingratitude, impatience in time of testing, and fear of death. Because of his corrupt nature, man is filled with negative affections, his heart is full of evil desires, and there is nothing he can do by himself to alter this situation. When confronted by the demands of the Law, he becomes aware of his powerlessness, and the Law constantly accuses him of lack of obedience. The Law directs its shafts towards his conscience and reminds him relentlessly of how poorly he fulfills God's will. The concept of the Law as judge and accuser is inextricably related to its demand for sincere faith and man's inability to fulfill this demand.

Unless one takes note of the enormous weight the Confessions attribute to the First Table of the Law, or the First Commandment, one will misunderstand both the anthropology of the Reformation and its concept of original sin. In comparison to civil law and philosophical, ethical systems, God's law is distinctive in that it demands a right attitude toward Him. But since man is unable to fulfill this demand, all his deeds are evil—even those which appear good to his fellowmen. When man does good deeds apart from the Holy Spirit, he sins—even then—for in such a case he does these with an unclean heart (AP IV 35). The Reformation concept of original sin is also tied in with the

[60] 160:20-29 (Ap IV 8).

[61] 186:20 — Illam aeternam legem et longe positam supra omnium creaturarum sensum atque intellectum: Diliges Dominum Deum tuum ex toto corde (Ap IV 131).

[62] 185:20 — Loquimur autem non de ceremoniis, sed de illa lege, quae precipit de motibus cordis, videlicet de Decalogo (Ap IV 124); 186:12-15 (Ap IV 130); cf. CR 21, 192 (*Loci,* 1521). With regard to the teaching about the affections see Chapter Five.

First Table of the Law.[63] In opposing the scholastic theologians of the high and later Middle Ages, the Confessions set forth two criticisms, both of which reveal the significance they attribute to the First Table of the Law. The first of these was directed at the scholastic tendency to confuse philosophical and spiritual righteousness, *iustitia civilis* and *spiritualis,* which caused theologians to ignore the fact that the Law demands more than good works (Ap II 43 and IV 12-16). As a result of this, in the second place, it was falsely assumed that man can fulfill the commandments of the First Table on the strength of his own ability. (Ap II 8)

God's law is directed at man's heart, and it says to his conscience: "You shall love the Lord your God with all your heart" (Deut. 6:5) and "You shall not covet" (Rom. 7:7). But when man discovers that he is unable to fulfill these demands, the Law — which was designed to be a help and a guide — becomes instead an accusing power,[64] a power which puts fear into his heart.[65]

The Law as norm and as a power of destruction need not, therefore, presuppose two distinct concepts of the Law; these two uses of the Law are rather based on the fact that it makes demands which no one can fulfill in his own strength. The reformers tried to prove from experience that man is unable to fulfill the Law, but their intention was to provide a commentary on St. Paul's exposition of the Law in Romans and Galatians. Their analysis of the Law as an accusing power rests on their interpretation of Rom. 4:15: "The Law brings wrath."

B. THE LAW AS NORM

In addition to its judging function, the Law in the Confessions also has a positive task — to serve as a guide. This follows of necessity from the connection between natural law and the Decalog. It may be sufficient at this point to refer back to what was said earlier about the Decalog's perpetual significance as a guide to those good works which God wants done.[66] By fulfilling a positive normative function in this way, the Law liberates the burdened conscience from the false demands of work-righteousness.

[63] 150:5-17 (Ap II 14).

[64] 385:13 — haec praecepta omnes sanctos accusent: Diligas Dominum Deum tuum ex toto corde tuo. Item: Non concupiscas. Propheta ait: Omnis homo mendax, id est, non recte de Deo sentiens, non satis timens, non satis credens Deo (Ap XXVII 25). Cf. *De sp. et litt.,* 13, 21 (CSEL 60, 173 ff.).

[65] 167:30 — Lex enim semper accusat conscientias et perterrefacit (Ap IV 38).

[66] 639:11-19 (LC I 311). Cf 302:19 — die rechte guten Werk, die Gott in zehen Geboten fordert (Ap XV 25).

There is a problem of terminology here, however — one which is related to the Law's judging function. It may be stated thus: To the degree that the Law not only does the work of condemnation but is also identified with condemnation, there seems to be no room left for a positive function. As accuser, it is instead something which must be overcome. Nevertheless, even in earliest Lutheranism the Law always had an accusing as well as a normative function.[67] Joest [68] has attempted to show that Luther's writings, which emphasized the negative, accusing function of the Law more strongly than other Reformation sources, also pointed to the positive use of the Law. Luther spoke of *observationes* and *remedia,* of *exemplum* and *Gebot.* One cannot deny that Luther and Melanchthon had differences of opinion concerning the Law. In spite of this, there is relative unity on the subject in the Confessions.

When they refer to the Law's positive function as norm, the Confessions choose to employ other terms than "law." They usually speak of *Gebot, praeceptum,* and *mandatum.*[69] Runestam [70] is correct in stating that "command," *mandatum,* has a much less hostile connotation than "law" in Reformation parlance. The Lutheran Symbols rediscovered the positive use of the Law in the Decalog. It is worthy of note that LC never refers to the Ten Commandments as "law"; it chooses to use other expressions. No "doctrine or social order" can be placed side by side with the Ten Commandments (LC I 317). Even in the places where one would expect to see the word "law," LC speaks of the Ten Commandments. In the passage where LC quotes the psalter's song of praise to the Law (Ps. 1:1-3), Luther paraphrased the original "law" with "God's Word and command." [71] There can be no doubt that the choice of words here was deliberate. If one compares Luther with Augustine, the difference is clear. Having learned from

    [67] L. Haikola, *Usus legis* (1958), pp. 30 f.

    [68] W. Joest (1951), pp. 71—78. Cf. P. Althaus (1952), pp. 7 f., 28 ff., and the same author (1962), pp. 232—38, and also the summary in Haikola, *Usus legis* (1952), pp. 5—12, of the discussion elicited by Karl Barth's critique of Lutheranism.

    [69] E. g., 290:9 — qui boni fructus, docent mandata. The corresponding German text puts it thus: was rechte gute Werk sein, lehren die zehen Gebot (Ap XII 174).

    [70] Arvid Runestam (1921), pp. 213 f.

    [71] 549:30 — Gottes Geboten und Worten (LC New Preface 10). It should be mentioned, however, that the word "Torah" in the original of Psalm 1 included quite a bit more than "law" in the strict sense of the term. All of God's Word was referred to as "Torah." Cf. G. von Rad, *Theologie des alten Testaments,* I (1957), 192—202, and H. J. Kraus, *Psalmen,* I (1960), 4 f.

Paul, Augustine, too, knew how to speak of the Law as a judging and accusing power,[72] but even so he did not hesitate to use the word "law" in referring to the Ten Commandments.

Mandatum is the term used most frequently in the Confessions to designate the positive, normative will of God. We have already made note of how this came about—in Chapter One—and we shall deal with it further in a later context. Both AC and Ap assert energetically that the Reformation doctrine of the Law includes nothing fundamentally hostile to the Law, or antinomian in its attitude. It was necessary for the confessional writers to find an expression also for the positive will of God. The "law" concept was freighted in a negative way as God's *opus alienum,* and because of this the authors sought for an expression for the normative will of God as found in Scripture's two-fold love commandment which summarizes the Decalog. The reformers looked upon two commandments as being particularly basic: to remain in one's earthly calling and to live in the marriage relationship. They drew support for their opposition to ecclesiastical ordinances from the commandments found in Scripture. These alone could liberate the conscience from the compulsion of carrying out futile and self-chosen deeds.

According to the Symbols the faithful Christian fulfills God's will with the assistance of the Holy Spirit. The Gospel is preached in order to empower the faithful to do what they are responsible for according to the Ten Commandments. "The Creed properly follows, setting forth all that we must expect and receive from God . . . . It is given in order to help us do what the Ten Commandments require of us" (LC II 1-2). This statement includes the twofold Law fulfillment: to trust God with the heart, and to do works of love toward one's neighbor in faith. In the same manner Ap repeats time after time that the Christian can fulfill the Law only with the aid of Christ or the Holy Spirit.[73] In his own strength man is certainly able to do it in an external way, but fulfilling the Law with the whole heart is possible only in faith with the help of the Holy Spirit.

Statements of this kind do not disregard the dialectic in the Law and man's inability to fulfill the Law by himself. As a Christian, man is at one and the same time righteous and sinful. This means that he can never fulfill the Law; he cannot satisfy God's demands in the First Table of the Law. The Law continues to accuse the conscience for

---

[72] *De sp. et litt.,* 5, 8—6, 9 (CSEL 60, 160 f.)

[73] 187:34 (Ap IV 132); 187:15-17 (Ap IV 135); 214:8 and 19 (Ap IV 269 f.); 258:48 (Ap XII 37).

failing to fulfill its requirements. But at the same time the will of God functions as a norm—as it is manifested in the Decalog and in the *mandata* of Scripture—which man should strive to fulfill in the power of the Holy Spirit. Thus the fulfillment of God's will is not man's own work, but God's work within him. This is his new option, provided to him by God. Nevertheless, the normative facet of the Law's activity has been pushed into the background as a result of Reformation theology's concentration on the Law as an accusing power. For the reformers nothing could compete in importance with their emphasis on the judging function of the Law, which serves to reveal man's sin to him and to drive him to Christ.

The Use of the Law

The term *usus legis* is not to be found in the confessional documents written by Luther and Melanchthon. The term *officium legis*, which is the equivalent in meaning of *usus legis*, is employed in SA,[74] but this term too is for the most part absent in the documents we are dealing with here. In the Book of Concord it first appears in FC,[75] but it was used in some of the earlier writings of Luther and Melanchthon. Ebeling [76] is of the opinion that it was Luther who coined the term, but this judgment overlooks the obvious origins in Augustine's *De spiritu et littera* (10, 16), where there is an analysis of how the Law is used by the unrighteous and the righteous (even though the term itself is absent). The terminology is fluid in the writings of both reformers, however, and at length both *officium legis* and *effectus legis* came to be used.

The absence of the *usus legis* formula in the Confessions does not necessarily imply, therefore, the absence of that matter toward which the reformers had to take a stand on the basis of their doctrine concerning the Law. In its original meaning the Law was thought to be the same as the active will of God, which appears dimly in natural law and confronts us more clearly in the Scripture's *lex moralis* and in the church's preaching of the Law. But since the Law is frequently identified with its accusing function and with the work-righteousness way of salvation, the question becomes inevitable: How and in what way should the Law be preached and taught? The Law was seen to have both an accusing and a normative function.[77] The attempt to give such

[74] 436:31 and 40; 437:37 (SA III II 4 and III III 1).

[75] 793:5 ff. (Ep VI), and 962:1 ff. (SD VI).

[76] G. Ebeling in ThLZ (1950), p. 242.

[77] Cf. L. Haikola, *Usus legis* (1958), pp. 30 and 108 f.

questions a systematic form has been subsumed under the rubric "The Use of the Law."

This question has been the object of intense discussion within Luther research. We cannot review this in all of its breadth here, but we shall illumine it with material at our disposal in the confessional writings. A few facts should be put on the record as background. Talk of the use of the Law developed gradually during the 1520s. The terminology was extremely fluid at first, but the sole purpose in asking the question was to explain both the reason for preaching the Law and the way in which the Law could be fulfilled.[78] At the outset both Luther and Melanchthon spoke of *two* uses of the Law (though their terminology was somewhat varied). In the second edition of *Loci* (1535) Melanchthon proceeded to speak of three uses. It is believed that he originated the later orthodox doctrine of the threefold use of the Law, *triplex usus legis,* which was accepted by the Lutheran Church. Elert [79] has shown that the statements on the three uses ascribed to Luther in the second antinomian disputation (1538) are a forgery. But beyond these facts there are many questions; we shall briefly touch upon two which are important for our investigation.

Number one: Did Luther and Melanchthon disagree about the use of the Law when the confessional writings began to appear (ca. 1530)? And in connection with that, number two: Did Melanchthon's transition *expressis verbis* from two to three uses signify a change in his point of view? Research in this area has been content for the most part to establish the change in terminology without going on to ask *why* this was done. The transition was certainly related to the antinomian controversies, which necessitated a more precise statement of earlier opinions. As far as Luther and Melanchthon are concerned, there is no recorded difference of opinion between them concerning the use of the Law; if they engaged in a polemical exchange on the subject, it has not been preserved. On the other hand, Luther in his dispute with the antinomians was still able to associate himself with Ap.[80] One must, however, take into consideration the possibility of differences of opinion which both reformers either were unaware of or successfully concealed through the use of devious formulations. The difficulties involved in evaluating this material can be highlighted by comparing two such eminent Luther researchers as Bring and Ebeling,

---

[78] Cf. WA 11, 31:7 ff. (*Predigten des Jahres 1523*), CR 26, 28 (*Articuli visitationis,* 1527), and CR 21, 405 (*Loci,* 1535).

[79] Werner Elert in ZRG (1948), pp. 168—70.

[80] WA 50, 470:21 f. (*Wider die Antinomer,* 1539).

who are in basic agreement with one another. Both assert that Melanchthon proceeded from the two- to the three-use concept around 1535. As far as Bring [81] is concerned, this transition signifies an altered theological position. But Ebeling [82] objects by saying, "Melanchthon already in *Unterricht der Visitatoren* (1528) and in Ap touches upon the idea of *tertius usus legis.*" There is much evidence to support the claim that Melanchthon's understanding of the Law did not change essentially, but that the transition from the two- to the three-use concept simply served to make more precise a position adopted earlier. Following the same line of argumentation, one can say that Luther sets forth a similar train of thought in LC. In opposition to Ebeling [83] one can also state that in one sense the Law for Melanchthon, as well as for Luther, was "not a static, revealed norm" [84] but something purely functional, one facet of God's activity among men. Joest [85] has sought to approach the *tertius usus* problem in Luther from a new point of view. He has concluded that a number of "*tertius usus* passages" can be found in the Luther material, even though the term itself was never used. Against this background, we can now proceed to our material in the Confessions, where the matter is dealt with even though the term *usus legis* is lacking.

In SA Luther asserts that God carries out a twofold activity through the Law. Its primary function is to restrain sin in man's external social life with threats of punishment and promises of mercy.[86] It thereby promotes civil righteousness, *iustitia civilis*. Melanchthon speaks of this righteousness here and there in both AC and Ap, where he refers to it also as "the righteousness of the law," *iustitia legis*.[87]

[81] R. Bring (1943), p. 48.

[82] G. Ebeling in ThLZ (1950), p. 240. Ebeling bases this in part on CR 26:53 — Darumb sollen abermals die zehen gebot vleissig gepredigt werden, darynn alle gute werck verfasset sind.

[83] 639:11 — So haben wir nu die zehen Gepot, ein Ausbund göttlicher Lehre, was wir tuen sollen, dass unser ganzes Leben Gotte gefalle . . . also dass ausser den zehen Gepoten kein Werk noch Wesen gut und Gott gefällig kann sein (LC I 311).

[84] ThLZ (1950), p. 243.

[85] W. Joest (1951), pp. 14 and 71—82. See also P. Althaus, *Gebot und Gesetz* (1952), and the same author reviewed by Joest in ThLZ (1955), pp. 44—48. Cf. H. Ivarsson (1956), pp. 115 ff. and 130 ff.; E. Schlink in *Festschrift für Karl Barth* (1956), pp. 333 ff., and L. Haikola, *Usus legis* (1958), pp. 130 f. and 141 f. It is typical of Haikola to point up the typological differences between Luther and Melanchthon.

[86] 435:18-20 (SA III II 1).

[87] 164:22 (Ap IV 21); 169:17 (Ap IV 47).

God certainly promotes this righteousness with the aid of the Law, and man himself is able to grasp with his powers of reason what God requires, and even to some extent to carry it out. These deeds are necessary and also praiseworthy, but they form no basis for claiming righteousness before God. The activity which God thus carries on through the Law serves human society. In the confessional writings both Luther and Melanchthon are agreed upon this function of the Law—though it is possible that Luther's statements are shaded with a significantly greater degree of pessimism. Because of the presence of sin and evil, God has not succeeded in realizing His goal with the first use of the Law; if anything, man gets worse, or seeks to bring about his own righteousness. (SA III II 1)

The second and the proper function of the Law is to reveal the depths of human degradation, to accuse man, and to convince him of the reality of God's condemnatory wrath (SA III II 4). As such, the Law is "the thunderbolt by means of which God with one blow destroys both open sinners and false saints" and drives them to despair.[88] This is what is usually referred to as the *usus theologicus, elenchticus,* or *spiritualis,* although these terms are not found in the confessional writings. In what was said above we learned to recognize that the Law's function as an accuser of *the conscience* results from God's demand for a complete and undivided love for Him in the First Table of the Law.[89] According to the Confessions, this second function is the proper use of the Law—as discussed by Paul in Romans and Galatians.[90] This accusing function of the Law forms the foundation of Christian righteousness, and it also serves to draw a line of demarcation between philosophy and Christian faith.

Besides these two uses of the Law, the Confessions presuppose in some way a positive, normative function of God's will, applicable also to the Christian. If the Law did not have such a function, it would imply one of the five following possibilities: (1) The Christian is released from the necessity of living in accordance with God's will (antinomianism). (2) He could comprehend with his natural reason what God demands of him, and decide what to do in actual situations. (3) He could comprehend what God demands of him with his reason

[88] 436:23-26 (SA III III 2).

[89] 436:8 — das Gesetz sagen muss, dass [der Mensch] keinen Gott habe noch achte oder bete frembde Gotter an — the First Table of the Law (SA III II 4); 638:43—639:5 (LC I 310).

[90] Cf. CR 15, 631 — Principio monendus est lector, Paulum non loqui de politico usu legis, aut de paedagogia, sed de usu legis in conscientia, agente cum Deo et quaerente iustificationem (*Com. in epist. Pauli ad Romanos,* 1532).

enlightened by the Holy Spirit, and decide what to do in actual situations. (4) He could live spontaneously in accordance with God's will as revealed in Biblical law. (5) He could live spontaneously according to God's will, which is synonymous with love to one's neighbor.

None of these alternatives is found in the Symbols, however. Neither, however, do they say directly that the Law is to be preached to Christians, nor do they assume the same position as FC VI with regard to the third use of the Law. But they do presuppose that God's will is mediated to us in the Ten Commandments and that the Christian is to live in accordance with them. This is emphasized most clearly in the sections written by Melanchthon, but the relationship is in fact the same in LC. The positive function of the divine will can be designated as "law" in Ap, though other expressions are usually sought.

As far as the reformers were concerned, it was self-evident that Christians should do good works. The criterion of such works is not only their benefit to our neighbor; God must also command and approve them.[91] Luther found the norm for good works in the Ten Commandments. If one of the Ten Commandments is ignored, no work can be acceptable to God, regardless of how altruistic it appears to men.[92] But Luther did not refer to the positive divine will as law; he chose instead to employ other designations, especially *Gebot, mandatum, praeceptum.* For Luther the Law was too closely related to God's wrath and judgment to be referred to as the positive will of God — which he undoubtedly recognized and accepted. The divine will accomplishes the positive function of helping the faithful avoid all self-chosen works. While the primary task of the Law is to accuse the old man of sin, it seemed to Luther to be unthinkable that the new man, who is born again through justification, should be accused in the same way. The new man is free from the Law, because he is free from God's accusation and wrath. But he is not free from good works, which the will of God also commands. Luther chose, however, not to refer to this positive will as law — as is commonly done. He used other designations (as listed above).

A similar point of view is to be found in the confessional documents written by Melanchthon. It must be remembered that as late as ca. 1530 Melanchthon still had not formulated his later doctrine of *tertius usus legis;* at that time he was speaking only of two uses, the civil and the spiritual. When, in Ap, he referred to "law" in a strict

91 WA 26, 204:6-8 (*Unterricht der Visitatoren*, 1527).
92 639:16-19 (LC I 311).

theological sense, he had in mind the entire and uncompromising devotion to God demanded in the First Table of the Law. The following propositions are implicit in the Law as understood theologically: (1) As a result of man's lack of ability in things spiritual, no one can fulfill the Law. (2) The Law always accuses us; it shows us the wrath of God. (3) The man who is justified can, with the aid of the Holy Spirit, begin to fulfill the Law (i. e., to trust in God and feel love for Him) — but he can never do this perfectly.[93] (4) The Christian must carry out the good works commanded by God in His law. Melanchthon too sought willingly for labels other than "law" for this positive, normative function in God's will. "True prayer, charity, and fasting have God's command; and where they do, it is a sin to omit them." [94]

We will have reason to return to the positive view of God's will in the chapter on the new life, and can here be content with these short intimations. The Confessions do not overlook the fact that the Commandments have a positive function in the Christian life. Even for Melanchthon the fact that there are good works commanded by God was a safeguard against the work-righteousness which the Reformation so powerfully rejected. The Law — by which is meant the will of God as expressed in the First Table of the Decalog — is obscured or transgressed every time it is conceived of as a way of salvation. This could be done in two ways (Ap XII 145), either by thinking that man is justified by observing the Second Table of the Law, or by concluding that man will be declared righteous before God by observing commandments other than those prescribed by Him. The Law is no way of salvation at all. But appropriate for justification by faith is not a rejection of the Law but instruction therein. This is to recognize its limitations at the same time that its positive function is also acknowleged. It goes without saying that the preaching of the Law has its necessary counterpart in the proclamation of the Gospel.

2. The Gospel

What the Gospel Is

The counterpart of the Law is the Gospel, which like the Law is a complicated entity and appears in a variety of contexts. Its many-

---

[93] 187:15 — Ex his apparet, non posse legem sine Christo et sine spiritu sancto fieri (Ap IV 135); 196:14 — Sed haec imperfecta iustitia legis non est accepta Deo nisi propter fidem (Ap IV 181); 201:21 (Ap IV 214).

[94] 283:9-13 (Ap XII 143).

sided nature is pointed out in FC,[1] but in the literature that has been written about the Confessions this is noted with surprising infrequency. Instead, scholars often falsely proceed on the basis of one fixed meaning. Schlink very definitely indicates that the Gospel can have varied meanings, but the only one he gives to it himself is "message, proclamation, the promise of forgiveness for the sake of Jesus Christ."[2] It is obvious that Schlink has here made use of learning which has become common property through the efforts of the form criticism school, i. e., that the basic meaning of the Gospel is "the preached eschatological message of salvation."[3] A number of other scholars have adopted the same position; they proclaim with one voice that the Gospel is a message concerning the forgiveness of sin.[4] This is certainly a vital facet of the Gospel in the confessional writings, but it does not cover the total content.

The Gospel has two or, if one desires, three clearly distinguishable basic meanings. In the first place, it is used with reference to the New Testament writings. In the second place, it refers to the total content of these writings, which is a living reality in the life of the church. And in the third place, it is used specifically with reference to the Word of promise as found in New Testament Scripture and as continuously actualized in the church's proclamation and administration of the sacraments. The first two of these are virtually synonymous and are hard to keep separate; we shall therefore treat them as one. But the emphasis on the Gospel as promise was specifically characteristic of the reformers and necessitates our special attention.

A. THE GOSPEL AS NEW TESTAMENT SCRIPTURE AND ITS CONTENT

This can be said to be the conventional meaning of the term, and it is primarily in this sense that it was used in Catholic literature. The Confutation refers to the Gospel in the singular—in contrast to Gratian, who also spoke of the four gospels.[5] But quite apart from this, "Gospel" in both of these documents refers to the writings of the four

---

[1] 952:20 — Dass das Wörtlein Evangelium nicht in einerlei und gleichem Verstande allwegen, sondern auf zweierlei Weise in heiliger göttlicher Schrift, wie auch von den alten und neuen Kirchenlehrern, gebraucht und verstanden worden (SD V 3).

[2] E. Schlink (1961), pp. 134, 7, 27, and 104.

[3] Cf. M. Dibelius in *Zeitschrift für alttestament. Wissenschaft,* 33 (1918), 146 and 125.

[4] F. Brunstäd (1951), p. 87; R. Josefson (1953), p. 45; Anders Nygren in STK (1957), p. 69, and in NTU, article on "Evangelium."

[5] *Decr. Grat.,* I, d.15, c.1.

evangelists as well as to the contents of the same. That "Gospel" in the singular refers to the four written gospels is due to the fact that the content is held to be one and the same in all. The Gospel in the sense of a distinct entity is older than the four written gospels, but when the Gospel message had been written down by the evangelists, it was natural to permit the word "Gospel" to refer to the four gospels as well. The Gospel is, therefore, the entire message about Jesus, His words and deeds, which the apostles and their successors were commanded to proclaim.[6] Furthermore, the Gospel is the Scriptures which contain this proclamation and instruction. In the Confutation "Gospel" refers above all to the content of the written gospels.[7]

The Lutheran Confessions took over this traditional understanding of the Gospel and made use of it many times. To every Chris.ian of the 16th century the idea that "Gospel" referred first and foremost to the New Testament writings about Jesus' life, His activities and proclamation, lay in the very nature of the matter. It was thus that the term was used in the Sunday worship services. The meaning of the Fifth Commandment is clear, we are told in LC, because Jesus Himself has explained it in the Gospel for the seventh Sunday after Trinity (Matt. 5:21-26).[8] The expression "according to the Gospel," *iuxta* or *secundum evangelium,* is above all a traditional formula, taken over from an older theology. It refers to the four gospels and appears, for the most part, in the discussion of what must obtain in the church. It is used directly as an argument for indicating the organization and authority of the ministry [9] — but also to settle the meaning of penitence [10] and a series of other controversial questions.

But the Gospel concept was soon broadened to include all of the New Testament writings, and it can easily be identified with Scripture as a whole, which naturally served as the deciding authority in questions of faith and doctrine. The Confessions frequently say "the Gospel teaches" or "Scripture teaches" in such a way that it would appear as though they had the same authority in mind. Melanchthon

---

[6] *Decr. Grat.,* I, d.21, c.2 — qui etiam iubente domino in toto orbe terrarum dispersi Euangelium praedicaverunt.

[7] CR 27, 111 — contra evangelium, contra Apostolos, contra Patres. 113 — contra expressum evangelium. See also 116, 117, 134, 135, 162, 163, 176, and 181.

[8] 606:15-27 (LC I 182).

[9] 121:13 f. (AC XXVIII 5), referring to John 20:21-23 and Mark 16:15.

[10] 447:11 — Von dieser Busse predigt Johannes und hernach Christus [auch] im Evangelio, und wir auch (SA III III 39); 250:29 f. (Ap XI 4); 277:38 (Ap XII 122). Cf. above, Chapter One, part 1.

can write in one place (Ap XII 157) "scriptura docet" and in another
(Ap XV 5) "evangelium docet" and mean one and the same thing. We
know that the ceremonial law has been abolished through the Gospel.
So says Ap XV 30, referring to Col. 2:16-17. From this point of view,
it was just as natural for Melanchthon to write "in der Schrift oder
Evangelio" (Ap XII 173) as for Luther to combine these expressions
(LC V 31). Luther often had the New Testament or a certain word
therein in mind when he spoke of the Gospel.[11] If the Gospel is
preached, then the words of Scripture are quite simply being preached
(LC III 47). Likewise, when the Confessions speak of the Gospel's
commands *(mandatum evangelii, evangelium iubet)*, they have New
Testament pronouncements in mind.[12]

In reading the Symbolical writings, however, one soon discovers
—as in reading older medieval documents—that the distinction between "Gospel" as New Testament Scripture and "Gospel" as the
content of the same can be very hard to maintain. The transition from
one to the other frequently occurs abruptly, as in the following statements derived from AC and Tr.

"Our teachers assert that according to the *Gospel* [*iuxta evangelium*] the power of keys or the power of bishops is a power and
command of God to preach the *Gospel,* to forgive and retain sins, and
to administer and distribute the sacraments." (AC XXVIII 5)

"The *Gospel* requires [*evangelium enim tribuit*] of those who
preside over the churches that they preach the Gospel, remit sins,
administer the sacraments, and, in addition, exercise jurisdiction."
(Tr 60)

The word "Gospel" appears twice in each of these quotations, but
it does not mean exactly the same thing. In both instances it refers
first of all to a certain New Testament passage (John 20:21-33), and
then to the total content of these writings in the spirit of Mark 16:15.
If we now proceed to look at the Gospel from the point of view of its
content, we soon find that it is something very comprehensive. It is
not simply associated with the New Testament; it also functions in the
church. The living God stands behind the Gospel, and what He commands and provides lives in the present. The Gospel, like the Law, is
the expression of an activity which is grounded in the active meaning

---

[11] 576:41 — im Evangelio verpoten ist zu schweren (LC I 65); 580:30 — im
Evangelio lieset (LC I 81); 630:9 — nach dem Evangelio, referring to Mark 18:15
(LC I 276); 632:19 — im Evangelio, referring to Matt. 7:12 (LC I 285); 658:13
— Trostsprüche des ganzen Evangelii (LC II 54).

[12] E. g., 289:33 and 37 (Ap XII 172 f.).

of the Biblical concepts. The church has been entrusted with something which is her distinctive mark; it is called the Gospel. The expression denotes, at one and the same time, both an entity closely related to the Bible as well as an activity. If one defines it as preaching, a purely formal point of view has been adopted, in total contrast to the ideas just quoted above from AC XXVIII 5 and Tr 60. While the Gospel mentioned there is to be preached, it cannot simply be identified with preaching without further clarification.

It is not at all difficult to find quotations in Reformation theology which support the claim that the Gospel is an oral proclamation. "The Gospel is not what one finds in books and what is written in letters of the alphabet; it is rather an oral sermon and a living Word, a voice that resounds throughout the world and is proclaimed publicly, so that one hears it everywhere." [13] In the Confessions too there are direct references to the Gospel as preaching. The entire Gospel is an oral preaching (LC IV 30); it appears or operates through spoken words.[14] It is more common, however, for the Confessions to speak of the Gospel's preaching, i. e., the way in which it is applied, the way it functions, in the church (e. g., LC II 38). Such terms as *Zuspruch* or *Botschaft* never appear in the confessional writings. In isolated instances they do employ the expression *Zusage* — in the pregnant sense of proclaiming the forgiveness of sins. The Gospel as *Zusage* is equated with the Word of promise.[15] But even though *Zusage* is used infrequently, this (as we shall see) did not prevent the idea from arising under a different name.

If someone defines the Gospel as preaching or message, he has made the proper and significant observation that the "Gospel" is more than the words of Scripture. It is a proclamation, a doctrine, and a way of life which is available in the church. Jesus' message was already in preparation in Old Testament times, and it is now at work in the church. There should be an identity between the preaching and teaching of the New Testament and of the church. The Gospel affects both man's faith and life; it points to the church's sacraments and to the necessary formation of the ministry. The source of the message is found in the New Testament. The essence of the Gospel is made

---

[13] WA 12, 259; LW 30, 3 (Epistel Sanct Petri gepredigt und ausgelegt); W. Elert, I (1962), 188 ff.; R. Prenter (1946), 127 f.; H. Ivarsson (1956), pp. 19 ff.

[14] 449:8 — durchs mundlich Wort (SA III 4).

[15] 172:4 — dieweil du verheissen hast Vergebung der Sünde, so halte ich mich an die Zusage, so verlasse und wage ich mich auf die gnädige Verheissung (Ap IV 60); 197:33 (Ap IV 188).

clear in the Bible, which is the source of revelation. What the Gospel contains in its totality is made clear by its actual application.

It is said in the article on Baptism (Ap IX 2): "Among us, the Gospel is taught purely and diligently. We have therefore received this fruit from it, by God's favor, that no Anabaptists have arisen in our churches." The people have been protected from the heretical teachings of the Anabaptists by the Word of God. It ought to be fully clear that there is in this statement a connection between the words of Scripture and the Gospel. The Gospel is based on the words of Scripture, but it is somewhat more comprehensive. It is the actual proclamation of salvation. According to the rest of the article quoted above, the essence of the Gospel consists partly in the promise of salvation, *promissio salutis,* which is given also to small children, and partly in the new birth which Christ through the Holy Spirit imparts only through Word and sacrament. The Gospel therefore contains instruction concerning the necessity of child baptism and the sacraments. This instruction is justified on the basis of a Bible passage (Matt. 28:19), but its more precise meaning and implications are made clear in the churches under the name of Gospel.

The expression "the chief article of the Gospel," *praecipuus evangelii locus,*[16] always refers to the doctrine of justification by faith—but what is the Gospel? It signifies either the writings of the New Testament or, what is more probable, *the teachings and instructions which these writings contain and which are continually proclaimed in the church.* It is certainly in this sense that the word is used in Ap XXI 35-36, which speaks of preaching and confessing the Gospel.

In the preface to LC Luther complains about the neglect of private devotions on the part of Evangelical pastors. Having been freed from the compulsion of reading the breviary every day, one could at least desire that "every morning, noon, and evening they would read, instead, at least a page or two from the Catechism, the Prayer Book, the New Testament, or something else from the Bible and would pray the Lord's Prayer for themselves and their parishioners. In this way they might show honor and gratitude to the Gospel, through which they have been delivered from so many burdens and troubles, and they might feel a little shame because, like pigs and dogs, they remember no more of the Gospel than this rotten, pernicious, shameful, carnal liberty." [17] As used here, "Gospel" points to the Reformation message

16 129:2 (AC XXVIII 52); 252:52 (Ap XII 3); 254:35 (Ap XII 10).

17 546:18-31 (LC New Preface 3). Cf. W. von Loewenich (1959), pp. 271 ff.

in its entirety, which includes among other things instruction concerning the Christian life. Many misused the Gospel, claiming a false freedom.

The Confessions provide us with an approximate idea of what the Gospel includes in its totality, although they never give us a precise definition. It deals with salvation through Christ, with the church, the sacraments and penitence, with the ministry, the life of the individual Christian, and eternal life. Melanchthon listed four characteristics of the Gospel. It speaks of the forgiveness of sin for Christ's sake, of the righteousness of faith, of true penitence, and of the works God has commanded.[18] It is often hard to decide when "Gospel" points to something in the New Testament and when it refers to the actual proclamation of the church. There could hardly be any interest in drawing such a line of demarcation. For the reformers the important thing was that the actual proclamation and teaching be in harmony with Scripture.

B. THE GOSPEL AS SCRIPTURE'S WORD OF PROMISE AND AS A DIVINE WORK OF SALVATION

So far we have considered the word "Gospel" as a designation for the New Testament Scriptures and their total content in the actual preaching and teaching of the church. But the term is used also in another, narrower sense as *the promise of the forgiveness of sins,* which is a reality in the life of the church and is therefore an expression of God's ceaseless work of salvation. FC points out that "Gospel" can denote in part Jesus' entire range of activity, and in part the Good News of God's grace in Christ. In this latter sense the term suggests above all a Word of comfort proclaimed to an agonizing conscience.[19]

In reminding us of this facet of the Gospel, FC points to something distinct in Reformation theology, the counterpart of which is hard to find in older theological literature. St. Augustine came the closest, it seems. In his *De spiritu et littera* he distinguished between letter and spirit, and set law and mercy in opposition to one another.[20] But Augustine never makes a direct reference to the Gospel as promise.

---

[18] 393:1 — evangelium de gratuita remissione peccatorum propter Christum, de iustitia fidei, de vera poenitentia, de operibus, quae habent mandatum Dei (Ap XXVII 54).

[19] 791:5-31 (Ep V 6).

[20] *De sp. et litt.,* 9:15 — de sapientia quippe eius dictum est, quod legem et misericordiam in lingua portet, legem scilicet, qua reos faciat superbos, misericordiam uero, qua iustificet humiliatos (CSEL 60, 167).

According to the Confessions, the Gospel, properly speaking, *proprie,* is the same as the promise of the forgiveness of sin.[21] It is another expression for God's gracious will.[22] They arrived at this specific definition of the Gospel as a result of their understanding of Scripture in its entirety. Alongside of the Law, the Promise is there with its assurance of forgiveness for Christ's sake. In his important statement on Law and Gospel (Ap IV 5) Melanchthon asserts that all of Scripture contains the promise of the forgiveness of sins. It can even be found in the Old Testament, in the form of a promise concerning partly the expected coming of Christ and partly the forgiveness of sins. The same promise remains valid and unchanged since Christ has come. So far as the Law is concerned, the Confessions represent the *heilsgeschichtliche* point of view, because they distinguish between the Old Covenant and the New. But so far as the Gospel as a Word of promise is concerned, they indicate no conclusive distinction. The same promise of salvation is found in the Old Testament as in the New; the promise of forgiveness was given not only to the Israelites but also to the heathen (Ap IV 262). This is clearly affirmed in all the books of the Bible, and therefore we can be sure that it is a promise from *God.*[23]

The reformers discovered that in Scripture the Gospel deals with the forgiveness of sin for Christ's sake. Inasmuch as God gives His promise of forgiveness in the Gospel,[24] an abrupt transition from the Gospel, which contains the promise, to an identification between the Gospel and the promise takes place. Thus the Gospel receives the definite and restricted character of a Word of promise. In SA's interpretation of Mark 1:15, "Gospel" is rendered as "promise," [25] and the promise is understood to be a personal statement, *Zusage,* con-

[21] 168:40 — evangelium, quod est proprie promissio remissionis peccatorum et iustificationis propter Christum (Ap IV 43); 226:47 — evangelium proprie hoc mandatum est, quod praecepit, ut credamus Deum nobis propitium esse propter Christum (Ap IV 345); 217:30 — evangelio seu promissione (Ap IV 287); 232:35 (Ap IV 388); 261:49 (Ap XII 53).

[22] Cf. CR 21, 402 — Est igitur Evangelium sententia de voluntae Dei ignota rationi. Vocamus enim proprie Evangelium promissionem, quod Deus propter Christum gratis velit ignoscere et iustificare (*Loci,* 1535).

[23] Cf. the same concept in Luther, WA 6, 560:24-35; LW 36, 107 (*De captivitate babylonica, The Babylonian Captivity of the Church,* 1520).

[24] 258:28 — evangelium de Christo, in quo promittitur gratis remissio peccatorum per Christum (Ap XII 35).

[25] 437:12 — Wie Christus spricht Marci 1:15 — "Tut Busse und gläubt dem evangelio, das ist: Werdet und macht's anders und gläubt meiner Verheissung" (SA III III 4).

cerning forgiveness of sin for Christ's sake.[26] As Luther maintains in his exposition of the Fifth Petition in LC III 88, the Gospel is the equivalent of forgiveness. To nullify the promise is the same as to ignore the Gospel. (Ap IV 264)

As the promise is founded on Holy Scripture, one need not seek for a definite Word of promise, for it is present whenever God promises to raise up and restore oppressed and grieving consciences. The confessors discovered the promise just as easily in Is. 1:18 ("Though your sins are like scarlet, they shall be white as snow; though they are red like crimson, they shall become like wool") as in Luke 6:37 ("Forgive, and you will be forgiven").[27]

Therefore the Gospel is the same as the divine work of raising up oppressed consciences. The Gospel is, so to speak, a mode of operation, a function of the Word.[28] Just as the Law can be thought of as the Word which judges, the Gospel becomes the Word which raises up. In connection with Is. 28:21, the Law is understood to be God's alien work, *opus alienum,* and the Gospel His proper work, *opus proprium* (Ap XII 51). The two things which God does above all vis-à-vis man is to frighten and to make alive. This latter activity is identified with the Gospel in the sense of "the promise of grace granted in Christ," *promissio gratiae in Christo donatae* (Ap XII 53). The promise is repeated throughout all of Scripture and is active in raising up the troubled and oppressed. "First it was given to Adam, later to the partriarchs, then illumined by the prophets, and finally proclaimed and revealed by Christ among the Jews, and spread by the apostles throughout the world" (Ap XII 53). The Gospel becomes the epitome of Christ's entire work of salvation, and it can quite simply be identified with Christ or with Christ's work (Ap XII 257 and 260). It is the name given the divine work of grace, which is manifested in the church's various sacred events. This more functional conception presupposes no new meaning of the Gospel, but is based upon the Word as promise. Apart from Scripture's Word of promise no penitent sinner could be certain of the forgiveness of sin.

How the Gospel Functions

With what was just said above we have crossed over the line to the

---

[26] 172:4 — dieweil du verheissen hast Vergebung der Sunde, so halte ich mich an die Zusage, so verlasse und wage ich mich auf die gnädige Verheissung (Ap IV 60).

[27] 211:7-31 (Ap IV 258 ff.).

[28] Cf. A. Gyllenkrok in NKT (1953), p. 79.

point where we have come to look upon the Gospel as a divine activity in the present.

The Gospel, like the Law, is not an expression for something which belongs only to the past. Rather it is through the Gospel (the promise) that God is now active to save, to help, and to raise up—just as in Biblical times. This means that Scripture's Word of promise must be set forth before contemporary man in the church's preaching and administration of the sacraments. In the proper sense of the term, the Gospel is the promise of the forgiveness of sin, and its most important function is to convey consolation to anxious consciences in preaching and absolution. But at the same time the Gospel also functions in some way as a norm—in its wider sense as the total content of the New Testament. If we are to do justice to the Gospel in the confessional writings, we must have both of these facets in mind.

A. THE LIBERATING AND RESTORING FUNCTION OF THE GOSPEL

That the Gospel as promise liberates and restores the conscience is the characteristic and dominant point of view in Reformation theology. In the Law God appears with His demands; He tells us what He wants done, and He frightens the conscience. In the Gospel, i. e., the promise of grace given in Christ, He assures us of His mercy. The divine promise is repeated throughout the Scriptures, from the first page of the Old Testament to the last in the Bible, and it is always valid. It is for this reason that the Confessions emphasize its oral reiteration. If the promise were simply something in the past, it would be sufficient to read of it in the Scriptures. But it is now as always an actual Word from the living God, and because this is the case it must orally assure the penitent conscience.

This function is frequently spoken of. The Gospel is functioning when it imparts solace and forgiveness.[29] This is God's proper approach to man, whereby He offers him the promise of forgiveness. This is done in a variety of ways, for God deals with us through the Gospel "in more ways than one" (SA III III 8 and III IV). In a well-known statement about the Gospel, SA describes how God operates: first of all through the spoken Word, then through Baptism, through the Lord's Supper, through the power of the keys, and finally through the mutually consoling conversation of fellow believers. (SA III IV)

The Gospel must therefore be active and be brought to sinful men. It is a Word that lives in the present, directed at man's heart. The Gospel in its totality has a point, a major thrust, which it unceasingly

---

[29] 437:27 f. (SA III III 8); 267:24 ff. (Ap XII 76).

seeks to set forth: forgiveness of sins in Christ. This chief doctrine is often referred to in the Confessions as *praecipuus evangelii locus.*[30]

The main purpose of preaching is to bring men to faith in Christ. For no one could know anything about Him or come to faith in Him if the Gospel in the form of promise were not set forth and proclaimed. Preaching is the special medium whereby the Holy Spirit can be active in the church (LC II 38). "For where Christ is not preached, there is no Holy Spirit to create, call, and gather the Christian church." [31] The proclamation of the promise of forgiveness is not the only task of preaching, however, for its content is determined by all the dogmatic and ethical instruction included within the framework of the church year (LC II 31-33). The preaching of the Reformation period certainly had a purely pedagogical function too, a fact which is seen most clearly in the many combinations of "preaching" and "teaching." [32] But the primary intention of all preaching is the presentation of the Gospel (promise), whereby men are led to faith in Christ. (Ap XXIV 32)

But this emphasis on preaching does not contain any negative attitudes towards the written words of the Bible. It is these very words which are to be proclaimed and actualized in the church day by day. The manner in which the Gospel is used is not so important, as long as it is preached and read or meditated upon.[33] The basic purpose of the preaching of the Gospel is to communicate the forgiveness of sins, so that consciences are healed and the assurance of God's mercy renewed.

The same Word of promise is actually set forth in Baptism and the Lord's Supper, each time these sacred acts are carried out. The sacraments are distinguished by the fact that they are commanded by God and related to a promise of grace (Ap XIII 3). The Word of promise is found both in Baptism (LC IV 36) and in the Lord's Supper (LC V 64). However, the Confessions seem to place the greatest weight on absolution and its personal declaration of the assurance of forgiveness. Inasmuch as the Gospel's promise-character is ex-

---

[30] E. g., 252:52 (Ap XII 3 and 10). In this statement "evangelium" must have reference to the entire content of the New Testament, the chief part of which is the forgiveness of sin through Christ.

[31] 655:29-32 (LC II 45); 713:39-42 (LC V 31).

[32] E. g., 662:4 (LC II 70); 671:24 (LC III 40); 305:52 ff. (Ap XV 44), which provide a concise summary of the rich content of Evangelical preaching.

[33] 583:36 — Welche Stund man nu Gottes Wort handlet, prediget, höret, lieset oder bedenket, so wird dadurch Person, Tag und Werk geheiligt (LC I 91); 259:30 — derselbige Glaub an das Wort soll für und für gestärkt werden durch Predigthören, durch Lesen, durch Brauch der Sakrament (Ap XII 42).

pressed most clearly in the words of absolution, it was easy to identify
the one with the other.

In order to describe how the Gospel brings about the forgiveness
of sins in those who receive it in faith, the Symbols employ the
graphic expression "the voice of the Gospel," *vox evangelii*.[34] The
actual message of the Gospel (i. e., the inner meaning of the entire
message of the New Testament) is the proclamation that penitent
sinners receive forgiveness in Christ. This *vox evangelii* speaks most
forcefully in the absolution,[35] and the Gospel came to be identified
with it (AC XII 5). Since the absolution is the Gospel's own voice, we
hear Christ Himself speak therein. Those who receive the words of
absolution, "Your sins are forgiven," can be sure they are hearing,
"not our word, but the voice and word of Jesus Christ, our Savior"
(Ap XII 2 German). This view of the Gospel as Scripture's Word of
promise active in the present is related to the fundamental concept
of the reformers that God deals with us in the present exclusively
through His Word. The reformers knew as little of a direct God-relationship as of a God-relationship provided through the church's
clergy. The Word of Scripture, the Gospel in the sense of promise, is
given by the Holy Spirit, who leads the heart of man from anxiety over
sin to faith. What the New Testament contains and speaks of lives in
the contemporary church. One and the same promise from the living
God is involved here, as well as one and the same work of salvation
through Jesus Christ. It was Melanchthon, not least of all, who was
concerned about establishing a continuity from the so-called *protevangelium* of Gen. 3:15 through the Old and New Testaments and
forward to his own time.[36] When the promise rings out, the conscience
is freed from guilt, and the heart turns from unbelief to faith. But for
it to be a promise, its consonance with Scripture is a necessary presupposition. A promise without support in Scripture would lack au-

[34] 259:39 — Haec est propria vox evangelii, quod fide consequamur remissionem peccatorum (Ap XII 2); 214:41 (Ap IV 274); 381:17 (Ap XXVII 13);
259:6 (Ap XII 39).

[35] 273:11 — absolutio, quae est vox evangelii (Ap XII 105); 214:28 (Ap
IV 371). Cf. H. Ivarsson (1956), 23. But the Confessions do not identify preaching and absolution for that reason — for that would make it appear as though
they were one and the same activity.

[36] 270:15 — Es ist Gottes Beschluss, Gottes Befehl von Anbeginn der Welt
her, dass uns durch den Glauben an den gebenedeieten Samen, das ist, durch den
Glauben um Christus willen ohne Verdienst sollen Sunde vergeben werden (Ap
XII 88). Cf. P. Fraenkel (1961), 41, 62 f., 133 f., and above, Chapter Two,
part 3.

thority. It is Scripture which gives the Word its character as promise and enables it to nourish faith.

The certainty of faith is found in the Gospel, which is to say, in the Biblical Word of promise (Ap XII 88). Because of this, there is an indissoluble connection between the Gospel in the Bible and in the present. The same God uses the same Word to accomplish man's salvation. "Especially amid the terrors of sin, a human being must have a very definite word of God to learn to know God's will, namely, that he is no longer angry" (Ap IV 262). Von Engeström [37] has properly pointed out that it is precisely the Gospel as promise which presupposes a clear Word in Scripture. The certainty of the forgiveness of sin is found in the Gospel, i. e., in Scripture.[38]

B. THE TEACHING FUNCTION OF THE GOSPEL

In the proper sense of the term, the Gospel is the promise of the forgiveness of sins. It has its source in the Bible, and in a Word which is repeated orally in preaching, in the administration of the sacraments, and in absolution. When it succeeds in doing what it was designed to do, it liberates the guilt-burdened conscience. The Gospel is looked upon as a message of freedom. LC glories in the fact that the Gospel brings release from papal coercion [39] by deflecting work-righteousness and by providing a positive view of the Christian vocation in everyday life. But LC also complains about the misuse of Evangelical liberty in the form of laziness and self-indulgence.[40] Such misuse was related to a false concept of the Gospel. As the promise of the forgiveness of sins, the Gospel speaks to the inner man, to the conscience—but it does not dispense with life in the power of the Holy Spirit,[41] with which the Gospel also deals. That the Gospel has a teaching function in addition to its forgiving function is quite naturally related to the fact that in a wider sense it is more than a promise of the forgiveness of sins. As an expression of the entire message of the New Testament it includes guidelines for the conduct of both the church and the individual.

We established the meaning of the Gospel as ecclesiastical norm

---

[37] S. von Engeström (1933), 42 f.

[38] 270:15 — Hanc certitudinem fidei nos docemus requiri in evangelio (Ap XII 88); 270:58 — das heilige Evangelium, alle klare Schrift der Aposteln, die göttliche Wahrheit (Ap XII 90).

[39] Cf. 715:38 (LC V 40).

[40] 501:13—502:19 (SC Preface 2 ff.); 546:28-31 (LC Preface 3).

[41] 726:40—727:1 (LC On Confession 5); 732:23-27 (LC On Confession 30).

when, in the first chapter, we investigated the significance of the expression "according to the Gospel," *secundum* or *iuxta evangelium*. In this time-honored expression, "Gospel" means the same as the New Testament Scriptures. It includes instructions concerning the responsibilities of bishops, and provides a critical authority which opposes their busying themselves with anything other than the preaching of the Gospel and the administration of the sacraments. The Gospel in its wider sense as New Testament Scriptures and their content assisted the reformers in taking a stand in the controversies they had with their contemporaries both on the right and on the left.

In opposition to Carlstadt and the "enthusiastic" tendency within the Reformation's left wing, they asserted that the Gospel provides directions concerning the Christian's relationship to the powers that be. "The Gospel . . . commands us to obey the existing laws, whether they were formulated by heathen or by others" (Ap XVI 3). "The Gospel does not overthrow civil authority, the state, and marriage but requires that all these be kept as true orders of God" (AC XVI 5). In setting forth these principles governing the Christian's relationship to secular authority, the Confessions employed arguments taken from the Gospel, i. e., from the New Testament Scriptures. The Bible passages which provided guidance here included Rom. 13:1 ff. and 1 Tim. 2:1 f. From the same source, i. e., the New Testament, they derived their conviction that even pagan authorities should be obeyed, as long as this could be done without conflicting with one's higher allegiance to God (Acts 5:29).[42] The Confessions here proceeded to build upon principles which the reformers, on the basis of the New Testament, had developed in other writings. God rules partly through secular and partly through spiritual rulers.[43] Secular as well as spiritual rulers are instruments for God's activity in the present (AC XXVIII 18). The non-Christian authority has some knowledge of God's will, derived from natural law.[44] On the basis of the Gospel as New Testament the Confessions also derived the principles that it is wrong to take revenge, that the execution of punishment is the duty of the state, and that a just war is permissible. (Ap XVI 7 f.)

Arguments in opposition to the monk-piety of the Catholic Church were also derived from the Gospel. According to the reformers' interpretation of the Gospel, every man is permitted to live in his secular

42 71:13-17 (AC XVI 6).

43 WA 19, 629; 17, 630:2 (*Ob Kriegsleute*, 1526); 123:10-13 (AC XXVIII 18); 306:4 (Ap XII 44).

44 CR 26, 17 (*Articuli visitationis*, 1527).

position and to care for the obligations entrusted to him. Since the Gospel is not opposed to everyday activities, man is encouraged to remain in his secular calling with a good conscience. "Our theologians have explained this whole matter of political affairs so clearly that many good men involved in politics and in business have testified how they were helped after the theories of the monks had troubled them and put them in doubt whether the *Gospel* permitted such public and private business." (Ap XVI 13)

It is just in the meaning of New Testament Scripture that the Gospel provides information about what the church is actually to teach. The teaching function of the Gospel is also emphasized in what the Confessions say about preaching. The double task of preaching is to make the Christ of the Gospel come alive partly as Savior and partly as Example. The first is most closely related to the Gospel as Word of promise, the other to the Gospel in its wider sense as the content of the New Testament. Ivarsson [45] has discovered a hortatory characteristic in preaching, as the extension and the natural consequence of the Gospel (p. 116). Exhortation does not harmonize with either of the two uses of the Law, and neither can it be identified with the Gospel as the faith-creating Word of promise. It is better to think here of preaching as instruction, about the necessity of which the Symbols are clearly conscious. Preaching is distinguished from absolution, inasmuch as the former also includes instruction on the basis of the New Testament. "If anyone refuses to hear and heed the warning of our preaching, we shall have nothing to do with him, nor may he have any share in the Gospel." [46] The Gospel is both something to have faith in and something to live by (LC Confession 5). In this way one can summarize the entire pedagogical function of preaching — about which the Symbols speak so often.[47]

That the Gospel has a teaching function is obviously related to the fact that it is not only thought of as a Word of promise but also as the New Testament Scriptures. According to the Confessions the New Testament provides both the promise of forgiveness and the source of Christian doctrine and teaching. We find in LC that preaching about the forgiveness of sins should include instruction regarding the Christian life. Such instruction is necessary in order to guide the

[45] H. Ivarsson (1956), pp. 113 ff. See also W. Joest (1951) and P. Althaus (1952); E. Schlink (1956), pp. 323—35.

[46] 732:23-27 (LC On Confession 30).

[47] This is done in the most detailed fashion in 305:52—306:9 (Ap XV 44), where Melanchthon summarizes the content of Evangelical preaching.

congregation into the truth of the Christian faith. During the course
of the church year, instruction in the chief tenets of the Christian faith
should be imparted (LC II 31 f.). One of the tasks of preaching is to
provide necessary exposition of the Scriptures. People will not recognize the distinction between Law and Gospel, and its importance
for understanding the Scriptures, unless they are instructed therein.
And without this, one can easily get trapped in what the Confessions
consider an erroneous imitation-piety. It is through instruction in
Scripture that the hearers are made aware of the unbiblical nature
of monk-piety, which is based on the false assumption that by imitating one of the great saints — a Bernard, a Francis, or a Dominic
— one can win righteousness before God. But these men were moti-
vated to withdraw from the world, not to win righteousness thereby,
but by a desire to have more time for the study of Scripture and for
other exercises. While they lived in the righteousness of faith, their
followers have imitated their way of life without recognizing its deeper
motivation.

Without instruction in the Gospel, i. e., the New Testament, one
cannot come to understand its true meaning (Ap IV 211 f.). Imitation-
piety is based on the imitation of certain conduct while ignoring its
inner motivation. Instruction is required in regard to other questions
too. What attitude shall a Christian have concerning military service
and capital punishment? In other words, what does the commandment,
"Thou shall not kill" really mean? No one needs to be in doubt about
this, asserts LC I 182, for Christ has cleared it up in the Sermon on
the Mount. Luther found occasion here to provide instruction on the
difference between what one is obliged to do in an official position and
as a private person (LC I 181). What is marriage? The Confessions get
their answer from the Gospel (Ap XV 42-43). All such questions require thorough instruction, the source of which is the Gospel. The
Confessions do not hesitate to use the Gospel in this way.

3. Civil and Spiritual Righteousness

There are two kinds of righteousness, the civil, *iustitia civilis,* and
the spiritual, *iustitia spiritualis,* which correspond to the distinction
between Law and Gospel (Promise). Righteousness is a philosophical
as well as a theological term, with roots in both Greek philosophy and
the Bible — though the content is different. These two expressions appear in the Lutheran Confessions first of all in AC's presentation on
the free will. "Our churches teach that man's will has some liberty for
the attainment of civil righteousness and for the choice of things sub-

ject to reason. However, it does not have the power, without the Holy Spirit, to attain the righteousness of God—that is, spiritual righteousness." [1] It was commonly held during the Reformation that an understanding of the two kinds of righteousness was of fundamental importance for anyone who would comprehend the Scriptures. [2] These two kinds of righteousness formed a practical application of the difference between Law and Gospel. If Law and Gospel are the forms through which God works among men, righteousness, *iustitia,* is an expression of man's reaction to this divine activity. But it is also another way of expressing what the Gospel means to man.

There was general agreement that an upright life was required of everyone. A naturalistic view of man is entirely foreign to the Confessions. Man is an ethical being; he is able to distinguish between good and evil, and he possesses a limited knowledge of God through the natural law written in his heart. Man can live on a high ethical level on the strength of his own powers. Aristotle was looked upon as the philosopher who had come the furthest in regard to ethical questions. [3] The best we can do by ourselves is to live an upright life. "As Aristotle correctly says, 'Neither the evening star nor the morning star is more beautiful than righteousness.' God even honors it with material rewards." [4] What man succeeds in accomplishing through rational deliberation upon natural law is referred to in the Confessions as civil righteousness, *iustitia civilis.* It is commonly given other names too, which define it more clearly. It is just as often referred to as philosophical righteousness. [5] Melanchthon defined it as "obedience in agreement with all the virtues, and as an honorable life, externally disciplined." [6] It is closely associated with a life of activity and is

[1] 73:2-8 (AC XVIII 1-2 German). The Latin reads: De libero arbitrio docent, quod humana voluntas habeat aliquam libertatem ad efficiendam civilem iustitiam et deligendas res rationi subiectas. Sed non habet vim sine spiritu sancto efficiendae iustitiae Dei seu iustititiae spiritualis.

[2] CR 15, 443 — Valde prodest in universae scripturae lectione observare, quod duplex sit iusticia. Altera est politica, sic enim docendi causa vocabimus, cum opera bona, seu civilia, ratio humana efficit. Nec videt aliam iusticiam ullam humana ratio. . . . At Evangelium longe aliam iusticiam ostendit, quae vocatur iusticia fidei (*Disp. orationis in epist. ad Rom.,* 1529).

[3] 161:36—162:1 (Ap IV 14). The allusion is to Aristotle's Nicomachean ethics.

[4] 165:3 (Ap IV 24); CR 15, 500 (*Comm. in epist. ad Rom.,* 1532).

[5] 149:36 (Ap II 12); 161:31 (Ap IV 13).

[6] CR 15, 499 — Apud Philosophos iusticia universalis vocatur obedientia iuxta omnes virtutes, id est, externa disciplina honesta, quam homo suis viribus efficere potest (*Comm. in epist. ad Romanos,* 1532).

frequently referred to as the righteousness of works, *iustitia operum*.[7] Since it comes under the domain of reason, it is often called rational righteousness, *iustitia rationis*,[8] and because it is a righteousness which man can produce by himself, it is also known as fleshly righteousness, *iustitia carnis*,[9] or as one's own righteousness, *iustitia propria*.[10] All of these designations serve to express the same thing: a morality of which man has knowledge through natural law and which he is able to carry out with his own powers. But in contrast to a purely rationalistic ethic, this morality is not autonomous; it implies obedience to natural law, which originates with God and which therefore includes directions that are related to the divine law. Therefore it is also frequently referred to as the righteousness of the Law.[11]

The writers of the Confessions do not analyze the content of philosophical righteousness more closely, but they share the Biblical and early Christian idea that God has made Himself known even apart from the Bible. All men possess a consciousness of a higher divine order, which is worthy of obedience. Reason is able to perceive what God, on an external level, commands through His law. Reason conceives of a law whose content agrees in large measure with the Second Table of the Ten Commandments. The Confessions do not know a pure so-called situation ethics[12] in which reason, in agreement with the love commandment, decides from case to case what is ethical. They rather think of a law which is present in man as a rational power, *iudicium*, and enables him to make decisions that concur with the divine will. Reason is capable, to a limited degree, of perceiving what God has ordained in His law.

This obviously does not exclude the frequent necessity of making decisions in concrete situations. The Law is more like a general standard of measurement than a norm which predicts the will of God in all individual cases. What reason is capable of understanding is generally illustrated with examples which correspond to the Second Table of the

---

[7] 311:27 (Ap XVIII 4).

[8] 160:37 (Ap IV 9); 164:37 (Ap IV 22).

[9] 311:37 — Id enim vocatur scriptura iustitiam carnis, quam natura carnalis, hoc est ratio, per se efficit sine spiritu sancto (Ap XVIII 4). Cf. CR 15, 453 — propter iusticiam carnis, id est, propter honesta opera, quae natura suis viribus efficit.

[10] 163:46 (Ap IV 20).

[11] 164:22 (Ap IV 21); 167:36 (Ap IV 39); 169:17 (Ap IV 47); 241:47 (Ap VII 31).

[12] For a discussion of situation ethics, see R. Josefson (1953), pp. 178—84; G. Wingren (1958), pp. 199 ff.; and L. Haikola, *Usus legis* (1958), pp. 92 ff.

Decalog. Melanchthon mentions the following: Do not be angry, do not kill (Fifth Commandment), do not lie (Eighth Commandment), do not commit adultery (Sixth Commandment), obey authority (Fourth Commandment), curb desire (Ninth and Tenth Commandments).[13] As Ap IV, points out, civil righteousness is related to the Second Table of the Decalog. Therein lies its merit—and its limitation. Reason's righteousness is worthy of high praise: It is good and profitable before men, *coram hominibus;* it is necessary for communal living. But its limitation is that it is not sufficient before God, *coram Deo,* inasmuch as it fails to take into account what God prescribes in the First Table of the Law.[14] Theologians leave themselves open to criticism, therefore, if they do not make a clear distinction between the different kinds of righteousness and speak only of *iustitia civilis.*

Although the Confessions recognize that reason has knowledge of God's will as expressed in the natural law, their characteristic emphasis is not upon reason's ability to live an honorable life by imitating the Law. The human ability to act morally is established above all to counter complaints about minimizing man's moral capacity. Reason's limitations are emphasized time after time. It can comprehend God's will only to a certain extent, *aliquo modo.*[15] In spite of all that the philosophers have written about philosophical righteousness, it is rare—even among the philosophers.[16] In principle, civil righteousness can be practiced in one's own strength, with the aid of reason, but frequently it is not realized because of "one's natural weakness" and because of the devil's temptations to a depraved existence.[17] Insights into an upright life are possible to a limited extent, but man's natural weakness is so great that his knowledge is seldom followed. Reason's knowledge is defective, and man's ability is restricted.

Philosophical righteousness can be discussed without any reference to a divine law. But the Confessions do relate it to God's law, the Decalog—and measured thus, it is judged. What the Confessions undertook to do, therefore, was to make a theological judgment of philosophical righteousness. The results of their analysis can be sum-

[13] These examples are derived from CR 15, 443 (*Disp. orationis in epist. ad Romanos,* 1529). Similar ideas are found in 311:26-32 (Ap XVIII 4).

[14] 166:28-30 (Ap IV 34). The expressions "coram Deo" and "coram hominibus" are used in a similar manner by Augustine in *De sp. et litt.,* 8, 14 (CSEL 60,166), where Augustine also distinguishes between spiritual and civil righteousness.

[15] 160:11 f. (Ap IV 7).

[16] 311:46-49 (Ap XVIII 5).

[17] 164:52-53 (Ap IV 24).

marized as follows: (1) Philosophical righteousness makes reference only to the Second Table of the Law; it overlooks the First. (2) It touches only upon external actions, and ignores the deeper motivations. It does not look into the heart, the inner life of man. (3) It is a legal righteousness, in the sense of work-righteousness. For when man discovers God behind the demands of the Law, he comes to believe that he can fulfill what God expects by doing good deeds. It is against this point that the chief criticism of *iustitia civilis* is made.

The Law then came to be thought of not as something good, but as the representative of a perverted way of salvation which, according to the Lutheran Confessions, was a distinguishing feature of both Judaism and contemporary Roman Catholicism [18] and was based on the false assumption that man, by his own powers, is able to love God above all things. When man discovers that God demands much more than the Second Table of the Law, he seeks to satisfy the demands of the Law with good works. He does this in the false belief that he possesses resources which enable him to fulfill the Law by himself. Behind the concept of work-piety one finds therefore an erroneous estimate of man's ability as well as of the depth of original sin.[19] The positive and negative evaluation of *iustitia civilis* is related to the Law's double function as accuser and as norm.

Philosophical righteousness stands in a dual relationship to God. God commands it, and it has His approval—but it does not qualify as righteousness before Him. It has its place before men, *coram hominibus*, where it receives the highest praise, but it will not do before God, *coram Deo*. In the First Table of the Law, God requires much more than man can accomplish alone; He expects the undivided loyalty of the human heart. Spiritual righteousness, *iustitia spiritualis*, like civil righteousness, *iustitia civilis*, has many names. To illustrate the connection between this righteousness and the inner life of man, it is frequently called the righteousness of the heart, *iustitia cordis*.[20] It is very closely related to the First Table of the Law, where, as we have seen, God demands something which man of himself is unable to produce—his wholehearted faith and confidence. Inasmuch as the Law and the Promise contrast with one another, *iustitia rationis*

---

[18] E. g., 164:22-28 (Ap IV 21); 241:42-49 (Ap VII 31).

[19] 165:16—Falsum est et hoc, quod ratio propriis viribus possit Deum supra omnia diligere et legem Dei facere, videlicet vere timere Deum, vere statuere, quod Deus exaudiat, velle obedire Deo in morte et aliis ordinationibus Dei, non concupiscere aliena etc., etsi civilia opera efficere ratio potest (Ap IV 27).

[20] 71:8 (AC XXVI 4); 242:15 and 23 (Ap VII 32).

definitely belongs to the Law, *iustitia spiritualis* to the Promise. Therefore the latter is also referred to simply as the righteousness of faith, *iustitia fidei*,[21] or is equated with faith.[22] It is called Christian righteousness, *iustitia christiana*,[23] or the righteousness of the Gospel, *iustitia evangelii*.[24] It is both the righteousness that the Gospel in the broad sense speaks of, and the righteousness the Gospel provides and supplies. As the work of the Holy Spirit, it is most often called spiritual righteousness, *iustitia spiritualis*.[25]

Implicit in the concept of righteousness is the idea of effort or performance. If man does right, he is righteous. It seems natural to think that God, who is Righteousness itself, should demand that man live an upright life, and it appears reasonable to translate the Biblical "righteousness of God," *iustitia Dei* (Rom. 1:17; AC XVIII 2), into "the righteousness which God demands." As the expression stands in the context of AC, it can only be interpreted in this way. This paraphrase is nevertheless quite improper, inasmuch as the Biblical *iustitia Dei*, according to the Confessions, is a righteousness that is *given*. God's demand for righteousness is altered to become a gift from God. In the language of the Reformation, *iustitia Dei* receives in its association with the Bible and St. Augustine a radically new meaning. It becomes not a *required but a bestowed righteousness*. The hallmark of Christian righteousness is that it attaches itself to what God gives, not to what He demands. To a certain degree, this naturally signifies the abrogation of the traditional concept of righteousness. Man is not able to fulfill what God requires, but God in His grace presents it to those who have faith in the promise of the Gospel.

The Lutheran Symbols presuppose that the righteousness which God has a right to expect of man is something which man, because he lacks insight and power, is unable to produce. Left to himself, man can achieve civil righteousness, but he lacks the ability to do the same with the only righteousness that is valid before God. As a result, *iustitia Dei* receives the completely new meaning that it is a given righteousness, not a demanded one. What man is unable to accomplish by himself is given him by a gracious God. The basic line of

---

[21] 76:21 (AC XX 8); 117:13 (AC XXVII 48); 130:35 (AC XXVIII 62); 233:7 (Ap IV 394); 167:39 (Ap IV 39).

[22] 242:22 — fidem seu iustitiam cordis (Ap VII 32). 179:44 — Fides igitur est illa res, quam Deus pronuntiat esse iustitiam (Ap IV 89).

[23] 78:12 (AC XX 18); 105:9 (AC XXVI 29); 161:22 (AC IV 12).

[24] 169:18 (AC IV 47).

[25] 73:7 (AC XVIII 2); 312:39 (Ap XVIII 9); 241:48-52 (Ap VII 31).

demarcation between the righteousness of the Law and that of the Gospel can be expressed thus: The former is achieved by man, the latter is given by God. Faith is a worship of God which accepts God's benefaction, *beneficia;* the righteousness of the Law is a worship of God which offers Him our merits, *merita.* God wants to be worshiped by faith in such a way that we receive from Him what He promises and offers.[26] In the righteousness of the Law, the way leads from man to God; in the righteousness of the Gospel, from God to man.[27] This difference runs through all the confessional writings and is fundamental to their understanding of the Word, the sacraments, and worship.

The reformers discovered this in Scripture. Luther found that *iustitia Dei* is the righteousness in which man is dressed by God.[28] God is the active agent; man is the one who receives. Because man lacks insight into and power to achieve the righteousness which is valid before God, it must be given to him by the Holy Spirit. It is the main theme in the Epistle to the Romans,[29] and it is confirmed throughout the entire Bible.[30] A characteristic argument, frequently repeated in the Confessions, is taken from Acts 10:43, where Peter says of Christ: "To Him all the prophets bear witness that everyone who believes in Him receives forgiveness of sins through His name." From this Ap draws the following conclusions: This passage is proof that righteousness by faith is taught in the entire Bible and has support both in the Old Testament and the New. Thus it can rightly be said that it has been confirmed by the whole church also.[31]

In addition to the Bible, a number of the church fathers also support the doctrine of righteousness by faith.[32] Above all, and with certain justification, the confessional writers fall back upon Augustine in his controversy with the Pelagians. It is not possible here to present a detailed account of their statements concerning Augustine and his anti-Pelagian literature. But this much can be said with certainty: The

---

[26] 170:13 — Fides est "latreia" (Rom. 9:4; 12:1), quae accipit a Deo oblata beneficia; iustitia legis est "latreia," quae offert Deo nostra merita. Fide sic vult coli Deus, ut ab ipso accipiamus ea, quae promittit et offert (Ap IV 49).

[27] 661:21-25 (LC II 67).

[28] WA 54, 185:12 ff. (*Praef. zu Gesamtausgabe*, 1545).

[29] 178:45-52 (Ap IV 87); CR 15, 445 (*Disp. orationis in epist. ad Romanos*, 1529).

[30] 178:33-37 (Ap IV 86); 181:22-26 (Ap IV 102).

[31] 177:18-34 (Ap IV 83); 265:20 — consensus prophetarum iudicandus est universalis ecclesiae consensus esse (Ap XII 66).

[32] Cf. CR 15, 495 (*Comm. in epist. ad Romanos*, 1532), and P. Fraenkel (1961), pp. 48 and 93—96.

Confessions do not repeat what Augustine says in detail. They rather take up some of his ideas and develop them more pronouncedly. It is obvious that a certain amount of change takes place. Augustine's philosophical background is ignored, the dialectic between Law and Gospel is treated differently, and so is the concept of grace. As he mentions in a well-known statement made in 1545,[33] Luther developed his view of *iustitia Dei* without depending upon Augustine, but he later found support in the latter's *De spiritu et littera*. The significance of this book for Lutheranism ought not be underestimated. In gratitude for what he had learned from it, Luther had it published in 1518, adding a preface of his own,[34] and it is frequently quoted in the Lutheran Symbols. Its importance for the Reformation doctrine of righteousness consists in that it (1) distinguishes between human or volitional righteousness on the one hand and *iustitia Dei* on the other;[35] (2) interprets the latter as a righteousness given by God; (3) teaches that righteousness is received by faith;[36] and (4) tells us that the Law frightens and faith gives hope.[37]

In the Lutheran Confessions the two kinds of righteousness are the consequence of the important Biblical distinction between Law and Gospel. The entire Christian message is concerned above all with righteousness before God. As a result, Ap refers to this teaching as "the main doctrine of Christianity," *praecipuus locus doctrinae christianae*.[38] Because it has support both in the Bible and in tradition,

[33] WA 54, 186:16 — Postea legebam Augustinum de spiritu et litera, ubi praeter spem offendi, quod et ipse iustitiam Dei similiter interpretatur; qua nos Deus induit, dum nos iustificat (*Praef. zu Gesamtausgebung*, 1545). Cf. *De spiritu et litt.*, 9, 15 — iustitia Dei, non qua Deus iustus est, sed qua induit hominem, cum iustificat impium (CSEL 60, 167). The course of Luther's development has often been analyzed. See, e. g., H. Bornkamm in ARG (1940), pp. 117—28, and ARG (1942), pp. 1—46; A. Gyllenkrok (1952), pp. 7—10; E. Bizer (1961), who represents a divergent point of view; and R. Prenter (1961). Luther developed his new insights in his controversy with Occamism, O. Scheel, II (1930), 164, 169, and E. Hirsch in *Festgabe für J. Kaftan* (1920), p. 150.

[34] A. Hamel, II (1935), 2. It can be pointed out that for A. Karlstadt too *De sp. et litt.* meant a great deal; he brought out an annotated edition of the same. See on this E. Kähler, *Karlstadt und Augustin* (1952).

[35] *De sp. et litt.*, 9, 15 — iustitia, inquit, Dei manifesta est — non dixit: iustitia hominis uel iustitia propriae uoluntatis (CSEL 60, 167).

[36] *De sp. et litt.*, 9, 15 — iustitia Dei sine lege est, quam Deus per spiritum gratiae credenti confert sine adiutorio legis (CSEL 60, 167), and 29:51 (CSEL 60, 207). Cf. *Die Bekenntnisschriften* (1963), 182:15-26 (Ap IV 106), and 77: 17-23 (AC XX 12-14).

[37] *De sp. et litt.*, 29, 51 — Ex lege timemus Deum, ex fide speramus in Deum (CSEL 60, 208). Cf. *Die Bekenntnisschriften* (1963), 182:29 (Ap IV 106).

[38] 159:1 (Ap IV 2).

it is consistent with both — although in somewhat different ways.

With regard to the Bible, one finds that it is never set forth as a superior critical principle. What the Confessions strive for above all is to demonstrate its harmony with Scripture on the basis of detailed exegetical arguments. But precisely because it is Biblical it serves as a key to Scripture. The Confessions have the conviction that the Biblical statements regarding righteousness cannot contradict one another. The Bible cannot teach righteousness by faith in one context and work-righteousness in another. When the Bible speaks of good works, these must be inserted into a larger context and consistently understood to be the fruits of righteousness and not its presupposition. On the other hand, the Confessions give no indication of a conflict between the righteousness of faith and the words of the Bible. Of the two, the Bible is the basic presupposition, inasmuch as it deals with the righteousness of God exclusively.

In relation to the contemporary church and church life, the righteousness of faith becomes a critical principle. The Confessions sharply oppose all that is known as human regulations, *traditiones humanae,* whose common trademark is that they stand under the sign of righteousness by the Law (AC XXVI 1 ff.). Since all the rules that have been proposed for achieving justification are contrary to the Gospel and Christian righteousness, they must be repudiated. Included here are a series of ecclesiastical ceremonies and, in general, the idea that bishops have been entrusted by Christ to think up new forms of worship designed to achieve justification. Such erroneous ideas will gain a foothold in the church as long as righteousness by faith is not proclaimed with sufficient clarity.[39] All churchly tradition which bears the stamp of its human origin, i. e., is contrary to the Gospel and righteousness by faith, is rejected. But at the same time another tradition, the doctrinal tradition, is approved. What was taught by the fathers in the early church [40] provides guidance to the extent that it is in harmony with Scripture. Because the righteousness of faith was itself an important part of the teaching and preaching of the uncorrupted church, the Confessions are concerned to point up this connection. The claim of the reformers that they represented the true Catholic Church was based on the conviction that this connection was real. The Reformation claimed to represent the truly Catholic tradition.

---

[39] 130:26—131:5 (AC XXVIII 61-64); 242:5—244:6 (Ap VII 32 ff.)
[40] 244:16-32 (Ap VII 38 f.)

This bifurcated attitude toward contemporary and early Christianity forms the background for everything the Confessions say about faith, life, and church organization. Their *Sitz im Leben* is the Western Church, out of which the Reformation sprang. Part of its tradition won the approval of the reformers; other parts were rejected. A practical expression of this can be found in the attitude they adopted regarding the dogma of the Triune God.

Chapter Four:

The Nature of God

When Luther wrote in SA that no disagreement existed between Catholics and Evangelicals with respect to "the sublime articles of the divine majesty," this was representative of the Reformation point of view. As Schlink [1] has said, "The doctrine of the Trinity is the basis for all statements of the Lutheran Confessions," because it is most intimately related to their doctrine of salvation as a work of God. Apart from Christ we can know nothing of the grace of God the Father, and apart from the Holy Spirit we cannot come to Christ (LC II 65). The concept of God is uniform here, in spite of the variations between the catechisms' pedagogical method of presentation and the more conventional theological approach of the other confessional documents. It is important to establish this uniformity, for according to an opinion frequently heard, the doctrine of the Trinity was nothing more than a formula inherited from the past, without any greater significance for Reformation theology.[2]

The primary cause of the exposition on the Trinity in AC I was John Eck's attack on Luther in the 404 Articles. There Eck accused Luther of denying the doctrine of the Trinity in his statement opposing Latomus (1521).[3] Eck's accusation was based on a misunderstanding, but it gave Melanchthon reason to clarify and emphasize the reformers' acceptance of the position held by the early church. The fact that the Evangelicals associated themselves (in AC I) with "the decree of the Council of Nicaea concerning the unity of the divine essence and concerning the three persons" may have had a secondary motive related to church politics, but the basic motive must have been something else. This is evident from the fact that neither Luther nor Melanchthon was content merely to repeat the Nicene Creed. Rather, they attached themselves even more distinctly to the Athanasian Creed. Like Augustine and the Athanasian Creed, they strove

---

[1] E. Schlink (1961), p. 62.

[2] For information on this question consult E. Schlink (1961), 62, n. 16; R. Prenter (1946), pp. 182 ff. and 245 ff.; E. Kinder in KuD (1955), pp. 185 f.; L. Grane (1959), pp. 15 ff.; and above Chapter Two, part 1.

[3] WA 8, 117:14—118:9 (*Rationis Latomianae Confutatio*, 1521).

to emphasize the unity of the divine essence: one God in three Persons. The doctrine of the Trinity must not be misunderstood as tritheism. In harmony with this intention, the Confessions ascribed the work of Creation to God as a whole (AC I 3 German, 2 Latin) — a position indicating their independence over against the Nicene and Athanasian Creeds. The statement that God has created all, both "visible and invisible" (AC I 3 German, 2 Latin) was taken from the Nicene Creed, but the terms which say that God is eternal, *aeternus,* and infinite, *immensus,* and that the three Persons in the Godhead are coeternal and coequal are taken from the Athanasian Creed.[4]

The picture of God as it appears in SA is virtually the same. Luther derived the formula which says that "the Son became man" [5] from the Nicene Creed, but the verbal agreements with the Athanasian Creed are numerous.[6] From AC to SA there is a uniform concept of the Godhead, a concept related to the Western dogmatic formulation, as this was codified in the confessions of faith of the early church. The concise formulations, the general doctrinal and verbal agreements with what the church had taught, reveal that the reformers were on familiar territory. On the part of the reformers there was no difference of opinion concerning the doctrine of the Triune God, and they sensed no need of analyzing a question on which all were of one mind. They were generally content to accept the word of the early church, and they took over the current formulations concerning the unity of the divine essence and the independence of the three Persons.

The stress on the divine unity did not hinder them in confessing the three Persons of the Godhead, and they add that "the word 'person' is to be understood . . . not as a part or a property of another but as that which exists of itself" (AC I 4). As seen from the point of view of the history of dogma, this implies a position in opposition to modalism. But here too they were content with intimations. They spoke of familiar things, about which the well-informed needed no detailed analyses. A more independent and pedagogical view of the dogma of the Trinity is set forth only in the catechisms. But these were meant for the people, designed to serve instructional purposes.

[4] 50:9-14 (AC I 2 German, 3 Latin), compared with 28:19 ff. (Athanasian Creed 6, 9, and 25).

[5] 414:38 and 39 (SA I), compared with 27:15 (Nicene Creed).

[6] 414:36 — Pater a nullo, filius a patre genitus est, spiritus sanctus a patre et filio procedit (SA I). Cf. 29:15 — Pater a nullo est factus, nec creatus, nec genitus. Filius a patre solo est, non factus nec creatus, sed genitus. Spiritus sanctus a patre et filio, non factus nec creatus nec genitus, sed procedens (Athanasian Creed 20-22).

Here it was that Luther's great teaching talents blossomed fully. The fact is that the catechisms do not vary from AC, Ap, and SA in their view of God as one substance in three Persons. To confess the Triune God is the common basis of all Christian faith. Those who do not do so have placed themselves outside the church of Christ (Ap I 2). The reason for holding fast to this faith is also clearly stated: It is believed to be clearly grounded in Scripture.[7]

One cannot stress strongly enough that the doctrine of the Trinity is the foundation of Reformation theology. And in spite of the variations in presentation between the catechisms and the other confessional documents, the basic position is uniform. The catechisms' explanation of the articles of faith is arranged according to the three Persons of the Godhead, and it deals with Their work — with the Father and creation, the Son and redemption, the Holy Spirit and sanctification. But the emphasis upon divine unity is not abandoned for this reason. God is the quintessence of Father, Son, and Spirit; there is "one God and one faith, but three persons." [8]

The same one God is at work in creation, redemption, and sanctification.[9] Just as it was natural for Luther to divide the work of God on the basis of the three Persons (for pedagogical reasons), so was it self-evident that the three Persons should point back to one and the same God: "He created us for this very purpose, to redeem and sanctify us." (LC II 64)

Knowledge of God is derived from the revelation given to us in the Gospel, a short summary of which Luther found in the Apostles' Creed.[10] It is true that man by himself possesses a general knowledge of God's existence, for the Ten Commandments are written on the hearts of all men.[11] But rational deliberations are not enough to provide man with the true insight into God's essence which is mediated to us through the Gospel and also in the First Table of the Decalog. The divine law written upon the heart provides knowledge of God

---

[7] 145:11 — eum habere certa et firma testimonia in scripturis sanctis (Ap I 2); 557:19-21 (LC Preface 18).

[8] 647:18 (LC II 7).

[9] 647:14 — I believe in God the Father, who created me; I believe in God the Son, who redeemed me; I believe in the Holy Spirit, who sanctifies me (LC II 7).

[10] Concerning Luther's terminology see J. Meyer (1929), pp. 256 ff. *Der Glaube* is used in LC and elsewhere in the conventional sense of human faith.

[11] 160:10 ff. (Ap IV 7); 660:21-23 (LC II 67). Cf WA 16, 372, 1-3 (*Predigten über das 2. Buch Mose, 1524—27*), and WA 39 I, 374:2-5, and 402:10-18 (*Die erste Disputation gegen die antinomer, 1537*).

only to a limited extent. What we can know about the divine essence is based upon knowledge received through revelation.

That man needs something to attach himself to is apparent in the universal existence of faith, for no group of people has ever appeared that did not establish the worship of God.[12] But outside of the Christian context the worship of God is generally perverted. Although God guides and upholds the created world, men do not acknowledge Him. The knowledge of God which man can have, theoretically, he has no longer, and as a result it cannot be the basis for faith and trust in God. Apart from the Gospel we find only an angry and terrifying judge;[13] apart from the Gospel we can only experience God's wrath and displeasure.[14] If man is completely dependent upon his own resources, he finds nothing but demands in his confrontation with God, demands he is powerless to fulfill. And standing before these impossible demands, he sees only God's wrath, not His love. The general knowledge of God says nothing about God's grace and love; it merely points to His existence. This is a knowledge based completely on Law, and as Law always does, it tells us what we must do—but unlike the Gospel, it says nothing of what God has done for us (LC II 67). Because this knowledge of God has all of the characteristics of the Law, it is not only inadequate but also promotes works of self-righteousness (LC I 22). Inasmuch as true knowledge of God comes only through the Gospel, the doctrine of the creeds is quite different from that of the Law. Only the Gospel provides us with correct information about God, and even enables us to receive what God gives. (LC II 67)[15]

Since the doctrine of the Trinity is thus connected to justification by faith, it also stands in an inner, organic relationship to the distinction between Law and Gospel. Reason apart from the Gospel cannot bring man true knowledge of God. Law and reason go together, but through them we see only a caricature of God. What God actually thinks of us we learn through the Gospel, and the Gospel has to do with Father, Son, and Spirit. The Son is the reflection of God's father-heart, but a saving knowledge of the Son comes to no one except by the Holy Spirit. Instruction and proclamation concerning the Triune

---

12 563:37-42 (LC I 16 f.); cf. D. Löfgren (1960), pp. 9 f.

13 660:42-43 (LC II 64).

14 661:31-32 (LC II 68); 651:46-47 (LC II 28).

15 It is not difficult to hear in this an echo of Augustine's well-known distinction between the law of works and the law of faith. The former says *fac quod iubeo,* and the latter *da quod iubes* (*De sp. et litt.,* 13, 22; CSEL 60, 175).

God fall within the sphere of the Gospel and revelation, which sur-
pass all human wisdom and reason. (LC II 63)

When one seeks to be more specific about what the Confessions
find essential in the work of the three Persons of the Godhead, two
things must be kept in mind. First, that the unity of the Godhead
is presupposed at all times, in spite of the threefold division, and
second, that knowledge about the Trinity is mediated through the
revelation of the Gospel. The proper attitude toward God is found
in the trust of the heart. The confidence of faith is superior to a theoretical knowledge of God, for only in faith does one receive God's
gifts. God is a power, from whom goodness and love pour forth to
meet us. But in order to come to faith, man needs something external
to attach himself to,[16] and also the support of the Holy Spirit, which
enables him to live up to his insight. This twofold purpose is accomplished in the summary of the Gospel found in the Apostles' Creed,
which deals with the essence and activity of the Father, the Son, and
the Holy Spirit.

The Father

The fact that the First Article stands under the sign of the Gospel
means that it has to do with what God has done for us and continues
to give us. It does not have to do with a natural theology about God
but with insights provided through the Gospel in regard to the heavenly Father, who is concerned about His creation. In the words of
AC, God is at one and the same time Creator and Sustainer of all
that is visible and invisible.[17]

The Lutheran Confessions vary from the Nicene Creed in as-
cribing the work of creation to God in His entirety, and in adding
that the God who created is also the Sustainer of His creation. This
creation-faith has as its object the Father who is active in the present,
and its nerve center is the conviction that all things are incessantly
dependent upon Him.[18] Schlink [19] has devised the term *creatio con-
tinuata* for this work of sustaining the creation. The fact that man is

---

[16] 696:31 — Das wöllen aber die Blindenleiter nicht sehen, dass der Glaube
[man's faith] etwas haben muss, das er glaube, das ist, daran er sich halte und
darauf stehe und fusse (LC IV 28).

[17] 50:11 — creator et conservator omnium rerum, visibilium et invisibilium
(AC I 2). Cf. the Nicene Creed: factorem coeli et terrae, visibilium omnium et
invisibilium.

[18] 648:1-32 (LC II 12 ff.)

[19] E. Schlink (1961), p. 38.

continuously dependent upon God the Father does not, however, contradict the Biblical idea that He created the world once and for all and in so doing gave expression to His divine will. This is seen most clearly in Ap's analysis of the Biblical account of creation, and of the creative Word as perpetually active in the order of nature, in the lives of plants, animals, and man.[20] If one accepts the idea that God ceaselessly creates anew, it can lead to the abrogation of the permanent order of God's will and to the setting aside of the natural law as it is known and referred to in the Confessions.[21]

God richly provides us with His gifts day by day. The First Article is a grateful song of praise to the Giver of many good gifts. We take creation-faith seriously when we look upon all that we have as gifts from the heavenly Father. What the Father has provided is to be used according to His will for the benefit of our neighbor. We must not hold on selfishly to what we have received, but through our service, and chiefly in our vocation, permit ourselves to be used as instruments of God and as channels of His love.[22] To confess faith in God the Father, Creator of heaven and earth, involves the application of the deepest purpose of the First Commandment. He who makes this confession has turned fully toward God in faith and undivided trust.[23]

The Son

We are led to true knowledge of the Father by the Son, who is the mirror of the father-heart of God (LC II 64). What the Confessions have to say about His person and work is very closely related to the tradition of the early church. AC, Ap, and SA are directly linked up with the dogmatic formulations of the early church by both words and phrases. The wording in AC is influenced above all by the Athanasian and the Chalcedonian creeds. The point of departure is God's Son, the Word, who became man by the assumption of human nature in the womb of the Virgin Mary. As is true with the Athanasian Creed, AC presents us with an "assumption Christology." [24] The divine has

---

[20] 335:14-31 (Ap XXIII 8-13).

[21] This characteristic of actuality is emphasized in a one-sided manner by D. Löfgren (1960), pp. 9, 25, 83 ff., and elsewhere. Cf. B. Lohse's critique in ThLZ (1961), pp. 928—31, and F. Laus in *Luther Jahrbuch* (1962), pp. 44—51.

[22] 566:20-26 (LC I 26).

[23] 563:6-10 (LC I 13 f.)

[24] 54:2 — Item docent, quod verbum, hoc est filius Dei, assumpserit humanam naturam in utero beatae Mariae virginis (AC II 1). Cf. the Athanasian Creed, 33 — Unus autem non conversione divinitatis in carne, sed adsumptione humanitatis

not been altered into something human, but it has incorporated the human into itself. The concept of unity is present here as in the Creed of Chalcedon[25] in the one Person, including both the divine and human natures of Christ. The Athanasian Creed seeks to illustrate by means of the relationship between the human soul and body how the divine, which corresponds to "reasonable soul," *anima rationabilis,* and the human, whose equivalent is "human flesh," *caro humana,* become one Christ.[26] Although AC III does not include this idea, it repeats the terminology of the Athanasian and Chalcedonian creeds: "united in one person . . . one Christ," *in unitate personae . . . unus Christus,*[27] "inseparably," *inseparabiliter,* united, "true God and true man," *vere Deus et vere homo.*[28] According to Luther's statement, there was no difference of opinion between the Catholic and Evangelical theologians with regard to Christology (SA I), and this was also confirmed by the Confutation.[29] Luther avoids a more precise statement in SA, professing only the virgin birth. In the words of the Nicene Creed, the Son "became man," *homo factus est.* In the same fashion, the catechisms pass over every attempt to explain the miracle of the incarnation. They simply make an unambiguous confession of faith in Christ as God's Son (LC II 27). In spite of the different terminology, one must not forget that all the confessional documents speak of the Christ who is true God and true man. On this point there is complete unanimity.

—The death of Christ as the work of atonement is a central point in Reformation theology.[30] It forms the presupposition for justification, and both the First and the Third Articles of the creed are, in their deepest meaning, connected with it. Through Christ's death on the cross we have a reconciled Father and can share in the Holy Spirit.[31] No doctrine of the atonement in the modern sense of the term appears. The formulations are conspicuously meager. If one

in Deo; also Ap III 1 — naturam humanam assumptam a verbo in unitatem personae.

25 1104 (*Decr. Chalcedonense*).

26 The Athansian Creed, 30 and 35.

27 54:6 f. (AC III 2). Cf. 30:2 and 8 (Athansian Creed, 32 and 35).

28 54:6 f. (AC III 2). Cf. 1105:16 and 22 (*Decr. Chalcedonense*).

29 CR 27, 90 — In tertio articulo nihil est, quod offendat, cum tota confessio, cum symbolo Apostolorum et cum recta fidei regula conveniat. Cf. Ap III, which makes the same assertion.

30 415:4-6 — the doctrine of Christ's death and resurrection is referred to as the chief article (SA II).

31 Cf. 366:24-28 (Ap XXIV 58).

should classify them according to Aulen's [32] well-known pattern, it would be easiest to assign them to the Latin type. They deal, in other words, with an actual atonement, a satisfaction (Ap IV 40) which Christ, as true God and true man, achieved on our behalf. Christ was born of the Virgin Mary, He actually suffered, was crucified, died, and was buried, in order that He might reconcile, *ut reconciliaret,* the Father to us by becoming a sacrifice, *hostia,* for our sin.[33] All men are confronted with the impossible demand to fulfill God's law. The meaning of the atonement is that Christ has fulfilled the Law for us, thus eliminating God's wrath (Ap IV 40-42). The Confessions are much less interested in the formation of an original theory of the atonement than in stressing the point that Christ alone is our Reconciler and Mediator. They develop this train of thought in clear opposition to work-righteousness, the worship of saints, and teaching of the sacrifice of the Mass.

That Christ alone by His death has made atonement therefore clearly contradicts the worship of saints and work-righteousness. For if anyone is to be the atoner, it is necessary (1) that there is a distinct passage in the Bible which tells us that God will have mercy upon those who call upon Him through this atoner, and (2) that the atoner has made satisfaction in such a way that his merits can be of value to others. It is only Christ who fulfills both of these conditions. There are distinct words of promise about Him in Scripture, and His merits are reckoned to our benefit. (Ap XXI 17-19)

There is also an inner connection between Christ's atonement on the one hand and justification and the Lord's Supper on the other, but there is no room left for the teaching of the sacrifice of the Mass. Inasmuch as Christ's work of atonement is the sole foundation of a new relationship to God, and since it is forever valid, all talk about human merit as the basis of atonement is excluded.[34] The Reformation catchword "for the sake of Christ," *propter Christus,* recognizes no other possibility. The possibility of a new fellowship between God and man is opened up only through the sacrifice of Christ, given once and for all. It is no accident that *hostia* is used so frequently in this connection. This term, which designates the bread in the Roman

[32] Gustaf Aulén, *Christus Victor* (1930); Hj. Lindroth, *Försoningen* (1935).

[33] AC III and Ap III. The main words here, *reconciliatio* and *hostia,* go back according to Ap's own interpretation to the Old Testament and even to extra-Biblical ideas concerning the necessity of a propitiatory sacrifice. (Ap XXIV 22-24).

[34] 355:34 — Non propter nostras iustitias, sed propter aliena merita, videlicet Christi, velit Deus nobis reconciliari (Ap XXIV 23).

Catholic Mass, is used in the Lutheran Symbols to refer to Christ's unique sacrifice on the cross. Christ is a sacrifice, *hostia,* for all of our sins (AC III 3); His death alone atones. "Only the death of Christ," *sola mors Christi,* is the counterpart of *sola fide,* and also its presupposition.[35]

According to the Roman Catholic position in the Confutation, Christ is presented as a sacrifice in the Mass. Just as Christ once and for all was offered up in the bloody sacrifice of the cross, so He is given up daily in the Mass as a sacramental sacrifice of peace.[36] The Lutheran Confessions opposed this energetically. Christ's death is a work of atonement done once and for all, and is the presupposition of our justification.[37] It is the Holy Spirit who enables us to believe this.

The Holy Spirit

The Third Person of the Godhead is the Holy Spirit. He is, as the Athanasian Creed puts it, of eternity, as are the Father and the Son — from whom He is said to "proceed" (in harmony with the Western tradition after the *filioque* controversy). This wording was taken over as self-evident; there was no need of clarification. Faith in the Spirit as a person was so natural that all further analysis was unnecessary. But the necessity of this faith is made clear by the many statements about the Holy Spirit. The entire Christian life is the result of His work. To come under His domination is the presupposition of the Christian faith and the Christian life. Christ struggled against the powers of evil with His Spirit, and the aid of the Spirit is necessary if the Gospel's cause is to win the victory.[38] Apart from the Holy Spirit, all men sin; they either "disdain God's judgment in their self-sufficiency, or they flee from punishment and hate the God who judges." [39] Even the good works a man does apart from the Holy

[35] 356:7 — sola mors Christi est vere propitiatorum sacrificium (Ap XXIV 24).

[36] CR 27, 155 — Tantum ergo semel oblatus est in cruce, effuso sanguine; hodie offertur in Missa, ut hostia pacifica et sacramentalis.

[37] 93:5—94:3 (AC XXIV 21). More will be said about the meaning of the sacrifice of the Mass in the chapter on the Lord's Supper below. It might simply be pointed out here that the Confutation strongly rejected the assertion, quod Christus sua passione satisfecerit pro peccato originis et instituterit missam, in quo fieret oblatio pro cotidianis delictis, mortalibus et venialibus (AC XXIV 21). The rejoinder in the Confutation goes thus: Hoc nunquam auditum est a catholicis (CR 27, 149).

[38] 204:17-18 (Ap IV 230); 432:18-20 (SA II IV 15).

[39] 166:36-39 (Ap IV 34).

Spirit are evil before God, inasmuch as they are done with an evil heart.[40] As long as He has no power over the human heart, it can know only God's wrath.

The Holy Spirit's foremost and proper activity is to lead us into a right relationship with God, according to the First Table of the Law. What God requires of man is not simply an external obedience to the Law; He expects the faith and confidence of the heart. Man can to a limited extent achieve *iustitia civilis,* but no one can by his own strength produce the spiritual righteousness demanded by the Law.[41] Without the help of the Holy Spirit, man is unable to fulfill what the New Testament considers to be the profoundest meaning of the Law—to love God with one's whole heart (Matt. 22:37). According to the Occamist theologians, man is capable of loving God above all things,[42] but the Lutheran Symbols sharply disagree. In order to enter into a right relationship with God in harmony with the First Table of the Law, the heart of man must be born anew of the Holy Spirit.

The root of sin is evil desire, *concupiscentia* (Ap II 38 ff.), which manifests itself in superstition, in hatred of God, in lack of trust in Him. With Augustine and the scholastics, this evil is summarized as evil desires, *mali affectus* (Ap IV 146), which man of himself is unable to alter. The foremost activity of the Holy Spirit is therefore to awaken that faith without which He cannot remain with a man.[43] When the Holy Spirit comes to occupy man's heart, a new work begins therein. In place of evil desires new activities are set in motion. When we receive the Holy Spirit by faith, a new life is born. This is described as spiritual impulses [44] or as new affections.[45]

---

[40] 166:43 — vere peccant homines etiam cum honesta opera faciunt sine spiritu sancto, quia faciunt ea impio corde (Ap IV 35).

[41] 73:3 — humana voluntas habeat aliquam libertatem ad efficiendam civilem iustitiam et deligendas res rationi subiectas. Sed non habet vim sine spiritu sancto efficiendae iustitiae Dei seu iustitiae spiritualis, quia animalis homo non percipit ea, quae sunt spiritus Dei (AC XVIII 1).

[42] 160:38-39 (Ap IV 9); 311:9-14 (Ap XVIII 2); 434:20-21 (SA III I 6). Cf. *De Bekenntnisschriften* (1963), p. 74, n. 2, with reference to Duns Scotus and G. Biel, plus O. Scheel, II (1930), 164, 169, 171, and 288 ff.; A. Gyllenkrok (1952), pp. 2 f.; H. A. Oberman (1963), p. 153.

[43] 173:12 — [fides] est opus spiritus sancti (Ap IV 64); 183:47 (Ap IV 115); 316:17 — fides non manet in his, qui amittunt spiritum sanctum (Ap XX 13).

[44] 185:23 — Quia vero fides affert spiritum sanctum et parit novam vitam in cordibus, necesse est, quod pariat spirituales motus in cordibus (Ap IV 125); 227:5-7 (Ap IV 349).

[45] 80:18 — quia per fidem accipitur spiritus sanctus, iam corda renovantur et induunt novos affectus (AC XX 29). More will be said about the affections or impulses below in Chapter Five.

Through the Spirit we enter into an entirely new relationship with God. *Concupiscentia* is driven away, and in its place come the new spiritual impulses; we receive knowledge of God, fear of God, hope, love,[46] and faith.[47] Theologically speaking, faith is a work of the Holy Spirit and the presupposition of His remaining. Psychologically speaking, faith is described as an impulse, *motus,* or affection, *affectus.*

Since God as Holy Spirit is now active among us, the new life is a reality to be reckoned with. In the First Table of the Law God directs His demands at the evil desires of the heart, but through the faith effected by the Holy Spirit it is possible to fight these evil desires. Inasmuch as the heart awakened by faith harbors "spiritual and holy impulses," it is possible to love both God and one's fellowmen.[48] Such talk about spiritual emotions must not, however, lead to misunderstandings. This is not simply an immanent psychological experience in the life of man, and the Holy Spirit cannot be identified primarily with human regeneration. The Spirit is not the same as "a movement which is produced in things," [49] and He cannot be identified with man's spiritual renewal. The Holy Spirit is the Third Person of the Godhead, who has taken up the fight against sin by putting evil desire to death and by creating new impulses in man.[50] This fight continues throughout life. According to a basic Reformation concept, the Christian is at the same time righteous and sinful, *simul iustus et peccator.* The Christian is not without sin, but he struggles against sin—or better yet, the Holy Spirit struggles within him against all that is opposed to God. The Spirit does not permit sin to get the upper hand, but hinders it from doing what it desires to do.[51] Sin is not driven out, but on the basis of what Christ has done for us, *it is not reckoned* against us.[52] The Spirit unceasingly carries on His fight

[46] 227:14 — motus spirituales: notitia Dei, timor Dei, spes, dilectio Dei (Ap IV 351).

[47] 256:37 — sine bono motu . . . hoc est sine fide in Christum (Ap XII 25); 295:7 — sine bono motu cordis, hoc est, sine fide (Ap XIII 18, 224).

[48] 185:20-35 (Ap IV 125)

[49] 51:12-13 — motus in rebus creatus (AC I 6).

[50] 154:11-14 (Ap II 35). It may be worth noting that Ap here sought to reproduce Luther's intentions as specified in *De captivitate babylonica.*

[51] 448:25 — der heilige Geist lässt die Sünde nicht walten und überhand gewinnen, dass sie vollnbracht werde, sondern steuret und wehret, dass sie nicht muss tun, was sie will (SA III III 44).

[52] 460:11 — Obwohl die Sünde im Fleisch noch nicht gar weg oder tot ist, so will er sie doch nicht rechnen noch wissen (SA III XIII 1); 154:18 f. (Ap II 36). At this point the Confessions refer to imputative justification. With regard

against sin—first, by leading us to Christ and renewing the assurance of forgiveness,[53] and second, by opposing evil desires.[54]

Forgiveness of sins came to possess the central position in the fight against sin. What hinders us from having fellowship with God is fear of His wrath, lack of faith, and ignorance of Him. To overcome this opposition the Holy Spirit must employ certain distinctive means: the Word, the sacraments, the keys, and also the church. The work and office of the Holy Spirit is "to begin and daily to increase holiness on earth through these two means, the Christian church and the forgiveness of sins." [55]

One of the chief ideas of the Reformation was that "the Holy Spirit works through the Word and the sacraments." [56] "One cannot deal with God or grasp him except through the Word" (Ap IV 67). Well-known and often quoted are the words of AC V: "Through the Word and the sacraments, as through instruments, the Holy Spirit is given" *(Per verbum et sacramenta donatur spiritus sanctus tanquam per instrumenta).* The confessional writers emphasized this everywhere. Because they placed such a strong accent on the external Word and sacraments, they were strongly opposed to opinions both on the left and the right whose common characteristic, they felt, was to obscure the Word and the sacraments. Among the "enthusiasts" and the Anabaptists this was done first, by teaching that the Spirit works directly upon man's heart, and second, by referring to spiritual experiences.[57] Among the Roman Catholics this was done by pointing to the power of the papacy.[58] Both of these positions were judged

to merited grace, the reformers deliberately rejected Augustine's concept of grace. Cf. WA 54, 186:18 (*Preface*, 1545).

[53] 658:75 ff. (LC II 54).

[54] 189:14 — in hac vita non possumus legi satisfacere, quia natura carnalis non desinit malos affectus parere, etsi his resistit Spiritus in nobis (Ap IV 146).

[55] 659:16-20 (LC II 58).

[56] 370:1 — per verbum et sacramentum operatur spiritus sanctus (Ap XXIV 70).

[57] 294:8 — Ac prodest, quantum fieri potest, ornare ministerium verbi omni genere laudis adversus fanaticos homines, qui somniant spiritum sanctum dari non per verbum, sed propter suas quasdam praeparationes, si sedeant otiosi, taciti, in locis obscuris, expectantes illuminationem, quemadmodum olim "enthousiastai" docebant et nunc docent Anabaptistae (Ap XIII 13); 58:14-17 (AC V 4); 713:1—714:11 (LC V 28 ff.); K. Holl (1923), pp. 428 ff.; R. Prenter, *Spiritus Creator* (1946), pp. 253 ff.

[58] 454:7 — Denn das Bapsttum auch eitel Enthusiasmus ist, darin der Bapst rühmet alle Rechte sind im Schrein seines Herzen und, was er mit seiner Kirchen urteilt und heisst, dass soll Geist und Recht sein (SA III VIII 4).

as *enthusiasmus*. The Reformation principle is stated in SA: "God gives no one his Spirit or grace except through or with the external Word." [59] And what is said of the Word of God as it is preached, read, or meditated upon in private [60] also holds true of Baptism and the Lord's Supper. The reformers were firmly convinced that the Holy Spirit is given both in Baptism—by which they always had in mind infant baptism [61] —and in the Lord's Supper, which was instituted to influence the heart to faith. "The Holy Spirit works through the Word and the sacraments." [62]

The entire activity of the Spirit is linked up with the church. The church is, on the one hand, a product of the Spirit's activity, and on the other the medium whereby He works and leads us to faith in Christ. "For where Christ is not preached, there is no Holy Spirit to create, call, and gather the Christian church, and outside it no one can come to the Lord Christ." [63] The church is the mother who feeds and nourishes her children through the Word.[64] As the Confessions see it, the entire work of the Triune God is concentrated in the church's activity through Word and sacrament. LC puts it this way: "Creation is past and redemption is accomplished, but the Holy Spirit carries on his work unceasingly until the last day. For this purpose he has appointed a community on earth, through which he speaks and does all his work." [65] Creation, redemption, and sanctification are God's work from beginning to end. God is now active among us in order to bring all to completion on the last day. As seen from the eschatological point of view, the doctrine of the Trinity is placed in its context with the creation of the world, salvation, and the ultimate consummation. The doctrine of the Trinity is therefore deeply involved in the Confessions of the Reformation. It can properly be said to form one of their main pillars.

---

[59] 453:17 — [es] ist fest darauf zu bleiben, dass Gott niemand seinen Geist oder Gnade gibt ohn durch oder mit dem vorgehend äusserlichen Wort (SA III VIII 3).

[60] 549:8 — dass der heilige Geist bei solchem Lesen, Reden und Gedenken gegenwärtig ist und immer neue und mehr Licht und Andacht dazu gibt (LC New Preface 9).

[61] 154:11 — spiritus sanctus, datus per baptismum, incipit mortificare concupiscentiam (Ap II 35); 700:39-47 (LC IV 48 f.).

[62] 369:44—370:2 (Ap XXIV 70).

[63] 655:29-33 (LC II 44).

[64] 655:3-5 (LC II 42).

[65] 659:45—660:3 (LC II 61).

Chapter Five:

The Creation and Fall of Man

Man in the Light of Psychology

The Lutheran Confessions do not provide us with a coherent description of man as he issued forth from the Creator's hands and now appears as a psycho-physical being. But by putting together the pieces of the puzzle as they appear here and there in the material at hand, one can fashion a general picture. It is the Confessions' intention to uphold the belief that salvation is by grace alone, without human assistance, and their anthropology is based upon this. Their view of man is organically related to their view of man's salvation. Unless one takes into consideration what they say about God's demands in the First Table of the Law, one cannot understand their pronouncements about man. At the same time, these statements had an immediate effect upon the concept of man as such—which explains the difficulties which FC later sought to resolve. As it turned out, however, the most consistent attempts to look at man only in his relationship to God, without reference to what he is in himself, proved to be abortive.[1] In order to be able to speak of God and man in relation to one another, something must be said about the two parties in this mutual relationship. Even though the Confessions concentrated on the soteriological facet, they could not avoid saying something about man as a psycho-physical being as well. As background for the anthropology of the Confessions, we must here take a brief look at Melanchthon's psychology.

This is based on the distinction drawn by Aristotle among the soul's three parts,[2] *anima vegetativa, sensitiva,* and *rationalis.* Of these three, theology is concerned with the soul's highest part, reason. Under Aristotle's influence Melanchthon refined his terminology, which also resulted in certain shifts in his point of view. But one feature is consistent: his teaching about the will and the affections,

[1] L. Haikola, *Studien* (1958), pp. 41—44 and 86—89; Löfgren (1960), pp. 61—94. A detailed anthropology is to be found in Bengt Hägglund (1959), pp. 55 ff. and 181 ff. Hägglund analyzes the change in Melanchthon's anthropology from the first edition of the *Loci* (1521) to the writing of *De anima* (1553).

[2] Siebeck, I, 2 (1884), 17—19. Cf. Hägglund (1959), p. 184, plus CR 13, 19 (*Liber de anima,* 1553).

affectus, which he conceived of as his "theological masterpiece." [3]
As early as in the first edition of his *Loci* (1521) Melanchthon connected this "discovery" about man with his teaching about Law and
Promise and with original sin.[4] The teaching about man's affections
is to be found in the Confessions, although the anthropology in the
background is not fully developed. Melanchthon was concerned with
the problem of satisfactorily determining the relationship between
the understanding, the will, and the affections.

In the *Loci* of 1521 Melanchthon reckoned with two distinct faculties in man, the rational powers and desire. For a long time he avoided
the use of the conventional labels *intellectus* and *voluntas* and referred to these faculties instead as powers of the soul. He called the
intellectual power *vis cognoscendi,* and desire *vis appetendi.*[5] In the
former he included sensual knowledge as well as the knowledge of
reason, in the latter both sensual desire and the desires of the higher
powers. In all of his writings Melanchthon clearly defined the relationship between desire and the powers of reason thus: knowledge
must in some way precede desire, for man cannot desire that of which
hs is ignorant.[6] On the other hand, he never said that man always
wills to follow, or is even able to follow, his knowledge. Such a point
of view would be incompatible with the Christian view of man and the
doctrine of original sin. By degrees, however, Melanchthon, under
the influence of Aristotelian psychology, adopted more precise terminology. As a result, in his *Loci* of 1543 he traditionally referred
to man's intellectual function as *mens* or *intellectus,* and to his desire
as *voluntas.* In his later work another alteration was introduced as
well, for in accord with traditional Aristotelian-Thomistic thought,
Melanchthon came to look upon the will as a rational power, capable
of desire. In other words, the will has a rational quality (CR 13, 153).
He also emphasized a stronger connection between knowledge and
will.[7] Intellect and will are joined together in that complex which is
called *liberum arbitrium* — a term which designates the power of the

---

[3] Olsson in STK (1944), p. 105.

[4] CR 21, 87 and 97 (*Loci,* 1521).

[5] CR 21, 275 (*Loci,* 1535). Cf. CR 21, 86 (*Loci,* 1521).

[6] CR 21, 87 — Vis e qua adfectus oriuntur, est qua aut aversamur, aut
persequimur cognita, hanc vim alias voluntatem, alias adfectum, alias appetitum
nominant (*Loci,* 1521). This concept comes through most clearly in *Liber de
anima* — considerandus est, motibus cordis antecedere cognitionem (CR 13, 124).
Hägglund does not mention the fact that there is, on this point, an inner continuity in Melanchthon's way of thinking.

[7] CR 21, 653 — In homine est pars cognoscens ac iudicans, quae vocatur

will to choose among recognized possibilities.[8] Rather than refer to *liberum arbitrium* as "free will," by the way, it would be better to translate it as "the freedom to decide." [9]

According to Melanchthon, the affections as well as the will are a part of the soul's desire-function. The affections were recognized by Aristotle, and they were of great importance both to his psychology and ethics. "For him an affection is a movement in the soul which comes to consciousness. The affections arise without deliberation or intent. Ethically they are looked upon as continually present dispositions to certain kinds of action, psychologically as emotional states." [10] Melanchthon also thought of the affections as irrational powers. He identified them with such feelings as love, hate, fear, anxiety, or trust, and he understood them to be expressions of the human personality. Their seat is in the heart,[11] which is an indication of their irrational character. They are involved in man's unfree will in relation to God [12] and have less to do with external conduct than with man's inner life and his fellowship with Him. In his external conduct man can contradict his affections, but it is impossible to rule them with intellect or will. They are related to the First Table of the Law and the demand there expressed for trusting in God without reservation. It is obvious that Melanchthon took great pains to determine their place in man's spiritual life as carefully as possible and to clarify the relationship between them and the will. Here one can see a change in his point of view.

In the *Loci* of 1521 there is a tendency to join the affections very closely with the will. Even here, of course, Melanchthon does not

mens, vel intellectus, vel ratio, in hac parte sunt notitiae. Altera pars appetens vocatur voluntas, quae vel obtemperat iudicio vel repugnat (*Loci*, 1543).

[8] CR 21, 653 — Vocantur autem liberum arbitrium Mens et Voluntas (*Loci*, 1543). Cf. CR 21, 87 (*Loci*, 1521), and 21:275 f. (*Loci*, 1535), plus Peter Lombard, 2, d. 24, c. 3.

[9] Cf. B. Hägglund (1959), p. 217, and Augustine, *Retract.*, I, 9, 1 — ex libero arbitrio voluntatis (MPL 32, 595).

[10] Siebeck, I, 2 (1884), 90. The counterpart in St. Thomas is formed by his theory of the emotions, STh 1, II, q. 22-44.

[11] CR 21, 90 — Siquidem scriptura potissimam hominis partem cor vocat, adeoque eam in qua nascuntur adfectus (*Loci*, 1521). Concerning the doctrine of the affections or emotions, see Olsson in STK (1944), 103 ff., Lindström (1944), pp. 165 ff., L. Haikola, *Gesetz und Evangelium* (1952), pp. 49 ff., the same author in *Studien* (1958), pp. 38 ff., Hägglund (1959), pp. 181 ff., and Löfgren (1960), pp. 75 f.

[12] This is most obvious in CR 21, 115 — in affectibus nullam esse libertatem experientia docet (*Loci*, 1521).

identify them with it;[13] he rather presupposes a distinction. The will is identified with the heart, but the heart is never identified with the affections. They are born out of the heart or the will (Melanchthon preferred the Biblical *cor* to Aristotle's *voluntas*).[14] But there is still a very close connection between the will and the affections. Both are involved in human desire, are clearly demarcated from the intellectual powers, and all rational content is denied them. But since the Scriptures point to the heart as "the chief part of man" (CR 21, 90 and 92), the affections are afforded a high estimate in spite of this limitation. They are not influenced by the will, for experience teaches that man cannot call forth love or hate through the exertion of the will. Affections can be altered only with the help of other affections. The error of nominalism was its assumption "that the will can by nature resist or produce affections, as often as the intellect urges or recommends." [15] In this sense the will, in alliance with the affections, is independent of the intellect. The latter must certainly make various external facts known, but neither the intellect nor the will is able to control the irrational powers of the affections.

Melanchthon continued to occupy himself with the problem of the affections, and his efforts led him to make a clearer distinction between them and the will, as well as a more careful determination of their nature. In his later work he referred to them as that inner ferment which results from thoughts and ideas. Their seat is the heart (he continued to say), and they give expression to man's total response to what he encounters. They are either positive (joy, hope, and love) or they are negative (sorrow, fear, and wrath).[16] They form a clearly demarcated group within man's ability to desire — to which the will also belongs. But as *appetitus rationalis*, the will is distinct from the affections. And yet the two are very closely related. Just as thoughts and ideas are present in the intellect, so are such affections as love, hate, and fear found in the will.[17] The heart receives ideas from the

[13] Thus in Hägglund (1959), pp. 182 and 190.

[14] CR 21, 92 — Quod si vocabulo cordis, quod usurpat scriptura, uti maluissemus, quam Aristotelico vocabulo voluntatis (*Loci*, 1521).

[15] CR 21, 90 — Fallunt autem scholae cum fingunt voluntatem per naturam suam adversari adfectibus, aut posse ponere adfectum, quoties hoc monet consultive intellectus (*Loci*, 1521).

[16] CR 13, 124 — Sunt autem adfectus qui proprie sic nominantur, motus cordis noticiam sequentes, prosequentes aut fugientes obiecta, qui cum aut iuvent naturam, aut destruant, semper comitantur extremi motus, aut laesa natura dolor ac destructio, aut suaviter mota, delectatio seu laeticia acquiescens in obiecto (*Liber de anima*, 1553).

[17] CR 13, 139 (*Liber de anima*, 1553).

intellect, and these give rise to affections. They, in turn, impel the will to act. They are not always under the control of the will. In man's original state there was complete harmony among the intellect, the will, and the affections. But this harmony has now been disturbed, and the affections are frequently opposed to the will.[18]

This Melanchthonian psychology is found throughout the Confessions, particularly in Ap. Of course, it is not treated as fully there as in the *Loci* and *Liber de anima,* but it forms the background for what the Confessions say about man both before and after the fall into sin. The psychology of the affections played a particularly important role in the development of the doctrines of original sin, justification, and faith.[19]

Man in His Original State

Evangelical theology had three traditional concepts to work with in this area: *imago Dei* and *similitudo Dei* from Gen. 1:27, and *iustitia originalis.* Within Catholic theology it was assumed that *imago* and *similitudo* are not identical. Thomas, like Augustine, distinguished between them for reasons of logic. Similarity is a broader concept than image. Two objects can be similar even though one is not the image of the other. But image always presupposes the idea of similarity, in either a higher or a lower degree.[20] There is complete similarity between the Father and the only-begotten Son, while between God and man this similarity is imperfect. Both Christ and man are the image of the Father, but they reflect Him with varying degrees of clarity. In the Bible this difference is stated thus: the Son is the image of God, while man, on the other hand, was created *in* the image of God.[21] The image of God appears in man's reason and free will. These are congenital faculties; man cannot be deprived of them. When Thomas uses *similitudo* (Gen. 1:27), he has in mind the higher degree of Godlikeness which man, by God's grace, originally pos-

[18] CR 21, 653 — Sub voluntate sunt adpetitiones sensuum seu affectus, quorum subiectum et fons est cor, qui interdum congruunt, interdum pugnant cum voluntate (*Loci,* 1543). CR 13, 164 (*Liber de anima,* 1553). The control of the affections is dependent above all on the aid of the Holy Spirit, CR 13, 130 (*Liber de anima,* 1553).

[19] See, e. g., 80:23-26 (AC XX 31); 186:12-15 (Ap IV 130); 438:34-35 (SA III III 11).

[20] STh I, q. 93, a. 1 and 9.

[21] STh I, q. 93, a. 1 and 2 — primogenitus omnis creaturae est imago Dei perfecta . . . ideo dicitur *Imago.* . . . Homo vero et propter similitudinem dicitur imago; et propter imperfectionem similitudinis dicitur ad imaginem.

sessed and reflected.[22] Then it was that man lived by God's grace and
was obedient to Him. At that time the proper order of things held
sway: God was the highest, and in man reason ruled the lower powers
of the soul. As Thomas emphasized, this *rectitudo* was completely
dependent on God's grace. A right relationship to God formed the
basis of man's inner harmony.[23] The righteousness of man's original
state, *iustitia originalis*,[24] manifested itself in obedience to God and
in the harmonious order of the soul.[25]

Iustitia originalis is one of the chief concepts in the Lutheran
Symbols. In Ap Melanchthon accused the scholastic theologians
of having misunderstood its meaning and having overlooked the connection between the First Table of the Law and original righteousness. In the primordial state God's demand for undivided trust was
already present, and man—with God's help—was able to fulfill this
demand. Man's relation to God in the original state is conceived of
in analogy with man's relation to God in faith.[26] Ap is interested above
all in man's relation to God, but also, and as a result of this, it is concerned about man in his original state. Soteriology precedes and is
superior to anthropology. Compared to Thomas, the order here is
altered, so that both *imago* and *similitudo* are understood to be not
the God-given presupposition of a right relationship to God, but the
results thereof.

> But what is righteousness? Here the scholastics quibble about philo-
> sophical questions and do not explain what original righteousness is.
> In the Scriptures righteousness contains not merely the second table
> of the Decalogue, but also the first, commanding fear of God, faith
> and love toward him. So original righteousness was intended to in-

[22] S. Silen (1938), pp. 115 f.; F. K. Schumann (1936), pp. 117 f. The German edition of St. Thomas (1941), p. 354. The fact that Gen. 1:26 cannot be
cited in an attempt to distinguish between *imago* and *similitudo* was, however,
conceded by the Catholic side.

[23] STh I, q. 95, a. 1 — "Deus fecit hominem rectum" (Pred. 7:30.). Erat
enim haec rectitudo secundum hoc quod ratio subdebatur Deo, rationi vero in-
feriores vires, et animae corpus. Cf. J. Finkenzeller, *Festschrift für M. Schmaus*
(1957), pp. 527 f. — Der Begriffsinhalt des Wortes "rectitudo" reicht schon bei
Anselm von Geradheit im geometrischen Sinne bis zur Rechtschaffenheit im Sinne
der Rechtheit des Willens.

[24] STh I, q. 100.

[25] STh 1 II, q. 82, a. 3 — Tota autem ordinatio originalis iustitiae ex hoc
est, quod voluntas hominis erat Deo subiecta; q. 82, a. 1 — [harmonia] in qua
consistebat ratio originalis iustitiae.

[26] Cf. H. Olsson (1944), p. 233.

volve not only a balanced physical constitution,[27] but these gifts as well: a surer knowledge of God, fear of God, trust in God, or at least the inclination and power to do these things. This the Scripture shows when it says that man was created in the image of God and after his likeness (Gen. 1:27). What else is this than that a wisdom and righteousness was implanted in man that would grasp God and reflect him, that is, that man received gifts like the knowledge of God, fear of God, and trust in God? So Irenaeus interprets the likeness of God. (Ap II 16-19) [28]

This statement on man's original state is of interest for more than one reason. In the first place, *iustitia originalis* is a major concept here, and it is understood to be a relationship to God. If Melanchthon in his polemic against the scholastics had wanted to strike at Thomas, this would have been improper, inasmuch as Thomas, too, conceived of the God-relationship as the primary factor in the righteousness of man's original state. But Melanchthon combined the God-relationship with the unconditioned trust in God demanded by the First Table of the Law, and this was given by far the dominant position.

Second, Ap combines *imago* and *similitudo* without distinguishing between them in the scholastic manner. The Confessions herewith adopt the point of view which characterized the entire Lutheran tradition in contrast to the Catholic. What consequences this would have, and what controversies it would lead to, remains hidden in Ap.

In the third place, it is significant that God's image and likeness are results of the God-relationship and are not conceived of as human qualities. "What else is this than that there were embodied in man such wisdom and righteousness as apprehended God, and in which God was reflected?" (Ap II 18 German). Because man lived in orig-

---

[27] 150:32 — aequale temperamentum qualitatum corporis (Ap II 17). Melanchthon is here referring to the Thomistic-scholastic classification of *iustitia* as the harmonic order of the soul.

[28] 150:18-21 — Quid est autem iustitia? Scholastici hic rixantur de dialecticis quaestionibus, non explicant, quid sit iustitia originalis. Porro iustitia in scripturis continet non tantum secundum tabulam Decalogi, sed primam quoque, quae praecipit de timore Dei, de fide, de amore Dei. Itaque iustitia originalis habitura erat non solum aequale temperamentum qualitatum corporis, sed etiam haec dona: notitiam Dei certiorem, timorem Dei, fiduciam Dei, aut certe rectitudinem et vim ista efficiendi. Idque testatur scriptura, cum inquit hominem ad imaginem et similitudinem Dei conditum esse. Quod quid est aliud, nisi in homine hanc sapientiam et iustitiam effigiatam esse, quae Deum apprehenderet et in qua reluceret Deus, hoc est, homini dona esse data: notitiam Dei, timorem Dei, fiduciam erga Deum et simila? Sic enim interpretantur similitudinem Dei Irenaeus et Ambrosius (Ap II 15-19).

inal righteousness in paradise, he reflected the image of God. He had received wisdom and righteousness from God, and his intellect and will were so directed towards God that he was able to live in a manner consistent with God's expectations. While Catholic theology interpreted *imago* to refer to man's resources as a created, rational being, and *similitudo* to refer to the supernatural likeness, given by grace, the Lutheran Confessions interpreted both as the consequences of man's unbroken relationship to God and the resulting reflection of God's essence.[29]

In the fourth place, the concentration upon the God-relationship also meant that the scholastic interest in original man as a psychological being was shunted aside. And yet it would be a mistake to conclude that this interest disappeared altogether. In view of the fact that the fall into sin had repercussions for human nature, something had to be said about original man as well. The psychology is found in the background. Ap presupposes that *iustitia originalis* also implies "perfect health and, in all respects, pure blood, unimpaired powers of the body" (Ap II 17 German). The use of the term *rectitudo* (in the corresponding Latin), which points both to a right relationship with God and to a proper balance of the soul's varied powers, indicates that Ap here does not draw a fundamental distinction between theology and psychology[30] but simply seeks to emphasize the point of view which it found to be obscured in scholasticism, viz., the primary significance of the God-relationship, as this is expressed in the Law's demand for entire and unfeigned devotion to God.

The obvious tendency to look upon man's original state more as a relationship between God and man than from the point of view of what it meant for man to be created in the image of God can also be discerned in the attempts of the confessional writers to gain support for their position from the early church fathers. As we can demonstrate, they make the claim that their anthropology is in harmony with the Scriptures and the fathers (Ap II 50-51), but this intention seduced them into making an overinterpretation. Ambrose, like the scholastic theologians, maintained that the image of God manifests itself in the rational soul, inasmuch as this is the organ with which man contacts God and comes to know Him. Ap II 19 interprets this

[29] Cf. S. Silen (1938), pp. 31 f. and 120 f., and also D. Löfgren (1960), p. 91 — Imago Dei bedeutet für Luther, das *der Mensch in Gemeinschaft* mit Gott als dem Geber lebt.

[30] Cf. WA 42, 46:16 ff. and 124:4 ff., plus S. Silen (1938), pp. 117 f., and D. Löfgren (1960), pp. 91 f.

statement to mean that only that soul is *imago Dei* in which God is always to be found, i. e., the soul which actually lives in fellowship with God.[31] It is perhaps less surprising that Ap II 20 does not get around to reproducing the New Testament's much more concrete concept of God, which has its basis in the Old Testament.[32]

The Fall and Original Sin

Against the background of man's original condition we can now go on to understand the fall into sin and its consequences for the human race. Here too the Confessions take a firm hold on the First Table of the Law and its demand for wholehearted trust in God. If before the fall into sin man lived in an undisturbed fellowship with God, the fall then signifies such a powerful interruption of this fellowship that all men lost the ability to enter into a right relationship with Him. The image of God, together with *iustitia originalis,* was lost. The description of the fall into sin serves as the background for the main thesis of justification, that man in himself lacks all the prerequisites for his salvation. The nominalist idea which held that man was able of himself to love God above all things if only he did his best, *facere quod in se est,*[33] was hereby contradicted. It was in their polemics against the nominalists that the Lutheran Confessions developed their doctrine of original sin. (Ap II 8)

Accordingly, original sin signifies the loss of man's unbroken relationship with God, original righteousness, *iustitia originalis.*[34]

---

[31] *Exameron,* VI, 8, 45 (CSEL 32, 1, 235 f.). Having set forth the thesis that the soul and not the body is created *ad imaginem Dei,* St. Ambrose demonstrated this by pointing out that we are able to have fellowship with God only as spiritual beings. In this context he raises the following rhetorical question: non est ergo ad imaginem dei in qua deus semper est? (236:17). This question is altered in Ap II 19 into a declarative sentence with a double negative — non est ergo anima ad imaginem Dei, in qua Deus non(!) semper est (150:47). Concerning Ambrose consult S. Silen (1938), pp. 83—93.

[32] Research scholars are continuously occupied with this problem. See J. Jervell, *Imago Dei* (1960), and E. Larsson (1962), pp. 113 f., 151—65, and 175 ff.

[33] G. Biel, II Sent., d. 27, q. 1, a. 3, dub. 3: O. Scheel, II (1930), 164 and 287; H. Bornkamm (1961), p. 127; H. A. Oberman (1963), pp. 132—34 and 468. The expression *quoad substantiam actuum,* used in Ap II 8 and elsewhere, reflects G. Biel, II Sent., d. 28, q. 1, a. 2, concl. 3. According to the opinion expressed there by Biel, man is able to carry out the deeds God commands in His law, e. g., to love Him above all things. Regarding this see H. A. Oberman (1963), pp. 460, 468, and 473 f.

[34] 149:11 — Nam propriis viribus posse diligere Deum super omnia, facere praecepta Dei, quid aliud est, quam habere iustitiam originis? Quodsi has tantas vires habet humana natura, ut per sese possit diligere Deum super omnia, ut confidenter affirmant scholastici, quid erit peccatum originis? (Ap II 9-10).

But it also implies a positive evil, a corruption of nature, which the Confessions, in harmony with Augustine and Luther, call evil desire, *concupiscentia*. The Reformation point of view as expressed in AC tells us that original sin is in part a lack of original righteousness and in part evil desire. "All men who are propagated according to nature are born in sin. That is to say, they are without fear of God, are without trust in God, and are concupiscent." [35]

This same thought is developed, with even greater precision, in Ap. According to the Confessions, the interpretation of original sin as a lack of original righteousness and as evil desire was supported by all of the well-informed older theologians. "Not the ancient theologians alone, but even the more recent ones – at least the more sensible among them – teach that original sin is truly composed of the defects that I have listed, as well as of concupiscence." [36]

In order to comprehend the position of the Lutheran Symbols on this point, we must take a look at the older doctrinal formulation of original sin. What immediately strikes the observer is the vagueness, perhaps even lack of uniformity, in the medieval doctrine of original sin. The key concepts employed by the previous theology were *concupiscentia* and *defectus iustitia originalis* – the same ones we find in the Lutheran Confessions. But a number of different interpretations appear. Gabriel Biel distinguished among three schools:[37] (1) The Augustinian, represented among others by Peter Lombard, according to whom original sin is *concupiscentia*. (2) The school of Anselm,[38] who saw in original sin a lack of *iustitia originalis*. Concupiscence was thought of as punishment for the absence of righteousness. (3) The mediating school, represented among others by Thomas, who identified the "form" of original sin with the absence of righteousness, and

---

[35] 53:3 — Omnes homines, secundum naturam propagati (i. e., all except Christ; see E. Schlink [1961], p. 82, and F. Brunstäd [1952], p. 49) nascantur cum peccato, hoc est sine metu Dei, sine fiducia erga Deum et cum concupiscentia (AC II 1).

[36] 152:32 — Neque solum veteres, sed etiam recentiores, si qui sunt cordiatores, docent simul ista vere peccatum originis esse, defectus videlicet . . . et concupiscentiam (Ap II 27).

[37] H. A. Oberman (1963), p. 122, plus the literature mentioned there. Cf. also Ch. Boyer in *Theologie du peche* (1960), pp. 271 ff. Boyer strongly emphasizes the ambiguity of the medieval teaching of original sin, p. 273.

[38] Anselm, *De conc. virg.,* cap. 6 and 27 (MPL 158, 440, and 461). Cf. STh 1 II, q. 82, a. 1 — originale enim peccatum est carentia originalis iustitiae, ut Anselmus dicit in libro de Concepto Virginali. This idea corresponds to the position held by G. Biel: H. Oberman (1963), pp. 122 f. and 130 f.

its "material" with concupiscence.[39] When the Lutheran Confessions define original sin as lack of righteousness and as evil desire, they would seem to share in the mediatory, Thomistic position—which they also quote and look upon as being Biblical.[40] But the agreement here is only apparent. The similar formulations conceal profound differences, which touch upon both parts of the definition of original sin. These differences are related to divergent concepts of man in his original state.

When Thomas referred to the lack of original righteousness as the "form" of original sin, he had two things in mind. First of all, the fundamental disturbance of man's relation to God—man's will is no longer submissive to God's will—and as a result of this, second, a dislocation of the harmonious unity of the soul, so that its lower powers are no longer submissive to the higher.[41] This lack did not, however, affect man as *imago Dei,* for he did not cease to be a rational, volitional being even after the fall into sin. It rather meant the absence of that higher degree of Godlikeness, *similitudo,* which man by the grace of God possessed in paradise.

As far as the Lutheran Confessions are concerned, the loss of *iustitia originalis* had much more radical consequences. Inasmuch as the original righteousness was so closely tied in with the image of God in man, its absence also involved the loss of *imago Dei.* Man was injured in his innermost being, and turned away from God in enmity. Lack of righteousness signifies the inability to fulfill the demands of the First Table of the Law. Active opposition to God has replaced love for God. Man's lack of righteousness refers, therefore, to his inability to love God and give Him obedience. The Confessions take great pains to point out that the defect in man means precisely this: "lack of ability to trust, fear, or love God" *(non posse Deo credere, non posse Deum timere ac diligere).*[42] It is therefore related to the First Table of the Law and its demand for spiritual righteousness.

But even though this lack is accorded such special significance, this does not mean that it is so total that man's ability to live in a moral

---

[39] STh 1 II, q. 82, a. 3 — Peccatum originale materialiter quidem est concupiscentia; formaliter vero, defectus originalis iustitiae.

[40] 152:36 (Ap II 27); 153:1 — Et hae sententiae consentiunt cum scriptura. Nam Paulus interdum expresse nominat defectum. . . . Alibi concupiscentiam nominat efficacem in membris (Ap II 30).

[41] STh 1 II, q. 82, a. 3.

[42] 152:25-27 (Ap II 26); 153:37 — cor naturaliter vacare amore, timore, fiducia Dei (Ap II 33); 153:10-14 (Ap II 31).

and rational way is disputed. The Confessions do not deny man's ability to achieve civil righteousness, which belongs to the realm of reason,[43] but they oppose the idea that a moral life makes man righteous before God. They do not say, either, that man has no knowledge of God, but rather that man has no *saving* knowledge of Him. As we have seen, they emphasize natural law throughout.[44] To a certain extent, all men can know God through the power of reason, but this knowledge is definitely limited. There is even knowledge of God apart from Christianity, but without Christ and the Holy Spirit no one can know what God thinks of us (LC II 66). Although the lack of righteousness also affects man's nature, it does not totally ruin his reason and will.

Reason is still found in man, taking the form of an ability to make judgments concerning the things it can grasp and understand. This means that every man is able, without special divine assistance, to make decisions about all the practical concerns of this world — whether these have to do with his work, leisure time, or family life — and choose what is good in the natural sense, i. e., what has come forth from God's creation.[45] A part of reason's legitimate task is to carry out those works which fall under the Second Table of the Law. Of and by himself man can be obedient to parents and authorities (the Fourth Commandment), in an external sense restrain himself from murder (Fifth Commandment), adultery (Sixth Commandment), and theft (Seventh Commandment), and in addition to this speak about God and worship Him in an external manner.[46] All these abilities are part and parcel of civil righteousness, *iustitia civilis*. But reason's capacity is limited to external things and events. It has nothing at all to do with righteousness before God, *iustitia spiritualis*, which is a divine gift and not a human achievement.

Reason has its sphere. Although human nature has been corrupted

[43] 149:36 — philosophica seu civili iustitia, quam et nos fatemus rationi subiectam esse et aliquo modo in potestate nostra esse (Ap II 12).

[44] 661:25-26 (LC II 67); 160:10 (Ap IV 7). Cf. 794:2-4 (Ep VI 2); 959:29 (SD V 22); 874:34-37 (SD II 9); and above, Chapter Three, part 1, Chapter Four.

[45] 73:13—74:10 (AC XVIII 4-6). The passage in question is a quotation from the pseudo-Augustine *Hypomnesticon contra pelagianos et coelestianus*, III, 4, 5 (MPL 45, 1623).

[46] 311:26 — Potest aliquo modo efficere iustitiam civilem seu iustitiam operum, potest loqui de Deo, exhibere Deo certum cultum externo opere, obedire magistratibus, parentibus, in opere externo eligendo potest continere manus a caede, ab adulterio, a furto. Cum reliqua sit in natura hominis ratio et iudicium de rebus sensui subiectis, reliquus est etiam delectus earum rerum et libertas et facultas efficiendae iustitiae civilis (Ap XVIII 4).

by sin, man does not lack the ability to arrange things wisely in his private life, home, and community. But when reason transcends the limits of its ability, it becomes an evil power. Luther had some harsh words to say about blind and insane [47] reason, which claimed to be able to understand and control God. Apart from the illumination of Scripture,[48] reason is unable to comprehend the depth of original sin and cannot achieve righteousness before God. The severe polemics against *ratio* were exclusively concerned with the fact that it claimed to be able to point the way to God. *Ratio* is a false way of salvation, identical with the work-righteousness which ignores Christ and the salvation He provides. Both Luther and Melanchthon were in agreement about the insufficiency of reason. Blind reason fumbles with the things of God and in its darkness looks to its own works for comfort. Reason understands work-righteousness and the righteousness of the Law, but it stands like a stranger in the presence of the righteousness that comes by faith.[49] The restrictions placed upon philosophy were always made in the interest of distinguishing between Christian righteousness, *iustitia spiritualis,* and civil or philosophical righteousness. When the Confessions refer to original sin as *ignoratio Dei,* they do not suggest that man lacks all knowledge of God, only the saving knowledge.

Neither does original sin exclude freedom of the will in every form. The ability to achieve civil righteousness presupposes freedom of the will. In regard to external conduct of life and the Second Table of the Law, man even after the Fall has limited freedom of the will. Employing his will, he can choose among those things which come under the domain of reason, but since the will is no longer sound, it cannot of itself do what is good as seen from God's point of view. The diminution of the intellect and the will makes man unable to fulfill the demands of the First Table of the Law. Man lacks "unimpaired power to love God above all things and to obey his commandments 'according to the substance of the act.' "[50] The possession of such power would mean that man still had the original righteousness, and

---

[47] 440:13 (SA III III 18); 693:23 (LC IV 13).

[48] 149:42-44 (Ap II 13); 434:8-10 — Solche Erbsunde ist so gar ein tief bose Verderbung der Natur, dass sie kein Vernunft nicht kennet, sondern muss aus der Schrift Offenbarung gegläubt werden (SA III I 3).

[49] 161:26-29 (Ap IV 12); 204:14 (Ap IV 230); 235:5 (Ap IV 394); 440:13 (SA III III 18).

[50] 149:7-10 (Ap II 8). Concerning the expression "quoad substantiam actuum" see n. 33.

this would be a denial of original sin. This is expressed negatively in the words *carentia iustitiae originalis* – the loss of original righteousness.

But this lack also affects man's *nature* in some way. The early Confessions do not analyze the precise significance of this corruption of human nature; this was not done until the Flacian controversy arose later on. The question which Flacius raised – as to whether original sin is to be thought of as a *substans* or an *accidens* – was certainly anticipated by Luther,[51] but the definitive confessional answer was not provided until FC was written.[52] The earlier Confessions assert only that original sin is a fault in human nature – human nature has surrendered to the power of the devil (Ap II 47); all are born with a faulty and defiled nature (Ap II 6). The Confessions do not, however, adopt a Manichaean view of man.[53] Sin does not utterly destroy man as a creation of God. FC's efforts to neutralize both Manichaeism and Pelagianism, in the interest of preserving faith in creation and salvation, were anticipated by the earlier Confessions. The fault in human nature was therefore limited to man's lack of knowledge and fear of God (Ap II 8), or in other words to man's inability to fulfill the First Table of the Law.

In addition to the absence of *iustitia originalis,* original sin is also *concupiscentia.* In the confessional writers' interpretation of this Biblical and Augustinian concept we see most clearly their deviation from contemporary Catholic theology. This has to do with the role of concupiscence both before and after Baptism. Inasmuch as concupiscence points to man's unfree will in spiritual matters, it is conceived of as an active tendency in opposition to God, "the continual inclination of nature" toward evil (Ap II 3). The Confessions consistently relate it to the First Table of the Law on the one hand and to the doctrine of human affections on the other.

The chief interest of the confessional writers at this point is to show how concupiscence involves active opposition to God and His demands for faith and obedience. All interpretations of concupiscence

---

[51] In his lectures on Genesis, 1535—45 (WA 42, 47:8 and 48:32 f.), Luther set forth the opinion that original sin is a substance which is intrinsic in the human essence. See Silen (1938), p. 118. Flacius, who formally represented the same point of view, nevertheless gave the substance concept a different meaning. See L. Haikola (1952), pp. 112—18; Ljunggren (1928), pp. 109 f.; Hägglund (1959), pp. 132 f.

[52] Ep I 19 (775:13 ff.) and SD I 59 (864:13) reject the idea that original sin is a substance. Cf. E. Schlink (1961), pp. 45 ff.

[53] 51:2 (AC I 5). Cf. to what follows E. Schlink (1961), pp. 44 ff.

as sheer sensuality are rejected. It rather signifies a striving away from God; its essence is "doubt about God's wrath, his grace, and his Word; anger at his judgments; indignation because he does not deliver us from trouble right away; fretting because bad people are more fortunate than good people; yielding to anger, desire, ambition, wealth, etc." [54] All of this illustrates, in the first place, disobedience against the First Table of the Law, and second, the transgression of the other commandments. Together with the loss of original righteousness, man also lost the ability to fulfill the Law as he should. This vacuum was filled by concupiscence—man's constant inclination to seek his own instead of that which belongs to God.

The reformers felt that their interpretation of *concupiscentia* was the correct intention underlying the Augustinian classification of original sin as evil desire—the Biblical support of which they found in Rom. 7:7: "I should not have known what it is to covet if the Law had not said, 'You shall not covet'" (cf. Ex. 20:17; Deut. 5:21).[55] That concupiscence has such consequences is related to the fact that it influences man's affections.

Before the fall into sin, man had positive feelings about God; after the Fall, they became negative and hostile. Even if man is able to do, in an external way, what God commands in the Law, he cannot satisfy the deepest demands of the Law in an internal way. His negative affections prevent it. What man was able to do in his original condition has now become impossible. This is the real meaning of *concupiscentia,* and the ultimate result of the fall into sin. Evil desire is combined with the unsettled affections that struggle against the First Table of the Law and stand outside the control of the will. Concupiscence is nature's perpetual inclination away from God.

It is true even within the sphere of civil righteousness that the dominion of evil desire over the affections is so great that judgment can be distorted.[56] But this is even more true with regard to the internal righteousness which the Law requires and man cannot achieve. In place of love, faith, and fear of God, man is filled with hate, ani-

---

[54] 155:35 — dubitare de ira Dei, de gratia Dei, de verbo Dei, irasci iudiciis Dei, indignari quod Deus non eripit statim ex afflictionibus, fremere, quod impii meliore fortuna utantur, quam boni, incitari ira, libidine, cupiditate, gloriae, opum, etc. (Ap II 42). Cf. 166:36-52 (Ap IV 34).

[55] *De sp. et litt.,* 13, 21 and 14, 24 (CSEL 60, 174 and 178); 155:5-6 (Ap II 39); 385:13-16 (Ap XXVII 25).

[56] 311:40 — tanta est vis concupiscentiae, ut malis affectibus saepius obtemperet homines quam recto iudicio (Ap XVIII 5).

mosity, anger, and faithlessness.[57] Apart from the Holy Spirit, human powers are filled with base affections.[58] Thus it is that man breaks the First Table of the Law.[59] The Law is directed at the inner feelings of the heart.[60] The commandment which says, "Thou shalt not covet" can be translated thus: "You shall not harbor affections that are in opposition to God." Instead of hate and animosity, man is expected to show God love and devotion. But this he cannot do by himself. As a result, he stands under judgment.

Because man's affections are not free, he cannot produce righteousness before God. God demands the heart's devotion in accordance with the First Table of the Law, but man is unable to fulfill this demand. The Lutheran Confessions therefore emphatically reject the idea that man of his own power should be able to love God above all things and his neighbor as himself.[61] If man could do this, then the grace of Christ would not be needed and man would still be in possession of original righteousness (Ap II 8 ff.). Man can carry out the external act, but he cannot control the attitude of the heart. He can refrain from theft and murder, but he cannot sway the inner feelings.[62] No one can completely fulfill the Law in this life, because the base affections never cease. Sin consists of the will's enmity to God.[63]

Man lacks the ability to influence the affections that are inimical to God. There is complete agreement on this point between Ap and SA. Since evil desires are in themselves sin, and not under the control of the will, it is pointless (according to SA) to request forgiveness only for voluntary sins.[64] The Biblical, Christian view of these things

[57] 438:34 — concupiscentia enim, vitiosi affectus, inclinatio, libido et affectio prava . . . sunt peccata (SA III III 11).

[58] 80:23 — humanae vires sine spiritu sancto plenae sunt impiis affectibus (AC XX 31).

[59] 186:13 — affectus cordis erga Deum, qui praecipiuntur in prima tabula, non posse fieri sine spiritu sancto (Ap IV 130); 194:47 — Plus quam coeci sunt, qui malos affectus in carne non sentiunt esse peccata. . . . Caro diffidit Deo, confidit rebus praesentibus. . . . Cum talibus affectibus luctatur spiritus sanctus in cordibus (Ap IV 169 ff.). Cf. 312:10-30 (Ap XVIII 7 f.).

[60] 185:22 (Ap IV 124); 187:30 (Ap IV 136).

[61] 434:20-23 (SA III III 6 f.).

[62] 74:31 — [Natura] potest enim continere manus a furto, a caede — tamen interiores motus non potest efficere, ut timorem Dei, fiduciam erga Deum, patienciam, etc. (AC XVIII Editio princeps, 1531).

[63] 189:14 — in hac vita non possumus legi satisfacere, quia natura carnalis non desinit malos affectus parere (Ap IV 146); 219:38 — horribiles motus voluntatis fugientis iudicium Dei (Ap IV 304).

[64] 438:15-18 (SA III III 11); 155:47 ff. (Ap II 43).

is said to be that with all his volitional tendencies man keeps turning away from God. In spite of the retention of external knowledge of God and freedom of the will, man is unfavorably disposed toward God. The evil desires of the soul are sinful under all circumstances, regardless of whether man consents to them or not.[65] It was the intention of the reformers to employ their doctrine of original sin to give expression to the idea that sin is something total and all-inclusive. Sin separates man from God in such a radical way that only God Himself, through Christ, can bridge over the abyss.

The Confessions claim to reproduce the Biblical and Augustinian doctrine of original sin,[66] but the question is more complicated than that. Von Loewenich's judgment that "Augustine has been better understood by the Catholic Church than by its opponents" [67] may well stand the test of time. The difference between Augustine and the reformers is not, as has often been maintained, that the former used *concupiscentia* only in reference to sexual desire. On the contrary, Augustine emphasized the idea that sinful man turns away in his pride from the godly and eternal to the temporal and emancipates himself from God.[68] The real contrast appears in what is taught about the role of concupiscence in those who are baptized, and with regard to the conditions that must prevail before a given act can be referred to as sin.

Luther and the Confessions, citing Augustine, are of the opinion that concupiscence remains as sin even in those who are baptized.[69] This, however, is not what Augustine meant. In the statement referred to in Ap II 36 Augustine asserts: "Carnal concupiscence is remitted, indeed, in baptism; not so that it is put out of existence, but so that

---

[65] 166:43 — vere peccant homines etiam cum honesta opera faciunt (Ap IV 35).

[66] 147:11 — ostendemus pluribus verbis, nostram descriptionem consentire cum usitata ac veteri definitione (Ap II 4).

[67] W. von Leowenich (1959), pp. 84 and 246.

[68] *De sp. et litt.*, 7, 11—8, 14 and 10, 17 (CSEL 60, 162 ff. and 169 f.), plus *De. lib. arb. voluntatis*, I, 16, 35 (MPL 32, 1240); S. Silen (1938), pp. 98 f.; J. Mausbach, II (1909), 174—78. It is in the manner given here that the confessors understood Augustine: Sigificat enim concupiscentiam successisse amissa iustitia (Ap II 24). For a somewhat different view see E. Dinkler (1934), pp. 116 f.

[69] 153:51 ff. (Ap II 35-37); WA 2, 160:34 — in puero post baptismum peccatum remanens negare, hoc est Paulum et Christum semel conculcare (*Disputatio et excusatio F. Martini Luther,* 1519). Luther's position was condemned in the papal bull *Exsurge Domine,* 1520 (Denz. 742), and repudiated in the Confutation (CR 27, 88).

it is not to be imputed for sin. Although its guilt, *reatus,* is now taken away, it still remains until our entire infirmity be healed by the advancing renewal of our inner man, day by day, when at last our outward man shall be clothed with incorruption." [70] What Augustine intended to say here is that concupiscence is not sin in itself, but only in connection with guilt, *reatus.* Inasmuch as guilt is forgiven in Baptism, the sin is no longer there. What remains is concupiscence as a weakness in those baptized. If this weakness enlists the aid of the will, [71] new sin is the result. So when the Confutation [72] refers to residual concupiscence as the cause of sin, *fomes peccati,* it properly reflects Augustine's point of view.

It cannot be said of the confessional writers, however, that they have altered the sense of the quotation from Augustine cited above by means of a slight retouching. While Augustine says that concupiscence is so abrogated in Baptism that it is no longer reckoned as sin (although the concupiscence remains in the form of a weakness), Ap maintains that the *sin,* which is forgiven, nevertheless remains after Baptism. [73] The difference therefore is that for Augustine postbaptismal *concupiscentia* is a weakness in human nature which can be the cause of sin, while for the reformers it is sin even after Baptism, although it is not counted.

This difference of opinion goes back to two completely dissimilar ways of looking at sin and grace. According to Catholic theologians sin was not sin unless carried out with the consent of the will. [74] To speak meaningfully of sin requires that man can be held responsible for his actions. All share in Adam's guilt, but there must be a way for the baptized to be held responsible for their actions. Grace, which

[70] *De nuptiis et concupiscentia,* I, 24, 28 (MPL 44, 430), quoted from *A Select Library of the Nicene and Post-Nicene Fathers of the Christian Church,* ed. Philip Schaff, trans. Peter Holmes, Vol. V, p. 275, sec. 28. J. Mausbach, II (1909), 185 ff.; S. Silen (1938), pp. 100 ff.; Ch. Boyer in *Theologie du Peche* (1960), pp. 272.

[71] *De peccatorum meritis et remissione,* II, 4, 4 (MPL 44, 152 f.).

[72] CR 27, 88; cf. G. Biel, II Sent., d. 30, q. 2, a. 3, dub. 2, and H. A. Oberman (1963), p. 469.

[73] Augustine: dimitti concupiscentiam carnis in Baptismo, non ut non sit, sed ut in peccatum non imputetur (*De nuptiis et conc.,* I, 24, 28). The Confessions: peccatum in baptismo remittitur, non ut non sit, sed ut non imputetur (Ap II, 36).

[74] Eck pointed this out in his 182 articles against the Reformation: Male distinguunt hodie inter veniale et mortale, cum omnis affectus concupiscentiae sit peccatum mortale, quia omne peccatum est mortale secundum naturam, sed veniale his, qui sunt in Christo. W. Gussman, II (1930), 125.

is a power from God for use in opposing the residual weakness in man, has a sanitary, healing influence; Augustine compared it to a medicine which cures the sick.

The reformers, on the other hand, saw in sin something which ineluctably separates man from God, so that only God can set things right again. Sin is a perpetual concentration upon oneself, turning away from God. To speak of will and the freedom of the will in this context is evidently meaningless (Ap II 43); salvation would then be dependent on man's will. The doctrine of original sin took form with an eye on the doctrine of justification by faith through grace alone (Ap II 33). Grace was given a different connotation. In the first place, it is not a power which heals and renews man; it is the attribution of God's righteousness. In consequence of this, Augustine and the reformers did not mean the same thing when they spoke of man as at the same time righteous and a sinner, *simul iustus et peccator.*

Chapter Six:

Justification — Man's Restoration

The Background of Justification

Fallen man is not free from God; the demand for righteousness still rests upon him. The *iustitia originalis* of man's primal state, which signified an uncorrupted trust in God and attachment to God, remains as an impossible demand.

The background and presupposition of justification is that man is conscious of this demand and of his inability to meet it. Its presupposition is, in other words, proper instruction concerning Law and Gospel (Promise). Here we have one explanation of why Melanchthon introduced his presentation on justification (Ap IV) with a reminder of the Scriptural distinction between Law and Gospel and why Luther in LC takes note of the impossible demands of the Law before he goes on — in the second major section, on faith — to show how the Triune God helps man fulfill them (LC II 1). The demands have to do with faith and trust in God: the righteousness in question is of an inner, spiritual nature — *iustitia spiritualis,* which is demanded in the First Table of the Law. The authors of the Confessions were convinced that in their concentration on the First Table they had rediscovered what the Bible and the discerning fathers meant by righteousness.[1] God requires more than external deeds. He wants man's heart; He expects *iustitia spiritualis.*

We can here make a direct connection with our previous analysis (Chapter Three, Part 3) of the different kinds of righteousness. The Confessions do not deny that man can perform noble deeds in an external fashion. He can do his work and use his reason to comprehend what God expects of him in the social context. With the aid of his volitional powers he can achieve civil righteousness. *Iustitia rationis* is therefore possible for man, although many fail to achieve it because of the power of sin and the devil's deceitful temptations (Ap IV 22-24). To make an estimate of Lutheran theology in general and of its anthropology in particular, it is important, yes necessary, to keep in

---

[1] 165:32 — Huius nostrae sententiae testimonia habemus non solum ex scripturis, sed etiam ex patribus (Ap IV 29).

mind this distinction between civil, rational righteousness on the one hand and the spiritual righteousness which God requires in the First Table of the Law on the other hand.

The impossible demands of the Law are related to the First Table. As long as man thinks only of the Second Table, the fulfillment of the Law is at least a theoretical possibility. But God demands a righteous heart, i. e., faith and love, which man cannot achieve. When measured against God's standard, all fulfillment of the Law is insufficient inasmuch as *the First Table of the Law is impossible of fulfillment for fallen man.* The reason for this is well known. By virtue of the loss of *iustitia originalis,* concupiscence dominates human life and, working through the affections, prevents the will from trusting in God as it should. Because the heart is turned away from God, man always sins, even when, apart from the Holy Spirit, he performs deeds which are in themselves honorable.[2] As we saw in the previous chapter, man does not have to will to do wrong in order to bring sin into being; his whole outlook is turned away from God. For the sake of justification as God's work, without human contribution or cooperation, the Confessions found it necessary to stress: "It is false, too, and a reproach to Christ, that men who keep the commandments of God outside a state of grace do not sin."[3] Even if someone should fulfill the Second Table in an external sense, man is not free from sin, inasmuch as the heart is turned from God. The reformers' fundamental belief in the impossibility of fulfilling the Law has nothing to do with a general downgrading of man, but it is related to their conviction that the commandments of the First Table far exceed man's abilities and powers.

When man, on the basis of the First Table of the Law, is confronted by the demand for faith in and love for God, his complete inability to fulfill this demand is revealed to him. This inability does not therefore reflect upon his ethical conduct in general; it rather has to do with the demand for the heart's devotion and faith. The Decalog requires that we truly love God with the whole heart, and it condemns the evil desires in our nature. But to produce love for God is just as

[2] 166:43 — vere peccant homines etiam cum honesta opera faciunt sine spiritu sancto (Ap IV 35).

[3] 165:27 — Falsum est et hóc et contumeliosum in Christum, quod non peccent homines facientes praecepta Dei sine gratia (Ap IV 28). The German parallel text has in an interesting manner modified this formulation: it is false and libelous vis-à-vis Christ that they do not sin "die Gottes Gebot allein äusserlich halten."

impossible as it is to get rid of evil desire. So, in this sense, we can never fulfill the Law. No one ever does as much as it requires.[4]

At this point the Confessions deliberately oppose the nominalists, who taught that man's powers were unsullied and that he can love God above all things. The Reformation developed as a result of controversy involving the nominalist doctrine of penance, according to which a man could prepare himself for the reception of grace through certain "dispositions," including love for God as well as others. The confessional writers continued the Evangelical criticism of nominalism and rejected the alleged ability of man to love God and harbor faith.[5] Apart from Christ and the Holy Spirit, the demands of the Law as contained in the First Table can never be fulfilled. Man is incapable of the righteousness which he knew in the original state and which God now requires of him.

In general, three reasons are set forth in support of this point of view. The testimony of Scripture is basic and decisive here—as always in the Confessions. Those who insist that they can in their own strength fulfill the Law—i. e., the First Table—have misunderstood Scripture. They fail to recognize what the Scriptures mean by law and righteousness. Instead, they confine their attention to the Second Table, overlooking the fact that the central point of the Law is to be found in the First Table's insistence upon wholehearted trust in God. Such men confuse civil and Christian righteousness. "Scripture cries out everywhere that we are far away from the perfection that the law requires"[6] and that we cannot fulfill the Law satisfactorily.[7] According to Scripture, the fulfillment of the Law is impossible.

The second argument is that if man can fulfill the Law in his own strength, Christ is unnecessary and salvation is based on merit rather than on grace. Christ then becomes a teacher of morality and a law-

[4] 168:25 — legem nunquam faciamus (Ap IV 42); 193:53 — nunquam legis satisfaciamus (Ap IV 164); 185:44 — lex non potest fieri sine Christo (Ap IV 126); 282:41 — nemo tantum facit, quantum lex requirit (Ap XII 142).

[5] 165:16 — Falsum est et hoc, quod ratio propriis viribus possit Deum supra omnia diligere et legem Dei facere, videlicet vere timere Deum, vere statuere, quod Deus exaudiat, velle obedire Deo in morte et aliis ordinationibus Dei, non concupiscere aliena etc., etsi civilia opera efficere ratio potest (Ap IV 27); 162:39-40 (Ap IV 17); 434:22-23 (SA III I 7). G. Biel taught that man is able "actum dilectionis dei super omnia elicere et suis naturalibus etiam si gratia non inpenderetur" (II Sent., d. 28, q.1, a.3, dub. 1 L; quoted in H. A. Oberman (1963), p. 153.

[6] 282:34 — Atqui scriptura ubique clamat, quod multum absimus ab illa perfectione, quam lex requirit (Ap XII 142).

[7] 194:16 — Tota scriptura, tota ecclesia clamat legi non satisfieri (Ap IV 166).

giver comparable to the great philosophers, but scarcely a Savior.[8] If it is argued that man can fulfill the entire Law of and by himself, then one must also take the consequences: Christ is transmuted into one of humanity's "great men."

A third argument against the assertion that we can love God above all things of and by ourselves is to be found in Christian experience. Love is an act of the will, but the will lacks the ability to love God. Experience, as well as Scripture and the church, clearly reveals how far removed we are from a proper fulfillment of the Law and how we lack love for God.

When man comes to understand through the preaching of the Law that God requires an upright life, he begins to do good things, falsely believing that he will thus please God. The false notion that we can by our own strength do what God expects promotes the attempt to achieve righteousness by the Law. The deepest motivation for monasticism, fasting, worship services, and holy days is the belief that man has the ability to make himself righteous before God on the basis of meritorious deeds. This opinion "has produced and increased many types of worship in the church, like monastic vows and the abuses of the Mass; someone has always been making up this or that form of worship or devotion with this view in mind." (Ap IV 10)

All work-piety is founded on a misunderstanding of the Law and an incorrect view of man. It is based on the false idea that we can by our own strength love God and perform works that He finds commendable. The Law directs its arrows at man's inner life, at the feelings of the heart, at the affections,[9] which no one can govern with his own will. When man comes to realize his inability, the Law is transformed from a pleasant guide into an accuser. Like Augustine,[10] the confessional writers emphasize that "the Law" always has the same meaning—the Decalog. Because it is impossible for man to fulfill it, he is confronted by God's wrath, which in turn strikes fear into his conscience. The Law becomes a wrathful power.

The confessional writers, like Augustine (*De spiritu et littera* 5, 8), sought to give expression to Paul's concept of the Law, particularly as found in Rom. 4:15: "The Law brings wrath"—it accuses and

---

8 161:19—162:13 (Ap IV 12 ff.); 232:46-54 (Ap IV 392); 149:18-20 (Ap II 10).

9 185:20 — Loquimur autem non de ceremoniis, sed de illa lege, quae praecipit de motibus cordis, videlicet de Decalogo (Ap IV 24).

10 *De sp. et litt.*, 13, 21 ff. (CSEL 60, 173 ff.).

frightens the conscience.[11] Different expressions were used, but the
same theme was repeated: The Law "always accuses the conscience,
which does not satisfy the law and therefore flees in terror before the
judgment and punishment of the law"—according to Rom. 4:15 (Ap
IV 270). Because of the Law, man "is terror-stricken and humbled,
becomes despondent and despairing, anxiously desires help but does
not know where to find it, and begins to be alienated from God, to
murmur, etc. This is what is meant by Rom. 4:15, 'The law brings
wrath'" (SA III II 4). "The law will always accuse us because we
never satisfy the law of God. As Paul says (Rom. 4:15), 'The law
brings wrath.'" (Ap XII 88)

For the theologians of the Reformation era, talk about the curse
of the Law was not so much theoretical booklore; they knew from
experience about the wrath of God and the judgment of conscience.
The whole of Scripture provided knowledge concerning the reality
of a distressed conscience,[12] but they also knew about it from personal
experience. As Schlink points out, the specific Reformation experience
had to do with the wrath of God.[13] The experience of God's wrath and
of the judgment of conscience was the primal experience in which the
Reformation had its origin. The Confessions often speak of the
anguished conscience.[14] God's demand for righteousness and man's
inability to fulfill this demand result in a distressed conscience. The
Reformation proclamation of justification by faith presupposes a
situation in which man is subjected to the demands of the Law and
can see no way out to salvation. "This whole teaching is to be referred
to that conflict of the terrified conscience, nor can it be understood
apart from that conflict."[15] Against those who opposed the Reformation doctrine of justification it was said that they must be entirely
ignorant of God's wrath as manifested in the chastened conscience.[16]
If one is aware of the judgment of conscience, he will also know how
impossible it is to love God by oneself. No one can love an angry
judge.

---

[11] 167:28-31 (Ap IV 38); 436:13 (SA III II 4).

[12] Both the psalter and the prophets have left us with a great deal of material
which sheds light on this question. See, e. g., 257:25-39 (Ap XII 31); 436:17—
437:2 (SA III III 1 ff.).

[13] E. Schlink (1961), p. 79. Cf. Werner Elert, I (1962), 17 ff.

[14] 254:21 (Ap XII 9); 163:37 ff. (Ap IV 20); 77:31 ff. (AC XX 15).

[15] 78:8 — Tota haec doctrina ad illud certamen perterrefactae conscientiae
referenda est, nec sine illo certamine intelligi potest (AC XX 17).

[16] 160:40-42 (Ap IV 9); 163:42 ff. (Ap IV 20).

The Meaning of Justification

The situation described above provides the background for the Reformation doctrine of justification, which is summarized most concisely in AC IV: "Our churches also teach that men cannot be justified before God by their own strength, merits, or works but are freely justified for Christ's sake through faith when they believe that they are received into favor and that their sins are forgiven on account of Christ, who by his death made satisfaction for our sins. This faith God imputes for righteousness in his sight (Rom. 3, 4)." AC's intent is to show—with the support of Romans 3 and 4—that man is justified not by works but by faith. Thus it establishes first of all that the righteousness in question is spiritual, the *iustitia spiritualis* which is valid before God, *coram Deo*. The article further asserts that this righteousness cannot be achieved on the strength of one's own good works. Apart from grace all works are sin and as a result cannot justify. All human merit must therefore be rejected.[17] Neither can man prepare himself for justification through penitence or remorse. He cannot point to a moral life of patience, purity, and obedience, and even less to his love for God, as a basis for justification.[18] The reformers saw a new form of Pelagianism in the nominalist teaching of a natural love for God. The fight against this was at the same time a battle against Pelagianism, and in waging it the reformers were certain that they were carrying on a tradition dating back to the early church.[19]

The doctrine that justification is wholly and completely God's work, a divine gift, is in harmony with the discovery of *iustitia Dei* as God's gift, not His demand. Righteousness is given to us *propter Christum,* i. e., because Christ has offered Himself as a sacrifice and reconciled the Father to us (AC II 3).[20] We receive the righteousness of God by faith, and *this faith* is reckoned by God as righteousness, valid before Him (according to Rom. 4:3 and 9).[21]

In order to comprehend this line of thought, we must bear in mind

---

[17] 265:5 — non propter ulla nostra merita atque opera (Ap XII 65); 276:3 — non propter nostra opera praecedentia aut sequentia (Ap XII 116); 177:25 — non propter nostra merita, non propter nostram contritionem, attritionem, cultus, opera (Ap IV 83).

[18] 189:49-57 (Ap IV 151).

[19] 163:26-29 (Ap IV 19).

[20] Above, Chapter Four.

[21] 56:9 — Hanc fidem imputat Deus pro iustitia coram ipso (AC IV 3). The language used here is unusual. Cf. *Die Bekenntnisschriften* (1963), p. 56, n. 3. Ap would have used the concept *reputare* instead.

the consequences of original sin. Original sin resulted in the loss of original righteousness, that unbroken relationship with God which is now required of us in the First Table of the Law. That man's faith is reckoned as righteousness must simply mean, then, that the condition of undisturbed fellowship with God has been achieved anew. Communication between God and man is resumed through faith. Those who believe live in a renewed relationship with God, and the deepest demand of the Law is thus fulfilled. The way to God has been opened by Christ. It is for His sake, and not because of human achievement, that the faithful live in the righteousness man knew before the fall into sin. It is through faith that judgment and agony of conscience are taken away; it is for Christ's sake that we can approach the Father and live in fellowship with Him. These points of view are further developed in Ap.

In 1884 Loofs published his well-known article on justification as explained in Ap,[22] and since that time there has been a lively exchange of opinion concerning the proper interpretation of Ap's doctrine of justification. The discussion has centered upon a difficult passage in Ap IV 72: "And 'to be justified' means to make unrighteous men righteous or to regenerate them, as well as to be pronounced or accounted righteous. For Scripture speaks both ways." [23]

While Melanchthon therefore felt able to prove that the concept of justification was used in two ways in the Bible, Loofs asks whether or not Melanchthon here represents two contradictory interpretations of justification: (1) the one current in original Lutheranism, and (2) the purely forensic interpretation of later Lutheran orthodoxy. According to the first, justification signifies the renewal which is given expression in the phrase "to make unrighteous men righteous or to regenerate them," *ex iniustis iustos effici seu regenerari.* The subsequent orthodox explanation of justification was anticipated in the phrase "to be pronounced or accounted righteous," *iustos pronuntiari seu reputari.* (Both Ap IV 72)

---

[22] F. Loofs in ThStK (1884), pp. 613—88. The discussion was summarized by H. Engelland (1931), pp. 541—68. See also *Die Bekenntnisschriften* (1963), p. 158, n. 2; E. Schlink (1961), p. 93, n. 12; F. Brunstäd (1951), pp. 73 ff.; Bengt Hägglund (1959), pp. 361 ff.; L. Haikola in *Festschrift till Hj. Lindroth* (1958), pp. 51—62; and H. Volk in *Festgabe für L. Jaeger* (1963), pp. 96—131. Also A. Peters, *Glaube und Werk: Luthers Rechtfertigungslehre im Lichte der Heiligen Schrift* (1962); and O. Pesch, *Theologie der Rechtfertigung bei Martin Luther und Thomas von Aquin* (1967), with extensive literary notations.

[23] 174:37 — Et quia iustificari significat ex iniustis iustos effici seu regenerari, significat et iustos pronuntiari seu reputari (Ap IV 72).

But if our attention is directed first of all to the question raised by Loofs, it is easy to overlook Melanchthon's primary concern in Ap IV.[24] The passage from which we have quoted bears the superscription "Faith in Christ Justifies" (Ap IV 61), and this is the theme of the presentation as it continues. Thus Melanchthon is developing the thought in AC IV 3 that God reckons our faith as righteousness in His sight. It is through faith alone, *sola fide,* that we are justified.

This interpretation of justification was disputed by the Catholic theologians. According to the Catholic point of view, faith alone can never justify, but only that faith which is active in love. When Paul says in Rom. 4:3 and 9 that faith is reckoned to us as righteousness, the Catholic understanding insists that this is a reference to faith active in love and good works.[25] Contrary thereto, the basic concern of Ap is to show why faith alone makes men righteous before God and is reckoned as righteousness.

The answer to the question raised by the opposition went as follows. Since man's way to God is closed, God must come to man. This He does through the Scripture's Word of promise, the Gospel, which can only be received by faith (Ap IV 43). Spiritual righteousness is given for Christ's sake (Ap IV 40) and is received by faith. Justification, as God's work in us, is a divine service performed by God Himself (Ap IV 49). God presents us with His righteousness through the Word of promise, to which faith corresponds. As Ap reminds us, Paul speaks of the promise and faith in the same way in Rom. 4:16.[26]

In justification man finds himself in a penitential situation. His heart is harassed by God's demands as seen in the First Table of the Law, and his conscience is anxious because he is unable to meet these demands and as a result experiences divine wrath. The promise of God's forgiveness for Christ's sake changes everything. Through the Word of promise the righteousness of Christ is imputed to him, and faith then restores his heart and brings about the new birth; on the basis of Christ's righteousness God declares him to be righteous.

According to Ap, justification includes the following elements. Its foundation is the righteousness of Christ, which is provided to us through the Word of promise. If man receives the promise of the

[24] See H. Engelland (1931), pp. 559 ff.; E. Schlink (1961), p. 91, n. 11; and L. Haikola in *Festschrift till Hj. Lindroth* (1958), pp. 55 f.

[25] CR 27, 96 f.

[26] 170:26 — [Paulus] sentit enim promissionem non posse accipi nisi fide. Quare inter se correlative comparat et connectit promissionem et fidem (Ap IV 50); 171:11-16 (Ap IV 55 f.).

Gospel in faith, his new birth takes place. This experience affects the inner feelings of the heart and enables the soul to rest in God. Through faith in Christ the Mediator, who is the Foundation on which the promise is based, God heals the wounds inflicted by sin: sins are forgiven, fellowship with God is restored, and the absolute dominion of concupiscence is broken. It is in this sense that Ap refers to justification as an effective process, for to be justified means "to make unrighteous men righteous or to regenerate them," *ex iniustis iustos effici seu regenerari* (Ap IV 72). On the basis of this regenerating faith, God can *declare* the sinner righteous in His sight.[27] In this sense justification is the same as the forensic "to be pronounced or accounted righteous," *iustos pronuntiari seu reputari.* (Ap IV 72)

There is no precise chronological order in which these various elements appear, but in analyzing them one does find a logical division. Our interpretation makes justification a coherent whole and also enables us to see why it is faith that justifies: because it seizes upon the promise of Christ's merits, which take the place of human achievement, and regenerates the heart. The righteousness of Christ, which is imputed to us by faith, enables God to declare man righteous.

As Haikola [28] has shown, this interpretation makes good sense out of the difficult passage in Ap IV 72. God could not declare man to be righteous unless man actually possessed righteousness. This is implicit in the *forensic* concept of justification. The declaration of justification is the seal of the fact that man has met the demands of righteousness, i. e., that righteousness is actually to be found in him. But this righteousness is not his own achievement; it is the suffering and death of Christ for his sake which man shares in through the Word of promise. When this Word is received, the heart of man is born again. Thus it is, as Ap points out, that we are first of all made righteous through the forgiveness of sin and the merits of Christ which are imputed to us by faith.

According to a common interpretation, forensic justification means a process completely apart from man and without any relation to him.[29] This common interpretation is correct in respect to the forensic concept as such, but it overlooks the fact that the precondition necessary to every declaration of righteousness is the existence of innocence.

---

[27] 178:33 (Ap IV 86); 183:42 — hac fide iusti reputamur propter Christum (Ap IV 114).

[28] L. Haikola in *Festschrift till Hj. Lindroth* (1958), pp. 51—62.

[29] Schmid (1843), p. 323, n. 5, par. 42. Loofs rejects this interpretation in ThStK (1884), pp. 619 f.

But there is a marked difference between the common juridical process and the justification of man before God. In the former it is a question of man's own innocence being the basis of the exoneration, but in the latter it is the righteousness of Christ, *iustitia aliena,* being imputed to man by faith through Word and sacraments.

When Melanchthon introduced the term forensic (in Ap), he was thinking of the kind of experience one would have in a regular court of law.[30] Just as a judge could not release someone who stands guilty before him, so also would it be impossible for God to exonerate a man who could not claim to be blameless. The fact that God absolves man is not dependent upon man's own achievements or merits (these have been shown to lie outside of man's capabilities) but upon the righteousness of Christ, reckoned to man by imputation, whereby the new birth takes place.

Ap here uses two concepts borrowed from an older theological tradition, viz., *imputatio* and *acceptatio.* The forensic declaration of righteousness is related to the idea of *acceptatio* in Scotism and nominalism.[31] In Ap, to be declared righteous is the same as to be accepted by God.[32] But whereas the basis of this acceptance within the medieval schools mentioned above was human merit, the Lutheran Confessions find it in the righteousness of Christ, which, through an act of imputation, is reckoned to us. The imputation concept is Biblical (Rom. 4:9), and it is closely related to the idea of righteousness as a divine gift. Augustine spoke of righteousness in the same way.[33] What is done, then, in Ap is that the New Testament and Augustinian concepts of imputation are combined with the idea of God's acceptance of the sinner. Justification as the forgiveness of sin and the imputation of the righteousness of Christ forms the presupposition of the forensic declaration of righteousness, of God's acceptance of man.

Against this background one can without difficulty understand Ap IV 305, a passage which has often puzzled interpreters. Here Melanch-

---

[30] O. Ritschl in ZThK (1910), p. 322 — Dieser Begriff aber besagt für Melanchthon noch gar nichts weiter, als dass Gott urteilend wie ein Richter zu denken sei. Cf. Loofs in ThStK (1884), p. 624, with reference to Prov. 17:15, and suggestions in Oberman (1963), p. 355, concerning the history of the concept.

[31] For further information see Dettloff (1954), pp. 84 ff., and (1963), plus Oberman (1963), pp. 160—84.

[32] 174:25 — ipsa fides illud, quo accepti sumus Deo (Ap IV 71); 183:50 — haec fides accipit remissionem peccatorum, et reddit nos acceptos Deo (Ap IV 116).

[33] *De sp. et litt.,* 9, 15 — iustitia Dei, non qua Deus iustus est, sed qua induit hominem, cum iustificat impium (CSEL 60, 167); ibid., 11, 18 — qua fide Jesu Christi, id est quam nobis contulit Christus (CSEL 60, 171).

thon explains Rom. 5:1 ("Since we are justified by faith, we have peace with God"): "In this passage 'justify' is used in a judicial way to mean 'to absolve a guilty man and pronounce him righteous,' and to do so on account of someone else's righteousness, namely, Christ's, which is communicated to us through faith. Since in this passage our righteousness is the imputation of someone else's righteousness, we must speak of righteousness in a different way here from the philosophical or judicial investigation of a man's own righteousness." [34]

Melanchthon therefore demonstrates that the term forensic has a fixed meaning. It is of course a juridical term, taken from the law courts, and it signifies that the accused is declared free of punishment — which can happen in a court of law only if he has actually been proved innocent.[35] Melanchthon was in agreement with this. When God in a forensic act of justification declares man to be free, this is dependent on man having a righteousness he can demonstrate. But — and here is where Christian righteousness is distinguished from the juridical type — the righteousness which man can claim is Christ's, which is a righteousness received by and imputed to us by faith. The forensic "to be pronounced or declared righteous," *iustum pronuntiari,* is accordingly preceded in part by the imputation of Christ's righteousness and in part by faith's acceptance of it. The imputation of Christ's righteousness does not coincide with the declaration of innocence, as some have claimed,[36] but is its logical presupposition. The imputation (forgiveness of sins), the new birth, and faith [37] all belong together in justification in the sense of "to be made righteous," *iustos effici.* The forensic "to be considered righteous," *iustos reputari,* takes place

---

[34] 219:43 — Iustificare vero hoc loco forensi consuetudine significat reum absolvere et pronuntiare iustum, sed propter alienam iustitiam, videlicet Christi, quae aliena iustitia communicatur nobis per fidem. Itaque cum hoc loco iustitia nostra sit imputatio alienae iustitiae, aliter hic de iustitia loquendum est, quam cum in philosophia aut in foro quaerimus iustitiam proprii operis (Ap IV 305 f.).

[35] This term is also used in the same way in Ap IV 252, where it serves to explain James 2:24. According to Ap, James does not describe how justification takes place, but rather why those who are already justified and born again are declared righteous before God, and how it is that they thereafter do good works. "Iustificari significat hic non ex impio iustum effici, sed usu forensi iustum pronuntiari. Sicut hic: Factores legis iustificabuntur" (Rom. 2:13). It was therefore exegetical reasons which gave rise to the idea that *iustificare* can have an imputative as well as a forensic significance.

[36] F. Loofs in ThStK (1884), p. 624, and O. Ritschl in ZTK (1910), pp. 312 ff. Melanchthon's choice of words in Ap is not, however, completely unambiguous, as we see in 179:38 ff. (Ap IV 89; 118 f.).

[37] 219:51 — fides est iustitia in nobis imputative, id est, est id, quo efficimur accepti Deo propter imputationem et ordinationem Dei (Ap IV 307).

on the basis of the righteousness of Christ received by faith. As a result of this, the Confessions speak of regeneration in connection with the forgiveness of sins. *Iustos effici* and the forgiveness of sins, *remissio peccatorum,* form a unit.[38] Here we find the otherwise hard to explain connection between the promise and the actual state of justification. Where the promise is, there is the life-giving forgiveness of sins.[39] For "where there is forgiveness of sins, there are also life and salvation" (SC VI 6). The righteousness of Christ imputed to man forms the basis of the forensic declaration of justification.

There is therefore *one* sustained idea which is found throughout Ap IV: faith alone justifies. The authors of the Confutation reacted to this with the strongest suspicions. As a result, Melanchthon felt constrained to show that the concept was Pauline and basic to the entire New Testament. In the development of his thought, he had to take two points of view into consideration: first, that justification denotes an actual new birth, and second, that this regeneration is a purely divine work without human contribution. Melanchthon took it upon himself to show that justification is a work in man but not of man. Both of these points are included in the *sola fide* formula.

The Meaning of Faith

What do the Lutheran Confessions mean by faith? In general it can be said that faith, like sin, has both a theological and a psychological facet, which are very closely related. Theologically speaking, faith is the converse of sin's broken relationship with God. It is a possibility for man to enter into a renewed relationship with God—a possibility created by the Holy Spirit.[40] Psychologically speaking, faith is an act of man's will and as such serves to break the power of sin over human affections.

In a psychological sense, the Confessions refer to faith as confidence, *fiducia* (AC XX 26). It has its locus in the heart,[41] where it

---

[38] 175:31 — Consequi remissionem peccatorum est iustificari . . . intelligendo iustificationem, ex iniusto iustum effici seu regenerari (Ap IV 76-78); 460:13 — Glauben, Verneuerung und Vergebung (SA III XIII 2).

[39] 176:19 — Igitur sola fide consequimur remissionem peccatorum, cum erigimus corda fiducia misericordiae propter Christum promissae (Ap IV 80).

[40] 168:53—169:20 (Ap IV 45 f.); 185:23-26 (Ap IV 125); 199:30 — At fides ostendit praesentiam Dei, postquam constituit, quod Deus gratis ignoscat et exaudiat (Ap IV 205).

[41] 715:19 — Der Glaube aber tut's des Herzens (LC V 37). Concerning Luther's similar understanding of faith I made reference to J. Meyer (1929), pp. 263—71.

efficaciously works to rehabilitate the frightened conscience. Exactly what this means can be clarified if we take note of the psychology the reformers accepted, and which was developed in particular by Melanchthon. He distinguished between faith as an act of reason, *notitia,* and faith as trust or confidence, *fiducia,* the so-called *fides specialis.*[42] *Notitia* is a purely intellectual act;[43] it believes that God is, but it does not presuppose the commitment of the heart or the new birth by the Holy Spirit. It merely denotes the acceptance of historical facts, e. g., "that merely the history concerning Christ should be known" (Ap IV 249 German). Since such faith is to be found among all men, regardless of whether they are Christian or not,[44] it can even be referred to as a universal phenomenon. Such a faith signifies an endorsement of incontrovertible historical facts as, for example, that Augustus succeeded Caesar as head of the Roman Empire.[45] It is based upon trust in authority.

Fiducia is an act of the will;[46] it has to do with man's inner life, his heart, and it is present "when my heart, and the Holy Ghost in the heart, says: The promise of God is true and certain. Of this faith Scripture speaks" (Ap IV 113 German). To have faith in the Christian and Biblical sense means much more than merely holding certain ideas about God. It means to say yes to God's promise,[47] to be willing to accept what God has promised man, to trust in the promise of God's mercy – a trust in God without reservation.[48] One cannot speak of faith in this sense apart from the Word of promise, or more specifically, the Gospel. Inasmuch as faith is "a good disposition in our heart" (Ap XIII 18), it serves as a remedy against sin and the evil and subversive affections. Just as the affections manifest themselves as reactions to external sense impressions,[49] so is it with faith. It too requires the

---

[42] 168:54 (Ap IV 45); 263:15 and 34 (Ap XII 59 f.); 295:35 (Ap XIII 21).

[43] 219:40 (Ap IV 304).

[44] 80:3 — notitia, qualis est in impiis (AC XX 26); 209:10 — otiosa notitia, qualis est etiam in diabolis (Ap IV 249); 260:9 — illa generalis fides, quam habent et diaboli (Ap XII 45).

[45] Cf. CR 13, 166 — Fides est noticia, qua adsentimur dicto sine dubitatione, victi testimoniis vel auctoritate (*Liber de anima,* 1553).

[46] 219:40 — fiducia in voluntate (Ap IV 304).

[47] 169:39 — Sed illa fides, quae iustificat, non est tantum notitia historiae, sed est assentiri promissioni Dei, in qua gratis propter Christum offertur remissio peccatorum et iustificatio (Ap IV 48).

[48] 563:8 — Mit dem Herzen aber an ihm hangen, ist nichts anders, denn sich gänzlich auf ihn verlassen (LC I 14).

[49] CR 13,124 (*Liber de anima,* 1553); Olsson in STK (1944), p. 103.

communication of knowledge of an external kind, such as that which comes through the Gospel, the Word of promise. (LC IV 30)

The emergence of faith therefore requires a divine promise which assures us of God's gracious disposition and can alter the will and so influence the affections that they change from a negative to a positive attitude vis-à-vis God. Such a transformation cannot take place unless one knows what God declares in His promises. In the Christian sense, faith is an act of the will, properly speaking, but its presupposition is a knowledge of God's promises mediated through the senses. This is most clearly expressed in *Liber de anima,* but it is already presupposed in the confessional writings. In the Biblical context, as Melanchthon said, faith is not simply the affirmation of historical events, but above all of the divine promise. "The will responds to this affirmation with trust, *fiducia,* and joy, *laetitia.* As a result, the will finds rest in God, in the good things which are offered in God's promise—just as Gideon's soul found peace when he was promised victory. Hence it is that faith is described thus: 'The assurance of things hoped for' (Heb. 11:1), i. e., confidence which is supported by the promise." [50]

Fiducia requires a promise in order to become a reality. It is not enough to accept certain historical facts; faith in the Christian sense must be able to support itself by the results of Christ's life, suffering, death, and resurrection—the promise of the forgiveness of sins.[51] Faith requires something external "so that it can be perceived and grasped by the senses and thus brought into the heart" (LC IV 30). The sacraments perform the same function. They are called "the visible Word," and they can influence the heart through the mediation of the senses: "As the Word enters through the ears to strike the heart, so the rite itself enters through the eyes to move the heart. The Word and the rite have the same effect" (Ap XIII 5). This must not, however, be thought of as a natural phenomenon, which can be explained simply with the help of psychology. Faith's new impulses in the heart are the work of the Holy Spirit.[52]

---

[50] CR 13, 166 (*Liber de anima,* 1553).

[51] 79:6 — Admonentur etiam homines, quod hic nomen fidei non significat tantum historiae notitiam, qualis est in impiis et in diabolo, sed significat fidem, quae credit non solum historiam, sed etiam effectum historiae, videlicet hunc articulum, remissionem peccatorum, quod videlicet per Christum habeamus gratiam, iustitiam et remissionem peccatorum (AC XX 23). The same thought occurs in 170:33-37 (Ap IV 51).

[52] 172:49-54 (Ap IV 63). Cf. above, Chapter Four, regarding the work of the Holy Spirit in man.

That faith is a divine act and not a human achievement is explained by the fact that it originates with a Word of promise. Faith is an act of the will which affects man's inner life, his heart,[53] and links his life up with God. It is a basic theological presupposition of the Lutheran Confessions that man is totally unable to influence his own will in spiritual matters. The will which is hostile toward God is strengthened in its opposition by the Law's demand for faith. Faith is given to man when he confronts and accepts the Gospel's Word of promise: "Your sins are forgiven." In the consequent coupling together of faith and the Word of promise, it is presupposed that faith is generated by God the Holy Spirit (Ap IV 115). Faith is a divine service, which receives God's benefactions.[54] It is "a strong, powerful work of the Holy Ghost, which changes hearts." (Ap IV 99 German)

Therefore faith also serves to regenerate human life. It is not a passive affirmation of external events; it is a divine power, whereby we are made alive and death and the devil are overcome.[55] Faith is capable of doing what lies beyond man's own resources; it conquers the pangs of conscience and the fear of God's wrath. It is "the new light and power which the Holy Ghost works in the heart, through which we overcome the terrors of death, of sin, etc." (Ap IV 250 German). Through faith we receive "a new and clean heart" (SA III XIII 1). So if one has faith, it is impossible to live in deliberate sin (Ap IV 48, 64, and 115). Above all else, faith signifies victory over the powers of destruction — sin, death, and the devil — as well as over divine wrath (Ap IV 142). "Such a faith is not an easy thing, as our opponents imagine; nor is it a human power, but a divine power that makes us alive and enables us to overcome death and the devil." (Ap IV 250)

Great difficulties appear, however, as we seek to define the meaning of regeneration more precisely. The Reformation's *sola fide* principle was characterized by its rejection of all human efforts. As a result, faith is separated also from love. Love is not the basis of justification, and neither does it play a role in justifying faith — as though man were justified on the basis of love active in faith.[56] The Confessions draw a sharp line of demarcation between faith and love. Love follows faith,

---

[53] See exposition of the First Commandment, e. g., 560:30-34 (LC I 4).

[54] 170:13 — Fides est "latreia" (Rom. 9:4; 12:1), quae accipit a Deo oblata beneficia (Ap IV 49); 220:9 (Ap IV 310).

[55] 209:16 — [fides est] divina potentia, qua vivificamur, qua diabolum et mortem vincimus (Ap IV 250); 258:25-33 (Ap XII 35 f.)

[56] This is what the Catholic theologians meant, CR 27, 96 f.

but it plays no role in the work of regeneration (Ap IV 74 and XII 82). Love presupposes faith. (Ap IV 36)

The difficulties involved in dealing with the meaning of regeneration are reflected in many of the suggested solutions. According to a commonly known Catholic interpretation, justification has no regenerating effect whatsoever,[57] which is in obvious conflict with the express pronouncements of the Confessions concerning regeneration. Kinder maintains that for Luther—in contrast to the older Melanchthon—justification meant absolution from sin (imputation) and an "incipient renewal," which consists of a new relationship with God.[58] Schlink [59] connects regeneration with renewal and good works, which are or ought to be the results of faith. It is quite obvious, however, that the Confessions [60] make a distinction between the new birth of faith and ethical renewal. Since concupiscence remains even after Baptism, the new birth cannot denote its annihilation either. Although man has been born again, he remains a sinner; he is *simul iustus et peccator*.[61]

The meaning of regeneration must be something quite different. It signifies the beginning of a new life, which is not man's own and yet is not detached from him. This new life is found in faith, which accepts the promise of the forgiveness of sins.

The Holy Spirit brings about the new birth of faith, through which Christ is present in man with His righteousness and man can accept the promise and live in a reestablished relationship with God. This in turn exerts an influence on man's entire attitude toward God, as well as on the tenor of his experience. Whereas before justification he found himself anguished by the judgment of his conscience, he now knows the confidence born of faith. His conscience finds consolation in the knowledge that the righteousness of Christ is imputed to him. This consolation is produced by the Holy Spirit. Regeneration is inextricably related to the fact that faith as *fiducia* is connected with

[57] Denifle, I, 2 (1906), 600; L. Ott (1957), p. 302.

[58] RGG B (1961), pp. 834 f. Cf. also Lindroth in NTU, III (1957), 433.

[59] E. Schlink (1961), pp. 105 ff.

[60] This holds true for all of the confessional documents written by Luther and Melanchthon which are analyzed here. 460:13 — Und auf solchen Glauben, Verneuerung und Vergebung der Sunde folgen denn gute Werk (SA III XIII 2); 185:29 — Postquam igitur fide iustificati et renati sumus, incipimus Deum timere, diligere, petere et exspectare ab eo auxilium, gratias agere et praedicare, et obedire ei in afflictionibus. Incipimus et diligere proximos, quia corda habent spirituales et sanctos motus (Ap IV 125). See also the summary in Engelland (1931), pp. 541 ff. and 117 ff., plus L. Haikola in *Festschrift till Hj. Lindroth* (1958), pp. 57 ff.

[61] 460:11-12 (SA III XIII 1); 195:43-44 (Ap IV 177).

the will and the affections. Psychologically speaking, regeneration signifies an alteration in man's emotional life,[62] since faith is a "good disposition," *motus bonus* (Ap XIII 18). Regeneration denotes a transition from fear to consolation and joy (Ap XII 60). This consolation *is the new spiritual life.*[63] Regeneration is rest and gladness in God.

When the Confessions speak of consolation, as they do in Ap, LC, and SA,[64] it is conditioned by the fact that man has been liberated from the external powers of evil. His situation has been altered through Christ; he has moved from guilt to righteousness. Consolation is not simply the expression of a subjective condition; it rather rests on an objective basis. The penitent man goes from damnation under the Law to the grace of the Gospel. The theological and psychological facets of regeneration postulate one another. "Amid such fears this faith brings peace of mind, consoles us, receives the forgiveness of sins, justifies and quickens us. For this consolation is a new and spiritual life." [65] What is said about an effective regeneration becomes easy to understand when seen against the background of penitence. When the judgment of the Law and the torment of conscience have been abolished, then regeneration has become a reality.

With this bifurcated theological and psychological view of regeneration in mind, the Confessions seek to explain how man can be both righteous and sinful at the same time. He is righteous because through faith he shares in the righteousness of Christ, who gives him the Holy Spirit and regenerates him. But he is also sinful, for he never succeeds in perfectly fulfilling the Law (Ap IV 177). We are reckoned as righteous because Christ and His righteousness are available through the Holy Spirit by faith. We are reckoned as sinners because we in ourselves are always inadequate.[66] In this sense, regeneration

[62] L. Haikola in *Festschrift till Hj. Lindroth* (1958), p. 60. In opposition to O. Ritschl in ZTK (1910), pp. 312—14, it must be said that this view of the role of the affections also appears in Ap.

[63] 172:46 — illa consolatio est nova et spiritualis vita (Ap IV 62).

[64] 437:28 (SA III III 8); 658:28-29 (LC II 55).

[65] 172:53 (Ap IV 63); 173:10 — [fides] non est otiosa cogitatio sed . . . a morte liberat, et novam vitam in cordibus parit, et est opus spiritus sancti . . . . Quid potest dici de conversione impii seu de moto regenerationis simplicius et clarius? (Ap IV 64 f.)

[66] 460:7 — Luther had always taught this about justification, that we "durch den Glauben" (wie S. Petrus sagt, Acts 15:9) ein ander neu Herz kriegen und Gott umb Christi willen, unsers Mittlers, uns für ganz gerecht und heilig halten will und hält. Obwohl die Sünde im Fleisch noch nicht gar weg oder tot ist, so will er sie doch nicht rechnen und wissen (SA III XIII 1). For more on this question consult, e. g., Gyllenkrok (1952), pp. 83 ff. and 125 f., plus R. Prenter in *Lutherforschung heute* (1958), pp. 64—74.

by faith is more than something that can clearly be experienced.[67]

Justification *sola fide* excludes all good works and merits. "The expression 'by grace' excludes merit and all works" (Ap IV 73 German). The concept of merit, so essential to the Catholic theology of that time, was excluded from the vocabulary of the reformers. On the other hand, the Confessions do not deny that good works ought to follow faith and "that if good works do not follow, our faith is false and not true." [68] Justification is exclusively a divine work of grace without human contribution. This was entirely in harmony with the Reformation's basic concept, which breaks through at nearly every point.

But the *sola fide* concept does not exclude the Word and the sacraments, because these are the presuppositions for the emergence of faith. Faith does not grow by itself, and man cannot produce it by his own powers. God the Holy Spirit must bring it to life through the Gospel's Word of promise. The Reformation phrase "through the Word" included a critical thrust directed at the *meritum* of the Catholics as well as at the spiritualism of the Anabaptists. Since the Word of promise in all its forms is the means God employs in making contact with man, justification is completely dependent thereon (Ap IV 66-68). In the controversies of the Reformation era the *sola fide* principle was understood by some as a polemic against Word and sacrament (CR 27, 96). In reply to this objection, the reformers made it clear that Word and sacraments are not excluded. "We exclude the claim of merit, not the Word or the sacraments, as our opponents slanderously claim" (Ap IV 73; cf. SA III III 8). The sacraments, like the Word, take their necessary place in Reformation theology.

[67] E. Schlink (1961), pp. 108 f.

[68] 461:5 (SA III XIII 4 [3 in Tappert]). See more on this below, Chapter Eleven.

Chapter Seven:

The Sacraments

1. What a Sacrament Is

God justifies and restores man through the Word and the sacraments. The Holy Spirit comes to man through these means.[1] Just as justification and spiritual righteousness are not something we offer to God, but something God gives to us, so are the sacraments God's work – exclusively. As a sign and evidence of God's will,[2] they belong to the Gospel's sphere. They are sacred acts, through which God provides what He has promised us in His Word. What the sacraments are and what they accomplish cannot be separated, for with God word and deed are one and the same. The sacraments are an expression of God's gracious disposition, and through them He makes us partakers of His gifts. Especially Ap utilizes words that denote an action, such as ceremony, rite, and work *(ceremonia, ritus,* and *opus)* [3] to emphasize how God speaks to His children through the sacraments. The same point of view is also found in the catechisms. Baptism, e. g., is referred to in LC as an act in which God baptizes us; God is the active one, and he who officiates at a baptism is serving in His stead.[4] The sacraments are a form of the Gospel, the promise, in action. So the sacraments, like the Gospel, are referred to as God's benefactions, *beneficia.*[5]

The Reformation took over the sacramental concept of the medieval church, but the reformers gave it a somewhat new content and

[1] 58:4 — per verbum et sacramenta tamquam per instrumenta donatur spiritus sanctus (AC V 2); 370:1 — per verbum et sacramenta operatur spiritus sanctus (Ap XXIV 70); 173:24-29 (Ap IV 66). Cf. H. Volk in *Pro Veritate* (1963), p. 117.

[2] 68:5 — signa et testimonia voluntatis Dei erga nos (AC XIII 1); 291:15 (Ap XIII 1); 369:23 (Ap XXIV 69).

[3] 292:14 — ritus (Ap XIII 3); 354:23 — ceremonia vel opus (Ap XXIV 18).

[4] 692:40 — Denn in Gottes Namen getauft werden, ist nicht von Menschen, sondern von Gott selbs getauft werden; darumb ob es gleich durch des Menschen Hand geschicht, so ist es doch wahrhaftig Gottes eigen Werk (LC IV 10); 354: 16-19 (Ap XXIV 18). Cf. WA 2, 694:14-16 *(Eyn Sermon von der Bereitung zum Sterben,* 1519); WA 6, 530:19-31 *(De captivitate,* 1520); and E. Roth (1952), p. 82.

[5] 170:12-18 (Ap IV 49), and 354:13-15 (Ap XXIV 18).

reduced the number from seven to two or three (there is a divergence on this point between the Confessions written by Luther and those written by Melanchthon).

In the medieval church it was said that the sacraments had matter and form, *materia* and *forma*.[6] The first of these words was used to refer either to an external thing, such as the water used in Baptism, or to some kind of action, such as the contrition, confession, and satisfaction of the sacrament of penance. In the latter instance, men spoke of the sacraments' *materia* in a figurative sense. This latitude in the *materia* concept explains why Luther and Melanchthon came to different conclusions regarding the number of sacraments. For whereas Luther followed the stricter interpretation and felt that material things must necessarily belong to the sacraments (the water in Baptism and the bread and wine in Communion), the wider interpretation of the *materia* concept opened up to Melanchthon the possibility of looking upon any one of the acts commanded by Christ as a sacrament.

When the medieval church spoke of the *forma* of a sacrament, it had in mind the words spoken in connection with the sacramental act, which were understood to be words of consecration. For the reformers these were words of promise as well as words of command. In Luther's catechisms one finds that the accent shifts from the promise to the command. But in Ap Melanchthon holds fast to the original Reformation concept which saw in the sacramental words first and foremost a Word of promise.

The *materia* and *forma* concepts go back to Aristotelian philosophy. The medieval church also used the terms "Word and element" instead of *forma* and *materia*.[7] The "Word and element" idea goes back in its origins to a well-known and often quoted statement made by Augustine in his exposition of John's Gospel: *Accedit verbum ad elementum et fit sacramentum*.[8] Luther[9] used this statement early, and it is frequently cited in the Confessions: *"Accedit verbum ad elementum et fit sacramentum*. This means that when the Word is added to the element or the natural substance, it becomes a sacrament, that is, a holy, divine thing and sign."[10] Word and element are both essen-

---

[6] Denz., 695; J. Brinktrine (1960), p. 36.

[7] Denz., 412; P.-Th. Camelot in RThom (1957), p. 443.

[8] *Tract 80 in Ioann.*, 15, 3 (MPL 35, 1840). Cf. *Sermo de sacr. altaris ad infantes*, 6, 1, 3 (MPL 46, 834 f.), and an analysis of these passages in P.-Th. Camelot in RThom (1957), pp. 440 ff.

[9] WA 7, 102, 11 (*Assertio omnium articulorum*, 1520).

[10] 694:29-34 (LC IV 17 f.) Luther frequently used the subjunctive form *ac-*

tial in the sacrament. Apart from the Word in Baptism the water is just water,[11] but without water there can be no sacrament. The question is: How do the Lutheran Symbols understand the relationship between Word and element? Or to be more precise: What is meant by saying that the Word comes to the element so that there can be a sacrament?

This question can be answered only after we have examined the meaning of Baptism and the Lord's Supper. Here we can point in a preliminary way to the fact that LC speaks of a union of the water and the Word—a parallel, if you will, to the Incarnation, in which the divine and the human entered into an indissoluble union.[12] The bread and wine of the Lord's Supper become Christ's body and blood through the Word.[13] What was most important to Luther was the emphasis that a sacrament is a work in which God Himself is present and active through the elements.[14] A more precise idea of what he meant by this can be seen in the lines of demarcation he drew against other opinions. In SA Luther criticized two such points of view. First of all, a so-called Thomistic concept which held that baptismal water possesses a spiritual power capable of washing away sins. And second, a Scotist idea which taught that it is neither the water nor the Word but God's unmediated will which performs the work of purification.[15] Even though these lines of demarcation (on the right against a "realistic" and on the left against a "voluntaristic" concept of the sacraments) are negative in nature, they give us an idea of SA's position. This position is based on the Word, which expresses what God commands, promises, and accomplishes through baptismal water and the bread and wine of the Lord's Supper. Like Augustine, Luther constructed his doctrine of the sacraments on Eph. 5:26.[16]

---

cedat instead of the indicative *accedit* employed by St. Augustine. See also 449: 18 f. (SA III V 2), and 709:37 f. (LC V 10). The designation of a sacrament as *signum* goes back to Augustine. P.-Th. Camelot, pp. 434 and 439 f.

[11] 516:16 — denn ohn Gottes Wort ist das Wasser schlecht Wasser und keine Taufe (SC IV 10); 693:33 (LC IV 14); 709:26-28 (LC V 8). Cf. *Tract in Ioann.* 4, 2 — Tolle aquam, non est baptismus; tolle verbum, non est sacramentum (MPL 35, 1512).

[12] 696:39 — dass [das Wasser] mit Gottes Wort und Ordnung verleibet ist (LC IV 29). Cf. R. Josefson (1944), p. 99.

[13] 709:42 — Das Wort muss das Element zum Sakrament machen, wo nicht, so bleibt's ein lauter Element (LC V 10).

[14] Cf. J. Meyer (1929), pp. 441 ff.

[15] 450:1-8 (SA III V 2-3). Cf. STh III, q.62, a.1 and 4, plus P. Brunner in *Pro Ecclesia* I, 149—50, where these problems are discussed.

[16] 449:17 (SA III V 1), and P.-Th. Camelot, p. 443.

Because in the catechisms Luther was fighting against a spiritualizing tendency that had no appreciation for the elements, he emphasized the external signs more there than in previous writings. The elements do not occupy the same dominating position in the statements written by Melanchthon. Even though Melanchthon was well acquainted with the Augustinian work Luther quoted so often, and even used it himself, he never cited the same passage.[17] As a result, the term *elementum* does not appear in AC or Ap. Melanchthon rather adopted other points of view—which are also found in Augustine. Thus Melanchthon avoided the necessity of taking a more specific position with regard to the controversial question as to how Christ is present in the Lord's Supper. By avoiding the element concept, the question of Christ's presence in the Sacrament was never a problem for him in quite the same way.

Melanchthon certainly believed that a sacrament consists of a divine Word and an external sign, but this need not be a thing such as the water of Baptism or the bread and wine of the Lord's Supper. On the basis of the figurative *materia* designation in scholasticism, Melanchthon could without difficulty permit the *ceremonia*, the sacred act, to constitute the sign.[18] He defined sacraments as "rites which have the command of God and to which the promise of grace has been added."[19] The key words in Melanchthon's concept of the sacraments are "sacred act" *(ceremonia, opus sacrum)*.[20]

In order to be called a sacrament, a religious act must fulfill two demands: it must be instituted by God, and be connected with a promise. These conditions are set forth in Ap for the purpose of distinguishing the sacraments from other seemingly similar acts which are not, however, instituted by God and connected with a promise.

The first requirement of a sacramental act is that it be commanded by God—which means, in concrete terms, that it has support in the

---

[17] *Tract 80 in Ioann.*, 15:3 — fit sacramentum etiam ipsum tanquam visibile verbum (MPL 35, 1840). 292:40 — praeclare dictum est ab Augustino esse verbum visibile (Ap XIII 5). 295:57 — ait Augustinus, quod fides sacramenti, non sacramentum iustificet (Ap XIII 23), in agreement with Augustine Ep. 98, 9 and 10 (MPL 33, 364).

[18] 369:37 (Ap XXIV 70). *Signum* can also be used to designate a sacrament in its entirety and not just the act itself to which the Word is attached. So also with Augustine.

[19] 292:14 — sacramenta vocamus ritus, qui habent mandatum Dei et quibus addita est promissio gratiae (Ap XIII 3).

[20] 354:12 (Ap XXIV 17). This point of view is strongly emphasized by P. Fraenkel in *Luther und Melanchthon* (1961), pp. 147—50.

Bible. Only those religious acts of which the Scriptures speak are instituted by God and can be designated as sacred acts.[21] A religious act without a Scriptural basis does not fulfill the primary requirement for a sacrament — that it be commanded by God. As support for the necessity of external signs the catechisms refer in particular to God's command and institution, *mandatum et institutio*.[22] The command is also cited on behalf of the promise. In order to be the sign of a promise, a sacrament must be traceable to God's express will, as this is proclaimed in Scripture. If one is baptized at God's command in the conviction that Baptism is a divine ordinance, he also receives the promise of salvation through the external sign.[23] Promise and command serve one another in a mutual fashion.

The other requirement for a sacrament is that God has attached a promise of grace to this sacred act. The Word which forms a union with the sign is a Word of promise. The specific content of the promise is the assurance of the forgiveness of sins,[24] and it is identical with the Gospel in the sense of promise, *promissio*.

The idea of the sacramental Word as a Word of promise is a genuine Reformation teaching, and it goes back to Luther's earliest writings. In his disagreement with the Roman Catholic doctrine of the sacraments, Luther placed great stress on the element of promise in the sacramental Word. The Mass is nothing other than the promise of the forgiveness of sins, which God has given to us and confirmed through the death of His Son.[25] The sacraments are one of the forms in which the Gospel, the promise, now confronts us. (Cf. SA III 4)

In emphasizing the promise as strongly as it does, Ap is being true to a basic Reformation principle. The purpose of the sacraments is to arouse faith; faith originates with and is nourished by the promise. The fact that a sacrament is a visible Word, *verbum visibile* (Ap here borrows a phrase from Augustine [26]), confirms its character as promise (Ap XIII 5). Sacraments are "signs of the promises." [27] To receive them, one is required to have faith.

[21] 292:1-4 (Ap XIII 2). Cf. Chapter One, part 1.

[22] 691:38 (LC IV 6).

[23] 698:16-20 (LC IV 36).

[24] 369:30 — Promissio novi testamenti est promissio remissionis peccatorum (Ap XXIV 69). Cf. E. Schlink (1961), pp. 180—87.

[25] WA 6, 513:34 — Vides ergo, quod Missa quam vocamus sit promissio remissionis peccatorum, a deo nobis facta, et talis promissio, quae per mortem filii dei formata sit (*De captivitate*, 1520).

[26] *Tract 80 in Ioann.*, 15:3 (MPL 35, 1840).

[27] 295:31 (Ap XIII 20); 259:24 — signa remissionis peccatorum (Ap XII

The connection between promise and faith also appears in the proposition which holds that it is not the sacrament as such, but faith in the sacrament, which justifies.[28] In Ap this idea is traceable back to Augustine,[29] and Luther had certainly borrowed from the same source in his earlier controversy with Catholic sacramental theology.[30] For Luther, this idea followed from Paul's teaching of justification by faith,[31] and it took form in his opposition to the teaching which says that the sacraments work by the outward act, *ex opere operato.* According to the scholastic interpretation, the sacraments are effective means of salvation as long as those who receive them do not interpose a hindrance. The technical term for this was *non ponere obicem,* "don't pull the bolt shut." [32] But both Luther and the Symbols criticized their opponents for ignoring the role of faith by saying that the sacraments are effective just as soon as the sacramental act is performed. Without the proper feeling in the heart, i. e., without faith, the sacraments cannot bestow grace upon man.[33] "Here we condemn the whole crowd of scholastic doctors who teach that unless there is some obstacle, the sacraments confer grace *ex opere operato,* without a good disposition [*sine bono motu*] in the one using them. It is sheer Judaism to believe that we are justified by a ceremony without a good disposition in our heart, that is, without faith." (Ap XIII 18) [34]

The entire Reformation critique of the Catholic sacramental doctrine is concentrated in these short sentences. The major concepts

---

42); 369:39 — Ergo sicut promissio inutilis est, nisi fide accipiatur, ita inutilis est ceremonia, nisi fides accedat (Ap XXIV 70).

[28] 295:57 (Ap XIII 23). Above, n. 17.

[29] *Epist. 98,* 9 and 10 (MPL 33, 364).

[30] WA 1, 544:40 — non sacramentum sed fides sacramenti iustificat (*Resolutiones disp. de indulg. virtute,* 1518); WA 2, 715:35 (*Eyn Sermon von dem Sacrament der Puss,* 1519); WA 7, 102:9 (*Assertio omnium articulorum M. Lutheri per bullam Leonis X,* 1520); WA 6, 532:29 (*De captivitate,* 1520).

[31] WA 7, 101:11-27 (*Assertio . . . ,* 1520).

[32] WA 1, 544:37 — nisi haereticam illam sed usitatam sententiam proferant, qua dicitur, sacramenta novae legis iustificantem gratiam dare illis, qui non ponunt obicem (*Resolutiones . . .* 1518). This statement, which was condemned in the papal bull "Exsurge, Domine" (Denz. 741), was defended anew by Luther in his *Assertio . . .* 1520 (WA 7, 101:10—103:7).

[33] WA 44, 719:29 — At vero nostrae doctrinae caput est: sacramentum non operari gratiam sine fide (*Vorlesungen über Genesis,* 1535—45).

[34] 295:1 — Hic damnamus totum populum scholasticorum doctorum, qui docent, quod sacramenta non ponenti obicem conferant gratiam ex opere operato sine bono motu utentis. Haec simpliciter iudaica opinio est sentire quod per ceremoniam iustificemur, sine bono motu cordis, hoc est sine fide (Ap XIII 18).

in the passage quoted above, *ex opere operato, non ponere obicem,* and *sine bono motu,* are technical terms taken over from scholastic theology. The confessional writers looked upon these as the subtle expression of a massive work-piety which was in glaring contrast to the righteousness of faith taught in the Scriptures (Ap XXIV 96 ff.). The *opus operatum* concept, they felt, implies that the very act of performing the sacraments is meritorious. If the sacraments do not require faith on the part of those who receive them, they can be carried out "without a good disposition" or change of heart. As a result, the Confessions also found unsatisfactory the idea that man must not interpose hindrances while receiving a sacrament, for it did not include an actual change of heart. The Mass was distorted into a sacrifice which was thought to justify simply by being enacted (Ap XXIV 5). It was also believed that the saying of the Mass was beneficial to those who were absent, and even for the dead (Ap XXIV 35 and 57). The result was a perpetual rise in the number of Masses offered both for the living and the dead.

In order to judge the value of their criticisms, and to understand the reformers' own concept of the sacraments, we must take a brief look at each of these three expressions, *ex opere operatum, non ponere obicem,* and *sine bono motu.* It will be seen that the confessional writers gave them a meaning which was different from what they had in scholastic theology.

When Duns Scotus and Gabriel Biel used *sine bono motu,* their intention was to emphasize the fact that the sacraments were effective without any preceding meritorious act of the will on the part of the recipients.[35] If human merit must be present as a precondition for the effectiveness of the sacraments, that would imply a restriction in their nature as means of grace. It is therefore the concept of grace that the expression *sine bono motu* seeks to protect; it says nothing, on the other hand, about the faith of the recipient (as the Reformation's critique falsely claimed). Ap based its critique of scholastic theology on ideas derived from Luther in his earlier controversy with the papacy,[36] but it is not clear whether Luther was there referring

[35] Biel, Sent. IV, d.1, q.3, a.1 — nisi impediat obex peccati mortalis, gratia confertur, sic quia praeter exhibitionem signi foris exhibiti non requiritur bonus motus interior in suscipiente, quo de condigno vel de congruo gratiam mereatur, sed sufficit, quod suscipiens non ponat obicem (quotation from R. Seeberg [1960], p. 517, n. 1). For more on this passage see Clark (1960), pp. 352 ff., and Pesch, *Theologie der Rechtfertigung bei Martin Luther und Thomas von Aquin* (1967).

[36] WA 7, 102:24 — Quidam enim ex eis dicunt, nec motum cordis requiri (*Assertio . . . 1520*).

to the faith which precedes or that which follows the reception of
a sacrament. A similar lack of clarity is to be found in the statements
in the confessional writings. Ap appears to use *sine bono motu* with
regard to the faith which is worked by the sacraments (Ap XIII 18
and 33), but whether this connotation is applied consistently is uncertain (cf. Ap XII 12). At any rate, the Confessions look upon
scholastic theology as representing a magical view of the sacraments:
they are of benefit to all to whom they are given, simply because they
are celebrated. However, the expression *sine bono motu* constituted
a fragile basis for such a critique.

The scholastic theologians had set forth a condition: no one who
desires the benefits of sacramental gifts can live in conscious, unfor-
given mortal sin. The sense of this is found in the phrase *non ponere
obicem*.[37] The Lutheran Confessions, however, did not succeed in
reproducing the relatively simple meaning of this phrase; they rather
gave the expression a vaguer and more general connotation, without
clearly stating what they had in mind when using it. Either they held
that according to scholastic teaching a man must cooperate with God
in receiving sacramental grace,[38] or else that the Catholic Church
does not require true penitence on the part of those who receive the
sacraments. It speaks for the latter interpretation that Ap criticizes
scholasticism for incorrectly holding that the Mass provides benefits
"for those to whom it is transferred, even for wicked people, if they
do not put an obstacle in its way." [39] A genuine change of heart is not
therefore required of those who receive the sacraments. A similar
critique is found in SA.[40]

The greatest lack of clarity surrounds the much-discussed expression *ex opere operato* — and this is true on both sides of the confessional line of demarcation. This expression goes back to the 13th
century and was designed to safeguard the idea of the sacraments
as means of grace. The sacraments are "instruments" of God, who
gives them their real power. They are the effective external signs
of an inner, invisible grace. Inasmuch as Christ is actively present
and giving us His salvation through these signs, the sacraments are

37 See n. 35. E. Thestrup Pedersen in *Festskrift til K. E. Skydsgaard* (1962),
p. 96.

38 Cf. Grane (1959), p. 125, and E. Thestrup Pedersen (1962), pp. 95 f.

39 367:27 — Item quod applicata pro aliis etiam iniustis, non ponentibus
obicem (Ap XXIV 63); 376:16-19 (Ap XXIV 96).

40 435:29 — Et si accedere velit homo ad eucharistiam, non opus esse bono
proposito recte faciendi, sed sufficere, si non adsit malum propositum peccandi
(SA III I 9). Cf. WA 6, 532:1 f. (*De captivitate*, 1520).

neither magical nor impersonal.[41] One finds, however, that the Lutheran Confessions never actually discuss this interpretation of *opus operatum;* rather, they look upon *opus operatum* as the highest and most refined form of work-piety, as a manifestation of a pre-Christian magical concept in which the sacrifice exerts an expiatory effect as soon as it is offered up.[42]

But the Catholic reply to the Reformation position was equally misleading. The Catholic theologians did not recognize that the reformers' chief objection to *opus operatum* had to do with the doctrine of good works. They considered it to be an attack on the objective nature of the means of grace. According to a well-known Catholic misunderstanding, the Reformation doctrine of justification leads to a denial of the sacraments as necessary means of grace.[43] Nothing, however, could be more erroneous (Ap IV 74). The Confessions strongly reject the idea that anything other than the Word and sacraments, received in faith, can bring us the Holy Spirit and righteousness before God.

In their view of the sacraments as acts of God both the Catholics and the Evangelicals represented similar points of view,[44] in spite of the fact that the Lutheran Confessions for natural reasons rejected the term *opus operatum,* which they related to work-righteousness. The Confessions say that the sacraments are the external means whereby God carries out His work of salvation; the sacraments are not what we do, but what God does. Baptism is God's gift to us; it is not a question of what we do.[45] God permits His will to be carried out through the sacraments (AC and Ap XIII 1). They are not human acts of confession, or symbols of something that once took place; they are faith-creating divine means.[46] This view of the sacraments as God's work can be traced back to the genesis of the Reformation, even in those writings in which God's promise and man's faith are emphasized in such a way that the sacraments could have been disregarded.[47]

[41] K. Algermissen (1957), pp. 248 f.; E. Thestrup Pedersen (1962), p. 95; F. Diekamp, III (1937), p. 34.

[42] 376:22—377:5 (Ap XXIV 97 f.).

[43] F. Clark (1960), pp. 350 f.; E. Thestrup Pedersen (1962), pp. 97 f.

[44] Cf. E. Thestrup Pedersen (1962), pp. 94, 96 f., and 107.

[45] 698:22 — Also siehest Du klar, dass da kein Werk ist, von uns getan, sondern ein Schatz, den er uns gibt (LC IV 36); 354:16-19 (Ap XXIV 18).

[46] 291:48-54 (Ap XIII 1); 369:23-25 (Ap XXIV 69).

[47] WA 2, 694:14-16 (*Eyn Sermon von der Bereitung zum Sterben,* 1519); WA 6, 530:19-31 (*De captivitate,* 1520).

The real line of separation between the Catholic and the Reformation points of view does not, therefore, run where it is frequently thought to be; the antithesis is rather based upon different opinions concerning grace and justification. According to the Catholic view, the church as an institution supplies the healing balm of grace through the sacraments and the priesthood. As a result, the accent is placed on the sacramental acts which surround the life of man from the beginning to the end. According to the Reformation concept, justification takes place through an act of imputation and acceptance. God, through the Word of promise, imputes the righteousness of Christ to those who receive the promise in faith and declares them righteous. It is for this reason that the Lutheran Confessions place such great stress on the connection between the promise and faith.

Only incidentally do the Confessions confront the difficult and perhaps basically insoluble problem of how the connection between the sacraments and faith can be clarified. In order to avoid an impersonal, magical view of the sacraments, the emphasis was placed on faith. But if faith is a human precondition for receiving the sacraments, one thereby may overlook the fact that salvation is the exclusive work of God. If, on the other hand, the intention is to say that faith as precondition for the reception of the sacraments is a divine work, the problem remains.

In extending the idea of the sacraments as the exclusive work of God, one confronts the concept of predestination—which also undeniably includes problems of its own vis-à-vis human responsibility. When Thestrup Pedersen analyzed the way Luther sought to master such problems in *De captivitate babylonica,* he quite properly rejected the idea that for Luther faith constituted a *condition* for the reception of the sacraments. Such an attitude could easily lead to synergism, which the reformers strenuously opposed, and would contradict the most basic Reformation presupposition, i. e., that justification is by faith alone without any human contribution. It is true that *De captivitate* includes passages which could be interpreted to mean [48] that faith is a precondition for receiving the sacraments beneficially, but these passages only serve to illustrate the difficulties involved in the problem here in question. On his own, Pedersen provides a solution which includes both the fact that God works unaided

---

[48] WA 6, 532:25 — verbum promissionis, quod fidem exigit (*De captivitate,* 1520); cf. WA 1, 544:37 — cum sit impossibile sacramentum conferri salubriter nisi iam credibus (*Resolutiones,* 1518), and E. Thestrup Pedersen (1962), p. 107.

in the sacraments, as well as the fact that man must be involved.[49]

The only place where the Confessions touch upon this question is in AC V, where it is said that the sacraments are a means by which the Holy Spirit creates faith "where and when it pleases God," *ubi et quando visum est Deo.* On the basis of this wording, a clear predestination concept is implied. The faith which is necessary for receiving the sacraments is created by God Himself through the Holy Spirit, who works through the sacraments. Word and sacrament are the instruments through which God works to touch the hearts and create faith.[50] Faith is bestowed through the free grace of God. No man, not even an unworthy person who administers them,[51] can influence the effectiveness of the sacraments; God alone decides. The concept of predestination is also in obvious agreement with Luther's earliest ideas.[52] That faith is dependent on God's grace was a principle for Luther completely in line with *iustitia Dei* as the righteousness given by God. But Melanchthon was conscious of the fact that a pure concept of predestination includes certain distinct problems. As a result, when in Ap he further discussed the sacraments and how they work, he did not repeat the proposition *ubi et quando visum est Deo.*[53] As we well know, he rejected the predestination concept in his later works.[54]

It cannot be said that the problem concerning faith as (1) a precondition for beneficial use of the sacraments and as (2) its result was solved in the Confessions. Their authors were not interested in this problem; they rather directed their attention and emphasis upon the necessity of faith. The recipient must have the *fides specialis*,[55] which takes hold of the promise. The emphasis in the Reformation concept of the sacraments is that they are true guarantees of the

---

[49] E. Thestrup Pedersen (1962), pp. 105—11. For the position of the Confessions on this, see E. Schlink (1961), pp. 152 f.

[50] 243:45 — Instrumenta, per quae Deus movet corda ad credendum, sicut verbum et sacramenta (Ap VII 36).

[51] 62:9 — Et sacramenta et verbum propter ordinationem et mandatum Christi sunt efficacia, etiamsi per malos exhibeantur (AC II 8).

[52] WA 7, 102:27 — non est in potestate nostra ponere incrudelitatem, sed solius dei, qui infundit solus fidem (*Assertio . . .* 1520).

[53] 369:48—370:2 (Ap XXIV 70).

[54] H. Olsson in STK (1944), pp. 89 ff.; Bengt Hägglund (1959), pp. 186 f.; L. Grane (1959), p. 54.

[55] 295:34 — et loquimur hic de fide speciali, quae praesenti promissioni credit, non tantum quae in genere credit Deum esse, sed quae credit offerri remissionem peccatorum (Ap XIII 21).

forgiveness of sins and justification for Christ's sake. They are signs of the promise. (Ap XIII 20)

According to the Confessions this faith, *fiducia,* cannot come into being as long as it has nothing external to attach itself to. It does, of course, have its seat in the will of man, in his heart, but it nevertheless requires an external assurance of God's grace mediated through the senses. The profoundest justification of the fact that Word and sacrament create faith is to be found here. "Yes, it must be external so that it can be perceived and grasped by the senses and thus brought into the heart, just as the entire Gospel is an external, oral proclamation. In short, whatever God effects in us he does through such external ordinances." [56]

The Catholic Church accepts seven religious acts as sacraments, Lutheranism two or three. Of the seven Catholic sacraments, the Lutheran Confessions conclude that two – confirmation and extreme unction – must be rejected because they lack Biblical support. Marriage belongs to the order of creation; it is older than the New Testament, and it was not at its institution connected with any special promise of grace. Ordination as a sacrament is also unknown in the New Testament, and must therefore go. Of the remaining three, opinions about the sacrament of penance were somewhat divided during the entire Reformation era. It is counted as a sacrament only in AC and Ap.

The Reformation way of thinking developed as a result of controversy with the late medieval, Occamist practice of penance,[57] and the results of this controversy are to be found in the Confessions. The Roman Catholic sacrament of penance was now divided into two parts. The *materia* of penance, i. e., contrition, confession, and satisfaction, was detached from the distinct sacrament of penance and was instead joined to Baptism. It was looked upon as a daily dying away from sin and a perpetual renewal of faith in Christ. Thus the effect of Baptism reaches throughout man's entire life. No other "last resort" measure, as the act of penance was called in a well-known statement attributed to Jerome,[58] is necessary. A return to one's baptism is sufficient.

[56] 697:4-10 (LC IV 30).

[57] Concerning this see C. Feckes (1925), pp. 59—89.

[58] *Ep 130 ad Demetriadem de servanda virginitate* — Illa quasi secunda post naufragium miseris tabula sit (MPL 22,115). Luther frequently criticized Jerome on this point. See *Die Bekenntnisschriften* (1959), p. 706, n. 9, and H. Rahner in ZKT (1957), pp. 129—69.

The *forma* of the Roman Catholic sacrament of penance, i. e., absolution, retains its sacramental character in AC and Ap. The sacrament of penance is constituted by the absolution (Ap XII 41). The statements concerning the sacramental character of absolution are, however, variable. The young Luther spoke of absolution as the third sacrament. In the catechisms he continued to emphasize individual absolution in private confession, but he no longer called it a sacrament. SC includes a special section on confession in immediate association with Baptism, but it does not consider it to be a sacrament, because the external sign is lacking. Absolution does not meet the requirements of being a sacrament. As a result, we will treat penitence in a special chapter. Even though it is not specifically included among the sacraments, its sacramental nature must be observed.

2. Baptism

All the sacraments are God's work. God acts, man receives. God offers His salvatory gifts through the sacraments; man receives them. God's grace is first and fundamental in the sacramental act. According to Ap a sacrament is a sacred act in which God gives us what He has promised.[1]

It is from this point of view that the Confessions consider Baptism. Baptism is a work in which God baptizes us through His servant, who acts in His place. Ap XXIV 18 asserts that Baptism in God's name means that one is baptized by God Himself. Although Baptism is administered by a man, it is God's work.[2]

The idea that Baptism is something God does runs like a red thread throughout LC. There is a connection here with the Confessions' general view of justification and divine righteousness, *iustitia Dei,* which is of course God's work and gift. As a means of grace, Baptism is an expression of God's act of salvation and is placed in contrast to all that man can think of doing in an effort to win righteousness before God. Baptism becomes an argument against monastic vows. While Baptism is something God has willed and commanded, monastic vows are looked upon as an expression of salvation by

---

[1] 354:13 — Sacramentum est ceremonia vel opus, in quo Deus nobis exhibet hoc, quod offert annexa ceremonia promissio (Ap XXIV 18). For contemporary literature on Baptism, see Grönvik, *Die Taufe in der Theologie Martin Luthers* (1968).

[2] 692:40 — Denn in Gottes Namen getauft werden, ist nicht von Menschen sondern von Gott selbs getauft werden; darumb ob es gleich durch des Menschen Hand geschicht, so ist es doch wahrhaftig Gottes eigen Werk (LC IV 10). "Name" here indicates the source from which salvation comes. (Ap IV 99).

human effort.[3] As is true of justification, Baptism is God's way to us, not our way to God. "Baptism . . . is not our work but God's," and "God's works . . . are salutary and necessary for salvation." [4]

The strongest expression of the fact that God Himself is at work in the sacrament of Baptism is infant baptism. If the basis of Baptism were found in man, presupposing a conscious faith in the one to be baptized, infant baptism would be absurd. But the Confessions speak of the necessity of infant baptism and tell us: "Children, too, should be baptized, for in Baptism they are committed to God and become acceptable to Him" (AC IX 2). For us, says Luther in LC, the important thing is not the presence or absence of faith in the one to be baptized, for the absence of faith does not invalidate Baptism; all depends on God's Word and command (LC IV 52). It is obvious that LC does not thereby intend to push faith aside as the precondition for a proper partaking of the sacrament—that would suggest the surrender of something essential to the Reformation view of the sacraments—but it simply serves to underscore the fact that Baptism is a divine accomplishment. There is a strong objective element in the Confessions' concept of the sacraments.[5] Baptism is not in itself dependent upon the faith of either the officiant or the recipient; in the power of Christ's institution and command both Word and sacrament are effective, even if they are communicated by an unbeliever (AC VIII 2). In the same way as "gold remains no less gold if a harlot wears it in sin and shame," Baptism remains valid even if faith is lacking (LC IV 59). God's ordinance cannot be nullified through our misuse of Baptism. (LC IV 55)

The idea behind all of these statements is the theocentric view: God is the active One, the Holy Spirit regenerates man through the Word and the sacraments. That infant baptism does in fact have God's approval is confirmed for the writers of the Confessions in the fact that also those who were baptized as infants have received the Holy Spirit. Among those baptized as infants are many men who have been sanctified by the Holy Spirit.[6] This argumentation is reminiscent of Peter's defense of the baptism of heathen in Acts 10:47, although the order there is reversed. In view of the fact that Cornelius and his house had received the Holy Spirit, Peter could think of no objection

---

[3] 693:9-25 (LC IV 11 f.).

[4] 698:6-10 (LC IV 35).

[5] J. Meyer (1929), p. 438, and E. Schlink (1961), p. 154.

[6] 247:26-32 (Ap IX 3); 700:39-46 (LC IV 48 f.).

to their baptism. Infant baptism is confirmed for the confessional writers by the fact that the Holy Spirit thereby comes to share His gifts with those so baptized.

The fact that the statements about Baptism as a divine deed are directed against the Donatists and the Anabaptists is the result of the confessional emphasis on the sacrament as something God does. If Baptism, e. g., were a sign or a confirmation of something that had happened earlier between God and man, it would not be a means of grace. As seen from the Confessions' realistic and antispiritualist point of view, Baptism must be understood to be a genuine means of grace, i. e., an instrument for God's active work of salvation.

The Confessions found support for their view of Baptism as God's work in the Biblical command. The argument is not a rational one in the usual sense of the term. On the contrary, it seems to have been clear to Luther that a symbolic view of Baptism is considerably easier both to justify and accept rationally. The Lutheran position on Baptism is based exclusively on what God has commanded in the Bible: "Go therefore and make disciples of all nations, baptizing them in the name of the Father and of the Son and of the Holy Spirit." (Matt. 28:19) [7]

There is a close tie between Baptism and justification by faith without works, but Baptism is not derived from justification; it is based on the Scriptural command. The command given in Matt. 28:19 is interpreted to mean (1) that salvation through Baptism must be shared by all, even young children, and (2) that God Himself achieves what He has commanded. LC looks upon the command to baptize in the name of the Triune God as an assurance from Him concerning His active cooperation. To be baptized in God's name means the same as to be baptized by God, not by man. [8] The authority in Baptism rests with God. Inasmuch as the one who administers Baptism has his commission from God, he simply executes a divine decree.

The catechisms strongly emphasize the necessity of the external sign, i. e., the baptismal water. The chief reason for this is that God gave His express command to use water. To ignore what God has commanded would denote disobedience vis-à-vis His express will, but to observe the command is to show one's obedience, as well as one's confidence that God through Baptism provides what He has

[7] 247:20 f. (Ap IX 2); 515:30-34 (SC IV 4); 558:9-14 (LC Preface 21); 691:27-30 (LC IV 4).

[8] 692:40-42 (LC IV 10); WA 6, 530:32-35 (*De captivitate*, 1520); J. Köstlin, I (1901), 410 f.

promised and accomplishes what He has said in His Word. If the pope can do much through his officially sealed bulls and letters, Baptism can do much more, for it comes to us from God (LC IV 8). To ignore the external sign would mean holding God in contempt. The basis for receiving the gifts of Baptism would also thereby be removed.

According to the definition provided in SA and LC, a sacrament consists of the Word and the elements. *Accedit verbum ad elementum et fit sacramentum,* i. e., the Word comes to the elements, and this makes a sacrament. In Baptism water is the element, and the Word, the command, has its primary significance as the words of institution [9] through which God has bound His saving presence to the water.

The water of Baptism has been called "a divine, heavenly, holy, and blessed water," [10] which man cannot praise enough since God has imbued it with His own power. This may sound as though the water as such were equipped with miraculous heavenly powers, but the Confessions reject such an interpretation as a misunderstanding (SA III V 2). Baptismal water has its special character as a result of the words of institution. Since God has commanded Baptism, He has bound Himself to it with His saving Word, and this "contains and conveys all the fullness of God" (LC IV 17). Water is the envelope into which the Word is inserted like nuts in a shell. As SA III V 1 puts it, reflecting Eph. 5:26, Baptism is "the Word of God in water." The water becomes one with God's Word, for through His name God has bound Himself to the water. Instead of a transubstantiation, one can visualize here a parallel to the Incarnation. Just as the Word became flesh in Christ, God has become incorporated with the water (LC IV 29), and therefore it possesses its power. It is extremely important that we do not belittle the water in Baptism but recognize it as an external confirmation of the truth of what God has instituted and ordained. He who does not honor the external order of Baptism intimates that he has contempt for God's will, clearly certified in the Bible, to save us through Baptism from the power of sin, death, and the devil.

Obedience to the *mandatum,* God's command, was an essential ingredient in Luther's experience. For him, it provided a safeguard against self-chosen works. In the catechisms the Fourth Commandment in a way occupies a unique place (LC I 115 f.), at the side of the

[9] 691:38 — hie stehet Gottes Gebot und Einsetzung; *Dei mandatum et institutionem* (LC IV 6); 692:18 — da stehet aber Gottes Wort und Gebot, so die Taufe einsetzet (LC IV 7).

[10] 694:22-23 (LC IV 17); cf. 693:36 (LC IV 14).

First Commandment. Luther understood it to be a guarantee against one's own works, which lead away from the tasks of the daily calling to a life within cloister walls. But the monastic life, unlike obedience to one's parents, has not been commanded by God. According to Luther, parents possess their special place as a result of God's commandment. As seen from a superficial point of view, one's parents do not seem appreciably different from other people, but on the basis of the Fourth Commandment "I see another man, adorned and clothed with the majesty and glory of God." [11] As the result of God's command LC looked upon the parental estate and the authority of government as God's earthly representatives. "God has exalted this estate of parents above all others; indeed, he has appointed it to be his representative on earth" (LC I 126). By analogy, this is related to Baptism. The water accomplishes nothing of and by itself, but it receives its unique function because God has given His command.

But there is more to it. Baptism is not only commanded, it is also equipped with a promise; this separates it from the commandments and gives it its sacramental character. The sacraments are sacred acts which God has ordained and to which He has added a promise of grace and forgiveness of sin (Ap XIII 3). The sacramental words are significant not only as words of institution but also as words of promise, and these two condition one another. By carrying out what God has commanded, man shares in what He has promised.

The very greatest stress therefore came to be placed on the promise, which is in harmony with what we now know about the Reformation view of the sacraments. It is not the sacraments *per se* but faith in their promises which justifies. As we know, Luther emphasized the Word of promise in his earliest writings. In *De captivitate babylonica* he reduced the number of the sacraments from seven to three by excluding all the church rites that did not possess an express Word of promise.[12] Melanchthon agreed. In AC and Ap he accented the Word of promise in the sacraments. It is not enough to show that a religious act has been commanded by God; the promise must be attached. The sacraments are signs of God's gracious will toward us. In Ap IX 2 infant baptism is justified by referring to God's promise, which applies even to small children.

In the catechisms, too, the promise constitutes an integral part of Baptism. It is the promise which gives it its character as a sacra-

[11] 694:43—695:8 (LC IV 20); 698:39—699:6 (LC IV 38). Note Luther's totally "unmodern" manner of motivating respect for one's parents.

[12] WA 6, 501:33 f. (*De captivitate*, 1520).

ment. Yet the promise has a considerably less prominent place here than in Luther's earlier writings,[13] in which he emphasized the Word of promise in a way that made it appear almost as though the external sign (the water) was being overlooked.[14] The catechisms, which have the opposite tendency, put the primary stress on the external sign God has commanded. As Josefson has shown, however, there is in fact no change in the point of view itself, but the shift of emphasis from the promise in the earlier writings to the command and the external sign in the catechisms is related to the polemical situation in which these different books appeared. In the catechisms Luther addressed himself first of all to the "enthusiastic," spiritualizing concept of Baptism with its low view of the external sign. In his zeal for God's command, the promise was seemingly forgotten. But in reality even in the catechisms Luther held fast to the promise as the most important part of Baptism; it is the promise that makes Baptism a sacrament, for God's gifts and gracious disposition are expressed in it. The sacramental Word has significance not only as command but also as promise, and it is the latter that makes Baptism a means of grace.

In the introduction to the section on Baptism in the catechisms we find the baptismal Word of promise ("He who believes and is baptized will be saved," Mark 16:16) alongside the words of institution taken from Matt. 28:19.[15] Baptism is compared to the Fourth Commandment. In both cases there is a distinct command from God. But Baptism is superior to the commandment, inasmuch as it is associated with a clear promise from God. "But here we have not only God's commandment and injunction, but also his promise. Therefore, it is far more glorious than anything else God has commanded and ordained." [16] The institution and promise of Baptism are very closely related. By being true to what God has commanded, man can be sure of the truth of God's promise. When we carry out the external act in obedience to God and with confidence in His promise, Baptism becomes Gospel.

As is true of the whole Gospel—the oral Word, Baptism, the Lord's Supper, and absolution—Baptism can only be received correctly through faith. Here as always when the Gospel is involved, faith and promise go together. Faith attaches itself to the promise

13 Cf. H. Grass (1954), pp. 87 and 90 f.

14 R. Josefson (1944), pp. 20, 23 f., and 107.

15 691:32-35 (LC IV 5); 516:4-9 (SC IV 7 f.)

16 699:10-14 (LC IV 38 f.); 516:2 — die Wort und Verheissung (SC IV 6).

which God has added to the water of Baptism (LC IV 33 f.). Baptism is a gift from God to man. It enables us to participate in His righteousness. But the gift must be received in faith.

Baptism *per se* is the work of God, wholly and completely; it is not dependent on man's faith or lack of faith. Its institution and promise remain, regardless of whether he who administers Baptism has faith or not. But to be received beneficially, faith must be present. What Baptism wants to impart can only be accepted by a faithful heart.

The Confessions here reject the "enthusiastic" view of Baptism, which denies both the external sign and Baptism as the work of God. God's Word and command, His institution, make Baptism what it is, and as such it is not dependent on the faith of the minister or the recipient. "My faith does not constitute Baptism but receives it" (LC IV 53). Thus Baptism is valid even if it is not received and used as intended; its validity does not depend on our faith but on the words of institution and promise (LC IV 53). Through the institution God has bound Himself to the water, and the Word of promise is also attached to the water. Baptism is in a sense a renewal of the Incarnation. The Word and the water become one in the same way that God and man are one in Christ (cf. LC IV 29).[17] Baptism as such is not dependent upon our faith. What God has determined and promised is not influenced by our changing attitudes.

But faith is necessary if Baptism is to be received in a way that brings salvation. The strong emphasis on Baptism as a work of God — whether men recognize it as such or not — did not lead the reformers to the *opus operatum* position. To share in the gifts of Baptism in a salvatory manner one must possess that faith which Baptism both effects and presupposes.[18] As a consequence LC came to assume the presence of a personal faith even in the little children carried to the baptismal font (LC IV 56), but this must be faith in a different sense from that of adults who trust in the promise of God. Without saying so specifically, LC here presupposes a new meaning in the concept of faith. If faith can be defined simply as the work and the presence of the Holy Spirit in man, it is not difficult to speak of faith even in a little child, who lives here on earth without being conscious of it. In much the same way one could conceive of the life of faith as a divine

[17] Cf. R. Josefson (1944), 126 f.

[18] E. Schlink (1961), 152 f. With regard to *fides infantium*, see Brinkel, *Die Lehre Luthers von der fides infantium bei der Kindertaufe* (1958), and Althaus' review in ThLZ (1959).

work in man even though he is not immediately aware of it. The presence of faith must be presupposed, since God has invited even children to Baptism and through the Holy Spirit has actually confirmed its legitimacy.

Baptism is a work of God, and it can be received only by faith.[19] It is emphasized throughout the Confessions that faith holds fast to the promises and thereby to God Himself, who has promised us salvation by instituting Baptism. Since God the Holy Spirit is bound to the water, our faith in Baptism concerns that God who meets us in this way with His salvatory gifts. Through the Word we can be certain of the divine presence.

Since Baptism is a divine work, it communicates specific gifts to those who hold fast in faith to God's command and promise. Baptism is aimed above all at the conquest of all the hindrances which stand in God's way. AC and Ap customarily refer to these hindrances as *terrores conscientiae,* terrors of conscience,[20] while the catechisms speak of the evil powers — sin, death, and the devil[21] — also including a frightened conscience.[22] There doesn't appear to be any factual difference between the catechisms and the other confessional documents. Our existence is dualistic; God is opposed by the powers of evil, sin, death, the flesh, the devil, the world, and hell.[23] Just how realistic this was for men of Luther's time is now difficult to imagine. The devil was much more tangible then than now. He is a personal power, constantly lurking in ambush to lead men into need and misery through sin.[24] The evil of the present time is the devil's work;[25] he has set up his kingdom in this world.[26] He is active not only among

---

[19] 698:9 — Gottes Werk aber sind heilsam und nicht zur Seligkeit und schliessen nicht aus, sondern fodern den Glauben, denn ohn Glauben künnde man sie nicht fassen (LC IV 35).

[20] 78:8-11 (AC XX 17); 163:38-42 (Ap IV 20).

[21] 696:1 — Sunden, Tod, Teufel (LC IV 25); 699:31-32 (LC IV 41).

[22] 673:35 — wider Sunde, Tod, und böse Gewissen (LC III 51); 683:29-35 (LC III 89); 684:21 (LC III 92).

[23] 506:29-31 (SC Preface 23). It is worth noting that the Confessions never include the Law among the powers of corruption.

[24] 578:19 — den Teufel, der immerdar ümb uns ist und darauf lauret, wie er uns möchte zu Sund und Schande, Jammer und Not bringen (LC I 71).

[25] 651:42 — Denn da wir geschaffen waren und allerlei Guts von Gott, dem Vater, empfangen hatten, kam der Teufel und bracht uns in Ungehorsam, Sunde, Tod und alle Unglück, dass wir in seinem Zorn und Ungnade lagen (LC II 28).

[26] 156:50 (Ap II 46); 157:16 (Ap II 50); 674:23 (LC III 54); 689:19 (LC III 114).

the ungodly; he attacks the faithful with tribulations,[27] and he seeks
to drive them over the deep end of despair. Man has been in captivity
to the devil ever since the fall into sin, and he cannot find release
without the aid of Christ. (Ap II 47 ff.)

In this struggle against the devil, Baptism has been introduced
on God's side. Its purpose is to free man from sin, death, and the devil
and bring man under the dominion of Christ, into His kingdom (LC
IV 24 f.). Since the command to baptize was given in the name of the
Triune God, the Father, the Son, and the Holy Spirit come to us in
Baptism to help us resist the evil powers (LC III 51). "In Baptism,
therefore, every Christian has enough to study and to practice all
his life. He always has enough to do to believe firmly what Baptism
promises and brings – victory over death and the devil, forgiveness
of sin, God's grace, the entire Christ, and the Holy Spirit with his
gifts" (LC IV 41). The catechisms summarize all of this under the
word salvation. The function of Baptism is to save. But "to be saved
. . . is nothing else than to be delivered from sin, death, and the devil
and to enter into the kingdom of Christ and live with him forever"
(LC IV 24 f.). These words, which are related to the explanation of
the Second Article of the Creed, must mean that Baptism is understood to be the consequence and the application of Christ's work
of salvation. Baptism, in other words, belongs with justification. This
is also confirmed by the fact that the catechisms, in harmony with
Paul in Romans 6, combine Baptism with Christ's death and resurrection.[28] Baptism is referred to in a common designation as the sacrament of the new birth [29] in connection with Titus 3:5. It has consequences which reach throughout one's life on earth and even into
eternity. The fact that water is poured upon the body is held to be an
anticipation of the resurrection from the dead (LC IV 43 f.). In this
sense Baptism also has an eschatological dimension. By enabling man
to share now in the new life of the Spirit, the resurrection life which
will finally be realized in the resurrection of the dead can be anticipated in faith.

There is no reason, however, to contrast this eschatological point
of view with a "psychological" one [30] and to look upon regeneration
as only sacramental-eschatological. The antinomy between the psychological and the theological is not found in the Confessions. Faith is

[27] 550:28-30 (LC New Preface 13); 551:10-11 (LC New Preface 14).

[28] 516:30—517:7 (SC IV 11 f.); 704:27-35 (LC IV 65).

[29] 516:21 f. (SC IV 10); 696:15 f. (LC IV 26); 712:13-14 (LC V 23).

[30] R. Josefson (1944), pp. 155, 157.

a work of the Holy Spirit in man, and the same is true of regeneration and the new life. Since Baptism is an instrument used by the Holy Spirit, the struggle against concupiscence is fought within man himself (SC IV 12). Anger, hate, envy, lewdness, indolence, pride, and faithlessness are fought against in order to make room for mercy, patience, and meekness (LC IV 66). Since Baptism confers the forgiveness of sins, it must also (rightly received) convey the fruits of faith. These are produced in man by the Holy Spirit, and in this limited sense man is involved as a psychological being—just as faith shows itself in man as confidence although it is worked by the Holy Spirit. Faith cannot therefore be described simply as God's appeal to man.[31] Because God comes to man through the Word and the sacraments, trust is born—and this is identical with faith.

Since Baptism enables the baptized to share in the life of the Triune God, they are thus led into the fellowship of the Christian church. At first glance it is surprising how little emphasis is given to the connection between Baptism and the church. While the New Testament clearly and frequently underscores the fact that we become members of the church, the body of Christ, through Baptism, the Lutheran Confessions nearly always suggest this connection only in passing, in subordinate clauses. LC points out, e. g., that Baptism is the sacrament "by which we are first received into the Christian church." [32] Justification of infant baptism is derived from the fact that the church continues to exist. If God had disapproved of this practice, the church would have died.[33] Because the statements here are so sparse, one could falsely draw the conclusion that Baptism was not looked upon as necessary for church membership. However, the Confessions demonstrate that the connection between Baptism and church membership is self-evident and hence requires no extensive explanation. LC's strong emphasis on Baptism in its controversy with the "enthusiasts" best reveals how essential it was to the reformers. Reformation theology is baptismal theology. The Christian faith is born in Baptism, whose effects are felt throughout the Christian life. The fundamental importance of Baptism is set forth as clearly as one could wish in the reformers' struggle against the Catholic sacrament of penance.

[31] R. Josefson (1944), pp. 122 and 158. Cf. 696:32 — dass der Glaube etwas haben muss, das er glaube, das ist, daran er sich halte und darauf stehe und fusse (LC IV 29), plus the section on faith in Chapter Six.

[32] 704:22-23 (LC IV 64); 691:12-13 (LC IV 2); 725:15-16 (LC V 86).

[33] 247:33-35 (Ap IX 3); 701:4-10 (LC IV 50).

In the Catholic Church the sacrament of penance was thought of as "a last resort" [34] for those who had fallen away from baptismal grace. One inescapable obligation for its members is to make an annual confession before a priest. For reasons noted above, the reformers broke with the Catholic concept of penance. Luther's first controversy involved the sacrament of penance, and it concluded, as far as he was concerned, with its complete demolition. The true meaning of penitence is found in contrition over past sins and in a renewed faith in the truth of God's promise to forgive sins for Christ's sake. The penitential act, therefore, really means nothing other than to actualize the meaning of Baptism. SC refers to Rom. 6:3-4 when it answers the question, "What does such baptizing with water signify?" by saying: "It signifies that the old Adam in us, together with all sins and evil lusts, should be drowned by daily sorrow and repentance and be put to death, and that the new man should come forth daily and rise up, cleansed and righteous, to live forever in God's presence" (IV 11-12). The Christian lives under the sign of Baptism so that he daily dies to sin in repentance and is raised in faith to the new life in the power of the Holy Spirit. According to the Reformation interpretation, penitence is a necessary consequence of Baptism because in spite of the new birth in Baptism "our human flesh and blood have not lost their old skin" (LC V 23). The Christian is *simul iustus et peccator*. Baptism fulfills its function when sin is opposed and faith with its fruits is brought to maturity. Faith is thought of not as so much passive knowledge; it rather exists in the penitential struggle against sin. (Ap IV 142)

Since Baptism was instituted by God and is effected by Him, its benefits accrue to man throughout his earthly life and forward to the day of resurrection in eternity. Baptism is properly used when the old man is opposed and the new man comes into being. This Lutheran point of view not only brings Baptism into tangible existence but also makes the conventional sacrament of penance superfluous. At the same time the nature of Baptism as a divine activity receives its strongest expression. The entire Christian life is lived under the protection God provides through Baptism.

3. The Lord's Supper

As is true of Baptism, the Lord's Supper is God's work and not our own. The basic point of view that the sacraments are "signs and

---

[34] Jerome, *Ep 130 ad Demetriadem de servanda virginitate* (MPL 22, 1115); 706:40-43 (LC IV 81); J. Meyer (1929), 438 f.

testimonies of God's will toward us, through which he moves men's hearts to believe" (Ap XIII 1) also holds true for the Lord's Supper. At the very beginning of his exposition of the Lord's Supper in LC Luther draws a parallel between it and Baptism. Both are based on what God has ordained and commanded, and God's order is unchangeable, independent of whether or not the recipient has faith, or if the one who administers the Lord's Supper does so in a worthy manner or not. This point of view is found throughout the Confessions; its presupposition is the conviction that God is at work in that which He has instituted and ordained. If the Lord's Supper were something other than a divine activity, the personal faith of the minister would naturally have a bearing upon the effect of the sacrament. But on the basis of their conviction that the sacramental act is God's work, both Luther and Melanchthon rejected all such ideas.[1] For them the decisive point was that the Lord's Supper be carried out in accordance with the order instituted by Christ. Among other things, therefore, the matter of giving the Sacrament under both the bread and wine or not was to them more than a question of convenience.[2] Observing the Biblical instructions shows respect for God's command and demonstrates the conviction that God is active when the Sacrament is administered as He has ordained.

As little as the order of nature can be changed by man's laws, so little can God's institution of the Lord's Supper be changed by human conduct. The Confessions see the will of God expressed in creation, and the order of creation confirms the correctness of what God has said in His Word. The ground bears seed and fruit every year because God in His Word (Gen. 1:11) has so commanded. The natural order will be in effect as long as the world endures.[3] The same is true of the Lord's Supper. Since it is God's work and not our own, it accomplishes what God has ordained, quite apart from the personal, spiritual qualifications of those who give or receive the Sacrament. If the Lord's Supper is made dependent on man's faith and worthiness, one would look upon the Sacrament as something that we do and not as God's work of salvation.[4]

There is another similarity between Baptism and the Lord's

[1] 62:8-11 (AC VIII 2); 710:34—711:20 (LC V 15 ff.). Regarding Luther's Lord's Supper theology, see Cleve, *Luthers nattvardslära* (1968), with an English summary.

[2] 451:9 (SA III VI 2 f.); 85:2-7 (AC XXII 2); 328:39 ff. (Ap XXII 1 f.).

[3] 335:22-31 (Ap XXIII 8).

[4] 709:1-12 (LC V 5 ff.).

Supper: both are said to be God's work on the basis of the divine institution or command found in the Bible. The words of institution for the Lord's Supper are understood to have a double meaning—part command and part promise. One can no more dispense with God's command than one can ignore the promise in the Sacrament. As a result, Ap XIII 3 sets forth the following as conditions for all sacraments: they must be *commanded* by God and connected with a *promise* of grace. Both of these also appear in the catechisms. The command is given the most attention there by far, but the promise is not overlooked either. "Of greatest importance [is] God's Word and ordinance or command," *Dei verbum, ordo et mandatum.*[5] The Lord's Supper is supported first and foremost by God's command in Scripture, which makes it a divine work. The command is to be found in such phrases from the words of institution as "take, eat," "do this, as often as you drink it, in remembrance of Me." [6] The promise becomes apparent in such phrases as "given for you," "poured out for you." (LC V 64)

The fact that Christ is present in the bread and wine depends, according to LC, upon His own command, for He said in the words of institution that the bread "is My body" and the wine "is My blood." Here, as in its section on Baptism, LC quotes Augustine: *"Accedat verbum ad elementum et fit sacramentum,* that is, 'When the Word is joined to the external element, it becomes a sacrament.'"[7] Luther's thinking here was centered upon God's active Word of consecration, whereby bread and wine become something other than ordinary bread and wine. "As we said of Baptism that it is not mere water, so we say here that the sacrament is bread and wine, but not mere bread or wine such as is served at the table. It is bread and wine comprehended in God's Word and connected with it. It is the Word, I maintain, which distinguishes it from mere bread and wine and constitutes it a sacrament which is rightly called Christ's body and blood." [8]

In his dissertation on the theology of worship in Luther, however, Vilmos Vajta does not understand this Word to be a Word of command but a Word of promise. "Luther," he says, "understood the Words of Institution as the pledge *(Verheissung, Zusagung)* by which

[5] 708:41-42 (LC V 4).

[6] 708:16-32 (LC V 3); 711:8-12 (LC V 17).

[7] 709:37-40 (LC V 10).

[8] 709:26-32 (LC V 9 f.); cf. 693:33-34 (LC IV 14); J. Diestelmann (1960), pp. 11 f. and 18 ff., presents an abundance of material which throws light upon the words of institution as words of consecration.

Christ has promised to be present." [9] According to Vajta's interpretation of Luther, Christ after the resurrection is everywhere present in all creation, but through the consecration "the omnipresent body and blood of Christ are revealed and promised to man." [10] The promise serves to reveal or disclose to those assembled for the Lord's Supper a presence which is already at hand in the power of Christ's ubiquity. The words of institution mean "nothing else but the promise of Christ's 'presence for us' in the Word." [11]

Two presuppositions serve as the foundation for what Vajta says here: (1) the concept of ubiquity, and (2) the promissory character of the words of institution. Through His ubiquity Christ is already present everywhere; the promise given in the words of institution contains the assurance of His presence for faith.[12] "As a matter of fact, it is the Word which attests to Christ's presence in the elements. To divorce the presence from the elements is contrary to Luther's intention." [13] The promise therefore says to the man of faith that Christ, in the power of His ubiquity, is present in the bread and wine of the Lord's Supper.

But does Luther express himself in such terms in LC? The answer must be no. In LC the words of institution are first of all divine command, not promise. Through these words Christ has bound His presence to the Lord's Supper; through the words of institution the whole Christ is present "in and under the bread and wine" (LC V 8). The reason why the words of institution ought to be thought of first and foremost as words of consecration is found in Luther's idea that the Word must *make* the elements into a sacrament; if this is not done, they are simply elements and nothing else.[14] In order to interpret the significance of these words, it can be helpful to look into the way Luther expressed himself in other writings which date from approxi-

[9] Vilmos Vajta (1958), p. 99; Regin Prenter in *Kerygma und Dogma* (1955), p. 56 — Das Sakramentswort ist . . . Gottes Verheissungswort. A. Peters (1960), pp. 86 f., adopts the same point of view.

[10] V. Vajta (1958), p. 100; p. 96 — For the real presence rests on God's presence in all his works.

[11] Ibid., p. 101.

[12] Ibid., p. 92 — Christ's presence is presence for the sake of our faith. A. Andrén (1954), p. 52, who deliberately reproduces Vajta's point of view, says that for Luther the consecration simply meant that the presence of Christ was revealed to faith; the presence was already a reality as a result of Christ's ubiquity.

[13] Vajta, p. 102.

[14] 709:42 — Das Wort muss das Element zum Sakrament machen, wo nicht, so bleibt's ein lauter Element (LC V 10).

mately this same time. On the other hand, it may be hazardous to try
to understand his conception of the words of institution at the time
of the appearance of the catechisms with the aid of quotations derived
from his earliest works.[15] The shifting of the main point from the
promise to the command, because of his controversy with the so-
called "enthusiasts," is something we have already shown to be significant in Luther's thinking about the Lord's Supper.

In a catechism sermon on the Lord's Supper dating from 1528,
which was preliminary to LC, Luther drew a comparison between
holy water and the Sacrament. Even though holy water is blessed,
it does not become a sacrament, for it lacks God's Word in the sense
of God's command.[16] It is this Word which makes the bread and wine
of the Lord's Supper into Christ's body and blood. "There the words
make the bread the body of Christ given for us" *(Ibi verba faciunt
panem zum Leib Christi traditum pro nobis).*[17] How this takes place
is an unfathomable mystery, whose solution is known only to God.
(WA 30 I, 54:23)

The same idea is expressed as clearly in *Vom Abendmahl Christi.*
The words of institution, which contain the statement "This is My
body," are divine words of command or consecration *(heisselwort),*[18]
which accomplish what they say. When the Lord's Supper is celebrated and the words of institution are read, Christ is present in the
bread and wine *in the power of these words.* The words used in the
first Lord's Supper were powerful words, *Machtworte* — they accomplished what they expressed. When Jesus said, "This is My body,"
it happened according to His saying, just as certainly as creation took
place as a result of God's Word as reported in the first chapter of
Genesis.[19] On the basis of Christ's command His body is present

15 V. Vajta did not take note of this change (1958), p. 99, n. 56. In H. Grass
(1954) this is clearly indicated.

16 WA 30 I, 54:14 — Papa consecrat aquam und wird weihewasser, so wird
doch kein Sakrament draus, quia es mangelt an dem andern stuecke, scilicet an
Gottes Wort. Man kans nicht deuten, das ein ander wasser sey, denn es ist, denn
es hat keinen befehl *(Katechismuspredigten, 1528).*

17 WA 30 I, 53:23. In my interpretation of this passage I concur with Grass
(1954), pp. 87 ff. In his critique of Grass, Vajta (1952), p. 185, n. 95, proceeds
on the assumption that *traditum* refers to *panem.* This is linguistically possible
but, for other reasons, improbable. Cf., e. g., WA 30, I, 54:5 — Haec verba in
Sacramento docent, quod panis sit corpus domini mei pro me traditum. "Heisselwort" connotes "word of command," just as "heissen" connotes "command," according to Grimm, *Deutsches Wörterbuch,* IV, 2, 908 ff.

18 WA 26, 283:31—284:4 *(Vom Abendmahl Christi,* 1528).

19 WA 26, 282:39—283:7.

in the Lord's Supper, for everything that He says is His will does in fact take place.[20]

Since Jesus has commanded that the words of institution be repeated, they still have the creative power they possessed from the beginning—and Christ's body and blood are truly present in the Lord's Supper. The minister who reads these words is only an instrument for Christ; he acts on Christ's orders and in His stead. He represents Christ in his function, but not in his person. He has no independent authority, but when he speaks the words of institution, he does so at Christ's command. The effective, consecrating power rests with Christ and in His Word, which the minister repeats and makes actual. The body of Christ is present in the Lord's Supper "by virtue not of our speaking but of his command, bidding, and action."[21] He "connects his command with our speaking."[22] Luther reminds us that water burst forth from the rock (according to Num. 20:8-14) when Moses struck his staff against it, as God had commanded him to do. This and other similar examples from the Old and New Testaments reveal to us that God expresses His will through His Word, even when it is spoken through human instruments, provided that this is done by God's express command. Even though God must make use of human hands and earthly things such as bread and wine, it is He who acts. God is everything and man is nothing when it comes to carrying out His institutions and commands. Therefore the Lord's Supper is altogether God's work.

And with this we return to a view of the sacraments as God's work with which we are already familiar. We have had reason on many occasions to recall LC's statement that to be baptized in God's name means to be baptized by God Himself (LC IV 10) and Ap's opinion that a sacrament is an act in which God gives us that which He has promised. Baptism is God's work through a human instrument (Ap XXIV 18). Similar thoughts are expressed elsewhere in the Confessions. The effectiveness of the sacraments is completely independent of the minister's spiritual qualifications, "for ministers act in Christ's stead and do not represent their own persons, according to the word (Luke 10:16), 'He who hears you hears me.'"[23]

---

[20] WA 26, 284:2 — denn es geschicht auch alles, was sie lauten.

[21] WA 26, 284:36-37, LW 37, 184; WA 38, 240:1-23 (*Von der Winkelmesse und Pfaffenweihe,* 1553); Diestelmann (1960), pp. 18—20.

[22] WA 26, 285:7, LW 37, 184 (*Vom Abendmahl Christi,* 1528).

[23] 246:16 — quia ministri funguntur vice Christi, non repraesentant suam personam, iuxta illud: Qui vos audit, me audit (Luke 10:16) (Ap VII 47).

One can make good sense out of Luther's short statements in LC only if the words of institution are interpreted as words of consecration. As we have already noted, the Word must make the elements into a sacrament, so that they are no longer ordinary bread and wine. Luther's position is that the body and blood of Christ are present in the Lord's Supper under the bread and the wine on the basis of Christ's command: "For as we have it from the lips of Christ, so it is; he cannot lie or deceive." [24] If one asks if an ungodly priest can administer the Sacrament properly, the answer is an unconditional yes, naturally. The basis of the Lord's Supper is the Word by which God has commanded and instituted it. We have the right to speak of a sacrament here "by virtue of these words" (LC V 18). Luther does not speak of the Word of promise, nor can the presence of Christ be adduced on the basis of the doctrine of ubiquity. The Word is the command which consecrates the elements and makes them into Christ's body and blood, for "what the words say, that it will be," *was die Wort lauten, das wirds sein.*[25]

All of the Lutheran confessional writings teach the real presence of Christ in the Lord's Supper, and they hold that this is an inheritance from the universal church.[26] Interpretations of the actual meaning of the Real Presence are, however, varied. A distinct difference of opinion between Luther and Melanchthon can be noted. Melanchthon did not relate the Real Presence to the elements in the same way as Luther—a result of his divergent definition of the sacraments. His contemporaries also noted a general vagueness in his explanation of the presence of the body of Christ in the Lord's Supper. As Fraenkel [27] points out, Melanchthon accepted the so-called functional view of the Lord's Supper and was less interested in the elements than in the Lord's Supper as an act. In other words, he associated the presence of Christ with the liturgical act, not with the bread and wine, and he

---

[24] 710:21-23 (LC V 13); 709:44 — Nu ist's nicht eins Fürstens oder Kaisers, sondern der hohen Majestät Word und Ordnung, dafür alle Kreaturn sollen zu Füssen fallen und ja sprechen, dass es sei, wie er sagt (LC V 11).

[25] WA 30 I, 24:12 (*Katechismuspredigten*, 1528); 710:21-23 (LC V 13).

[26] 248:11 — Et comperimus non tantum romanam ecclesiam affirmare corporalem praesentiam Christi, sed idem et nunc sentire et olim sensisse graecam ecclesiam (Ap X 2). To get Luther's point of view one can refer to WA 23, 145:26 — Das aber die veter und wir zu weilen so reden: "Christi leib ist im brod" (*Dass diese Worte Christi . . . noch fest stehen*, 1527); WA 26, 442:39—443:7 (*Vom Abendmahl Christi*, 1528). So also in Köstlin, I (1901), 479.

[27] Fraenkel in *Luther und Melanchthon* (1961), pp. 147 ff. Cf. Peters (1960), pp. 92 f.

felt that the functional view was closer to the doctrinal position of the early church fathers. His unwillingness to define the Real Presence more precisely was related to his aversion against going beyond what he considered the position of the church fathers.

Fraenkel's observation is in complete agreement with the definition of a sacrament found in AC and Ap. In contrast to Luther, Melanchthon in the Confessions never referred to the elements used in Baptism and the Lord's Supper; instead, he saw sacred acts, *ceremonia, ritus,* in the sacraments. In so doing he connected the divine presence with the sacred acts as such, not with the water of Baptism or the bread and wine of the Lord's Supper. As a result of this, AC X points out with regard to the Real Presence "that the body and blood of Christ are truly present and are distributed to those who eat in the Supper of the Lord." [28] As one notes immediately, the wording is extremely cautious. Melanchthon avoids making a precise definition of the Real Presence, and he relates it not directly to the bread and wine but to the sacramental act. His formulations in AC and Ap were so general that they could be accepted not only by Luther [29] but by the authors of the Confutation as well.[30] Melanchthon like Luther wanted to emphasize the actual presence of the body of Christ in the Lord's Supper, but he deviated from Luther in his manner of explaining it.

That Luther disagreed with Melanchthon can be explained by the great weight he attached to the elements in the Lord's Supper. The bread and wine, like baptismal water, are the means whereby God's saving presence comes. "We hold that the bread and the wine in the Supper are the true body and blood of Christ and that these are given and received not only by godly but also by wicked Christians" (SA III VI 9). The real presence of Christ in the bread and wine can hardly be accentuated more strongly than that. In the year before these words were set down, Luther, in deliberations with Bucer in the Wittenberg Articles,[31] had agreed to a somewhat milder statement and said that even the unworthy (although to their judgment; cf. 1 Cor. 11:27-29) receive Christ's body and blood. The stronger statement in SA reveals the great weight he came to attach to the Real Presence. For

[28] 64:2 — quod corpus et sanguis Christi vere adsint et distribuantur vescentibus in coena domini (AC X 1).

[29] Grass (1954), p. 137.

[30] CR 27, 106 f.

[31] The text is reprinted in *Die Bekenntnisschriften* (1963), p. 65:27-46 and 977:11—978:48.

Luther it was an objective presence, independent of faith or lack of faith on the part of priest or recipient.[32] The Real Presence depends on the creative words of institution, which accomplish what they say.

LC and SA teach the Real Presence with equal clarity. All communicants receive the body and blood of Christ, regardless of whether they are worthy or unworthy (LC V 18). The bread and wine of the Lord's Supper are Christ's body and blood.[33] "The Sacrament of the Altar . . . is the true body and blood of the Lord Christ in and under the bread and wine" (LC V 8). The formulations are symptomatic of Luther's view of the Lord's Supper. He was interested in (1) watching over and standing up for the real presence of Christ's body and blood, and (2) avoiding thought patterns tending in the direction of transubstantiation. Christ is present in the bread and wine of the Lord's Supper, but the bread remains unchanged in its substance. "That bread is and remains there agrees better with the Scriptures, as St. Paul himself states, 'The bread which we break' (I Cor. 10:16), and again, 'Let a man so eat of the bread' (I Cor. 11:28)." (SA III VI 5)

The bread and wine become Christ's body and blood on the basis of the Word. What we have in the Lord's Supper, according to LC, is Christ's body and blood by virtue of His words of institution, which have been added to the bread and the wine.[34] If one wishes to use the Incarnation as a model here,[35] one could draw a parallel between the elements of the Lord's Supper and Christ as man, and another parallel between the Word and Christ as God, and permit Word and element to form a unity just as Christ, true God and true man, is one person. In LC's baptismal theology it was shown that a similar analogy could be applied rather well, but the situation is more complicated in the case of the Lord's Supper. The "this" in the phrase "This is My body" refers, according to Luther's exegesis, to the bread.[36] A sacramental union takes place between the bread and Christ's body, so that the Lord's Supper becomes Christ's body and

[32] Köstlin, I (1901), 481, and Grass (1954), pp. 150 f.

[33] 710:5-6 (LC V 12); 713:3 — von solchem Brot und Wein, das Christus' Leib und Blut ist (LC V 28).

[34] 711:13-15 (LC V 17). In the Latin translation *virtute verborum* reads *verbi* (LC V 18 and V 10).

[35] If it is possible to draw a parallel between Baptism and the Incarnation, the parallel between the Lord's Supper and the Incarnation is even clearer. Luther reflected upon this possibility in his *Vom Abendmahl Christi*, 1528 (WA 26, 443:12 ff.).

[36] WA 26, 445:9 — "Das ist mein Leib" mit dem wörtlich "Das" auffs brod zu deuten (*Vom Abendmahl Christi*, 1528).

blood under the bread and wine. The Word makes the bread and wine into Christ's body and blood by enabling Christ's resurrected body to be present in them and to unite itself with them.

This difference between Baptism and the Lord's Supper has its basis in Luther's Bible exegesis. The Bible says, "This is My body" with reference to the bread, and Luther could not overlook this. He explained the union between Christ's body and the bread and wine on the basis of the power-filled words of institution. When these words are applied to the elements, they accomplish what they say — not on the basis of the priest's authority to consecrate, but on the basis of the divine will, according to which God "connects his command with our speaking." [37] "If you take the Word away from the elements or view them apart from the Word, you have nothing but ordinary bread and wine. But if the words remain, as is right and necessary, then in virtue of them they are truly the body and blood of Christ. For as we have it from the lips of Christ, so it is; he cannot lie or deceive" (LC V 13). Christ's Word works what it says. Through the union with Christ's resurrected body the bread and wine of the Lord's Supper become the body and blood of Christ.

But just how does the Real Presence take place? The Confessions are extremely reticent on this point. Inasmuch as the Real Presence was considered inflexibly certain on the basis of the words of institution, and since transubstantiation could not be accepted for exegetical reasons, Luther took the position that Christ's resurrected body is in the bread of the Lord's Supper, even though the substance of the latter remains unchanged. Theologians commonly refer to this theory as consubstantiation.[38] The term is not found in the Confessions, however. FC [39] speaks about a sacramental union, *unio sacramentalis,* with direct reference to Luther's linguistic usage (WA 26, 445:8). For Luther the bread is united with Christ's body without ceasing to be bread.[40] But is it plausible to say, "This is My

[37] WA 26, 285:7, LW 37, 184; Diestelmann (1960), pp. 22 f.

[38] Cf. Vajta (1958), p. 95, n. 41 (lit.); Andrén (1954), p. 48; Grass (1954), p. 58. Vajta criticizes this terminology and insists that Luther did not use it. Aulén (1956) feels the same way, and Peters (1960), p. 97.

[39] 798:1 (Ep VII 7).

[40] WA 26, 445:2 — denn ob gleich leib und brod zwo unterschiedliche naturn sind ein igliche fur sich selbs, und wo sie von einander gescheiden sind, freylich keine die ander ist, Doch wo sie zu samen komen und ein neu, gantz wesen werden ist, da verlieren sie yhren unterscheid, so fern solch new, einig wesen betrifft, und wie sie ein ding werden und sind, also heisst und spricht man sie denn auch fur ein ding, das nicht von nöten ist, der zweyer eins untergehen

body" with regard to Christ's resurrected body in union with the bread? Luther said yes and referred to other similar forms of expression. One can, e. g., point without risk of misunderstanding to a purse with a hundred gold coins and say, "This is a hundred guilders." [41] To say, however, that money and purse form a "substance" would be more peculiar.[42] The philosophical concept of *substans* had, in general, an ontological meaning, and so Luther had to give it another content.[43]

But Christ, according to the Bible and the Apostles' Creed, is to be found "at the right hand of God the Father." How can He at the same time be in the bread of the Lord's Supper? Luther confronted this question in his controversy with the so-called "enthusiasts," who held to a spiritualizing concept of the Lord's Supper and rejected the Real Presence. In replying to their objections he referred to the doctrine of ubiquity, which was developed in his antispiritualistic writings between 1526 and 1528. This doctrine is not mentioned in LC and SA but is hinted at in FC in the references to Luther's polemical writings dating from the last half of the 1520s.[44] The doctrine of ubiquity means that the body of Christ can be everywhere present as a result of the communication of attributes. Since His human nature participates in the omnipresence of the divine nature, the human nature too is everywhere present. The assertion that Christ is seated at the right hand of God was not interpreted by Luther as referring to a specific locality; he rather understood it to be an expression of God's omnipotence and omnipresence. The doctrine of ubiquity provided Luther with a weapon to be used against the "enthusiasts." It allowed him to demonstrate the possibility of holding that "Christ's body and blood is at the same time in heaven and in the Lord's Supper." [45] In this doctrine Luther discovered a theoretical possibility of explaining the Real Presence; it had no additional significance.[46]

---

and zu nicht werden, sondern beide brod und leib bleibe (*Vom Abendmahl Christi,* 1528).

[41] WA 26, 444:1-21.

[42] WA 26, 443:29-31.

[43] P. W. Gennrich (1929), pp. 64 ff.; V. Vajta (1958), p. 95. Cf. above, Chapter Five, n. 51.

[44] 1005:1-18 (SD VII 91), and 1006:9-10 (SD VII 95).

[45] WA 23, 137:4 (*Dass diese Worte . . .* 1527). Cf. A. Peters (1960), p. 74, n. 36.

[46] In this I concur with B. Gollwitzer in *Theol. Aufsätze für Karl Barth* (1936), p. 289, and H. Grass (1954), pp. 59 f.

It is perfectly clear that Luther at first attached somewhat greater weight to the doctrine of ubiquity than he did in *Vom Abendmahl Christi* and in later works. The reason for his growing caution is also clear. The doctrine of ubiquity could easily lead to undesirable pantheistic consequences. But the risk of pantheism declined as it became more apparent that this doctrine served only to justify the possibility of Christ's body being present both in heaven and in the Lord's Supper. The words of institution tended to counterbalance the pantheistic tendencies. To the degree that their creative, power-filled nature became evident, the undesirable results of the doctrine of ubiquity diminished. If the words of institution did not include anything more than a promise concerning Christ's already existing presence in the bread and the wine, the risk of pantheism would obviously not have been avoided. The Word must effect the Real Presence in an objective manner, as is said in both LC and *Vom Abendmahl Christi*. The doctrine of ubiquity demonstrates the possibility of the Real Presence, but Christ's presence, according to the Confessions, is brought about through the power-filled words of institution, which, as seen above, have the character of words of consecration. When the Lord's Supper is celebrated according to Christ's institution, the Triune God is present to carry out His work. "So his word surely is not merely a word of imitation, but a word of power which accomplishes what it expresses." [47]

When the words of institution are read, the presence of Christ's body is effected, inasmuch as He in His Word has proclaimed this to be His will. But the words of institution are not only addressed to the bread and the wine; they are also addressed to the communicants in the form of a *promise*. The Lord's Supper is a fellowship, and it can never be celebrated unless there are communicants. It receives its character as a means of grace because it transmits a promise concerning the forgiveness of sins, and in this sense the Lord's Supper is also Gospel. One receives the gift of forgiveness through participation in the sacred act of the Lord's Supper.

The Confessions find the Word of promise in the words of institution, viz., "given for you," "shed for you." [48] As in Baptism, the promise is here related to the elements. The words of institution make the body of Christ present in the Lord's Supper, and at the same time

[47] WA 26, 283:4; LW 37, 181 (*Vom Abendmahl Christi*, 1528).

[48] 720:45-52 (LC V 64); 714:27-33 (LC V 34). The element of promise in the words of institution is overlooked in J. Diestelmann (1960). Cf. K. Haendler in ThLZ (1961), pp. 374—78.

they contain the assurance that Christ is here given for the forgiveness of sins. The words of institution contain the assurance both of the real presence of Christ in the Lord's Supper and of the fact that forgiveness of sins is afforded us as a gift. The Real Presence comes first, the gift is the result. If Christ were not present under the bread and wine, the Lord's Supper could not mediate forgiveness. Through the Word of promise the Lord's Supper is clearly directed to those who partake of it in faith; thus it has a functional significance.

In modern Protestant theology there is a clearly discernible tendency to emphasize one-sidedly the functional aspect of the Lord's Supper.[49] The stronger the stress upon the Word of promise, the more obvious this tendency becomes. This is in full harmony with the attempt to interpret the Gospel as nothing but oral proclamation, or to see in the Law merely a judging function or define it as salvation by one's own works. Such one-sided views lack support in the Confessions, and so it is misleading to look at the Lord's Supper only from the functional viewpoint of the forgiveness of sins. The Lord's Supper provides us with the assurance of forgiveness on the basis of the fact that God, through the Word of consecration, has made the bread and wine Christ's body and blood. The Word of promise therefore includes no assurance of the real presence of Christ in the Lord's Supper, but on the basis of the presence of Christ's body and blood the Lord's Supper promises us forgiveness.

LC provides us with a crystal-clear distinction between the essence of the Lord's Supper [50] and its effect (LC V 20 ff.). The essence of the Lord's Supper constitutes the basis and presupposition of its effect. Before LC can analyze the "power and use" of the Lord's Supper, it clarifies its essence. It is of no use to speak only about the treasures of the Lord's Supper, i. e., of its essence, or only of its effects; both facets are essential. "Yet, however great the treasure may be in itself, it must be comprehended in the Word and offered to us through the Word, otherwise we could never know of it or seek it." [51] The Word

---

[49] Vilmos Vajta ponders this tendency in a very pronounced way. To him [Luther] the decisive question was not the "how," but the "why" of the real presence, and he found the answer in the "for-us," that is, "for our salvation" (1958), p. 96.

[50] 709:22—711:20 (LC V 8 ff.). This passage is introduced with the significant question: Was ist nun das Sakrament des Altars?

[51] 713:20-23 (LC V 29); 713:8 — von solchem Brot und Wein, das Christus' Leib und Blut ist und die Wort bei sich hat (LC V 28). That the material here deals with a Word of promise is evident from the text in WA 29, 198:5—199:2 *(Predigten des Jahres 1529)*. See J. Meyer (1914), p. 158.

of promise assures us that the treasures of the Lord's Supper—forgiveness of sins, life, and salvation—are ours. Therefore the Lord's Supper includes "both truths, that it is Christ's body and blood and that these are yours as your treasure and gift." (LC V 29)

The words of institution have meaning both as creative words of command, words of consecration through which God makes the bread and the wine into Christ's body and blood, and as words of promise, through which He says to the Christian receiving Communion that the gifts are his possession. The Gospel's Word of promise must come to the body and blood of Christ under the bread and wine in the Lord's Supper. In the Sacrament of the Altar Christ's presence under bread and wine is united with the Word of promise—Christ's Gospel (the promise) is joined with the bread and the wine.[52] By referring as they did to the Word of promise, the Confessions sought to negate not only all ideas relative to *opus operatum,* but also the objections of the spiritualists, who denied the possibility of receiving forgiveness through the bread and wine of the Lord's Supper. Their counterargument was that Christ died on the cross, not in the Lord's Supper.[53] LC replied by drawing a parallel between what happened on the cross and what takes place in the Lord's Supper. The work of atonement was carried out on the cross, and there it was that forgiveness of sin was won for us. But apart from the preaching of the Word no one can share in what happened. "How should we know that this has been accomplished and offered to us if it were not proclaimed by preaching, by the oral Word?" (LC V 31). In the Lord's Supper, by analogy, we have knowledge of Christ's forgiveness only through the promise, which belongs to the Sacrament and is directed orally to every communicant. "Now, the whole Gospel and the article of the Creed, 'I believe in the holy Christian church, the forgiveness of sins,' are embodied in this sacrament and offered to us through the Word."[54] In the Lord's Supper we hear the same promise of the forgiveness of sin by grace for Christ's sake that we hear in all the other forms the Gospel takes. The Lord's Supper is God's work for our salvation.

[52] WA 29, 200:13 — suum evangelion ist an wein und brod gebunden *(Predigten des Jahres 1529).* The opinion quoted is involved in the hard-to-interpret section 713:31—714:11 (LC V 31 ff.).

[53] WA 29, 199:11 — Christus mortuus in cruce, non coena. Ideo remissio peccatorum est in cruce, non in coena *(Predigten des Jahres 1529);* 713:31 — Darümb ist's auch nichts geredt, dass sie sagen, Christus' Leib und Blut ist nicht im Abendmahl fur uns gegeben noch vergossen, drümb künnde man im Sakrament nicht Vergebunge der Sunde haben (LC V 31).

[54] 713:46 ff. (LC V 32). "The Word" here is the same as a Word of promise.

But as we have found, the gifts of the Lord's Supper must be received in faith. Here, as everywhere else in the Confessions, promise and faith are inextricably related. Christ's presence in the Lord's Supper is independent of man's faith, but the gifts of the Lord's Supper can be received only by those who come in faith (Ap XIII 18 ff.). Faith is an active power in the heart. It nourishes new impulses in the heart and gives new courage to the uneasy conscience.[55] The bread and wine received in faith are the medicine for soul and body that the Lord's Supper was designed to be. It is "a pure, wholesome, soothing medicine which aids and quickens us in both soul and body. For where the soul is healed, the body has benefited also" (LC V 68). Grass [56] reports on other similar statements, in which Luther in association with Irenaeus and Hilary of Poitiers speaks of the Lord's Supper as the medicine of immortality. But Grass harbors grave doubts about such expressions, for he feels they contradict the Reformation insight which holds that God approaches man in a personal and spiritual rather than in a physical way. It must be remembered, however, that the idea that the Lord's Supper is medicine for body and soul means only that the Lord's Supper, like Baptism (LC IV 43 ff.), saves the whole man from the powers of evil—"death and the devil and all evils." [57] The Lord's Supper has an eschatological meaning. The body will share in eternal life too. That which will be fully realized then begins now, when the Lord's Supper is received in faith.

Faith can have such an effect only if the Word of promise is true and if it continues to be valid. The great importance the Confessions attach to the words of institution is connected with both of these points. Since no one but God can forgive sins, it is significant that the promise is given by Him. The strength of the Sacrament depends on Christ's institution and promise. When Jesus says "given for you," He has in mind every communicant, regardless of time and place. All communicants are included in the divine promises through Jesus' Word; they are included in Jesus' self-giving on the cross. Dimensions of time and space no longer apply. At the altar the treasures are accessible, and all that is required of the communicant is that he receives and holds fast to the truthfulness of God's promise in faith.[58]

[55] 331:11 — Sacramentum institutum est ad consolandas et erigendas territas mentes, cum credunt carnem Christi datam pro vita mundi cibum esse, cum credunt se coniunctos Christo vivificari (Ap XX 10).

[56] H. Grass (1954), pp. 106—10. A. Peters (1960) is of a different opinion.

[57] 722:3-4 (LC V 70); A. Peters (1960), pp. 146—53. Cf. above, Chapter Seven, nn. 21—24; and E. Schlink (1961), 164 f.

[58] 714:23 f. and 43 ff. (LC V 33); 720:42—721:2 (LC V 64 f.).

Faith and promise belong together. The promise of the Lord's Supper is directed at man, who receives it by faith. Every celebration of the Lord's Supper presupposes Communion, for there must be communicants to whom the promise can be directed. The celebration of the Lord's Supper is an application of justification by faith. Every such service is useless if it does not succeed in healing frightened consciences,[59] or if with the Spirit's help it does not fight against the works of the flesh and bring about regeneration to a new life. *Mortificatio* and *vivificatio*,[60] death and resurrection, the Christian life in anxiety and faith—all belong to the Lord's Supper, in its extension, so to speak. The Lord's Supper has a practical, soul-curing purpose: it is a weapon in the struggle against sin. It is used in a completely erroneous manner when faith does not succeed in restoring frightened consciences to health so that the new life in the Spirit can grow. The celebration of the Sacrament of the Altar, done in remembrance of Christ, is not therefore the passive enjoyment of a drama or pageant. "It is rather the remembrance of Christ's blessings and the acceptance of them by faith, so that they make us alive" (Ap XXIV 72). Faith is the spiritual power which regenerates the heart and provides righteousness before God. In the emphasis on the connection between the Lord's Supper as promise and faith we also find a strong polemic against the Catholic *opus operatum* teaching. The Mass must be Communion; it requires a worshiping congregation which in faith accepts the Word of promise.

Catholic theology, as we have seen, employed the *opus operatum* concept in an effort to stress the objective nature of the sacraments. God uses them as "instrumental causes," wholly independent of the spiritual qualifications of minister or recipient. The Lutheran Confessions do not, however, discuss this facet of the *opus operatum* doctrine; they rather give it a different interpretation. They conceive of the mass as an independent, justifying act. It is capable of *ex opere operato* gaining grace for those for whom it is said, whether they are present or not; [61] it can even be said for the dead (Ap XXIV 89 ff.). The

---

[59] 369:41 — inutilis est ceremonia, nisi fides accedat, quae vere statuat hic offeri remissionem peccatorum. Et haec fides erigit contritas mentes (Ap XXIV 70).

[60] 360:1-3 (Ap XXIV 34); 361:47-48 (Ap XXIV 39); 370:10-11 (Ap XXIV 71).

[61] 351:35 — quod missa ex opere operato conferat gratiam, aut applicata pro aliis mereatur eis remissionem venialium et mortalium peccatorum, culpae et poenae (Ap XXIV 9). According to Ap XXIV 10, this was the main question, the vortex of the controversy.

misuses which accompanied the many private Masses originated with such ideas, which were in turn based on the erroneous supposition that the Mass is a sacrifice distinct from Christ's sacrifice on Golgotha. The Mass became a meritorious achievement, which was thought to remove the sins both of the living and the dead.

The Confessions had no trouble in criticizing this supposed Catholic point of view. They said first of all that the *opus operatum* idea was in conflict with the Scriptural teaching that Christ had given Himself as a sacrifice once and for all (Heb. 9:12). In the second place, they contended that this idea contradicted the doctrine of justification. The concept of the Mass as a sacrifice is incompatible with what the Bible says about sacrifice and justification (AC XXIV 24 ff.). Christ alone is the sacrificial gift, *hostia,* and His death is the only sacrifice that can make atonement.

One can find a covert critique of the concept of the Mass as sacrifice as early as AC III 3: Christ was "a sacrifice not only for original sin but also for all other sins." [62] This criticism is developed at length in the rest of the confessional writings. The *opus operatum* concept of the Mass shunts faith aside (AC XXIV 29); through the sacrifice of the Mass men think they can bring about atonement and procure the grace that forgives sin (SA II II 7). Lacking Biblical support, the Mass becomes a human work in the service of work-piety, as is true in general of all forms of worship that are established without God's command [63] and promise. The sacrifice becomes our attempt to draw near to God; it is "a ceremony or act which we render to God to honor him" (Ap XXIV 18). According to the Confessions, there is a fundamental contradiction between *sacramentum,* which is God's work and gift to us, and *sacrificium,* which is our work and gift to God (Ap XXIV 16 ff.). To make the Lord's Supper into a sacrifice involves the elimination of this important boundary line between two completely different acts of worship. A worship service is supposed to be a meeting place between God and man; God comes there to provide us with His gifts. A worship service is a *sacramentum;* justification by faith functions within it.[64] The contrast between *sacramentum* and *sacrificium* is a consequence of the difference between New Testament justification and non-Biblical work-righteousness.

[62] 54:10-12 (AC III 3). See above, Chapter Four. The term used here for sacrifice is *hostia.*

[63] 373:41 — Neque vero est leve peccatum, tales cultus sine mandato Dei, sine exemplo scripturae in ecclesia instituere (Ap XXIV 89).

[64] Cf. Regin Prenter in *Kerygma und Dogma* (1955), p. 45.

The Lutheran Symbols based their critique of sacrifice on the inappropriate presupposition that the sacrifice of the Mass must be entirely separate from Jesus' sacrifice on the cross. Jesus offered Himself there once and for all, but in the Mass He is offered anew every day. There is no inner connection between these two events. As a result, the Symbols emphasized that only the death of Christ, *sola mors Christi,* reconciles us with God, and this was their chief objection to the concept of the Mass as sacrifice. Justification is ours for the sake of Christ's sacrificial death, and not by the power of the Mass, *ex opere missae.*[65] Passages from Hebrews seemed to provide an effective argument in support of the Evangelical position: Christ "entered once for all into the Holy Place . . . securing an eternal redemption" (9:12), and "by a single offering He has perfected for all time those who are sanctified." (10:14) [66]

As Prenter [67] has shown, the Reformation's critique in the Lutheran Confessions is built upon presuppositions which are no longer valid. For contemporary Catholic theologians it is self-evident that the Mass is not a new, independent sacrifice; it is only an actualizing of Christ's sacrifice on the cross, which the worshiping congregation can share in here and now. Iserloh [68] puts it this way, that the sacrifice of the Mass signifies a re-presentation, *Gegenwartigsetzung,* of the sacrifice on the cross. In this view the Mass does not, therefore, repeat Christ's sacrifice, but the latter is sacramentally present in the form of a meal using bread and wine. The development of such ideas has also led to the result that Evangelical theology has come to reveal a greater understanding of the sacrificial motif in the Lord's Supper.[69] So the question is: Did the Lutheran Symbols base their critique on a correct understanding of Catholic doctrine?

Catholic theologians take widely divergent attitudes toward the Protestant critique. Clark is entirely unable to understand the difficulties the reformers had with the concept of the Mass as sacrifice. As he sees it, their conception of the Mass as a renewed sacrifice was based on a misunderstanding which they should have been able to

[65] 356:7 (Ap XXIV 23); 94:13 (AC XXIV 29).

[66] 93:28—94:3 (AC XXIV 26 f.); 355:20-22 (Ap XXIV 22).

[67] R. Prenter in KuD (1955), pp. 46—48.

[68] E. Iserloh in *Abendmahl und Opfer* (1960), pp. 83 and 97. Cf. E. Schlink (1961), pp. 159 ff.

[69] With regard to the sacrifice motif in the Lord's Supper see Gustaf Aulén (1956); Hermann Sasse (1959); P. Meinhold (1960); Laurenthal, *The Eucharist as Sacrifice in the Faith and Order Movement* (1968).

avoid if they had had a correct insight into the contemporary teaching of the Mass as sacrifice. Two of the leading pre-Reformation theologians, Gabriel Biel and Cardinal Cajetan, had clearly stated that the sacrifice of the cross and that of the Mass are the same sacrifice. There is no question here about two separate sacrifices, but of one and the same, made once in a bloody manner and now in an unbloody manner.[70]

Iserloh presents a different point of view. He studied the polemic theology of the Reformation era for many years and discovered that the theologians involved never spoke of the Lord's Supper as a representation of Christ's sacrifice on Golgotha. They never succeeded in answering the objections to the idea of the Mass as another sacrifice, distinct from Christ's sacrificial act carried out once and for all.[71] "In spite of all zeal and efforts the controversial theologians of the 16th century . . . did not succeed in fully explaining the Catholic doctrine and thus giving Luther a sufficient answer to his difficulties." [72] Iserloh is of the opinion that the Protestant critique was justified, inasmuch as Catholic theology, under the influence of nominalism, did not give full expression to the connection between Christ's sacrifice on Golgotha and its sacramental presence in the Lord's Supper.

This is confirmed by a study of the historical material. Nicholas Herborn, who used Biblical material exclusively in his *Enchiridion,* did not succeed in demonstrating a unity. He definitely held fast to the idea that the same Christ is offered up both on the cross and in the Mass,[73] but he did not confront the objection which held that the sacrifice of the cross could not be repeated. It is interesting to note that Herborn did not in any way discuss the important Heb. 9:12 and 10:14 passages. The authors of the Confutation emphasized the Mass as sacrifice in such terms that accusations of teaching a renewed sacrifice could not be avoided.[74]

Suspicions about a repetition of Christ's sacrifice were heightened by the fact that the Confutation adduced Old Testament texts along-

---

[70] F. Clark (1960), pp. 73—98, 243—68, and 314—18.

[71] E. Iserloh (1950), pp. 144 ff. — Wegen seiner ungenügenden Argumentation fanden die Prostestanten bei Eck auf einen gewichtigen Einwand keine befriedigende Antwort, p. 148.

[72] E. Iserloh (1952), p. 59.

[73] N. Herborn, *Enchiridion,* 70:2 — Nam idem Christus est, immo eiusdem oblatio quamvis alio atque alio modo.

[74] CR 27, 150 — Quod iterum [adversarii] insinuant in Missa Christum non efferri . . . omnino reiiciendum est (Confutation, 1530).

side New Testament ones without distinguishing between them and without taking a position in regard to what Hebrews says about Christ's once and for all sacrifice. According to the Confutation, the Hebrews texts referred only to the sacrifice on the cross. Once and for all Christ was offered up on the cross; daily He is offered up in the Mass as a sacramental, peace-creating sacrifice.[75] Biblical support for this was taken from, among other places, the prophets Malachi and Daniel! Eck set forth the same arguments. What Iserloh says about the untenable nature of Eck's reasoning also applies to the Confutation in its defense of the Catholic point of view. In Hebrews Christ's one unique sacrifice is set over against the many sacrifices in the Old Testament. Christ's sacrifice made all others superfluous.[76]

Since, therefore, the Lutheran Confessions' critique of a renewed and repeated sacrifice was based on a position which many Catholic theologians would not recognize, the criticism can no longer be maintained in its traditional form. Still there is a radical difference of opinion between Catholics and Evangelicals with regard to the entire nature of worship. According to the Catholic position, the fruits of Christ's sacrificial death accrue to man not primarily because they are received in faith, but because Mass is said. We must certainly add that the element of fellowship is strongly accented even in Catholic theology, so that a congregation of the faithful, actively cooperating with the priest in the presentation of Christ's one sacrifice, is presupposed. Nevertheless, practices such as saying Masses for the dead reveal that the actualizing of the sacrifice of Christ in the Mass has a very special meaning for Catholics. Through the sacrifice of the Mass the unique sacrifice of Christ is made available every day, so that unlimited grace comes to the church and mankind. The Eucharist is therefore the center of the church's life. The sacrifice of the Mass stands in the most intimate relationship with the mystery of the Incarnation. God's eternal love, which in the fulness of time took visible expression in Christ's incarnation, continues in the life of the church and attains its zenith in the Mass, where the sacrifice of Christ is made present and effective through the priest (as Christ's ordained servant) and the

[75] CR 27, 155 — Tantum ergo semel oblatus est in cruce, effuso sanguine; hodie effertur in Missa, ut hostia pacifica et sacramentalis (Confutation, 1530).

[76] E. Iserloh (1950), p. 145 — Auf den Einwand seiner Gegner, Paulus stellte den vielen, immer wiederholten Opfern des AT aber doch das eine Opfer schlechthin, neben dem es fürderhin kein anderes Opfer mehr geben solle, gegenüber, auf diesen sicher schwerwiegenden und ernst zu nehmenden Einwand gegen das Messopfer geht Eck überhaupt nicht ein. Hätte er das versucht, dann wäre die Haltlosigkeit seiner Beweisführung deutlich geworden.

congregation.[77] Christ's sacrifice is not something that belongs to the past; it belongs to the present. As Christ became man, men must be active in the actualizing of Christ's sacrifice. They form, so to speak, an extension of Christ's human nature.

This reasoning is related to two fundamental Catholic principles: mediation and cooperation.[78] Salvation comes to man through visible and tangible means in analogy with the Christ who became man to mediate God's grace. The church, through the priest and the congregation, must now cooperate in this event. The Mass is understood as an *opus operatum* which mediates grace to those who do not interpose a hindrance. It is an instrument of God's salvation; through it the sacrifice of the cross is made available to all men in all ages.[79]

The Lutheran Confessions also teach that Christ's sacrifice can be said to be present in the Lord's Supper in and with the fact that He is present with His promise of forgiveness under the bread and the wine. Schlink says: "The same Christ who once gave his body on Calvary now gives his body in the Lord's Supper and this makes us contemporaneous with his death on the cross." He also speaks of "the identity of the giving of the body, once on the cross and now in the Lord's Supper." [80] It was equally clear to the confessional writers that Christ's work of atonement is of no value to anyone apart from the external mediation of the Word and sacraments. But they rejected the idea of the Mass as a good work which conveys salvation simply because it is read. They had no understanding for the Roman ideas of mediation and cooperation. God has not bound His salvatory work to any human activity; He rather uses men as instruments for His own work. The church is not some kind of intermediate authority cooperating with God. God Himself carries out His own work through men who obey His commands. God is the active one; man is merely a tool used for His purposes. Man or the church can never cooperate

---

[77] K. Algermissen (1957), pp. 255 f.; P. E. Persson (1961), p. 78; F. Clark (1960), pp. 350 ff. Clark is mistaken, however, in his judgment of Luther, who did not deny "the objective value of the sacraments," p. 351. Our presentation shows what is misleading about Clark's point of view.

[78] F. Clark (1960), pp. 105 ff. The English terms are "mediation and participation." E. Iserloh in *Abendmahl und Opfer* (1960), pp. 99, 105, and 109. P. E. Persson (1961), pp. 14 ff.

[79] F. Clark (1960), pp. 105 f. — In this economy of mediation through the church, the Mass is a principal instrument of Christ's saving action. Through its Eucharistic counterpart the sacrifice of the cross is made available for all men in all succeeding ages. Cf. Clark, p. 346.

[80] E. Schlink (1961), pp. 160 and 161.

with God; they can only carry out His mandate. But God comes to individual believers through the Word of promise He has attached to the Lord's Supper. It can therefore never be used to benefit others, but must be received in faith by those who hold fast to the truth of God's promises.

Chapter Eight:

Penitence

All the reformers were agreed in attaching great importance to penitence. Ap even calls it "the principal doctrine of the Christian faith" (XXIV 46), an honor usually accorded to justification. Indeed, there is a close relationship between penitence and justification.[1]

In the Lutheran Symbols the doctrine of penitence is highly complicated, however, as a closer look reveals. This is true in part because they attach various meanings to it, and in part because its status as a sacrament was uncertain. In conformity with the two uncontested sacraments, Baptism and the Lord's Supper, penitence was looked upon as God's work in man, condemning him through the Law and restoring him via the Gospel (the Promise). As such, penitence was another expression of the Law and the Gospel in function. This point of view was emphasized with equal weight in the confessional documents written by Luther and those written by Melanchthon, and it contributed to some extent to the dissolution of the old sacrament of penance, which the reformers criticized as man's work instead of God's. The Reformation developed not least of all as a result of the controversy with the medieval sacrament of penance.

Penance had had a long history before its content was clarified at the Council of Florence in 1439.[2] Like all of the Catholic sacraments, it had its matter and form, *materia* and *forma*. As far as its *materia* is concerned, one can speak only in a figurative sense, *quasi materia,* for it is constituted not of a thing but of the act of penance, i. e., the penitent's contrition, *contritio,* confession, *confessio,* and his satisfaction for sin, *satisfactio.* The *forma* consists of the absolution granted by the priest. The sacrament's effect, *effectus,* is the forgiveness of sin through priestly absolution.

As a consequence of the principles named in the previous chapter concerning mediation and participation in regard to Christ's work of

---

[1] 263:23 — Sunt enim loci maxime cognati, doctrina poenitentiae et doctrina iustificationis (Ap XII 59).

[2] Pope Eugene IV's bull *Exultate Deo,* Nov. 22, 1439. Mirbt (1924), pp. 236 f.; Denz., p. 699. Concerning the history of penance see B. Poschmann (1940); E. Roth (1952); L. Klein (1961).

salvation, the Catholic Church looks upon the priest functioning in the sacrament of penance as Christ's representative and deputy. He is equipped with Christ's authority both to bind and to loose. In the sacrament of penance he exercises the jurisdictional authority bound up in the pastoral office. At Christ's command and in His stead the priest absolves the penitent from sin and decides what he will have to do to make satisfaction. The priest fulfills through his person and in his office the charge once given by Christ to His apostles (John 20:22 f.) to possess the key which binds and looses. He has received from Christ the authority to absolve, *auctoritatem absolvendi,* and the need to make satisfaction is levied according to the priest's judgment, *arbitrium.* On the basis of his examination the sinner is declared free of guilt and is obligated to make satisfaction.

The Lutheran Confessions rejected this view of penance. But the antithesis between the Catholic and the Evangelical views does not lie where people have often wanted to find it, opposing Rome's tripartite division of penance (contrition, confession, and satisfaction) with the reformers' twofold division (contrition and faith).[3] The antithesis is deeper than this. Apart from the fact that talk about the Catholic tripartite division of penance is erroneous, inasmuch as it omits absolution, the antithesis is based upon a completely different view of penitence. According to the Evangelical position, repentance is God's direct work in man without human mediation or cooperation; according to the Roman Catholic position penance is a divine work in which the priest joins as an intermediate authority. Forgiveness of sin is given to the penitent not directly for Christ's sake, but on the basis of the authority Christ has given to His servant, the priest, to bind and to loose. This antithesis permeates all the forms in which penitence appears in Evangelical theology.

In the Lutheran Confessions penitence has both a sacramental and a nonsacramental form. While AC and Ap refer to *sacramentum*

---

[3] This point of view from L. Grane (1959), p. 112. Grane writes thus: "Early in the middle ages, the three-fold division of the sacrament became common, and at the council of Florence Pope Eugene IV fixed this as follows: the contrition of heart *(cordis contritio),* the confession of the mouth *(oris confessio),* and the satisfaction made for sin *(satisfactio pro peccatis)* according to the judgment of the priest. With that the tripartite division became the teaching of the church." This division has to do with the act of penitence, and not with the sacrament of penance; the latter also includes absolution. The same misunderstanding was also expressed in *De captivitate babylonica,* 1520 (WA 6, 544:22-25), and frequently during the time of the Reformation. There was talk of the three parts of penance even in Catholic circles (e. g., Denz., p. 745).

poenitentiae,[4] LC looks upon penitence as nothing other than a consequence of Baptism; it is simply Baptism in function.[5] Confession,
after all, is also involved in the act of penitence, and Luther (if possible)
attaches even greater weight to confession than Melanchthon does—
though neither considers it to be a sacrament. What the Lutheran
Symbols have done, in brief, is this: they have divided the medieval
sacrament of penance into three different parts which, although they
do in fact belong together under the concept of penitence, yet must be
distinguished: penitence as existential act, penitence as sacrament,
and penitence as confession.

That such a division could be possible is related to something that
was well known to both Gratian and the young Luther. Penance had
both an inner and an outer side. Men spoke of *poenitentia interior,*
i. e., the contrition of the heart, and *poenitentia exterior,* i. e., the
outer expression of the inner penitence in the form of an ecclesiastical
act.[6] As divine act in us and with us, the Evangelical concept of penitence therefore received both an existential and a sacramental meaning.
On the one hand, it is an expression of the Christian way of living.
A Christian life means a life of contrition and faith, *contritio et fides.*
But penitence can also be understood as God's means of restoring the
oppressed conscience. The main point is then shifted from contrition
and faith to absolution from sin, which is the presupposition of faith.
As seen from this point of view, penitence in AC and Ap has a sacramental meaning. Finally, penitence can include pastoral aspects, and
it is at this point that confession comes into view. The Evangelical
concept of penitence as it appears in the Symbols can therefore be
looked upon partly as a description of the Christian life, partly as
a sacrament, partly as confession. To avoid misunderstandings about

---

[4] 259:18-19 (Ap XII 41); 292:24-27 (Ap XIII 4).

[5] 705:47—706:25 (LC IV 74 ff.). A similar point of view can be found as
early as in *De captivitate babylonica,* 1520 (WA 6, 528:13-16).

[6] *Decr. Grat.,* II, De poenitentia, d.1, c.87 — Est enim poenitentia alia interior, alia exterior. Interior poenitentia est illa, de qua Augustinus ait: "Omnis
qui suae voluntatis arbiter est constitutus, non potest inchoare novam vitam, nisi
poeniteat eum veteris vitae." Item de eadem Petrus in Actibus Apostolorum
(2:38) legitur dixisse. . . . De exteriori vero poenitentia Ambrosius ait super
epistolam ad Romanos: "Gratis Dei in baptismate non requirit gemitum vel
planctum, non opus aliquod, sed solam confessionem cordis, et omnia gratis
condonat." WA 1, 98:24 — Duplex est poenitentia, scilicet signi et rei. Rei est
illa interior cordis et sola vera poenitentia, de qua Christus dicit: Poenitentia
agite, et Petrus Act 3[:19]: Poenitemini et convertimini. Signi est illa exterior,
quae frequenter est facta, cum illa interior sit ficta saepe, et haec habet duas illas
partes: Confessionem et satisfactionem (*Sermo de indulgentiis,* 1516). L. Klein
(1961), p. 11; H. A. Oberman (1963), p. 159.

this division, one must never forget that we are here constantly dealing with an action in which God crushes man through the Law and restores him through the Gospel.

Penitence as the Christian Way of Living

Supported by Scripture, the Symbols refer to penitence first of all as inner repentance, *poenitentia interior,* the act of penitence itself as an expression of the Christian way of living. The Christian lives his life in continual repentance. With Luther, "the Confessions understand penitence as 'the whole of human existence,' which includes both a repudiation of sin and a complete turning towards God." [7]

Penitence in this sense has two parts, contrition and faith, in connection with such New Testament passages as Mark 1:15, "repent, and believe in the Gospel," and Luke 24:47, "that repentance and forgiveness of sins should be preached in His name to all nations." [8] The fruits of penitence could be added as a third part to these two, but the Symbols do not consider it necessary to do so, since both contrition and faith produce renewal.[9] Penitence consists, properly, of contrition and faith.

The first part of the act of repentance is contrition, which has two characteristics. First of all, it is God's work and achievement in us. It is not something we do out of love for God or out of fear of His punishment; it is God's work in us through the Law. As SA says of contrition, "This is not *activa contritio* (artificial remorse), but *passiva contritio* (true sorrow of the heart, suffering, and pain of death)." [10] In contrition man is therefore the object of God's judging power. In the second place, contrition is understood as the terrors of a conscience frightened by God's judgment.[11] Both of these major points of view tell us that penitence must be understood as God's work in us. The origins of contrition rest with God; God is the active cause of contrition, not its object. God's activity does not, however, take place outside of us, but rather, so to speak, in our inner being. This means that contrition can be evaluated both theologically and psychologically.

[7] E. Kinder in EKL, I, 636.

[8] 260:4-6 (Ap XII 46); 257:23-25 (Ap XII 30); 437:13-14 (SA III III 4); 437:21-23 (SA III III 6). In all of these instances the Latin *poenitentia* is used for repentance.

[9] 257:4-8 (Ap XII 28); 67:8 — Deinde sequi debent bona opera, quae sunt fructus poenitentiae (AC XII 6).

[10] 437:2-3 (SA III III 2).

[11] 257:11 — dicimus contritionem esse veros terrores conscientiae, quae Deum sentit irasci peccato et dolet se pecasse (Ap XII 29).

Theologically speaking, it is God's work through the Law; psychologically it is profound grief, the pangs of death, and an anxious conscience.

In strongly emphasizing contrition as God's judging work in man, and in referring to it as *contritio passiva,* a contrition which man suffers and endures under the wrath of God, the Symbols conceive of it in complete analogy with Christian righteousness, *iustitia Dei passiva,* which is God's gift and not man's active accomplishment.[12] Luther associated his discovery of *iustitia Dei* with his study of Rom. 1:17. Other Biblical concepts also tell us that God is the active one, man the passive recipient. This holds true of such expressions as God's work, *opus Dei,* His wisdom, power, and Word, "which He works and speaks in us, according to the clear statement of Paul in Rom. 1:16-17."[13] In the sacraments God is the active one; He carries out His judging work through the Law, and His saving work through the Gospel. It therefore seems natural also to conceive of contrition as God's work in man.

The Reformation developed in controversy with Occamism's practice of penance, according to which the act of penance is a presupposition for absolution and a preparation for it. Contrition is an act of the will, with various stages and forms. *Contritio* was the designation for the perfect contrition of love for God, and *attritio* for the imperfect contrition based on fear of God. What Occamism demanded under all circumstances as the presupposition for forgiveness was the abomination of past sins, *detestatio peccati,* sorrow for having committed them, and the will to sin no more, *nolle peccare.*[14] *Contritio* emerges out of love for God. In harmony with the Catholic theory concerning man's cooperation with God in salvation, this kind of contrition should not have been understood as a purely natural act, but both as something caused by supernatural grace and also as something man achieves. Contrition presupposes faith in Christ, asserted the Confutation.[15] But according to Gabriel Biel, an Occamist, it is a natural act. Biel spoke about man's ability to produce by his own efforts that love and

[12] WA 54, 185:12—186:20 (*Praefatio,* 1545). Cf. above, Chapter Three, part 3.

[13] WA 10 I, 2, 37:5-6 (*Adventspostille,* 1522); WA 54, 186:10-13 (*Praefatio,* 1545).

[14] C. Feckes (1925), 60—64. For more on the concept *attritio* in Biel see H. A. Oberman (1963), pp. 152, 460, and 464. See also 256:7-14 (Ap XII 18 ff.); 439:18—440:4 (SA III III 16).

[15] CR 27, 111 — fidem praeviam esse poenitentiae: nisi enim quis crediderit, non poenitebit (Confutation, 1530).

contrition which are the presupposition of the forgiveness of sins.[16]

The young Luther opposed this Occamist position, and the Symbols also criticized it sharply.[17] Because of the depths of sin's depravity man is unable even with the help of grace, and much less so on his own, to prepare himself for the reception of the forgiveness of sins. One result of Luther's difficulties with *contritio* was that he turned his attention to God and came to look upon contrition as God's work in man and not as a human achievement. One can trace Luther's development in his lectures on the Psalms (1513 – 15), for here, on the basis of the tropological interpretation of the Bible, he identified the Biblical *iudicium Dei* with Christian contrition (WA 3, 29:9 ff.). This means that Scriptural statements about God's judgment, *iudicium Dei*, are directed first of all to the judgment which God pronounced upon the crucified Christ and then upon the Christian man. The cross of Christ reveals the meaning of God's judgment, but what happened to Christ on Golgotha is repeated in a spiritual way in the life of the Christian. According to Romans 6 and 8 the Christian must die with Christ in order to arise with Him in Baptism and faith. The judgment of God which overtakes the old man in this life, resulting in the death of fleshly deeds, was identified by Luther with man's repentance.[18] In other words, man's contrition is God's work, in analogy with *iustitia Dei* in the sense of man's faith effected by God through the Holy Spirit.[19]

The Symbols set forth a similar view. Man's contrition is God's work in him; it is an expression of how God puts the old man to death so that the new man can arise and live. A significant Biblical foundation for this point of view is found (as we have seen) in Is. 28:21, where a distinction is drawn between God's alien work, *opus alienum,* and His proper work, *opus proprium.* God's alien work is seen in the activity of the Law, whereby man's conscience is tormented because of sin.[20] Contrition as God's work in man can also be referred to as

16 R. Seeberg, III (1930), pp. 538—40; C. Feckes (1925), pp. 27—39, 57, 73 (n. 216), and 80; H. A. Oberman (1963), pp. 153—57; Th. M. McDonough (1963), pp. 32—45.

17 267:3-15 (Ap XII 75); 440:17 (SA III III 17).

18 WA 3, 463:15-20 (*Dictata super psalterium,* 1513—15); E. Vogelsang (1929), pp. 122—29; A. Gyllenkrok (1952), pp. 32—35; A. Brandenburg (1960); L. Klein (1961), p. 28.

19 WA 3, 463:1 — Iustitia tropologice est fides Christi (*Dictata super psalterium,* 1513—15).

20 261:22 — Et Esaie 28: Dominus irascetur, ut faciat opus suum. Alienum est opus eius, ut operatur opus suum (Ap XII 51). See above, Chapter Three,

mortification, God putting the old man to death. The Symbols look upon 1 Sam. 2:6, "The Lord kills and brings to life; He brings down to Sheol and raises up," or Romans 6, where we read of the death of the old man through Baptism, as Biblical verification of the Christian's experience in penitence.[21] Contrition is God's work in man. When Luther groups Baptism and penitence together in LC, the reason is the same. Baptism as God's work must be continued (figuratively speaking) throughout one's entire life; this daily baptism is daily repentance. "This act or observance consists in being dipped into the water, which covers us completely, and being drawn out again. These two parts, being dipped under the water and emerging from it, indicate the power and effect of Baptism, which is simply the slaying of the old Adam and the resurrection of the new man, both of which actions must continue in us our whole life long. Thus a Christian life is nothing else than a daily Baptism, once begun and ever continued" (LC IV 65). "What is repentance but an earnest attack on the old man and an entering upon a new life? If you live in repentance, therefore, you are walking in Baptism, which not only announces this new life but also produces, begins, and promotes it." (LC IV 75)

Contrition is God's work in man, accomplished through the Law. The judgment of conscience is identical with contrition. Contrition cannot therefore be a human presupposition for the forgiveness of sins, but it is God's work through the Word of the Law in man's inner being.[22] After the fall into sin, Adam was reproached and his conscience knew fear. David was accused by Nathan for his sin with Bathsheba, and he was filled with dread of God's wrath and judgment. This, according to the Lutheran Symbols, is contrition,[23] i. e., God's work in man through the Law, not man's work. The contrite man is conscious of God's wrath; he becomes aware of God's judgment upon his old life. God's activity is not mediated through man's cooperation, neither does He accomplish it directly; He rather uses the preaching of the Law as the means whereby He works. The mediatory element is found in the Word, which convicts us of sin. Theologically speaking, contrition is God's work in man; psychologically speaking, man experi-

part 1. The teachings of *opus alienum* and *opus proprium* originated with the Reformation and were characteristic of it.

[21] 260:28—261:37 (Ap XII 46 ff.)

[22] 260:56 — lex est verbum, quod arguit et condemnat peccata (Ap XII 48). For more information see the entire section 260:53—261:3 (Ap XII 48), and above, Chapter Three, part 1.

[23] 262:11-13 (Ap XII 55); 262:26-28 (Ap XII 56).

ences contrition as a tormented conscience, *terrores conscientiae*.[24] Contrition is man's reaction to the preaching of God's wrath in the Law. (SA III III 33-35). It is something that man, as a result of his sin, must endure; it is a *contritio passiva*.

That contrition is identified with an anguished conscience is related—as we have seen—to the opposition to Occamism's doctrine of *contritio*. Contrition is not under any circumstances a disposition for grace. Because he is held in thrall by sin, man cannot by himself produce genuine contrition. He cannot depend upon his own will. SA is of the opinion that "the false repentance of the papists" is based on the erroneous idea that man possesses unbroken powers which enable him to be genuinely penitent, that by using his reason and will properly he is able to avoid sin, and that theoretically he can therefore stand without guilt before God. But this is sophistry, based on a false conception of sin. None is righteous, all are full of "unbelief, blindness, and ignorance of God and God's will" (SA III III 32). When God works proper repentance within us through the preaching of the Law, we learn to understand "that we are all utterly lost, that from head to foot there is no good in us, that we must become altogether new and different men" (SA III III 35). Total judgment falls upon our lives through the preaching of the Law.[25] There is nothing in ourselves that we can point to or claim. In SA's description of contrition as an anguished conscience there is no room for psychological nuances, no room for a question about man's responsibility for his deeds. Evil desire is sin whether sanctioned by the will or not.[26]

Lutheran anthropology and the doctrine of the affections make their presence felt here. Since man, because his affections come into play, is unable to fulfill God's demands in the First Table of the Law, his entire life is under judgment. From the Law he must hear this judgment: "You are all of no account. Whether you are manifest sinners or saints, you must all become other than you now are and do otherwise than you now do, no matter who you are and no matter how great, wise, mighty, and holy you may think yourselves. Here no one is godly" (SA III III 3). All men stand under God's judgment; Scrip-

[24] 67:2 — contritio seu terrores incussi conscientiae (AC XII 4); 168:59 (Ap IV 45); 188:16 f. (Ap IV 142); 257:12 f. (Ap XII 29); 257:39 and 49 (Ap XII 31 and 34).

[25] 282:36 — Sed isti [the adversaries] fingunt legem Dei contentam esse externa et civili iustitia, non vident eam requirere veram dilectionem Dei ex toto corde, etc., damnare totam concupiscentiam in natura. Itaque nemo tantum facit, quantum lex requirit (Ap XII 142).

[26] 438:8-18 (SA III III 10); 166:43-45 (Ap IV 35).

ture has included everything human in sin, so that God's gift through Christ should be all the more abundant. (Gal. 3:22; Ap XII 81)

In addition to the just-mentioned anthropology, there are exegetical and dogmatic reasons for looking upon contrition as God's total judgment upon man. The exegetical reasons are found in the reformers' interpretation of what the Bible says about the judgment of God. *De his terroribus loquitur Scriptura* — "Scripture speaks of these terrors," especially in the Psalter and in the prophets (Ap XII 31). The dogmatic reason is found in justification by faith. We can be released from sin only through faith in the promise concerning forgiveness. There is also a pastoral motif here: No one with a tormented conscience can find forgiveness in anything other than God's mercy in Christ. It was the intention of the reformers to turn men's attention away from themselves and to Christ. When experiencing a truly anguished conscience, man is unable to determine whether his contrition has originated in an upright heart — he cannot tell if the motivation is fear of punishment or love for God.[27] Thus it was that Lutheranism drew a heavy line through all such questions. Contrition as a conscience anguished over sin is God's total judgment over all things human.

But at the same time contrition, just like faith, is understood as an activity that takes place in man. Although it is *contritio passiva,* man is not entirely passive. He can examine himself and come to see that he is guilty of transgressing God's law. Defining contrition as *contritio passiva* does not exclude man's involvement. To better understand this, we can take a look at the exposition of Col. 2:14 in Ap XII 48: "Paul says in Col. 2:14 that Christ cancels the bond which stood against us with its legal demands. Here, too, there are two parts, the bond and the cancellation of the bond. The bond is the conscience denouncing and condemning us; it is the voice that says with David (II Sam. 12:13), 'I have sinned against the Lord.' Wicked and smug men do not say this seriously, for they neither see nor read the sentence of the law written in their hearts. The sentence is understood only amid genuine sorrows and terrors. The bond therefore is contrition itself, condemning us." [28]

---

[27] 254:21 — Quando autem territa conscientia praesertim in seriis, veris et illis magnis terroribus, qui describuntur in psalmis ac prophetis et quos certe degustant isti, qui vere convertuntur, iudicare poterit, utrum Deum propter se timeat, an fugiat aeternas poenas? (Ap XII 9); 257:8-11 (Ap XII 29).

[28] 260:53 — Et deinde in Colossensibus inquit, Christum delere chirographum, quod per legem adversatur nobis. Hic quoque duae sunt partes, chirographum et deletio chirographi. Est autem chirographum conscientia arguens et condemnans nos. Porro lex est verbum, quod arguit et condemnat peccata. Haec igitur vox,

Melanchthon here intended to show that the judgment of conscience is the same as contrition and that it manifests itself in the
form of self-accusation: "I have sinned." Even though contrition is
God's work, man is able to see that he has not fulfilled what God requires in His law. David is the standard Biblical example of a man
brought to recognize sin as a result of God's judgment. David was
reproached by God after he committed sin. He was aware of the judgment of conscience in his inner being, and this necessitated a confession of sin: *Peccavi Domino,* I have sinned against the Lord.[29]
SC IV 20 permits the Ten Commandments to serve as a mirror of
confession in connection with the examination of conscience. Contrition can therefore take the form of the confession of sins, which
means that each can be identified with the other (Ap XII 107). A mark
of true contrition is that in its wake one sees the death of the flesh and
the fruits of the Spirit,[30] which take the place of making satisfaction
in the Catholic sacrament of penance. The section on confession in
both catechisms also indicates that the human role is not simply
passive. The fact that contrition is God's work, putting to death the old
man, does not exclude human activity by any means. And yet contrition is never a precondition for the forgiveness of sins. As seen
from man's point of view, the most profound meaning of contrition is
the recognition that God is just and fair in revealing to us His wrath
in the form of tribulations, suffering, and need. In such recognition
there is also a prayer for God's mercy. (Ap XIII 107 ff.) [31]

The other part of the act of penitence is faith. Apart from faith,
God's judgment leads to despair. The difference between the contrition
of Peter and that of Judas was that the former had faith, the latter
did not. Contrition without faith leads to even deeper despair. So when
Scripture speaks of repentance, it always includes contrition and faith.
In Jesus' invitation, "Come to Me, all who labor and are heavy laden,
and I will give you rest" (Matt. 11:28), faith is implied. According
to the Symbols, to come to Christ means the same as to have faith in
Him (Ap XII 44). This is expressed even more clearly in Mark 1:15:

quae dicit: Peccavi Domino, sicut David ait, est chirographum. Et hanc vocem
impii et securi homines, non emittunt serio. Non enim vident, non legunt scriptam
in corde sententiam legis (Ap XII 48).

29 262:26 — Sic David obiurgatur a Nathan et perterrefactus inquit: Peccavi
Domino (Ap XII 56).

30 279:52 — Nec potest esse vera conversio aut vera contritio, ubi non
sequuntur mortificationes carnis et boni fructus (Ap XII 131).

31 274:12 — Ideo pronuntio te iustum esse, cum condemnas et punis nos (Ap
XII 108).

"Repent, and believe in the Gospel." Faith must follow contrition.

Both contrition and faith are God's work in man. But while in contrition God frightens and demolishes, in faith He brings the oppressed conscience to life. The paradigm for this experience is derived from Scripture: "The Lord kills and brings to life; He brings down to Sheol and raises up" (1 Sam. 2:6; Ap XII 50). Faith is God's own life-giving work, His *opus proprium,* whereby He comforts broken hearts and brings forth new life.[32]

What is said about faith is already well known to us from Chapter Six and we need not therefore give it further attention at this point. Since the doctrine of penitence is closely related to the doctrine of justification, we have already covered the essential facts about the faith which is able to restore the conscience oppressed by contrition. Faith is not simply historical knowledge, and neither is it an act of the human will or intellect; it is rather God's work in man through the Holy Spirit.

The fact that faith is God's work does not, however, exclude the human facet of the experience. Faith can be described theologically as God's life-giving activity, and psychologically as an act in the human will. God's active involvement in faith does not exclude its human side, but how to conceive more precisely of the relationship between what God accomplishes and what man does is not analyzed. Man's volitional powers cannot influence salvation, because it is entirely God's work.[33] But it is precisely in its capacity as a divine activity that faith is something which occurs in man; it gives birth to new affections, replacing those evil sentiments that are hostile to God. Inasmuch as the Symbols also in their doctrine of penitence oppose the Catholic *opus operatum* concept and criticize it for permitting penitence to take place "without a right attitude in the recipient," [34] faith as a psychological act in man must be accorded the greatest significance. Faith as God's work in man provides a defense against work-piety. The basis of justification is God's grace in Christ, not

---

[32] 258:32-33 (Ap XII 36); 266:44 — fide corda eriguntur et fiunt tranquilla per spiritum sanctum (Ap XII 74); 172:43-46 (Ap IV 62); 173:9-12 (Ap IV 64).

[33] The question concerning the relationship between God's grace and man's will was dealt with in later orthodoxy, in Pietism, and in the Herrnhut school. The tendency was to mitigate this in a synergistic manner, i. e., that God's grace liberates man's will (in an incipient sense) so that it has the ability to choose to believe or not. Cf. L. Aalen (1952), pp. 169 and 301; H. Fagerberg (1952), pp. 258 ff., the same author in STK (1955), pp. 159 and 168; Th. Kliefoth (1854), pp. 245 ff.

[34] 255:11-16 (Ap XII 12); 256:36-39 (Ap XII 25); 172:51-54 (Ap IV 63).

contrition or some other human activity. Faith as a psychological phenomenon is "the proper attitude" in man and comforts the anguished conscience.[35] In addition, it provides a safeguard against the severely criticized *opus operatum* idea.

Penitence as a Sacrament

In penitence God works through Law and Gospel, i. e., the promise of the forgiveness of sins.[36] This promise is found throughout Scripture. It was given first of all to Adam, then to the patriarchs; the prophets repeated it and explained what it meant. In Christ it was renewed and made vital. The apostles proclaimed it anew, and it lives on now in the preaching of the church (Ap XII 53 f.). The proclamation of God's grace in Christ in the Reformation did not in principle signify anything new; it was rather the continuation of something willed by God from the beginning of the world. Here too, as always in the Lutheran Confessions, faith and the promise go together. God's promise can only be received in faith.

But in the context of penitence the promise has the special meaning of absolution. It was true even in the medieval sacrament of penance that absolution was the most important part of the sacrament—its form. After the priest had determined that the penitent was properly contrite and willing to make satisfaction, he would in the power of his jurisdictional authority confer the forgiveness of sins in the absolution.

Melanchthon held fast to the sacramental character of absolution. Luther too accorded it great importance, but he did not refer to it as a sacrament—as he had done in his earlier writings.[37] Melanchthon nevertheless felt that absolution met the requirements of a sacrament. It is an act of worship which is commanded by God and furnished with a promise of grace. Melanchthon held that "absolution may properly be called a sacrament of penitence, as even the more learned of the scholastics say." [38] But he gave absolution a different meaning and released it from its connection with the older sacramental act of pen-

[35] 437:28 (SA III III 8); 441:10-12 (SA III III 20); 728:45 (LC On Confession 14).

[36] 437:11 — Aber zu solchem Ampt tut das Neue Testament flugs die trostliche Verheissung der Gnaden durchs Evangelion, der man gläuben solle (SA III III 4).

[37] WA 2, 717:1-2 (*Eyn Sermon von dem Sacrament der Puss,* 1519).

[38] 259:17 — Et absolutio proprie dici potest sacramentum poenitentiae, ut etiam scholastici theologici eruditiores loquuntur (Ap XII 41); cf. L. Klein (1961), p. 81, who nevertheless overlooks the fact that absolution and confession are not identical.

ance. Although absolution can be tied in with private confession of sins, this need not be the case. This means that absolution as a sacrament must be considered in and of itself, apart from an unconditional connection with private confession and absolution.[39]

Absolution is the oral proclamation of the promise regarding the forgiveness of sins; absolution is the Gospel's Word of promise in function. It cannot simply be coordinated with preaching,[40] inasmuch as the sermon must also take the proclamation of the Law into consideration. Absolution deals exclusively with the oral promise of forgiveness for Christ's sake, which is a precondition for the emergence of faith. For when the Gospel or absolution is heard, the conscience can take new courage and comfort (Ap XII 39). The purpose of absolution is to awaken and strengthen faith.

Absolution has this in common with the uncontested sacraments: It is God's own work, without human intervention or mediation. We hear God's own voice in absolution. God must certainly use a human instrumentality as His voice, but the task of this instrumentality is simply to express the words of forgiveness. "It is not the voice or word of the man who speaks it, but it is the Word of God, who forgives sin, for it is spoken in God's stead and by God's command" (AC XXV 3 f.). Just as God in Baptism carries out His work of salvation through the water of Baptism, so in absolution He permits a sinner to be freed from sin and guilt through the voice of a man. The Word, in this case the Gospel's Word of promise, is the means God uses to bring life to the oppressed and anxious. Since God uses the Word as a means to forgive and to bring new life, "we must believe the voice of the one absolving no less than we would believe a voice coming from heaven" (Ap XII 40). In this and in similar contexts the Symbols frequently remind us of Luke 10:16—"He who hears you hears Me." In absolution God's own voice is heard. This concept of absolution as a sacrament can be readily harmonized with what we have found to be characteristic of Baptism and the Lord's Supper. The effective power comes from God, who works through the spoken Word, the promise.

That what is mediated is found exclusively in the Word and not in

---

[39] Schlink does not take note of the fact that (1) absolution is the third sacrament on the basis of Melanchthon's functional view of the sacraments, and (2) absolution is not necessarily connected with confession. He is therefore in error to say: "Already at this point it becomes clear why the absolution in Confession is really no sacrament because to the promise of grace no visible sign has been added by *God's* institution" (1961), p. 186. This is a direct contradiction of Ap XII 41 (see preceding note).

[40] Thus in H. Ivarsson (1956), pp. 23 and 29 f., and G. Wingren (1958), p. 14.

the person who speaks the words of absolution is also made clear in the position taken on the office of the ministry. Absolution belongs to the power of the keys, which "administers and offers the Gospel." [41] When the Symbols speak of the power of the keys, they refer to the office of the ministry or a function of the same. The threefold task of the pastor is to preach the Gospel, administer the sacraments, and have charge of the keys which bind and loose.[42] But the concern here is not to ascribe to the pastor any unique position or authority. He is subject to the Word and is to fulfill the mission given him by God, to proclaim the forgiveness of sins.

In the Evangelical sacrament of penitence — absolution — the pastor does not function as a judge; he is in the service of the Gospel, not of the Law. "The ministry of absolution is in the area of blessing or grace, not of judgment or law. The ministers of the church therefore have the command to forgive sins; they do not have the command to investigate secret sins" (Ap XII 103 f.).[43] This statement is pointed directly at the Roman view of the priest's jurisdictional authority to be a judge at Christ's command and in His stead, a judge who requires satisfaction and announces absolution for past sins. The Lutheran Symbols are completely unable to understand such a concept of the ministry. The pastor's God-given function in the sacrament of penitence is to absolve those who confess their sins and to excommunicate the impenitent. (Matt. 18:18) [44]

The entire emphasis centers upon the mission entrusted to the office of the keys. The interest of the Symbols is concentrated not upon the person, but the office. Certain persons must naturally occupy this office,[45] but the important thing is that *God* works through them (Ap XIII 12) — which means, in practice, that they are to teach and proclaim God's Word as certified in Scripture. In granting absolution,

[41] 259:5 — Porro potestas clavium administrat et exhibet evangelium per absolutionem, quae est vera vox evangelii (Ap XII 39). Cf. E. Kinder in ThLZ (1952), p. 548, n. 22, and L. Klein (1961), 45 and 69.

[42] 121:12-17 (AC XXVIII 5); cf. 120:27 — So ist nun *potestas clavium* allein geistlich Regiment, das Evangelium predigen, Sund strafen und vergeben, Sacramenta reichen. Dies allein soll der Bischof oder Priester Ampt sein (Vorarbeit zu AC XXVIII).

[43] 273:4 — quia ministerium absolutionis beneficium est seu gratia, non est iudicium seu lex. Itaque ministri in ecclesia habent mandatum remittendi peccata, non habent mandatum cognoscendi occulta peccata (Ap XII 103).

[44] 290:43—291:2 (Ap XII 176).

[45] 293:50 — Denn die Kirche hat Gottes Befehl, dass sie soll Prediger und Diakonos bestellen (Ap XIII 11); 294:4 — Habet enim ecclesia mandatum de constituendis ministris (Ap XIII 12).

they are simply to release from sin at Christ's command. When the pastor exercises his office, he functions in Christ's stead and represents Him in the spirit of Luke 10:16: "He who hears you hears Me." [46] The representation is found not in the person who proclaims the Word but in the Word of God which the pastor proclaims. The Symbols do not recognize any human mediator between God and man.

This means in practice that absolution as a sacrament in the Lutheran Church is completely different from what it is in the Catholic Church. Since a sacrament is God's gift to man, it has nothing to do with a juridical act. God has already judged the conscience through the Law, and the purpose of absolution is to release the burdened conscience. The precondition for absolution is therefore the contrition which is worked by God. This can be associated with confession in the sense of individual confession before the pastor, but it need not be. Absolution provides full forgiveness, and the forgiveness of sin is unreservedly valid in the presence of God, *coram Deo*. "For if the power of the keys does not console us before God, what is there that will finally bring peace to the conscience?" [47] Sacramental absolution in this form is *iure divino,* i. e., commanded by God in Scripture, and can nourish and strengthen the faith to which all the sacraments point. Inasmuch as absolution is that element in the act of repentance which gives rise to faith, it can rightly be designated as the sacrament of penitence.

Confession

Confession was included as the second element prior to absolution in the medieval sacrament of penance. Confession was to be made before a priest at least once a year.[48] The penitent was obligated to confess all sins, as far as that was possible.[49] On the basis of the confession, the priest as the servant of Christ and in His stead could determine the genuineness of the penitent's contrition and impose suitable satisfactions upon him. As a result of the penitent's earnest examination of conscience the priest could at last pronounce the words of absolution, which was the ultimate goal of the sacrament of penance.

In the Lutheran Symbols the term "confession" includes both

---

[46] 246:17 — ministri funguntur vice Christi, non repraesentant suam personam juxta illud: Qui vos audit, me audit (Ap VII 47).

[47] 254:6-8 (Ap XII 7).

[48] Denz., 437 — CR 27, 108 (Confutation, 1530); 249:5-11 (Ap XI 1).

[49] CR 27, 108 and 159 (Confutation, 1530).

confession of sin and absolution.[50] Confession of sin is our responsibility, impelled by the Law, while absolution is God's work and also the very heart of the act of confession. The Symbols retained confession for the sake of private absolution, but they detached it from the old sacrament of penance and did not give it a sacramental character, as absolution has in Ap. Absolution as a sacrament and confession are not identical, therefore, and neither are confession and penitence. Instead, confession is an application of Evangelical penitence and absolution on an individual basis.

The confession we are discussing here is usually referred to as secret or private. It is done either before a fellow Christian or a clergyman. Its purpose is to provide assurance of the forgiveness of sins. In his early writings Luther said expressly that confession can take place before any fellow Christian, and the same is true in LC.[51] SC, Ap, and Luther's later writings emphasize more strongly that confession should be made to a pastor,[52] but no absolute demand was made. In case of necessity any Christian at all can absolve.[53] The tendency to emphasize the role of the pastor in confession was associated with an alteration in the concept of the function of confession. In addition to its place in connection with absolution, it also came to be used as a means of maintaining church discipline. Confession assumed the character of an examination, in which the pastor could find out how well the confessors knew the catechism and the meaning of the Christian life.[54]

The heart of aural confession is private absolution, which nevertheless is not identical with absolution as a sacramental act. The *absolutio* which Ap calls *sacramentum poenitentiae* is commanded by

---

[50] 729:10 — So merke nu, wie ich oft gesagt habe, dass die Beichte stehet in zweien Stücken. Das erste ist unser Werk und Tuen, dass ich meine Sunde klage und begehre Trost und Erquickung meiner Seele. Das ander ist ein Werk, das Gott tuet, der mich durch das Wort dem Menschen in Mund gelegt, losspricht von meinen Sunden, welchs auch das Furnehmste und Edelste ist, so sie lieblich und tröstlich machet (LC On Confession 15). 517:10-17 (SC IV 16). Cf. WA 30 III, 570:7 and 566:9 ff. (*Sendschreiben an die zu Frankfurt a. M.*, 1533).

[51] 728:27-36 (LC On Confession 13); WA 8, 183:28 — Darumb so ist eyn iglich Christen mensch eyn beycht vatter der heymlichen Beycht (*Von der Beicht*, 1521); K. Aland (1960), p. 461.

[52] The rubric "Wie man die Einfältigen soll lehren beichten" (SC IV 15) is later altered to "Eine kurze Weise zu beichten für die Einfältigen, dem Priester" (WA 30 I, 343:1 3; Der Kleine Katechismus, 1529). In WA 30 III, 565:17 f., Luther says that his statements in the Small Catechism had reference to confession before a pastor or priest (*Sendschreiben an die zu Frankfurt a. M.*, 1533). K. Aland (1960), p. 468.

[53] 491:20-21 (Tr 67).

[54] K. Aland (1960), 465—71.

God in the Scriptures and is therefore *iure divino*.[55] It can be pronounced even apart from a preliminary confession of sin before a
pastor. Private confession before a pastor cannot be required of Christian people, inasmuch as it was a later custom developed without
Biblical support. Private confession is therefore *iure humano*.[56] The
fact that the Symbols nevertheless accepted and emphasized confession is related to two factors. First, confession is an expression of
Law and Gospel in action, and second and above all, it is of great
importance for the sake of private absolution. "For we also keep confession, especially because of absolution, which is the Word of God
that the power of the keys proclaims to individuals by divine authority"
(Ap XII 99). Because of this, confession is frequently referred to quite
simply as *absolutio privata*.[57] Chiefly because it is a useful means of
consoling oppressed consciences, it ought to remain in the church.
"Since absolution or the power of the keys, which was instituted by
Christ in the Gospel, is a consolation and help against sin and a bad
conscience, confession and absolution should by no means be allowed
to fall into disuse in the church, especially for the sake of timid consciences and for the sake of untrained young people who need to be
examined and instructed in Christian doctrine." (SA III VIII 1)

The reservations about confession which still remained were related to three factors. First, private confession (as the *glossa ordinaria*
on the writings of Gratian had already noted)[58] cannot be found in the
New Testament.[59] Second, it can contradict the principle that no human mediator dare step between God and man as was the case in the
traditional practice of confession, where the priest functioned in
Christ's stead and as His representative. Third, the demand for a complete confession of sin before a clergyman can lead to the misunderstanding that the forgiveness of sin is dependent upon the candidness
and completeness of the confession.[60] In such a case the confession
itself and not Christ would be the cause of justification.

[55] 255:10 — de absolutione, quae vere est iuris divini (Ap XII 12).

[56] 99:21 — fatetur humani iuris esse confessionem (AC XXV 12).

[57] 66:2 f. (AC XI 1); 274:47 and 50 (Ap XII 100 f.); 453:12 (SA III VIII 2).

[58] *Glossa ad Decr. Grat.*, De poen., d.5, c.1 — Confessionem ex traditione
ecclesiae potius institutum, quam authoritate veteris vel novi testamenti.

[59] 100:3 — dass die Beichte nicht durch die Schrift geboten, sondern durch
die Kirchen eingesetzt sei (AC XXV 13); 728:37-39 (LC On Confession 13). Cf.
WA 1, 98:31. De privata (confessione) nescio ubi Scriptura loquitur (*Sermo de
indulgentiis*, 1516); WA 8, 183:17—185:2 (*Von der Beicht*, 1521); L. Klein
(1961), pp. 11 f., 16, and 70.

[60] 441:1-3 (SA III III 19); 725:31—726:19 (LC On Confession 1 ff.)

This third point was emphasized with special care. AC maintains "that private absolution should be retained and not allowed to fall into disuse. However, in confession it is not necessary to enumerate all trespasses and sins" (XI 1). This point of view was repeated throughout the entire Reformation period and in all of the symbolical writings which include statements on confession.[61] One cannot require a complete cataloguing of all sins in confession. Such an enumeration is, for various reasons, impossible. Under such a requirement forgiveness of sin would always have to be conditional, for it would be dependent upon the completeness of the confession. The emphasis would switch from absolution to man's contrition and confession, which would lead to coercion of the conscience and work-righteousness.[62] Inasmuch as everything in man is sin, no one can fully know just how often he has sinned (Ps. 19:13).[63] Being specific about cataloguing one's sins is not basically necessary for the mature Christian;[64] a general acknowledgment of sin is sufficient. "As long as we are in the flesh we shall not be untruthful if we say, 'I am a poor man, full of sin.'" (SA III VIII 2)

Anthropology and the concept of sin explain why the enumeration of all sins in confession is an impossibility. But another strong argument is that the clergyman is not Christ's deputy, executing punishment and releasing from sin. Contrition and confession are a matter between God and man; the task of the pastor is simply to pronounce orally the words of absolution to those who request forgiveness. The mediation is accomplished not by the pastor but by the Word he speaks, which comes from heaven. Since in confession the pastor appears not as a judge but as God's voice of forgiveness,[65] he need not investigate the sinner. Absolution covers all sins unconditionally,

[61] 98:27 ff. (AC XXV 7 ff.); 259:55 ff. (Ap XI 6 ff.); 255:2 ff. (Ap XII 11); 272:51 ff. (Ap XII 102 f.); 404:25 ff. (SA III III 19); 453:8 ff. (SA III VIII 2); 726:14 f. (LC On Confession 3).

[62] 98:11-19 (AC XXV 5 f.); 440:25—441:13 (SA III III 19 f.). Cf. 98:31-34 (Torgau Articles). Concerning these articles consult G. Hoffmann in ZST (1938), pp. 482 ff.

[63] This passage from the Psalms is frequently quoted, e. g., 99:3 (AC XXV 7); cf. WA 26, 220:3 f. (*Unterricht der Visitatoren*, 1528), and 99:24 (the Torgau Articles).

[64] Cf. WA 26, 216:28-33 (*Unterricht der Visitatoren*, 1528), and 30 III, 566:31-32 (*Sendschreiben an die zu Frankfurt a.M.*, 1533).

[65] 729:2 — dass ihn Gott durch ein Menschen von Sunden entbindet und losspricht (LC On Confession 14); 98:11 — dieser Absolution zu glauben, nicht weniger, denn so Gottes Stimme vom Himmel erschulle (AC XXV 5). Cf. WA 8, 183:34 f. (*Von der Beicht*, 1521), and WA 30 III, 569:14 f. (*Sendschreiben an die zu Frankfurt a. M.*, 1533). L. Klein (1961), p. 21. Absolution is God's work, just as much as is Baptism and the Lord's Supper.

even those which are not acknowledged in confession. "Absolution, which is the voice of the Gospel forgiving sins and consoling consciences, does not need an investigation [of sin on the part of the pastor]." (Ap XII 105)

Such a point of view implies in principle the dissolution of the traditional form of confession, whose purpose was to prepare man for the communication of forgiveness in absolution on the basis of a sincere confession in the presence of a priest. In the Evangelical form of confession there is a desire to retain the personal pronouncement of absolution, but the act of confession itself is more or less pushed into the background. It certainly belongs in confession, but it can be shaped in a very general way. Since the act of private confession is not commanded by God, the theological justification of confession is eliminated. Confession ought to be retained for the sake of absolution, but absolution can be communicated in other forms just as well. In spite of Luther, who unquestionably placed a high value upon confession,[66] the practice soon disappeared. The efforts of individual theologians and pastors to bring about its renaissance cannot obscure the correctness of this judgment.[67]

A new view of private confession also began to take shape during the Reformation era. Confession was used in church discipline and in testing people's knowledge of the chief tenets of the Christian faith. LC contains an exhortation to confession, but also a related warning about the misuse of Evangelical freedom. For experienced Christians, confession served to provide private absolution, but for the young and the unschooled populace it was placed in the service of church discipline. The confession of sins was transformed into a confessional examination. In a letter dated 1533 Luther wrote as follows:

> But since young people are growing up every day, and in general have little understanding, for their sake we observe this custom, that they may be trained in Christian discipline and knowledge. For such confession is not undertaken only so they can confess sins, but to examine them as to whether they know the Lord's Prayer, the Creed, the Ten Commandments, and the rest of the catechism. For we have experienced all too well that the common people and the youth learn little from the sermon, if they are not especially asked and examined. But

[66] 729:37 — die liebe Beichte (LC On Confession 17); 730:42—733:24 (LC On Confession 23 ff.); cf. WA 8, 181:3-4 (*Von der Beicht,* 1521), and WA 26, 216:35 ff. (*Unterricht der Visitatoren,* 1528); E. Roth (1952), pp. 42 f.

[67] K. Aland (1960), pp. 452—519.

where is there a better opportunity to do this, and where is it more necessary, than if they wish to go to the Sacrament? [68]

Beginning with Luther's *Formula missae* of 1523 [69] one can see how the connection between confession and examination in the Christian faith was gradually established.[70] In *Unterricht der Visitatoren* (1528), which was an important forerunner of AC,[71] this connection is fully developed.[72]

This second justification for confession is found throughout the Symbols. SA provides two reasons for the retention of confession: first, the original one, that it is necessary for the sake of absolution, and second, the last-named, that it is also necessary "for the sake of untrained young people who need to be examined and instructed in Christian doctrine" (SA III VIII 1). A connection between confession and church discipline is also hinted at in AC XXV 1 and in Ap XI 5.[73] It goes without saying that the stronger the tie between examination and confession became, the further confession was removed in the mind of the people from its original purpose as a function of absolution on the personal, individual level. This could only contribute to the disappearance of private confession. What remained of penitence was its two other facets, the act of repentance itself and the general absolution.

[68] WA 30 III, 566:33—567:2 (*Sendschreiben an die zu Frankfurt a. M.,* 1533).

[69] WA 12, 215:18 ff. (*Formula Missae et communionis,* 1523).

[70] K. Aland (1960), pp. 462 ff.; L. Klein (1961), pp. 77 f.

[71] G. Hoffmann in ZST (1938), pp. 419—40.

[72] WA 26, 7—9, plus Luther's contribution, ibid. 216:27 ff. (*Unterricht der Visitatoren,* 1528).

[73] This is most precise in Ap's German text, 250:32 — So wird auch von unsern Predigern allzeit daneben gemeldet, dass sie sollen verbannet und ausgeschlossen werden, die in öffentlichen Lastern leben, Hurerei, Ehebruch, etc. Item so die heiligen Sakrament verachten (Ap XI 5).

Chapter Nine:

The Ministry

The Meaning of the Ministry

In order that the Word, the sacraments, and absolution might come to men, the church has the office of the ministry. Few questions, however, have prompted greater arguments than has the concept of the ministry in the Lutheran Confessions. This discussion, which was carried on in the middle of the 19th century, has not yet been concluded but has, on the contrary, once again become a matter of great interest.[1] And although the theologians involved worked to a large extent with the confessional writings and thus had a common basis for their studies, they produced widely varying results.

On the one wing stood Höfling, who nearly combined the professional ministry with the universal priesthood. He conceived of the ministry properly speaking as a function, an activity involving the preaching of the Gospel and the administration of the sacraments. This belongs *iure divino* to all Christians, but for the sake of order it has been delegated to those who have been properly called by a congregation.[2] Höfling's critics looked upon this as an abrogation of the special, divinely instituted ministry, which they in turn strongly emphasized. Stahl found the original form of the ministry in the apostolate of the New Testament, and claimed that it is still to be seen in the actual preaching office.[3] Vilmar attributed extraordinary significance to the pastor's person. He conceived of the ministry as a representation of Christ; the pastor is Christ's representative in his person.[4] Vilmar therefore emphasized the difference between the person and the function in the ministry. The call to service goes out to certain persons, who are obligated to carry out the functions involved.[5]

[1] See, e. g., J. Heubach (1956), pp. 11 ff.; H. Lieberg (1962), pp. 113 ff., 271 ff., 386, etc.; H. Wittram (1963), pp. 92 ff.; E. Kinder (1958), pp. 147.

[2] J. W. F. Höfling (1853), pp. 62, 225, 219, etc. H. W. Tottie (1892), p. 86. H. Fagerberg (1952), pp. 275 ff. W. Brunotte (1959), pp. 13 ff., 130 ff.

[3] F. J. Stahl (1862), p. 109.

[4] A. F. C. Vilmar (1872), p. 10; same author, II (1874), 30; same author (1870), p. 111. J. Heubach (1956), p. 30. H. Fagerberg (1952), p. 311.

[5] A. F. C. Vilmar (1870), 14 — Im Apostolat [geht] entschieden die Er-

These various points of view also serve to state our problem. What do the Confessions mean by *ministerium ecclesiasticum,* the ministry of the church? It is a function which basically can be exercised by all believing Christians? Or is it a special service which is entrusted to servants who are called and ordained thereto? Or is it a function in the church, exercised by persons who are called for this purpose?

The answer to these questions is commonly sought for in AC V. This article now bears the title "The Office of the Ministry" *(Vom Predigtamt; De ministerio ecclesiastico),* but its content corresponds poorly with this rubric. It seems to deal more with the preaching of the Word and the administration of the sacraments than with the office of the ministry. The authors of the Confutation, e. g., read it in this way and did not understand it at all as referring to the office of the ministry [6] (which may be explained by the fact that the rubric is of a later date).[7] Translated from the German, the article reads as follows, in full:

> To obtain such faith God instituted the office of the ministry, that is, provided the Gospel and the sacraments. Through these, as through means, he gives the Holy Spirit, who works faith, when and where he pleases, in those who hear the Gospel. And the Gospel teaches that we have a gracious God, not by our own merits but by the merit of Christ, when we believe this.
>
> Condemned are the Anabaptists and others who teach that the Holy Spirit comes to us through our own preparations, thoughts, and works without the external word of the Gospel.[8]

The Latin *ministerium* is here reproduced by *Predigtamt,* and the problem is, does it refer to an office or to an activity? Has Christ (according to AC V) instituted an office which is to be entrusted to persons especially called thereto, or has God through His institution

wählung (Berufung) der Person voran, und die Function folgt der Person. For more on this see J. Heubach (1956), p. 30, n. 105. H. Lieberg (1962) has attempted in his large volume, *Amt und Ordination bei Luther und Melanchthon,* to set the 19th-century debate within a larger theological and historical context.

[6] CR 27, 97 (Confutation, 1530).

[7] G. Plitt, II (1868), 160.

[8] 58:2 — The Latin reads as follows: Ut hanc fidem consequamur, institutum est ministerium docendi evangelii et porrigendi sacramenta. Nam per verbum et sacramenta tamquam per instrumenta donatur spiritus sanctus, qui fidem efficit, ubi et quando visum est Deo, in his, qui audiunt evangelium, scilicet quod Deus non propter nostra merita, sed propter Christum iustificet hos, qui credunt se propter Christum in gratiam recipi. Gal. 3: Ut promissionem spiritus accipiamus per fidem. Damnant Anabaptistas et alios, qui sentiunt spiritum sanctum contigere hominibus sine verbo externo per ipsorum praeparationes et opera (AC V).

simply made provision for the work of preaching the Gospel and administering the sacraments?

Present-day representatives of the latter interpretation (which is closely related to Höfling's functional concept of the ministry) include, among others, Wingren and Persson. What Christ has instituted according to the New Testament is not an office but "activities" which are necessary to the life of the church: Baptism, the Lord's Supper, preaching, announcing absolution.[9] What the New Testament means is "that these activities must go on, Baptism must be given, the Gospel proclaimed, the bread and wine distributed. This has been commanded; it is thus that Christ's salvation is spread abroad — and it was to save that He came into the world (John 3:16)." AC V does not refer to a special office, "but to activities which are necessary to the church." The office of the ministry is identified with the preached Word.[10]

This trend of thought has been further developed by Persson, who is of the opinion that when the Confessions refer to *Predigtamt,* they have in mind "nothing other than the continuously active and life-giving Gospel, regardless of who it is who presents it." "When the Gospel's Word of promise is proclaimed, by whomever this may be, there is the 'office,' for when one speaks here about the 'office,' he is not speaking, properly, of the 'bearer of the office' . . . but of the Word in whose service he stands." The office of the ministry is to be found wherever the Word in its various forms such as Baptism, the Lord's Supper, preaching, and absolution is in action. The office is identified with the activities themselves — preaching, baptizing, pronouncing the absolution, and giving the Lord's Supper. As seen from the Evangelical view of the ministry, the accent falls upon the activities themselves.[11]

The term *ministerium* goes back to the New Testament word *diakonia,* and it points both to the office itself and to the activities for which this special office was designed. These meanings are closely related to each other, but the Confessions clearly emphasize the latter. Activity as such need not presuppose an office in the conventional sense, but an office must always carry out a distinct activity — and that is what the Confessions accent in particular.[12]

---

[9] G. Wingren (1958), pp. 6, 9 f. and 15 f. Same author, *Gospel and Church* (1964), pp. 121 ff.

[10] G. Wingren (1958), pp. 12, 21, and 22.

[11] P. E. Persson (1961), pp. 297, 271, and 272 f.

[12] Vilmos Vajta (1958) strongly emphasizes the functional character of the

An obvious example of the functional use of *ministerium* in the Symbols can be derived from Ap XXVII 22, where it is said that even the cloisters are inhabited by good men "serving the ministry of the Word," *qui serviunt ministerio verbi.* In the parallel German text mention is made not of an office but of an activity — "reading and studying." A similar use of *ministerium* is found in Tr 67, where in connection with Eph. 4:12 we read that God entrusted the church with shepherds and teachers "for the work of ministry and for building up the body of Christ," *ad ministerium ad aedificationem corporis Christi,* which is translated into German as *zu Erbauung des Leibs Christi,* "for edification of the body of Christ." [13] AC XXVIII 9 also uses *ministerium* with reference to the activity which must be carried on for the sake of faith and eternal life. Man can receive the Holy Spirit only through the *ministerium verbi et sacramentorum.* The corresponding German text gives this as follows: *durch das Amt der Predig und durch die Handreichung der heiligen Sakrament,* "through the office of preaching and of administering the holy sacraments" (AC XXVIII 9). The meaning is: Through the proclamation of the Word and the administration of the sacraments we partake of the spiritual treasures God offers us. The functional aspect of *ministerium* is also to be seen in a comparison of the secular and the spiritual spheres. The Confessions say quite simply that the *ministerium evangelii,* i. e., activity in the service of the Gospel, implies a function quite different from that of the secular sphere.[14]

The Confessions usually translate *ministerium* as *Predigtamt,* and this expression too is used in the for us somewhat strange sense of "preaching activity." When we read that bishops impart spiritual gifts "only through the office of preaching," it is the very act of preaching the Gospel that the confessional writers have in mind (AC XXVIII 10). The statement that the preaching of the Word "is the highest office in the church" (Ap XV 44 German) points in the same direction. Here again Melanchthon has in mind the actual proclamation of the Gospel. A direct intimation of the fact that *Amt* must refer to a distinct activity is found in LC, where it says about Sunday: "The special office *(Ampt)* of this day, therefore, should be the ministry of

---

ministry, pp. 109 ff. Cf. E. Kinder (1958), pp. 150 ff.; J. Heubach (1956), pp. 67 ff.; H. Lieberg (1962), pp. 35, 94 ff., 105, 226, and elsewhere.

[13] This passage in the Vulgate reads as follows: in opus ministerii, in aedificationem corporis Christi.

[14] 123:19 — Haec interim alia functio est quam ministerium evangelii (AC XXVIII 19).

the Word *(Predigamt)* for the sake of the young and the poor common people" (I 86). It would be meaningless to think here of the ministry in the modern sense. In a free interpretation, this sentence says that the preaching of the Word is the proper activity for Sunday. The transition from *Predigtamt* to Word or Gospel is less surprising when seen from this point of view.[15]

The Confessions stress the point that the proclamation of the Word must be carried out. Emphasis is given to Word and sacraments, to which the *ministerium verbi et sacramentorum* stands in service. The seventh Schwabach article, which anticipated AC V, used "the oral Word" as an alternative to the preaching office. In order that men might come to believe, God has established "the preaching office or the oral Word, viz., the Gospel." [16] The expression "the power of the keys," *postestas clavium,* has the same functional connotation. When the Confessions speak of it, they are thinking more of the activity of binding and loosing sins than of the office or the person who occupies the office.[17] By the way, it was natural to use the term *ministerium* in a functional sense in the Catholic Confutation too.[18]

All of this is closely related to Melanchthon's (and also Luther's) functional view of the sacraments. The sacraments have been shown to be divine deeds, whereby God is active in the interest of human salvation. *Ministerium* is simply used to express the train of thought which is basic to the understanding of Baptism, the Lord's Supper, the Word, and absolution. God is the subject of Baptism; He is the active one in the Lord's Supper; and in absolution it is not "the voice or word of the man who speaks it, but it is the word of God, who forgives sin" (AC XXV 3). The Word in its separate distinctions as Law and Gospel is an expression of divine activity. The Gospel is God's own work, *opus proprium,* and the Law is His alien work, *opus alienum. Ministerium* has the same connotation, for it too bears the

---

[15] 175:7 — multo maxime ornamus ministerium verbi (Ap IV 73), which reads thus in the German translation: so preisen wir das Predigamt und Wort höher und mehr denn die Widersacher (Ap IV 74). 278:50 — This same church has these external signs: the preaching office or (!) the Gospel and the Sacraments (Ap VII 22). 294:9-11 (Ap XIII 13).

[16] 59:3-5 (Schwab. VII). Cf. 279:31 — Wort und Ampt (Tr 27), and P. E. Persson (1961), p. 274.

[17] 254:14-15 — Aus der Absolution, aus Gewalt der Schlüssel (Ap XII 8). 290:43—291:9 (Ap XII 176). 452:8-20 (SA III VII).

[18] CR 27, 179: Episcopos non solum habere potestatem ministerii verbi, which reads thus in the German version: das die Bischoff nit allain Gewalt haben zu raichen Gotes Wort und die Sacrament (Confutation, 1530).

mark of an activity. It is an expression for a necessary activity in the church, which God has commanded and approved. We know, Ap says, that "God approves this ministry [*ministerium*] and is present in it." (Ap XIII 12)

If the interpreters who have observed the functional significance of the ministry are therefore undoubtedly correct, the question is: How, exactly, shall this activity be understood? God is certainly the subject of the activity which goes on in the church — the preaching of the Word and the administration of the sacraments — but man must do these things. Does "the ministry of teaching the Gospel and administering the sacraments," *ministerium docendi evangelii et porrigendi sacramenta* (AC V 1) point to a special service or to a task which in principle belongs to all? Höfling chose the latter alternative, in principle combining the special office with the universal priesthood. Persson is more complex. On the one hand he defines the office as God's (Christ's, the Spirit's) continuous activity through the external Word. The ministry is nothing other than "the Word" itself, active in the church, i. e., Christ Himself. "The office of the Word" is identical with the Gospel as it is active in its various forms — and this work can be carried out in principle "by whomever it may be." [19] On the other hand, Persson emphasizes that it is executed "through the words and deeds of men called thereto by the church." [20] But the question remains: What has been instituted — a special service, or something else? And if a special service, how shall it be understood?

Certain statements in Tr play the greatest role in Höfling's argumentation. He has built upon the assertion that Christ "bestows the keys especially and immediately on the church, and for the same reason the church especially possesses the right of vocation." [21] On this basis Höfling draws the conclusion that the ministry, by divine right, belongs to all who "exercise it in faith and in harmony with its institution." [22]

It must be noted about Höfling's argument, however, that this passage in Tr does not discuss what the ministry is or is not, but rather the papal claim of primacy over the other bishops. Inasmuch as all the apostles received the same power of the keys as Peter, the papal claim is without basis. From the thesis that Peter was not superior to the

[19] Persson (1961), pp. 271, 277, 288, 293, and 297.

[20] Persson, pp. 278 and 299 ff.

[21] 478:27 — Tribuit igitur claves ecclesiae principaliter immediate, sicut et ob eam causam ecclesia principaliter habet jus vocationis (Tr 24).

[22] Höfling (1853), p. 219.

other apostles Tr draws two important conclusions—first, that the power of the keys belongs to the church (and not to Peter or the pope alone); second, that the church has the right to call men into ecclesiastical office. The German parallel text says "that the church has the authority to ordain its servants" (Tr 24). There is no polemic here against the special service (or ministry); rather, Tr opposes only the claim of papal primacy.

Persson bases his position on another portion of Tr, which includes an exposition of the so-called "primary passage," Matt. 16:18. "As to the statement, 'On this rock I will build my church' (Matt. 16:18), it is certain that the church is not built on the authority of a man but on the ministry of the confession which Peter made when he declared Jesus to be the Christ, the Son of God. Therefore Christ addresses Peter as a minister and says, 'On this rock,' that is, on this ministry." Melanchthon goes on to compare Peter's ministry with the Levitical priesthood, *ministerium Leviticum,* from which it differed in that it was not confined to certain persons (i. e., the descendants of Levi) or to a certain place (i. e., Jerusalem). The text then continues: "Nor is this ministry valid because of any individual's authority but because of the Word given by Christ." (Tr 25-26)[23]

In his interpretation of this passage Persson underscores the statement which says that the New Testament ministry is independent of person or place, and he concludes from this "that where the Gospel's Word of promise is proclaimed, *by whomever it may be,* there the 'ministry' is also in operation." [24] In order to give even greater weight to his concept, he quotes the corresponding German text: *"The person*

---

[23] 479:13 — Quod vero dictum est: "Super hanc petram aedificabo ecclesiam meam," certe ecclesia non est aedificata super autoritatem hominis, sed super ministerium professionis illius, quam Petrus fecerat, in qua praedicat Jesum esse Christum, filium Dei. Ideo alloquitur eum tanquam ministrum: "Super hanc petram," id est super hoc ministerium. Porro ministerium Novi Testamenti non est alligatum locis et personis sicut ministerium Leviticum, sed est dispersum per totum orbem terrarum et ibi est, ubi Deus dat dona sua, apostolos, prophetas, pastores, doctores. Nec valet illud ministerium propter ullius personae autoritatem, sed propter verbum a Christo traditum (Tr 25—26).

[24] Persson (1961), p. 271. As I have remarked earlier, Persson limits the scope of the statement concerning the right of all to exercise the ministry, particularly in the Lutheran section of his book (pp. 299 ff.). All Christians have the "power" to do this, inasmuch as the distinction between priest and layman was abolished, but the majority lack the right to do so, because of the fact that no one can exercise the ministry publicly unless he has a call — even though the ministry, fundamentally, belongs to all. Nevertheless the ministry, in Persson's opinion, is identified with the Word, the Gospel, in function. The term "ministry"

adds nothing to this Word and office commanded by Christ. *No matter who it is who preaches and teaches the Word,* if there are hearts that hear and adhere to it, something will happen to them according as they hear and believe because Christ commanded such preaching and demanded that his promises be believed." [25]

Yet, like the one cited by Höfling, this passage from Tr contains no statement of principle to the effect that the ministry can be executed "by whomever it may be." Melanchthon was only opposing the *papal* claim to primacy over the other bishops. By drawing a parallel between *ministerium Novi Testamenti* and *ministerium Leviticum,* Tr 26 clearly intimates that Melanchthon had in mind a special ministry in the church, although it naturally differed from the priestly service of the Old Testament. The citing of Origen, Ambrose, Cyprian, Hilary, and Bede (Tr 27) confirms that it was the papal claim of primacy which was being rejected, and not the ministry in the sense of a special service. Melanchthon repudiated the pope's special authority over the other bishops. The ministry of the church is bound neither to any special place (Rome) or person (the pope). Should the opposite be true, that would imply a relapse into a Jewish custom—and the confessional writers opposed this here as elsewhere.[26]

What Tr is telling us, therefore, in the passages cited is not that preaching and the administration of the sacraments can be taken hold of in principle "by whomever it may be," but only that the ministry is independent of every human authority, that it is based exclusively upon Christ's institution. Since the ministry has been given a different justification and meaning, the Lutheran Confessions refer to it as "the ministry of the Word," *ministerium verbi,* in which a functional significance is emphasized. "The ministry of teaching the Gospel and administering the sacraments," *ministerium docendi evangelii et porrigendi sacramenta* (AC V 1), is the technical term for this functional view of the ministry.

Ministerium in a technical sense refers to a special service, with the emphasis on activity. This is seen clearly in Ap XIII 7-13, one of the few passages in the Confessions where a logically consistent analysis of the church's ministry is given. The opposition to the Church of Rome does not concern the obligation to call and ordain servants of

is retained, but it is provided with a meaning which is at variance with the current usage.

[25] 479:30-34 (Tr 27). The italics here are mine.

[26] 126:26-33 (AC XXVIII 39); 295:5-7 (Ap XIII 8); 298:9 f. (Ap XV 4). Cf. 580:40—581:3 (LC I 82).

the church, inasmuch as the church is commanded to do so;[27] what Ap rejects is the Roman Catholic interpretation of the ministry as a service of sacrifice. The ministry of the church is called "the ministry of the Word or the administration of the sacraments to others," *ministerium verbi et sacramentorum aliis porrigendorum* (Ap XIII 7). It is looked upon as a limited service, to which certain men are called and in which the emphasis is placed not upon the person but upon the service he renders. "The church has the command to appoint ministers" (Ap XIII 12), inasmuch as "God wishes to preach and work through men and those who have been chosen by men" (Ap XIII 12 German). God has established a special office, in which the crucial point is the resulting activity. The special office, the church's ministry, is looked upon from a functional point of view in analogy with the concept of Word and sacraments as divine activities. The only legitimate ministry is one which functions in a manner consistent with God's intentions.[28]

Another indication that the confessional emphasis on the functional view of the ministry was not designed to abolish the concept of the special office is seen in the stress placed on the call to the office of the ministry. The Confessions attach conspicuous importance to the church's duty and right to place men in the office of the ministry by call, choice, and ordination.[29] Apart from a proper call, without being *rite vocatus* (AC XIV), no one may publicly exercise the duties of the ministry. The Confessions base the church's right and obligation to do this upon New Testament statements about the office of the ministry. It is not the ministry but the various ranks of clergy that are called into question. Among the gifts entrusted to the church the Confessions also include "pastors and teachers" (according to Eph. 4:11).[30] In

---

[27] 294:4 — Habet enim ecclesia mandatum de constituendis ministris (Ap XIII 12).

[28] P. Fraenkel (1961), pp. 156—58. H. Lieberg (1962), pp. 289 ff.

[29] 491:5 — Quare necesse est ecclesiam retinere jus vocandi, eligendi et ordinandi ministros (Tr 67). 492:19-20 (Tr 72).

[30] 491:13 — sicut et Paulus testatur ad Ephesios, cum ait: "Ascendit, dedit dona hominibus." Et numerat inter dona propria ecclesiae pastores et doctores et addit dari tales ad ministerium ad aedificationem corporis Christi (Tr 67). Cf. 479:29 f. (German text) and WA 50, 632:35 — kennet man die Kirche eusserlich da bey, das sie Kirchendiener weihet oder berufft oder empter hat, die sie bestellen sol, Denn man mus Bisschove, Pfarrher oder Prediger haben, die öffentlich und sonderlich die obgenanten vier stück odder heilthum (i. e., the Word, Baptism, the Lord's Supper, and absolution) geben, reichen und uben, von wegen und in namen der Kirchen, viel mehr aber aus einsetzung Christi, wie St. Paulus in Eph. 4 sagt: "Dedit dona hominibus" (*Von den Konziliis und*

case of necessity, laymen too have the right to carry out this service, but under normal conditions the church is to provide the office with properly called incumbents (Tr 67). As Prenter has pointed out,[31] talk about "necessity" must presuppose an office which under normal circumstances is in operation. Otherwise, such talk would be meaningless. The right of emergency implies a departure from a valid right. The church has been commanded by God to appoint ministers, whom God uses as His instruments under very definite conditions (Ap XIII 11 f.). The idea that the office of the ministry is identical with the Gospel in action has no support in the Lutheran Confessions.

The Confessions do not deny the special ecclesiastical office, but they do oppose the idea that the office *iure divino* has different ranks. As seen from the functional point of view such ranking appears meaningless, inasmuch as the accent has shifted from the human instrument to the divine subject. According to the Confessions the difference in rank between a bishop and a priest was not in effect originally; it grew by degrees. In the New Testament, *episcopos* and *presbyteros* can denote the same person. The Symbols conclude from this that an ordinary pastor can on the basis of fundamental equality of rank officiate at ordination.[32] For the reformers it was somewhat of a necessity of life to be able to establish Biblical support for the original unity of the ministry. If the difference in rank between bishops and priests could be traced back to Christ's institution, the bishop alone would have the right to ordain — and in that case the Evangelical church would lack a proper ministry. But the right to ordain belongs not to the bishop but to the church. The Symbols do not deny the church's need of pastors. Rather they emphasize the church's right and duty to provide itself with servants who can proclaim and teach the Gospel, administer the sacraments, and pronounce absolution.

To support their position, the confessional writers derived assistance both from the New Testament, where *presbyteros* and *episcopos* cannot as a matter of fact be distinguished, and from the fathers of the early church — chiefly from Jerome and his letter to the

---

Kirchen, 1539). Regin Prenter in AUU (1960), p. 12; (1961), p. 85, and in ThLZ (1961), pp. 321—32. Melanchthon ascribed unusual importance to Ephesians 4:11 as grounds for the divine origins of the ministry and of the church's need for pastors. See CR 8, 1 (Preface to Luther's German work), and P. Fraenkel (1961), pp. 153—61.

31 R. Prenter in AUU (1960), p. 12; (1961), p. 90, n. 6.

32 490:37 — Sed cum jure divino non sint diversi gradus episcopi et pastoris, manifestum est ordinationem a pastore in sua ecclesia factam jure divino ratam esse (Tr 65). 296:17 (Ap XIV 1).

priest Evangelus, which was often quoted during the Reformation period.[33] Jerome's position can be summarized under the following points: (1) the entire New Testament (Acts 20:28; Phil. 1:1; 1 Tim. 4:14; Titus 1:5 ff.; 1 Peter 5:1 f.; 2 John 1) reveals that bishops and priests were on an equality from the beginning. (2) In order to avoid schism and division, one of the elders was later chosen to be the leader of the others, and he was called "bishop." As an example of this procedure, mention is made of the appointment of the first bishop of Alexandria. (3) At the time Jerome wrote (ca. A. D. 380) bishop and priest were still the same, but with one exception: only the bishop could ordain. (4) All bishops and priests are the successors of the apostles, *apostolorum successores*. (5) Between bishops and priests on the one hand and deacons on the other, there is according to the New Testament an original distinction.

Of these five points, the Confessions accepted only the first two and drew these conclusions: (a) that bishops and pastors are similar *iure divino* and (b) that an ordination performed by a pastor is as valid as that performed by a bishop.

As a result, the Confessions show a conspicuous lack of interest in the Biblical names given to those who hold ecclesiastical office. Mention of apostles, prophets, evangelists, pastors, and teachers (Eph. 4:11) is taken as proof that God has given servants to the church (Tr 27). The confessional writers identify these with their own *Pfarrherren* and *Lehrer* (Tr 67), and they oppose the idea of a graded clergy with a uniform clergy. God has instituted a service, the office of the ministry. All who occupy this office are fundamentally alike. Authority to exercise ecclesiastical functions is common to all, whether they are called pastors, priests, or bishops (Tr 61). This similarity has its final justification in the fact that there was no difference in authority between Peter and the other apostles. When Peter confessed Jesus as the Messiah (Matt. 16:16), he spoke as the representative of the other apostles. The same authority he received from Jesus was given to the remaining apostles. (Matt. 18:19; John 20:23; Tr 22-24)

The picture is therefore completely uniform. God has instituted an office through which He works. The church must have its called and ordained servants, but the title they bear has no real significance. Every such distinction is secondary — it is *iure humano*. According to divine right all are the same. But this lack of interest in hierarchical gradations does not indicate a setting aside of the office of the ministry. Its

---

[33] *Epist. 146 ad Evangelum* (MPL 22, 1193 f.); *Decr. Grat.*, I., d. 93, c. 23. A passage from this letter is quoted in 489:43—490:20 (Tr 62).

necessity is best revealed by the way the Confessions emphasize that this office must be filled. They would never have been able to refer to Jerome if their basic purpose for doing so had been to provide the word "ministry" with a new and until then unknown meaning.

Because the men who hold ecclesiastical office are placed on the same level, it doesn't matter what they are called. The most common designation is *minister (Kirchendiener)*.[34] Another is *pastor* or *pastor ecclesiae (Seelhirt)*.[35] Tr 72 speaks about *pastores et ministri (Pfarrherren und Kirchendiener)*. Since *Predigtamt* is without doubt the most common German translation of the Latin *ministerium*, the term "preacher," *Prediger*, is commonly used in the Confessions, especially in the material written by Luther. The title *Pfarrherr* is used frequently.[36] Since preachers are to proclaim the true Gospel, they are also known as "teachers," *Lehrer*.[37] While "priest," *Priester*,[38] is uncommon and used only in a few instances, the title "bishop," *Bischof*,[39] appears here and there with greater frequency. As noted, there seems to have been no difference between bishops and ordinary "priests" in New Testament times, and the Lutheran Confessions desired to maintain this fundamental similarity between them. The Confessions certainly did not reject the episcopal office, but they accorded it no special significance. The tasks of the bishop are the same as those entrusted to other ordained servants of the church. Thus it was that SC included a single table of duties for "Bischöfen, Pfarrherren und Predigern."

The confessional writers draw two conclusions from their inter-

[34] 273:6 (Ap XII 104); 241:5 (Ap VII 28); 291:6 (Ap XII 176); 473:10 (Tr 8); 474:15 f. (Tr 11); 491:7 and 9 (Tr 67); 456:22 (SA III 9).

[35] 273:41 and 47 (Ap XII 106).

[36] 294:1 — Prediger und Diakonos (Ap XIII 12); 426:13 (SA II III 1); 502:30 (SC Foreword 6); 547:30 (LC Foreword 6); 626:45 (LC I 263).

[37] 246:20 (Ap VII 48); 205:15 (Ap IV 234); 479:30 (Tr 27), and 491:19 — Pfarrherrn und Lehrer (Tr 67).

[38] 62:9 (AC VIII 2); 363:38 (Ap XXIV 48).

[39] See, e. g., the whole of AC XXVIII and Ap XXVIII 12, plus Tr 60 ff. Any attempts to justify a specific episcopal constitution on the basis of the Lutheran Confessions must be looked upon as futile. One might with better reason cite the Swedish church order of 1571. Although the fundamental equality between bishops and pastors is not questioned there, it is stated that the distinction between bishop and pastor ought to be preserved, since that is good church organization, a subject introduced under the rubric "God the Holy Spirit" (Church Order, chap. 25). This higher estimate placed upon the office of the bishop is one explanation of the fact that the post-Reformation Swedish church tradition was distinctive. There is no counterpart to what is said in this Swedish document in either AC, Ap, or Tr. For further information on this matter the

pretation of *ministerium* (the Greek *diakonia*): (1) The term denotes a special service, or office, and (2) the difference in rank between bishops and priests is abolished in principle. All ministers are called to serve the Word and the sacraments. The purpose of the ministry is to give expression to God's activities. This follows from the functional view of the office of the ministry.

The Tasks of the Ministry

One of the fundamental ideas in Roman Catholic theology is that the priests and bishops of the church continue here on earth the work of the incarnate but now exalted Christ in the time between the Resurrection and the Second Coming. They are placed in office by Christ to lead the faithful to eternal life. The office of the ministry was established to guide the faithful and the church in new situations. In the power of their ordination, priests and bishops function at Christ's command and in His stead as His representatives.[40]

Christ worked on earth with divine power and authority. He has entrusted His *potestas* to His successors, the bishops and the priests, through whom He now continues His work. In harmony with canonical law, the Catholic theologians of that time set forth a twofold ministerial authority, *potestas ordinis* and *potestas iurisdictionis*.[41] These two forms of authority resulted from Christ's twofold activity as priest and king.

Potestas ordinis, the priestly authority, includes everything related to the worship service and the administration of the sacraments. When the bishop in the ordination service says "Receive the power to offer sacrifice in the church for the living and the dead, in the name of the Father and of the Son and of the Holy Spirit," *Accipe potestatem offerendi in ecclesia pro vivis et mortuis, in nomine Patris et Filii et Spiritus Sancti*, the priest receives authority to offer the sacrifice of the Mass and to administer the other sacraments.[42] *Potestas iurisdictionis* includes all that the ministry requires in order to teach and govern the church. The Confutation expresses both of these aspects of the minis-

---

reader is referred to P. Brunner (1955), pp. 43 ff., and to H. Lieberg (1962), pp. 153 ff., 216 ff., 308—13 and the literature mentioned there.

[40] P. E. Persson (1961), pp. 10 ff. Cf. Denz., 699, and N. Herborn, *Enchiridion*, chaps. 13 and 15.

[41] *Codex iuris canonici*, can. 118, 196, and 948. CR 27, 178: Nam sufficientissime probatur, potestatem ecclesiasticam in spiritualibus esse iure divino fundatam. J. B. Sägmüller I, 1 (1925), 45 f.

[42] Denz., 701. Dom C. Lialine in *En bok om kyrkans ämbete, A Book on the Ministry of the Church* (1951), pp. 127 f.

try in such a way that bishops not only have the authority to present God's Word and the sacraments, but also to rule, to punish, and to show the faithful the way to eternal blessedness.[43] But to execute this commission, the bishop requires "the power to judge, define, distinguish, and establish what is helpful or conducive to the goal of eternal bliss." [44] This seemingly necessitates a degree of independence on the part of the bishops. They must make new decisions from time to time, and they can do that on the basis of Christ's promise in John 16:12 f. They act in Christ's stead. Bishops and priests function in the present as another Christ, *vice Christi,* in His stead. They are His co-workers, *cooperatores,*[45] God's assistants.[46] Through the priest Christ offers the sacrifice of the Mass,[47] and in the sacrament of penance He exercises His jurisdictional authority.

The Lutheran Confessions accepted the conventional division of *potestas ordinis* and *potestas iurisdictionis,* but they criticized (1) the interpretation of what these concepts mean, and (2) the scope of the assigned responsibilities. Approval of the old division of episcopal authority into *potestas ordinis* and *potestas iurisdiction's* is found in Ap XXVIII 13. As far as the Confessions are concerned, the former means only that the bishop or priest has the *ministerium verbi et sacramentorum,* i. e., that he is called to "the ministry of Word and sacraments" (Ap XXVIII 13). *Potestas ordinis* is therefore the summary expression of what AC V and all other pertinent confessional statements consider the essential task of the ministry. By interpreting *potestas ordinis* as they do, the Confessions reject the idea of the ministry as a service of sacrifice. As we have seen in a previous chapter, they repudiate every thought of sacrifice in connection with the Lord's Supper. By defining the ministry as "the ministry of the Word and the administration of the sacraments to others," *ministerium verbi et sacramentorum aliis porrigendorum* (Ap XIII 7), they at the same time take a position in opposition to the Roman Catholic

[43] CR 27, 179 — Episcopos non solum habere potestatem ministerii verbi Dei, sed etiam potestatem regiminis et coercitivae correctionis ad dirigendum subditos in finem beatitudinis aeternae. Cf. Ap XXVIII 6, where this formulation is subjected to a critical analysis.

[44] CR 27, 225 translated from the German. The corresponding Latin text reads as follows: potestas iudicandi, definiendi, et statuendi ea, quae ad praefatam finem expediunt aut conducunt (CR 27, 179).

[45] N. Herborn, *Enchiridion,* 80:11, 27 and 33.

[46] Ibid., 64:23.

[47] Denz., 698: sacerdos enim in persona Christi loquens hoc conficit sacramentum.

view of ordination. Pastors are called not to offer sacrifice but to preach the Gospel and distribute the sacraments to the people.[48]

The Confessions assign everything connected with the exercise of the power of the keys to the jurisdictional authority—but they impose strong limitations on this authority. A bishop has "a definite command, a definite Word of God, which he ought to teach and according to which he ought to exercise his jurisdiction" (Ap XXVIII 14).[49] The legitimate *potestas iurisdictionis* includes the power "to forgive sins, to reject doctrine which is contrary to the Gospel, and to exclude from the fellowship of the church ungodly persons whose wickedness is known, doing all this without human power, simply by the Word." [50]

The jurisdictional authority of the bishops is therefore limited to a few specific areas. All secular power is excluded. The spiritual and secular spheres must not be confused.[51] Both certainly originate with God (AC XXVIII 14), but their tasks are completely unlike. Priests and bishops do not have the right to involve themselves in secular government (AC XXVIII 2); they cannot impose secular punishment (AC XXVIII 20); they lack authority to judge court cases involving marriage (AC XXVIII 29). Spiritual and secular power is to be kept separate.

But even in ecclesiastical matters the jurisdictional authority is limited to the just-named responsibilities. Bishops cannot proceed on their own, without Scriptural support, to promulgate religious decrees and then proclaim that they are necessary to salvation. The Confessions consign all regulations regarding liturgy and church ceremonies, holy days and hierarchical gradations, eating and drinking, to the concept *traditiones humanae*—which according to Matt. 15:9 ought not be observed when they encroach upon justification by faith. In general the Symbols adopt a liberal attitude toward ecclesiastical customs and usages. They can and should be retained as long as they do not

---

[48] 293:34 — Ideo sacerdotes vocantur non ad ulla sacrificia velut in lege pro populo facienda . . . sed vocantur ad docendum evangelium et sacramenta porrigenda populo (Ap XIII 9).

[49] 400:18 — habent certum mandatum, certum verbum Dei, quod docere, iuxta quod exercere suam iurisdictionem debent (Ap XXVIII 14).

[50] 124:5 — remittere peccata, reiicere doctrinam ab evangelio dissentientem et impios, quorum nota est impietas, excludere a communione ecclesiae, sine vi humana, sed verbi (AC XXVIII 21).

[51] 122:21 — Non igitur commiscendae sunt potestates ecclesiastica et civilis (AC XXVIII 12). 239:49—240:2 (Ap VII 23 f.).

hinder freedom of conscience. However, all traditions introduced for the purpose of justification must be repudiated.[52]

The radically different views of the jurisdictional authority of the ministry (which Ap looked upon as one of the major facets of the controversy)[53] are glaringly apparent to anyone who takes a closer look at the arguments on both sides. According to the Catholic concept the bishops receive their jurisdictional power from Christ. Since they act in Christ's stead, they must also have the right to make judgments and issue decrees which affect the faith and lives of men. Of greatest significance for this point of view is the fact that the apostles (according to Acts 15:20) issued commands having to do only with church order, and that the church even went against the commands of the Decalog by moving the Sabbath from Saturday to Sunday.[54] Bishops therefore have the right to act in new situations; they are not bound in an absolute way by a word of Scripture.

In opposition, the Lutheran Confessions submit the thesis that the jurisdictional power of the bishops must not go contrary to the Gospel (AC XXVIII 34). For when they teach or decide anything contrary to the Gospel, then the church has God's command to deny them obedience (AC XXVIII 23). When the Confessions use the word "Gospel" here, it has reference to the New Testament writings. This is clear from the context, and quotations from Augustine and Gratian serve to underscore it.[55] Scripture takes precedence over ecclesiastical authority. To establish this principle, the Confessions refer to Gratian, who cites the practice of the early church fathers.[56]

But a line of argument based exclusively on Scripture could produce complications. One finds that the apostles repeatedly issued temporary commands for the good of the congregations. Acts 15:20 is. without question a striking example of a Biblical precept which neither of the contesting parties during the Reformation looked upon as binding. The Catholic theologians used it to support their view of

[52] 69:6—70:6 (AC XV); 297:31—307:23 (Ap XV). With regard to the expression "traditiones humanae" see Chapter Two above.

[53] 398:16 — De hoc articulo controversia est (Ap XXVIII 6).

[54] 125:13-30 (AC XXVIII 30 ff.). Cf. the argumentation in CR 27, 91: Et tamen recte pie ac vere ita credimus, non quod in scripturis habeatur expressum, sed quia sic per spiritum sanctum edocta tenet pia mater Ecclesia (Foreword to the Confutation, 1530).

[55] *Epist. ad catholicos,* 11, 28: qui nec catholicis episcopis consentiendum est, sicuti forte falluntur, ut contra canonicas dei scripturas aliquid sentiant (CSEL 52, 264). *Decr. Grat.,* I, d. 9, c. 8-10.

[56] W. Maurer (1957), p. 86.

episcopal power. For their part, the Lutherans emphasized the words of Peter found earlier in the same chapter of Acts, that no one should put "a yoke upon the neck of the disciples" (Acts 15:10).[57] These words are considered a statement of principle, superior to the commands of more or less incidental nature that are found here and there in Scripture.[58] The apostles themselves admitted that certain of their decrees were temporary and could be abrogated.[59] Scripture is therefore superior to the bishops.

According to the Confessions, the *potestas iurisdictionis* of the bishops does not include the right to establish laws regarding faith and life which are said to be necessary for salvation but which cannot be traced back to Scripture. For the Catholic theologians the shifting of the Sabbath to a new day of the week was proof of the church's right to alter even the commands of the Decalog.[60] But here too the Lutheran Symbols stress the priority of Scripture: It is not the church through its bishops but Scripture itself which has abolished the Jewish Sabbath.[61] The confessional writers are thinking not primarily of Jesus' statements about the Sabbath (e. g., Matt. 12:8) but of the general rule that the ceremonial law, to which the Sabbath command belongs, has been abolished through the Gospel (Ap XV 30). Bishops have the right to establish rules in the interest of order, but what they decide can be set aside if this can be done without giving offense (AC XXVIII 53 f.). The concern of the Confessions is to set limits upon the independent authority of the ministry.

The fact that the ministry was defined as the office of the Word and sacraments means that there is an authority set over it — the Scriptures. What this really signifies has been established in previous chapters on Baptism, the Lord's Supper, and absolution. When, e. g., a pastor celebrating the Lord's Supper reads the words of institution

[57] This Bible passage is often used in connection with the interpretation here set forth. 127:16 ff. (AC XVIII 42); 303:31 ff. (Ap XV 31); 398:37-40 (Ap XXVIII 8). Cf. WA 18, 76:9-18 (*Wider die himmlischen Propheten,* 1525).

[58] In the present-day discussion it is not infrequently asserted that the Bible, according to the reformers' point of view, is completely lacking in authority as far as questions relating to church order are concerned. But if this were true, one might well ask: Why does AC look to the Bible for guidance in the matter of episcopal authority? Or why does Tr appeal to the Bible so frequently for support of its position regarding equality between bishops and pastors? Cf. Chapter One above.

[59] 401:7 — pleraque ordinaverunt ipsi apostoli, quae tempore mutata sunt. Neque ita tradiderunt, ut mutare non liceret (Ap XXVIII 16).

[60] Cf. CR 27, 177—83 (Confutation, 1530).

[61] 130:13 — Scriptura abrogavit sabbatum (AC XXVIII 58).

according to Christ's instructions and command, they receive consecrating significance, not because it is the pastor who reads them but
because he reads the very words which include both Christ's command
and promise.

This can be most clearly illustrated by another sacramental act,
absolution. In the sacrament of penance the Catholic priest appears as
another Christ. He is robed in Christ's jurisdictional power. After the
penitent has been examined, he is chastised and then absolved from
guilt. The priest must have such authority in order to appear as judge.[62]
In the Evangelical practice of penitence the pastor's task is significantly reduced. He is to pronounce the words of absolution, but he
has no right to require a full enumeration of all sins on the part of the
penitent. The penitent's contrition is a matter between God and himself. God, the true judge,[63] works genuine contrition through the Law.
Since the pastor therefore lacks the right to judge, he does not need to
know about all the sins involved in order to speak the words of absolution.[64]

We can now better understand the consequences of the functional
view of the ministry. The pastor in his ministry is to let God's work be
expressed—and this can happen only if the pastor understands that
he is an instrument in God's hands. Bishops and pastors have the twofold *potestas ordinis* and *potestas iurisdictionis*, but they possess no
independent authority in office. They are strictly subordinated to the
Gospel or Scripture,[65] and when they act contrary thereto, no one
owes them any obedience.[66]

The Evangelical view of the tasks of the ministry is revealed even
more clearly against the background of the different ways in which the
reformers and their Catholic opponents understood another basic New

---

[62] Denz., 699. CR 27, 179 (Confutation, 1530). N. Herborn, *Enchiridion*,
81:14-40.

[63] 99:16 — Ergo tua confitere peccata apud Deum, verum iudicem (AC
XXV 11). 452:14 f. (SA III 7).

[64] 273:1 ff. (Ap XII 103); 99:11-19 (AC XXV 10 f.). In AC Melanchthon
buttresses his position by quoting from Chrysostom, as found in *Decr. Grat.* II,
c. 33, q. 3, c. 87, par. 4.

[65] 402:14 — Nec debent episcopi traditiones contra evangelium condere (Ap
XXVIII 20). 402:34 — Darum wenn sie unchristlich und wider die Schrift
lehren, soll man sie nicht hören (Ap XXVIII 21). Cf. CR 21, 224 — Primum
ergo si doceant scripturam, sic audiendi sunt ut Christus. Iuxta illud (Luke 10:16):
Qui vos audit, me audit (*Loci*, 1521).

[66] 124:13 — At cum aliquid contra evangelium docent aut constituunt, tunc
habent ecclesiae mandatum Dei, quod prohibet oboedire (AC XXVIII 23).

Testament passage, Luke 10:16–"He who hears you hears Me." [67]
It had long been held that this passage refers to the ministry. The
Catholic theologians found in this passage additional proof that Christ
had made the apostles and their successors participants in His priestly
and kingly authority, so that they could appear as another Christ and
guide people in questions of doctrine and life.[68] For the reformers it
was precisely this passage that included a definite limitation upon the
tasks of bishops and pastors. The apostles did not receive an unre-
stricted commission from Christ. They were called to proclaim His
Word and not their own. When we hear their words and believe in
them, it is because they speak Christ's Word. Christ demands that all
His apostles and followers preach and teach in such a way that men
hear Him – Christ. "For Christ requires them to teach in such a way
that he might be heard, because he says, 'hears me.' Therefore he
wants his voice, his Word to be heard, not human traditions" (Ap
XXVIII 19).[69] We are to believe the servants of Christ, not because of
their own words but because of Christ's Word, which they set forth.
In Luke 10:16 Christ confirms the fact that the Word conveyed to us
through the apostles is effective "and that we should not look for another word from heaven." (Ap XXVIII 18)

In practice this means that when the Gospel's Word of forgiveness
is spoken by the pastor in absolution, we hear God's own voice, according to Luke 10:16. "Because God truly quickens through the
Word, the keys truly forgive sin before him, according to the statement (Luke 10:16), 'He who hears you, hears me.' Therefore we must
believe the voice of the one absolving no less than we would believe
a voice coming from heaven" (Ap XII 40). Absolution deserves all of
our confidence, "because it is the voice of God and is spoken by God's
command."[70]

The various tasks of the ministry can therefore be consolidated
into this one: to make the voice of Christ heard through preaching
and through the administration of the sacraments and the power of
the keys. If this is done, the pastor's personal qualifications are of

[67] Luke 10:16 is quoted remarkably often: 124:9 (AC XXVIII 21). 240:45
(Ap VII 28). 246:19 (Ap VII 47). 259:14 f. (Ap XII 40). 401:25 (Ap
XXVIII 18). Cf. H. Lieberg (1962), 304 f.

[68] CR 27, 161 f. (Confutation, 1530). N. Herborn, *Enchiridion*, 89:18-21,
115:17—116:3, and 116:33—117:7, plus chap. 13.

[69] 401:38 — Requirit enim Christus. ut ita doceant, ut ipse audiatur, quia
dicit: Me audit. Igitur suam vocem, suum verbum vult audiri, non traditiones
humanas (Ap XXVIII 19).

[70] 98:3 — quia sit vox Dei et mandato Dei pronuntietur (AC XXV 3).

secondary importance. The decisive thing is not what the pastor is but what he preaches and teaches. We are not to listen to false prophets, for they come from Antichrist. But the sacraments do not lose their efficacy if they are administered by unworthy pastors who have been properly called by the church. These men do not function as private persons but *vice Christi,* in Christ's stead – according to Luke 10:16: "He who hears you hears Me." [71]

God's actions through the office of the ministry cannot be illustrated more clearly. The functional view of the ministry implies that the office is to exercise its churchly duties in Christ's stead. The pastors are in this sense His representatives. In performing the duties of their office "they do not represent their own persons but the person of Christ, because of the church's call, as Christ testifies (Luke 10:16), 'He who hears you hears me.'" (Ap VII 28)

The Confessions clearly introduce a functional view into the concept of *ministerium* and use it to give expression to God's existential activity in preaching, in the administration of the sacraments, and through the power of the keys. But they never express the same fear as do modern interpreters with regard to the idea that certain men must be called to this activity, execute God's mandate, and articulate His promises. On the contrary, "it is God's will to preach and work through men and those who have been chosen by men." [72] Bishops and pastors are necessary for the execution of Christ's commission "to preach the Gospel and administer the sacraments to the people" (Ap XIII 9). But they have no independent position in relation to Christ, i. e., in relation to His Word. They are to let His voice be heard, and not their own. If they do so, God is present in the office of the ministry. (Ap XIII 12)

Against this background, it is fully understandable why the Confessions so frequently make the transition from *ministerium* to the Word. A few examples can best explain this. According to AC XXVIII bishops are to promote spiritual good and spiritual righteousness. "These gifts cannot be obtained except through the office of preaching and of administering the holy sacraments, for St. Paul says, 'The gospel is the power of God for salvation to everyone who has faith.'" The Latin text also refers to Psalm 119:50: "Thy Word gives me life." For the expression "through the office of preaching and of

[71] 240:46 f. (Ap VII 28 German). 246:17 ff. (Ap VII 47). 238:11-13 (Ap VII 19).

[72] 294:3 (Ap XIII 12 German). H. Lieberg (1962), pp. 270—85, rightfully emphasizes this point of view.

administering the holy sacraments" the Latin text reads "through the ministry [*ministerium*] of Word and sacraments" (AC XXVIII 9). This passage deals with the duties of bishops, and the idea is that when these men fulfill their responsibilities, the Holy Spirit is given through the Word and the sacraments. The mediation is not to be found in the office but in that which the office administers.

The same point of view is found in Ap XIII. After stating that God has established the preaching office, reference is made to two Bible passages which deal with the Word (Rom. 1:16 and Is. 55:11). Immediately thereupon follows the explanation: "The church has the command to appoint ministers" (Ap XIII 12). *Ministerium* refers to the activity which the persons thereto called are to carry out. But the mediation is accomplished not through the persons but through the Word and sacraments they offer. Neither is it true that these persons, through an authority conferred by ordination, make the Word and sacraments effective means of salvation. He who works is God; the pastor simply fulfills a necessary obligation. When the pastor does what he is called to do, God the Holy Spirit is Himself present. The functional view of the ministry, which emphasizes the Word, does not exclude the ordaining of individuals to the office of the ministry. The concept of their tasks and their position, on the other hand, is radically altered. Pastors do not mediate grace; they are servants of the Word and the sacraments. Through their acts God's work is to be expressed.

Against this background we can now understand AC V. This article says more about the Word and sacraments than it does about the office of the ministry, because the Holy Spirit comes to man through these and not through the office. When Melanchthon formulated AC V, he did not exclude the special office of the ministry, but he was anxious to give expression to its new meaning as an instrument for the Word and the sacraments. As a result, he shifted the emphasis from the ministry to the means of grace.

One consequence of the functional view of the ministry is that the men who hold this office are not accorded a special spiritual position superior to the other members of the church. Through the sacrament of ordination Catholic priests receive a *character indelebilis,* i. e., a spiritual mark which cannot be eradicated.[73] A difference in spiritual worth arose between priests and laymen, as seen among other things in the fact that laymen were denied the chalice in the Lord's Supper.[74]

[73] Denz., 695 — characterem, id est, spirituale quoddam signum a ceteris distinctivum, impriunt in anima indelebile.

[74] G. Biel (1510), Lectio 84, fol. 251/R: Ex illo autem errore, quod com-

The Lutheran Confessions were completely opposed to any inequality between pastors and laymen. They are the same in spiritual worth; the difference between them has to do only with their tasks. This equality led to the restoration of the chalice to the laymen – as was the practice in the early church.[75] The abolition of enforced celibacy was another result of this spiritual equality (AC XXIII). It was as natural for the reformers to see that the pastor occupies a special office as to see that the prince had his specific mission in the state. Both the spiritual and the secular estates are of God. But men are needed to serve within them.

Appointment to the Ministry

The concept of the universal priesthood doesn't play nearly as important a role in the Confessions as in Luther. According to a common and oft-mentioned idea, Luther derived the special office of the ministry from the universal priesthood, which empowers all baptized and believing Christians to preach the Word and administer the sacraments. The special office was delegated out of the universal priesthood in the interest of order, since all do not have the requisite gifts for publicly exercising the duties of the ministry. As a result, suitable persons must be called to do this.[76]

But another line of thought can be found in Luther alongside this one. The functionally conceived ministry is a divine institution. Luther thought of the actual ministry as an independent institution, which is a part of the essence of the church, based on God's express will and command. How these two trends of thought can be combined into one is a problem which has been solved in various ways.[77]

The problem is less ambiguous in the Confessions, inasmuch as they follow through on the latter line of thought, thereby achieving

munio sub utraque specie esset de necessitate salutis, sequuntur alii non minus periculosi errores, ut recitat Gerson. Scilicet primo quod tanta esset dignitas laicorum circa sumptionem corporis Christi sicut sacerdotum. With regard to the spiritual distinction between pastors and laymen consult the critical presentation by F. Arnold in *Universität Tübingen: Reden bei der feierlichen Übergabe des Rektorates zu Beginn des Sommersemesters am 7 Mai 1954*, pp. 23—45, and also Y. Congar (1954), pp. 29 ff. and 64 ff.

[75] 330:22-39 (Ap XXII 6 ff.). *Conc. Constantiense*, 1415 (Denz., 626), sets forth, with approval, the alteration here stated.

[76] H. Lieberg (1962), pp. 40—103; G. Hök in *En Bok om kyrkans ämbete* (1951), pp. 146 f.; H. Lyttkens in NKT (1958), pp. 8 ff.

[77] W. Brunotte (1959); H. Lyttkens in NKT (1958), pp. 14 ff., 81 ff.; Regin Prenter in AUU 1960:12 (1961), pp. 95 ff.; H. Lieberg (1962), pp. 104—32; and Persson (1961), pp. 299 ff.

logical consistency in their statements. The universal priesthood is given a subordinate place.[78]   The classical Bible passage for this doctrine, 1 Peter 2:9, is quoted only once (Tr 69), with the correct observation that the "royal priesthood" refers to the whole church, not only to the ordained clergy. The New Testament's "universal priesthood" is just another expression for the church as the true people of God.[79] But the Confessions do not claim that the universal priesthood is to replace or take over the functions of the ministerial office, but rather that it has the right and the duty "to choose and ordain servants of the church." (Tr 70)

It is true that a number of scholars insist that AC V points to the universal priesthood.[80] The article, however, does not in fact refer to it, but rather to the function of administering Word and sacraments, which is regularly taken care of by persons called thereto — persons who are discussed in detail in AC, Ap XIII and XIV, and in the Confessions in general. If AC V is interpreted in the same way, one can avoid all the problems concerning the relationship between the universal priesthood and the special office of the ministry — which Melanchthon wanted to avoid[81] — and at the same time gain what was above all important to the reformers, viz., to oppose the hierarchical system and the cleavage between clergy and laity. Through the functional view of the ministry all such barriers are eliminated.

But the ministry must have its incumbents. The Confessions never cease to emphasize Christ's command to the church to call, choose, and ordain its servants.[82] Apart from a proper call, no one can publicly serve in the church (AC XIV). According to Ap XIV the call also includes a form of ordination. Using examples derived from the early church, SA speaks of the right and the duty to ordain persons suited to the service of the church (III X 1-3). According to Ap the church is

[78] R. Josefson in *En Bok om kyrkans ämbete* (1951), p. 184. H. Lieberg (1962), pp. 259—67, plus the literature there referred to.

[79] Y. Congar (1954), pp. 19 and 38; E. Kinder in *Schriften des theologischen Konvents Augsburgischen Bekenntnisses* (1953), pp. 5—23.

[80] R. Sohm (1892), p. 491, n. 18. and p. 499, n. 31; W. Maurer (1957), pp. 67 ff.; E. Kinder (1958), p. 152.

[81] Eck had attacked the reformers for falsely teaching that every Christian has the right to ordain pastors and confirm children, etc. Eck, art. 267—68 in W. Gussmann, II (1930), 134.

[82] 491:4 — Ubicunque est ecclesia, ibi est jus administrandi evangelii. Quare necesse est ecclesiam retineri jus vocandi, eligendi et ordinandi ministros (Tr 67). Concerning what follows see the excellent presentation in L. Grane (1959), pp. 127 ff.

commanded by God to set in office preachers and deacons. (XIII 11)[83]

Lieberg has collected a variety of material to throw light upon the call and ordination to the ministry, but the impression one gets from the sources is how timidly new and distinctive forms were sought. No one was ordained (for certain) prior to 1535,[84] and then at the request of the Elector of Saxony. The Confessions shed very little light upon the forms used for the installation of pastors and preachers, a fact which is even more obvious when compared with contemporary Catholic documents. Herborn underscores the importance of being sent into service through laying on of hands and prayer by the bishops. He refers to the apostolic succession and seeks to prove from Scripture that this form of sending men into the ministry was used since the time of the apostles.[85] One looks in vain for such instructions in the Confessions. For information about appointment to clerical office one must look elsewhere, including contemporary church handbooks.[86] Call, election, and ordination normally belonged together, and of these three the call was no doubt looked upon as most essential.[87] Ordination was thought of as a confirmation of the call in the presence of the worshiping congregation, but the form it took was a matter of indifference. The laying on of hands was recommended by both reformers, but it was not held to be expressly commanded in Scripture and therefore did not have the character of a *ius divinum*. Attempts to attribute a sacramental significance [88] to it on the basis of XIII 12 are not correct. What Melanchthon says there must be seen as a benign attempt to be courteous to his opponents, but it lacks fundamental significance. The fact is that the Confessions with their functional view of the ministry must attribute relatively minor importance to ordination, since their emphasis lies not upon the servant but upon the mission he is called to carry out.

How indifferent the confessional writers were to the form used in placing a pastor in office can be seen from the fact that they were even willing to concede to the Catholic bishops the right to ordain for the

---

[83] 294:4 — Habet enim ecclesia mandatum de constituendis ministris (Ap XIII 12).

[84] H. Lieberg (1962), pp. 177 f. and 185.

[85] N. Herborn, *Enchiridion,* chap. 15.
to 28, and G. Rietschel (1889). WA 38, 220 f., and 401 ff.

[86] *Die evangelischen Kirchenordnungen des XVI. Jahrhunderts,* I (1902), 24

[87] G. Hök in *En bok om kyrkans ämbete* (1951); H. Lieberg (1962), pp. 340 ff.

[88] Cf. the attempts in this direction made by H. Lieberg (1962), pp. 348 ff.

sake of love and unity—if they would only be true bishops and take care of the church (Ap XIV; SA III X 1). This is also a meaningful testimony to Luther and Melanchthon's strong concern for the unity of the church. Because of the fundamental equality of bishops and pastors, any pastor at all can carry out this commission. More important than the form used for ordination is that the church not be left without ministers. The statements concerning the call and ordination confirm that the confessional writers can never have questioned the office of the ministry as such. They saw in episcopal ordination a human contrivance without support in the Holy Scriptures and the procedure of the early church. Hierarchical distinctions among the clergy are not necessary for the survival of the church. On the other hand, the ministry must remain and function, so that through its services the Word, the sacraments, and absolution may be made available for the church's life and growth.

Chapter Ten:

The Church

The consequences of the Lutheran view of justification, the sacraments, and the ministry are revealed in the doctrine of the church. Just as the Word, the sacraments, and the ministry are thought of as divine activities without human mediation, so in the church the emphasis is placed upon what God the Holy Spirit does. What this meant, concretely, was the demolition of the institution of the Roman Catholic Church. According to the Catholic view, Christ has delegated His spiritual power to the church and its ministry, with the pope at the apex. Here on earth the pope is the vicar of Christ, *vicarius Christi,* and thereby the mouth through which Christ now speaks. The church is accorded an independent significance in the sense that through its clergy it guides men in matters of faith and life. When the clergy speak, Christ speaks, for He has entrusted the Holy Spirit to the church and has furnished it with His authority. According to the Lutheran Confessions the church has no such mission or authority. What is necessary for faith and life is found in the Holy Scriptures. The church is the creation of God the Holy Spirit through Word and sacrament, and its only task is the function of providing these means of grace to men so that they might believe and be incorporated into the fellowship of Christ—for which "the church" is another expression. That the church is conceived of at all points as God's direct work through Word and sacrament without itself mediating grace is the basic view of the church's essence and membership, its origins and unity.

The Essence of the Church

In its seventh article AC refers to the church as *congregatio sanctorum, in qua evangelium pure docetur et recte administrantur sacramenta.* The church is "the assembly of saints in which the Gospel is taught purely and the sacraments are administered rightly." [1] This definition has its closest prototype in the Schwabach Articles,[2] and it

---

[1] 61:4-7 (AC VII 1).

[2] 61:23 — Solche Kirch ist nit ander dann die Glaubigen an Christo, welche

goes back to a statement from Luther in his great confession of 1528: "Next, I believe that there is one holy Christian Church on earth, i. e. the community or number or assembly of all Christians in all the world, the one bride of Christ, and his spiritual body of which he is the only head." [3] These statements are based upon similar expressions from the beginning of the 1520s, when Luther's concept took firm shape. The church is most clearly defined in *On the Papacy in Rome* (1520) as "a community or assembly of the saints in faith." [4] Luther put it the same way in SA: The church is "holy believers and sheep who hear the voice of their Shepherd." [5]

What all these statements have in common is that the church is the fellowship of believers. The chief words in AC VII are *congregatio sanctorum*, in the German version *die Versammlung aller Glaubigen* ("the assembly of all believers"). Nonetheless, one often finds strong reservations about this definition of the church in the pertinent literature. These reservations can be traced back to the confessional theology of the previous century, which sought to come to grips with the collegial concept of society propounded in the Age of the Enlightenment. According to this concept, communities are built up from below and developed on the basis of each member's free choice.[6] In contrast to this, leading spokesmen for confessional theology looked upon the church as something other than the sum of individual members. These theologians had good reason for their criticism, but the institutional concept they employed had sources other than those of the Reformation and therefore has little value for illuminating the concept of the church.

When the Confessions use the word *Versammlung,* "assembly," they do not thereby have "association" in mind. The alternatives for *Versammlung* in Luther's confession of 1528, quoted above, are "the

obgenannte Artikel und Stuck halten, glauben und lehren und daruber verfolgt und gemartert werden in der Welt.

[3] WA 26, 506:30-33; LW 37, 367 (*Confession Concerning Christ's Supper,* 1528).

[4] WA 6, 301:1-2, LW 39, 75. See also WA 6, 293:1-5, LW 39, 65; and WA 7, 683:10, LW 39, 218 (*Answer to the Hyperchristian . . . Book by Goat Emser,* 1521).

[5] 459:21-22 (SA III XII 2).

[6] See, e. g., F. Delitzsch (1847), pp. 3 f.; F. J. Stahl (1862), pp. 42 ff.; G. Billing (1876—78), pp. 241 ff. Cf. E. Troeltsch in *Die Kultur der Gegenwart* (1909), pp. 436 ff. Gustaf Aulén (1912), pp. 25, 28 ff., and 80 ff. Opposition to the collegial system is particularly marked in Stahl. Cf. H. Fagerberg (1952), pp. 197 ff., and the literature there listed, plus E. Hirsch, V (1954), 160 f. and 171 ff.

bride of Christ" and "the body of Christ"; these same expressions
are found in Ap[7] and LC.[8] Such observations indicate how alien
modern ideas of "association" must have been to the reformers. When
AC VII was written, the purpose was to interpret the meaning of what
the New Testament says about the church as the body of Christ. The
phrase "the assembly of all believers" implies the presence of the
Holy Spirit, for He works through the Word and sacraments to lead
men to fellowship with Christ, who is the Source of faith and the Head
of the church. The article on the church in AC VII follows the articles
on justification and its means, the Word and the sacraments. Since
Christ is the Foundation of faith, this connection must also be made
in defining the church. In "the assembly of all believers" (AC VII) it
is presupposed, therefore, that the church is the body of Christ. This
point of view is developed further in Ap, where *congregatio* serves as
an explanation of the New Testament's *corpus Christi*.[9] In order not
to misunderstand the Confessions' definition of the church, one must
bear in mind how self-evident the transition from the body of Christ
to the congregation was.

In using *congregatio sanctorum,* the confessional writers also
intended to reproduce the meaning of *communio sanctorum* in the
Apostles' Creed.[10] Ap tells us this definition was added to the creed
in order to confirm that the church refers to "the assembly of saints
who share the association of the same Gospel or teaching and of the
same Holy Spirit, who renews, consecrates, and governs their hearts"
(VII 8). The thought here is in complete agreement with LC's doctrine
of the church. *Communio* is misunderstood, said Luther, if it is
translated by the abstract *Gemeinschaft,* communion; its real meaning
is *Gemeine,* congregation or community, and it is used in the creed as
an explanation for *ecclesia,* church, which appears in the previous

[7] 235:1 and 5 — corpus Christi (Ap VII 5); 236:5 — Christi Braut (Ap
VII 10); 241:14 — corpus Christi (Ap VII 29); 236:32 — corpus Christi (Ap
VII 12).

[8] 657:26 — Ich gläube, dass da sei ein heiliges Häuflein und Gemeine auf
Erden eiteler Heiliger unter einem Haupt, Christo, durch den heiligen Geist
zusammenberufen (LC II 51). Cf. a similar allusion to the body of Christ in
670:43 (LC III 37).

[9] 234:34 — Et haec ecclesia sola dicitur corpus Christi, quod Christus spiritu
suo renovat, sanctificat et gubernat, ut testatur Paulus Eph. 1 cum ait: Et ipsum
dedit caput super omnia ecclesiae, quae est corpus eius [whereupon Ap com-
ments] videlicet integritas, id est tota congregatio ipsius, qui omnia in omnibus
perficit (Ap VII 5).

[10] 235:29 — Et videtur additum, quod sequitur, sanctorum communio, ut
exponeretur, quid significet ecclesia, nempe congregationem sanctorum (Ap VII 8).

phrase. ". . . someone wished to explain what the Christian church is. But some among us, who understand neither Latin nor German, have rendered this 'communion *(Gemeinschaft)* of saints,' although no German would use or understand such an expression. To speak idiomatically, we ought to say 'a community *(Gemeine)* of saints,' that is, a community composed only of saints, or, still more clearly, 'a holy community.' This I say in order that the expression may be understood; it has become so established in usage that it cannot well be uprooted . . ." (LC II 49-50). He had earlier [11] made the observation that *communio sanctorum* is lacking in the so-called Symbolum Romanum and that it must therefore have been added to the Apostles' Creed relatively late.[12] His view was that at the outset it had been an elucidating gloss in the margin of the ancient handwritten documents but that it had gradually worked its way into the text itself. Two things are worthy of special attention.

First of all, the reformers' interpretation of *communio* as *congregatio (Gemeine)* is certainly incorrect. *Communio* signifies fellowship with, participation in something. The older German translation which Luther assailed had the proper conception of the word's true meaning.[13]

Second, the reformers gave a new and previously unknown meaning to the genitive *sanctorum* by translating it as "the believers." In AC there is an abrupt transition from "the saints" to "the believers"; the German text reproduces *congregatio sanctorum* with *die Versammlung aller Glaubigen,* "the assembly of all believers" (AC VII 1), and the same language is employed in Ap, SA, and in Luther's private writings.[14] What *sanctorum* originally signified is still being debated, and we can hardly decide it with complete certainty. The choice is between the masculine "the saints" and the neuter "the holy," i. e., the sacraments.[15] In the former case *communio sanctorum*

[11] WA 2, 190:20-26 (*Resolutio Lutheriana super propositione XIII de potestate papae,* 1519). W. Kohler I:1 (1900), 82—84.

[12] F. Kattenbusch I (1884), 59—62. A. Hahn (1897), par. 18 and 19. The much-mentioned *communio sanctorum* is presumably of Gallic origin. See A. Hahn (1897), par. 61, and J. N. D. Kelly (1950), pp. 388—90.

[13] J. Meyer (1929), p. 95. Cf. F. Hofmann (1933), p. 244, n. 134, which indicates that Augustine was aware of this meaning.

[14] E. G., WA 6, 292:37 — das die Christenheit heysset eyn vorsamlunge aller Christgleubigen auff erden, wie wir ym glauben betten, 'Ich gleub in den heyligen geyst, ein gemeynschafft der heyligen' (*Von dem Papstthum zu Rom,* 1520), and WA 50, 624:14—625:15 (*Von den Konziliis und Kirchen,* 1539). E. Schlink (1961), pp. 203 f.

[15] This was supported by Th. Zahn (1893), pp. 88 ff., and F. Kattenbusch,

should be translated as "the fellowship of saints," in the latter as "participation in the sacraments." Various factors, including Greek texts, argue for the second of these possibilities, but complete certainty cannot be achieved. The Confessions, however, consistently maintain that the church is the same as the congregation of believers.

The reformers found support for their interpretation in the Greek *ekklesia,* which means "assembly of the people" in both secular and sacred contexts. In Acts 19:32 and 39 this word is used in reference to the civil assembly in Ephesus,[16] and in other passages, where "God's" or "Christ's" is added, it refers to the Christian congregation. If *ekklesia* is translated as "church," its meaning, according to Luther, is obscured. He attacked the "un-German," "blind," and "unintelligible" word "church" with great zeal because it is such a poor explanation of the New Testament *ekklesia.*[17]

Luther was sure as early as in his lectures on the Psalms (1513 to 1515) that *ecclesia* should be translated as *congregatio,*[18] and he discovered some years later that John Hus was of the same opinion. In his major statement on the church—which Luther came to know well after the Leipzig debate [19]—Hus emphasized that *congregatio* is the proper interpretation of *ecclesia,* whose basic meaning is "assembly." [20] Hus anticipated Luther in rejecting the erroneous

II (1900), 931 f. J. N. D. Kelly (1950) represents a contradictory interpretation: "The dominant conception, at any rate between the fifth and eighth centuries, was 'fellowship with holy persons.' "

16 G. Kittel, III (1938), 516. Cf. WA 50, 624:21 (*Von den Konziliis und Kirchen,* 1539).

17 WA 50, 624:18-20, and 625:5 and 32 (*Von den Konziliis und Kirchen,* 1539). Cf. 655:44 ff. (LC II 47 f.).

18 WA 3, 184:3 — sanctorum congregatio seu Ecclesia, and 488:12 — congregationis tuae (scil.) ecclesiae (*Dictata super Psalterium,* 1513—15).

19 WA Br I, 514:27-29 (An Joh. Staupitz 3/10/1519). Cf. 419:24-25 (Wenzel von Rozdalowsky an Luther, 17/7/1519). WA 6, 587:21—588:3 (*Von den neuen Eckischen Bullen und Lügen,* 1520), and WA 5, 451:29—452:9 (*Operationes in Psalmos,* 1519—1521), in which he goes so far as to accept Huss' definition of the church as *universalis praedestinatorum universitas!* This book was published in Germany in 1520. See W. Köhler I:1 (1900), 195 ff., and A. Ebeneter in ZKT (1962), pp. 20 f. Huss is quoted here from an edition dating from 1558.

20 J. Huss, *De ecclesia* (1588), p. 196 b — Sed quia secundum Graecos dicitur congregatio, sub uno legimine contenta, ut 2. Polit. chap. 7 docet Arist. ubi dicit: Ecclesia autem participant omnes. Ideo secundum istam significationem congregatio omnium hominum dicitur Ecclesia. Huss is referring here to Aristotle, *Politica,* 2, c. 7:4.

identification of church with church building [21] and clergy.[22] Hus and Luther disagreed at certain points in defining the church,[23] but they were agreed in saying that *congregatio* must be the right interpretation of *ecclesia*. As a result, LC is also critical of using "church" *(Kirche)* as a translation of the creed's *ecclesia*. If one does so translate *ecclesia,* said Luther, the unlearned will inevitably think of the church building. "But the house should not be called a church except for the single reason that the group of people assembles there. For we who assemble select a special place and give the house its name by virtue of the assembly." The Greek *ekklesia* means "a common assembly," and the creed's *sancta ecclesia catholica* must be translated as "a Christian congregation or assembly," *ein christliche Gemeine oder Sammlung* – or better yet, "a holy Christian people," *ein heilige Christenheit.* (LC II 48)

Our investigation has shown that during the entire era of the Reformation there was complete uniformity in speaking of the church. She is the *congregatio sanctorum,* the congregation of believers. This expression is designed to reproduce the creed's *communio sanctorum* and the Bible's pictures of the church as the body of Christ (Ap VII 5), the bride of Christ (Ap VII 10), and the true people of God (Ap VII 14). All of these metaphors make clear that the church was never thought of as a union of likeminded, believing men. Ap VII 7 tells us directly that AC VII was intended to be an exposition of Eph. 5:25-27 and of the creed's doctrine of the church:

> We have not said anything new. Paul defined the church in the same way in Eph. 5:25-27, saying that it should be purified in order to be holy. He also added the outward marks, the Word and the sacraments. He says, "Christ loved the church and gave himself up for it, that he might sanctify it, having cleansed it by the washing of water with the word, that the church might be presented before him in splendor, without spot or wrinkle or any such thing, that it might be holy and without

[21] Ibid. — Ecclesia primo significat domum Dei, factam ad hoc, ut in ea populus excolat Deum suum.

[22] Ibid. — Secundo, Ecclesia significat ministros ad illam domum Dei pertinentes, isto modo Clerici pertinentes ad unam materialem Ecclesiam vocant se Ecclesiam. (As a result of the clericalization of the church, this identification lay near at hand. See above, Chapter Nine, n. 74, and WA 2, 190:18 (Resolutio Lutheriana, 1519). In *Von dem Papstthum zu Rom* (1520) Luther, as W. Köhler has rightly pointed out — I:1 (1900), 201 — took over Huss' schema (WA 6, 292:35—297:35).

[23] According to Huss, the church is *numerus omnium praedestinatorum,* while according to Luther it is *congregatio sanctorum.*

blemish." We have repeated this statement almost verbatim in our Confession. The Creed also defines the church this way, teaching us to believe that there is a holy, catholic church. (Ap VII 7) [24]

The attitude of the Confessions toward the Bible and tradition, which was presented in Chapter Two (above, p.   ), is here confirmed. The reformers recognized their continuity with the church of the fathers, which was the work of God the Holy Spirit through Word and sacrament. The *congregatio sanctorum* includes the faithful as well as their living Head, Christ, who now works among His own through the means of grace. To use another Biblical concept, the church is the new people of God.

In thus analyzing the church, the writers of the Confessions (like the young Luther) intended to say something basic about its structure. As the people of God, the church is not an external kingdom with laws, regulations, and earthly government; it is rather an internal and spiritual kingdom, of which Christ is king. In *On the Papacy in Rome* Luther pointed out the antithesis between the internal and the external. Both Judaism and Catholicism are characterized by their efforts to construct external congregations, regulated by laws and rites.[25] The church of Christ, in contrast, is an internal spiritual kingdom. The same ideas can be found in Ap. The Israelite people of God formed an external kingdom; the observance of laws and ceremonies was required for membership (Ap VII 14). The confessional writers discerned an analogous situation in the Church of Rome. This church accepted an Old Testament point of view which they generally rejected. They never denied that the church must have an external form, but the true church of which the Bible and the Apostles' Creed speak is something internal. In the final analysis, the church is the fellowship of faith and the Holy Spirit in the heart.[26] The essence of the church is

---

[24] 235:13 — Neque novi quidquam diximus. Paulus omnino eodem modo definivit ecclesiam Eph. 5, quod purificetur, ut sit sancta. Et addit externas notas, verbum et sacramenta. Sic enim ait: Christum delixit ecclesiam et se tradidit pro ea, ut eam sanctificet, purificans lavacro aquae per verbum, ut exhibeat eam sibi gloriosam ecclesiam non habentem maculam neque rugam aut aliquid tale, sed ut sit sancta et inculpata. Hanc sententiam paene totidem verbis nos in confessione posuimus. Sic definit ecclesiam et articulus in symbolo, qui iubet nos credere, quod sit sancta catholica ecclesia (Ap VII 7).

[25] WA 6, 293:13—296:13, LW 39, 65—69 (*On the Papacy in Rome,* 1520). Luther here refers to John 18:36 and Luke 17:20, among others.

[26] 234:26 — At ecclesia non est tantum societas externarum rerum ac rituum sicut aliae politiae, sed principaliter est societas fidei et spiritus sancti in cordibus (Ap VII 5). 236:36—237:9 (Ap VII 13 ff.).

the result of the spiritual righteousness God gives us for Christ's sake. As is the case with both the sacraments and the ministry, the structure of the church is determined by God's own activity. The two components of the church are God's activity through the Word and sacraments and the reception of the same by faith. The unity of the church does not require uniformity in external forms — which are the work of man — but agreement concerning Baptism and faith, which come from God.[27] The church is the fellowship of believers, over whom Christ alone rules through the Word and sacraments, without human mediation.

Because of the Word and sacraments, the church cannot be referred to as invisible. The reformers were by no means ignorant of this term, and they were well aware of its many meanings.[28] The fact that it is not used in the Confessions must be interpreted as a specific repudiation. There were charges of a spiritualized concept of the church in the air, and the confessional writers specifically dissociated themselves from this by pointing out that the church is not some kind of a Platonic state.[29] The rejection of the Catholic view of the church was related to the fundamental concept that the Word and sacraments are the mediators of God's grace. Christ alone exercises dominion in the church, apart from the mediation of the clergy. He is the Head of the church, and the church is His body, which He renews, sanctifies, and guides through the Holy Spirit.

The intention of the Confessions is to describe the church which, according to Eph. 5:27, is without "spot or wrinkle." The relationship between this and the empirical church is a problem which theologians have wrestled with from the beginning of Christian history. In *Glossa ordinaria*[30] there is the suggestion of an idea which the confessors

---

[27] 61:9 — Nec necesse est ubique similes esse traditiones humanas seu ritus aut cerimonias ab hominibus institutas; sicut inquit Paulus: Una fides, unum baptisma, unus Deus et pater omnium etc. (AC VII 3 f.). Cf. WA 6, 293:1-5 (*Von dem Papstthum zu Rom*, 1520).

[28] With regard to this problem consult E. Kinder (1958), pp. 93—103, and the literature there mentioned.

[29] 238:17 — Neque vero somniamus nos Platonicam civitatem, ut quidam impie cavillantur, sed dicimus existere hanc ecclesiam (Ap VII 20). Cf. WA 7, 683:8-26 (*Antwort an Emser*, 1521), where the definition of the problem is developed.

[30] *Glossa ord. ad Decr. Grat.*, II, c. 33, q. 3, d. 1, c. 70: Sol. ecclesia quandoque large sumitur, ut granum and paleam complectatur. The gloss here can be directly associated with Augustine. See F. Hofmann (1933), p. 237.

also found very useful [31] – the distinction between the church in the wide sense and in the narrow sense. In the wide sense the church includes both the good and the bad, wheat and chaff, while in the narrow and proper sense it refers only to the faithful and sanctified.

This difficulty must be noted however: while the *Glossa* uses the word church to point to the historical church, the Catholic Church,[32] the reformers have the congregation of believers in mind. But to define "the church" as the congregation of believers and then go on to refer to it in a wider and a narrower sense can produce complications, inasmuch as the wider church, by definition, does not fulfill the conditions of being a "church" and therefore has no reason to be referred to as such.

In order to avoid these difficulties, the confessional writers defined their position more specifically and explained that the church is an external association to the extent that to its true essence belong the Word, the sacraments, and a functionally conceived ministry.[33] Since the Word and sacraments are the means by which the Holy Spirit works, they are the sole and true marks of the church. Word and sacrament are the external means whereby Christ exercises His dominion, and they reveal at the same time where the true church is to be found.[34] In this way the church becomes the true people of God, Christ's living body, which exists in the true believers all around the world (Ap VII 20). In this definition of the church the emphasis lies upon the fellowship of believers, the body of Christ, which becomes recognizable here in time through Word and sacraments. Interest is concentrated on what Christ accomplishes by His Spirit when the heart is awakened to faith. We are here dealing primarily with a spiritual fellowship, which is held together through the proclamation of the Word and the administration of the sacraments.

The difference in structure is seen best in a comparison with contemporary Catholic theology. The latter emphasized that the church is a visible and obvious external entity, identical with the

[31] 236:7 — ecclesiam large dictam (Ap VII 10). 240:31 — ecclesiam proprie dictam (Ap VII 28).

[32] *Decr. Grat.,* I, d. 21, c. 3 — Est ergo prima Apostoli Petri sedes Romana ecclesia non habens maculam neque rugam, nec aliquid eiusmodi. The words *ipsa congregatio fidelium hic dicitur ecclesia* suggest, however, another interesting train of thought, which may point forward to the coming reformation. They are found in *Glossa ord. ad Decr. Grat.,* II, c. 24, q. 1, c. 9.

[33] Cf. E. Schlink (1961), pp. 200 f.; and R. Josefson in *En bok om kyrkans ämbete* (1951), pp. 185 ff.

[34] 61:3 (AC VII 1); 236:1-5 (Ap VII 10).

Catholic Church. It is governed in an invisible manner by the Holy Spirit, and visibly by the church's ministers, with the pope at the apex, as they make the Word and sacraments available under common external forms. The church, conceived of in this way, is universal — spread throughout the entire world.[35] Similar formulae were employed by both of the contending parties, though with different meanings. Both recognized the connection between the church and the Holy Spirit. Catholic theology did this in such a way as to place the church under the guidance of the Spirit through the work of the clergy, while the Lutheran Confessions referred to the Word and sacraments. Both parties emphasized the catholicity of the church with very similar expressions, although the Catholics referred to their own church in so doing, while the Lutherans had the company of true believers in mind. According to the Confessions the church is the kingdom of Christ, not "a papal kingdom," *regnum pontificium* (Ap VII 26). Catholic theology, on the other hand, pointed out that the church, precisely as Christ's kingdom, stands under the guidance and jurisdiction of the pope.[36]

The Members of the Church

Since the Confessions define the church as "the assembly of saints," *congregatio sanctorum* (AC VII 1), the question concerning her members must be one of great importance. Do only the faithful belong to the church, and do unbelievers simply drop out? The Confutation gave close attention to this problem and said that the church cannot decide that those who do not fulfill certain qualifications should immediately be separated from its fellowship. God will separate the wheat from the chaff on the Day of Judgment, but this process should not be anticipated here in time.[37]

The theological controversy here touched a problem which had been of great concern since the days of the early church; it is known as the Donatist problem. In his controversy with Donatus and his

---

[35] N. Herborn, *Enchiridion* 43:4 — Ecclesia catholica quamvis Spiritu Christi regatur, est tamen palam cognita, quippe quae dum eisdem sacramentis, eodem verbo Dei, iisdem ministris ceremoniarumque varietate dignoscitur, manifestarium est hanc non solum in occultis angulis latitare, sed totum per orbem terrarum, id quod et ethnici atque Judaei fatentur, diffusam.

[36] Ibid., 55:30-32 and all of chap. 31, plus 107:10 ff., where we read the following: Unam summam oportet in ecclesia Christi esse autoritatem, quam in vicario Christi Petrique successoribus agnoscimus. Luther attacked this point of view vehemently, as in *Von dem Papstthum zu Rom*, 1520 (WA 6, 290:20 ff.).

[37] CR 27, 102—3.

followers, Augustine upheld the opinion that the godless and sinful men in the church militant cannot be sifted out, for that will be God's responsibility when the harvest is in.[38] In order to clarify the problem elicited by the Donatist struggle, Augustine began to speak of two kinds of church membership, one as *numero et merito*, the other simply as *numero*. Some belong to the Catholic Church in name only, i. e., *numero*, while others combine external church membership with an inner, spiritual element and are in this way church members *numero et merito*. Augustine presented this idea in connection with John 13:21: "One of you will betray Me." Judas belonged to the disciple band only in a nominal sense, without sharing in the spiritual fellowship.[39] Apart from this spiritual membership one does not really share in the life of Christ and in the spiritual gifts made available through the church. But the inadequate type of church membership which characterizes the evil, indifferent, and godless men does not invalidate the church and its unity.

Augustine's concept of two kinds of church membership was handed down through the Middle Ages; in Luther it appears in his early lectures on the Psalms as well as in later writings.[40] *Glossa ordinaria* [41] refers to the difference between belonging to the church both nominally and actually, *nomine et re,* and just nominally, *nomine,*[42] but it sought to establish this distinction more precisely by distinguishing between those who are of the church, *de ecclesia,* and those who are merely in the church, *in ecclesia.* To be of the church signifies that one is a true and actual member of the same, combining an inner participation with the external.[43]

[38] F. Hofmann (1933), pp. 233 ff. W. Kamlah (1951), pp. 140 ff. J. Ratzinger (1954), p. 146.

[39] *Tract in Joann.,* 62, 2: Unis ex vobis [John 13:21]: numero, non merito, specie, non virtute; commixtione corporali, non vinculo spirituali; carnis adjunctione, non cordis socius unitate (MPL 35, 1799). Cf. F. Hofmann (1933), pp. 243 f., and J. Heckel (1950), p. 14.

[40] WA 3, 68:9; 194:17 f. and 33 f.; 226:2 f.; 273:34 f.; 632:5. WA 4, 24:35 ff.; 129:7 ff.; 138:35; 197:11 ff.; 210:1 f.; 240:13 ff.; 284:25 and 352:24 (*Dictata super Psalterium,* 1513—15). WA 51, 521:31-34 (*Wider Hans Worst,* 1541).

[41] *Glossa ord. ad Decr. Grat.,* II, c. 33, q. 3, d. 1, c. 70.

[42] Altogether, the *Glossa* in the passage referred to sets forth four kinds of church membership: (1) nomine et re ut boni catholici; (2) nec nomine, nec re, ut praecisi; (3) nomine tantum; (4) re tantum. These ideas were developed by John Huss, *De Ecclesia* (1558), 200 a. Huss' commentary on the first alternative is characteristic: Quidam enim sunt in Ecclesia nomine & re, ut praedestinati(!) oboedientes Christo catholici.

[43] *Glossa ord. ad Decr. Grat.,* II, c. 33, q. 3, d. 1, c. 70: aliud esse de ecclesia,

The Confessions picked up these ideas and also spoke of a double church membership, which was combined with the wide and narrow concepts of the church. The living members of the church, those who have received the Word and sacraments in faith, possess the Holy Spirit and belong to the church *nomine et re*, both nominally and actually (Ap VII 10). Only these are included in the congregation of the faithful and form and true church. "Thus those in whom Christ is not active are not members of Christ."[44] Church membership is conditioned by the righteousness of faith; to belong to the church *nomine et re* is the same as to share in Christ. Everyone who receives the Word and sacraments in faith belongs to the church and lives under Christ's dominion in His kingdom. Since the church, properly speaking, not only includes but is composed of the faithful, the godless must be excluded. They cannot belong to the assembly which the Confessions define as "church"; they rather belong to the devil. The Symbols strongly emphasize the difference between the kingdom of Christ and the kingdom of the devil. Since the wicked are led by the devil and not by the Spirit of Christ,[45] they cannot constitute the church, which comprises the faithful. On the contrary, a sharp line of demarcation must be drawn between the latter and those who dwell under the devil's scepter.[46]

But this line can be drawn only by God, on Judgment Day. For the time being, Christ's kingdom is hidden beneath the cross, suffering, and ungodliness.[47] The communion of saints exists in the midst of ungodliness. A whole and perfect church cannot be found here. Lest anyone despair about the presence of the true church, these conditions for its existence in time must be kept in mind (Ap VII 9) — which implies, as a matter of principle, a strongly critical attitude toward the external congregation. This is a result of the new structure given the church in Reformation theology. But there are other reasons to refrain

---

quod hic negatur de malis; aliud esse in ecclesia, quod in contrariis conceditur. Huss also commented on this, *op. cit.,* 199 b, as did Luther in WA 51, 521:33 ff. (*Wider Hans Worst,* 1541).

[44] 235:7 — Quare illi, in quibus nihil agit Christus, non sunt membra Christi (Ap VII 5).

[45] 237:22-38 (Ap VII 16). 241:16 — Constat enim impios ad regnum et corpus diaboli pertinere (Ap VII 29). Cf. E. Schlink (1961), pp. 194 ff.

[46] 237:41 — Si ecclesia, quae vere est regnum Christi, distinguitur a regno diaboli, necesse est impios, cum sint in regno diaboli, non esse eccelsiam (Ap VII 17).

[47] 237:50 — regnum Christi . . . tectum cruce (Ap VII 18). 238:9-10 (Ap VII 19).

from an attempt to separate the evil from the good. One is found in the Biblical parables, which have traditionally been interpreted to refer to the church: the weeds and the wheat, which grow together until the time of harvest (Matt. 13:24-30),[48] the fishnet in the sea (Matt. 13: 47-50), and the ten virgins (Matt. 25:1-13; Ap VII 19). Another excellent reason is found in the Lutheran view of the sacraments. Since they are a divine work and are independent of the officiating clergyman's spiritual worthiness, one cannot for the sake of the sacraments attempt to ascertain who has faith and who does not.[49] In this world the church must include both living members and dead ones. (Ap VII 5)

The result of this is a tension between two incompatible tendencies, caused by the desire to combine an anti-Donatist point of view with a concept of the church as the fellowship of believers. The empirical church which appears before our eyes is not the congregation of believers in the sense in which the Confessions use this term. But since it is only this fellowship which merits the name church in the Biblical and apostolic sense, the empirical congregation can be called a church only in an improper sense. In order to refer to the empirical organization as a church in some sense, the Confessions were forced to accept the wider concept of the church (Ap XII 10) — with the difficulties included therein.

The chasm between this and the true church could be reduced if the church, like a people or a nation, was thought to be something more than a gathering of private individuals. With its laws, institutions, traditions, and language a nation is more than the sum of its citizens, without whom, however, it could not exist. The confessional theology of the previous century recognized this and used it in criticizing the Symbols.[50] To be sure, the latter are at least partially protected against this criticism by their obvious acceptance of the Biblical concepts of the church as the body of Christ, the bride of Christ, and the people of God. But these metaphors do not say anything specific about the external congregation. On the other hand, they can very well have been said, theoretically, about an inner, invisible congregation. As a

---

[48] 237:54-58 (Ap VII 19). The Confessions emphasize in particular that the field in the parable refers to the world and not to the church.

[49] 238:11-13 (Ap VII 19). This is the foremost point of view in AC VIII and is frequently emphasized, e. g., 234:5-11 (Ap VII 3).

[50] See, for example, F. J. Stahl (1862), pp. 43 f. Cf. E. Schlink (1961), p. 202, n. 7, and W. Maurer (1957), p. 82.

result, the writers of the Symbols sought in two other ways to nullify the obstacles that arose.

For one thing, they (like the *Glossa*) drew a distinction between being in the church and of the church. Only the true believers are *of* the church, those who have been made alive in the Spirit of Christ. *In* the church are the impious and ungodly, which can even include those who hold office in the church and administer the Word and sacraments. The Symbols do not, however, make any strong, systematic use of this distinction; they rather refer to it more or less in passing.[51]

On the other hand, and most important, all the members of the church are held together in an actual unity through the Word and sacraments. This is true primarily of the church in its proper sense, which is "called together by the Holy Spirit" (LC II 51). But the Holy Spirit never works apart from certain means, and it is for this reason that the Word, the Spirit, and the church condition one another in a mutual interdependence. "Where Christ is not preached, there is no Holy Spirit to create, call, and gather the Christian church, and outside it no one can come to the Lord Christ" (LC II 45). A presupposition for becoming a living member of the church of Christ is that one hears God's Word in faith.[52] Word and sacrament serve to protect the church from spiritualizing tendencies and to make of it a "historical community,"[53] i. e., they guarantee its existence in time and space. Through the proper preaching of the Word and the administration of the sacraments the church is born and kept alive. The Word and sacraments also form a bond of unity with the dead members of the church, who are numbered among the faithful in a nominal way and belong to the church in its wider sense.[54] The nonbelievers live in the Christian fellowship only in an external manner, and sometimes in such a way that they oppress and persecute the true members of the church. (Ap VII 9)

The loose relationship between the true members of the church and the others prompted later Protestant theology to make an attempt to bind them closer together. This was made possible through the order of divine grace. The Christian life was thought of as a series of stages, a way upon which some went so far, others farther. The concept of

---

[51] 235:45 — Infinita multitudo est impiorum in ipsa ecclesia (Ap VII 9). 237:47 (Ap VII 17). 238:28 (Ap VII 20).

[52] 657:35 — durch den heiligen Geist dahingebracht und eingeleibt dadurch, dass ich Gottes Wort gehört habe und noch höre (LC II 52).

[53] Cf. Gustaf Aulén (1912), p. 80.

[54] 234:5-11 (Ap VII 3). 236:7-8 (Ap VII 10). 240:34-40 (Ap VII 28).

faith was bifurcated, so that reference was made to a preliminary faith and a perfect faith. The former was described as a desire, longing for Christ, the latter as the perfect understanding of Christ as Mediator and Redeemer.[55] Under the influence of Pietism and the Herrnhut movement a new concept of justification with synergistic tendencies was set forth. An attempt was made to preserve the idea of God's unlimited grace while still protecting human responsibility, and this had a bearing on church membership as well. When Kliefoth distinguished in the orthodox manner between the assembly of the called, *coetus vocatorum*, and the assembly of the truly believing, *coetus vere credentium*, in connection with the confessional distinction between the church in the narrow and in the broad sense, he attached a much more positive significance to the congregation of the called than did, e. g., J. Gerhard.[56] This was done in deliberate opposition to the orthodox position.

Later theologians also pointed out the weakness which is undeniably present in the Confessions' attempt to combine two basically conflicting points of view. Aulén has taken note of "a dualistic train of thought" in their definition of the church. The church is not only a fellowship of faith but something else as well. "Both circles are thought of as distinct, each existing for itself. Their connection with the church, as well as the church's with them, is merely apparent."[57] Aulén's terminology is misleading, inasmuch as he overlooks the fact that the church is precisely the same as the congregation of believers, but his critique is symptomatic of the difficulties involved in the Confessions' definition of the church. Aulén sought for a new starting point, and found one in his definition of the church as "a congregation created by the Gospel." [58] He prefers to look upon the church from the point of view of its activity rather than of its essence.[59] This in fact means that Aulén would rather talk about the church's origins than its essence — about where it is found rather than about what it is. He says nothing about the question of the church's members, which so occupied the reformers and later theology.

55 Cf. J. F. Fresenius (1763), p. 395. A. Nohrborg (1771), pp. 407, 475 ff. Th. Kliefoth (1854), pp. 236, 241, 244 f., 262 f., 266, and 273 ff. G. Hök (1949), 27 ff. H. Fagerberg in STK (1955), pp. 159—64.

56 Th. Kliefoth (1854), pp. 252 f. H. Fagerberg (1952), pp. 260—67.

57. G. Aulén (1912), pp. 85 and 50.

58 Ibid., pp. 17, 49, 83, and elsewhere.

59 Ibid., p. 85. A similar point of view can be found in E. Schlink (1961), p. 198 — the church is defined as the assembly of all believers, and the assembly, in turn, is defined by what is done in its midst.

The Origin of the Church

The church is not a human society; it is the work of the Holy Spirit through Word and sacrament. The connection between the Holy Spirit, who "calls, gathers, enlightens and sanctifies" (SC II 6), and the church is Biblical and early Christian. This is reflected in the Third Article of the Creed, concerning the Holy Spirit, in which the church is also mentioned. Like the Word, the sacraments, and the ministry, the church is God's own creation. This is true both in the sense that God calls and gathers the church and in the sense that He works through it. The means used by God the Holy Spirit are the Word and sacraments. As seen from this point of view, the functional concept of the ministry must also be included in the church, inasmuch as its task is the presentation of the Word and sacraments.

The basic point of view regarding the origin of the church is, therefore, that it is the work of God the Holy Spirit. Only the Holy Spirit is able "to create, call, and gather the Christian church" (LC II 45). LC summarizes what the Third Article of the Creed says about the church thus: "I believe that there is on earth a little holy flock or community of pure saints under one head, Christ. It is called together by the Holy Spirit in one faith, mind, and understanding. It possesses a variety of gifts, yet is united in love without sect or schism." (II 51)

To the end of time God's congregation, the church, is nourished through the activity of the Holy Spirit. The Holy Spirit is not therefore bound to the church; rather, the church is the result of the Holy Spirit's activity and is at the same time the way by which He comes to man. The church "is the mother that begets and bears every Christian through the Word of God" (LC II 42). In speaking in this way about the church as the means whereby the Holy Spirit works, LC points to the church as the agent for the Word and sacraments. These are not only the means by which the Holy Spirit works among men (AC V; Ap IV 67; SA III VIII 3), but it is through the church that He does the work of proclaiming the Word and administering the sacraments. "The Holy Spirit carries on his work unceasingly until the last day. For this purpose he has appointed a community on earth, through which he speaks and does all his work" (LC II 61) "and brings us to Christ" (LC II 37). Where forgiveness of sins in Christ's name is not preached, "there is no Holy Spirit to create, call, and gather the Christian church, and outside it no one can come to the Lord Christ." (LC II 45)

It is remarkable that the Confessions are so definitely temperate in this context on the subject of Baptism. In medieval theology Baptism was the self-evident way of entrance into the Christian life and the church.[60] Does the Confessions' relative silence imply a conscious depreciation of Baptism as a necessary presupposition for church membership, or does it simply point up the fact that a living faith, which is the precondition for all sacraments, must be a part of Baptism? One certainly need not hesitate in answering this question. Word and sacrament are the distinctive marks of the church, and the guarantee of her unity (AC VII 2). The promise of salvation "does not apply to those who are outside of Christ's church, where there is neither Word nor sacrament, because Christ regenerates through Word and sacrament" (Ap IX 2). We are received into the Christian fellowship through Baptism (LC IV 2). It is clear from such statements that Baptism is a necessary qualification for church membership. It seems all the more peculiar that Luther quietly bypasses Baptism in LC's analysis of the origins and growth of the church. The only explanation must be that Baptism is not in and of itself a sufficient qualification for the true church membership about which the Confessions are concerned.

One can find an intimation of this in one of Luther's early writings, in which he says that the church has three distinctive marks — Baptism, the Lord's Supper, and the Gospel.[61] The Gospel in this instance refers to the oral proclamation of justification by faith,[62] and of the three the preaching of the Gospel is the indispensable condition for church membership and for the church in general. If the Gospel is absent or lacking, so is the church, even though Baptism and the Lord's Supper are present. The Gospel is the church's ultimate basis and source of life.[63] If there is any meaning in what the Confessions say

---

[60] Denz., 696 — Primum omnium sacramentorum locum tenet sanctum baptisma, quod vitae spiritualis ianua est: per ipsum enim membra Christi ac de corpore efficimur Ecclesiae.

[61] WA 7, 720:34 — Signum necessarium est, quod et habemus, Baptisma scilicet, panem et omnium potissimum Evangelium; tria haec sunt Christianorum symbola, tesserae et caracteres (*Ad librum . . . Ambrosii Catharini . . . responsio,* 1521).

[62] WA 7, 721:15 — Non de Euangelio scripto sed vocali loquor . . . quod fidem Christi veram, non informem et Thomisticam doceat.

[63] WA 7, 721:4 — Ubi vero Euangelium non esse videris (sicut in Synagoga Papistarum et Thomistarum videmus), ibi non dubites Ecclesiam non esse, etiam si baptisent et vescatur de altari, nisi parvulos et simplices exceperis . . . . Euangelium enim prae pane et Baptismo unicum, certissimum et nobilissimum Ecclesiae . . . symbolum est, cum per solum Euangelium concipiatur, formetur, alatur, generetur, educetur, pascatur, vestiatur, ornetur, roboretur, armetur, servetur,

by way of distinguishing between genuine and nominal church membership, Baptism must provide the framework. But Baptism must be the expression of the Gospel in the form of promise, received in faith. The Confessions remind us of this by pointing out that the Gospel overshadows everything else in its importance for church membership.

The Unity of the Church

Word and sacrament are the means used by the Holy Spirit to begin and increase the church; they are also the marks of the true church. Ap in particular attaches great importance to Word and sacrament as marks of the church, *notae ecclesiae*. The church is primarily the fellowship of faith and the Holy Spirit in the heart, but it "has outward marks, the pure teaching of the Gospel and the administration of the sacraments in harmony with the Gospel of Christ." [64] Tschackert and Aulén [65] agree in finding the term *nota* less than satisfying, since according to their interpretation it does not give adequate expression to the indissoluble relationship between the means of grace and the church. Word and sacrament are much more than a "basis of recognition" for the church; they are its "actual basis" and its "principle components." This critique, however, which is based on the presupposition that the Gospel is an act of God apart from doctrinal content,[66] overlooks a number of important factors.

In the first place, AC and Ap tell us as clearly as LC that Word and sacraments are the instruments of the Holy Spirit.[67] In replying to the questions concerning man's justification and the origins of the church, the Confessions consistently refer to the Word and sacraments. There is no lack of agreement on this point between those parts written by Luther and those written by Melanchthon.

In the second place, Luther too looked upon the means of grace as the distinguishing marks of the church. Melanchthon may have coined

breviter, tota vita et substantia Ecclesiae est in verbo dei [Matt. 4:4]. W. von Loewenich (1959), pp. 200—2.

[64] 234:30 — tamen habet externas notas, ut agnosci possit, videlicet puram evangelii doctrinam et administrationem sacramentorum consentaneam evangelio Christi (Ap VII 5).

[65] P. Tschackert (1910), p. 340. G. Aulén (1912), pp. 84 f.

[66] Cf. G. Aulén (1912), pp. 73 ff.

[67] 243:45 — instrumenta, per quae Deus movet corda ad credendum, sicut verbum et sacramenta (Ap VII 36). The Confessions look upon the brushing aside of Word and sacraments as fanaticism — 294:8-13 (Ap XIII 13); 453:16—454:12 (SA III VIII 3-4).

the term *nota ecclesiae* for use in Ap,[68] but as an alternative he employed the term used by Luther, *signum ecclesiae,*[69] which implies factual agreement.

That the question concerning the marks of the church came to the fore here is related to the fact that the reformers, like Augustine in his controversy with the Donatists,[70] felt compelled to state where the true church is to be found and what its marks are. For Catholics the answer was found simply by referring to the church under papal leadership, but since the reformers did not accept the pope as the visible head of the church, they had to form their answer in another way. Since Christ is the only head of the church, working among us now through Word and sacrament, these also serve to indicate where the true church is to be found. The connection between Word and sacrament as the church's "actual basis" and as its "basis of recognition" is very firm. Where Word and sacrament are absent, there is no salvation, and neither is there any church. "We know that the church is present among those who rightly teach the Word of God and rightly administer the sacraments." [71]

It is also necessary to take note of a significant detail in the formulations. References to Word and sacrament here point to the preached Word and the administration of the sacraments. The church is understood to be a product of the Word, the Gospel, and of the sacraments — in function. The true people of God, the church, consist of those who have received the promise of the Holy Spirit (Ap VII 16), and the church is found only "among those who rightly teach the Word of God and rightly administer the sacraments." [72] It is against this background that the classical definition of the unity of the church (in AC VII) must be read and understood:

[68] P. Tschackert (1910), p. 340.

[69] WA 7, 720:32-36 (*Ad librum . . . Ambrosii Catharini . . . responsio,* 1521). WA 6, 301:3-5 (*Von dem Papstthum zu Rom,* 1520). WA 50, 629:19 (*Von den Konziliis und Kirchen,* 1539). 238:14 f. (Ap VII 19).

[70] *Ep. ad catholicos de secta donatistarum,* 2, 2 — Quaestio certe inter nos versatur ubi sit ecclesia, utrum apud nos an apud illos (CSEL 52, 232:7 f.).

[71] 297:17 (Ap XIV 3 f.). 233:32 — nos sciamus ecclesiam Christi apud hos esse, que evangelium Christi docent, non qui pravas opiniones contra evangelium defendunt (Ap IV 400). Cf. Augustine, *Ep. ad catholicos de secta donatistarum:* ubi sit hoc corpus, id est ubi sit ecclesia, quid ergo facturi sumus? In uerbis nostris eam quasituri an in uerbis capitis sui domini nostri Iesu Christi? (CSEL 52, 232:23).

[72] 297:18 — Et ecclesiam esse scimus apud hos, qui verbum Dei recte docent et recte administrant sacramenta (Ap XIV 3).

For the true unity of the church it is enough to agree concerning the teaching of the Gospel and the administration of the sacraments. It is not necessary that human traditions or rites and ceremonies, instituted by men, should be alike everywhere.[73]

This passage has long created differences of opinion among interpreters. Delitzsch and Stahl have found it unsatisfactory to combine the proper administration of Word and sacrament with faith. "An active, believing congregation can exist in spite of serious doctrinal errors, and even more is it possible for a congregation with correct doctrine to exist without a living faith." [74] In response to this, other interpreters [75] deny that AC and Ap could have set forth a demand for pure doctrine as a condition for the unity of the church. The Gospel of which the Confessions speak, they maintain, is not a doctrine but a dynamic, powerful Word, "God's mighty work for man's salvation," the proclaimed Word. "If the Gospel and the sacraments are in operation, there it is that Christ is found, and He is Himself the unity of the church." [76]

The legitimacy of this solution is said to be found in the observation that the Gospel is something other and more than purely theoretical statements. If this solution were correct, it would eliminate a large number of hindrances to church unity in a single blow. For then such controversial questions as the meaning of justification, the number of sacraments, the propriety of infant or adult baptism, and the meaning of the Lord's Supper could be set aside as nonessential. But the problem is not solved that easily. The "Gospel" certainly does frequently denote the oral presentation of the forgiveness of sins,[77] and faith certainly is an act of the will, but the Gospel, the promise that gives birth to faith, must in some sense be true in order to be able to awaken

---

[73] 61:7 — Et ad veram unitatem ecclesiae satis est consentire de doctrina evangelii et de administratione sacramentorum. Nec necesse est ubique similes esse traditiones humanas seu ritus aut ceremonias ab hominibus institutas (AC VII 2 f.). Cf. 300:47-50 (Ap XV 18).

[74] F. J. Stahl (1862), p.42. Cf. F. Delitzsch (1847), pp. 3 f.

[75] L. Grane (1959), p. 74. Anders Nygren in STK (1957), pp. 65—74. Nygren here brings to fulfillment an idea broached in an earlier writing, *Christ and His Church* (1955), pp. 97 f. Also consult Vilmos Vajta in STK (1957), pp. 1—23.

[76] A. Nygren in STK (1957), p. 69. Nygren attributes this to E. Schlink (1961), p. 198: "The Gospel in its essence is the oral proclamation of forgiveness." According to Schlink (1961), pp. 206 ff., every church must be a confessional church.

[77] 449:8 (SA III IV). Cf. WA 7, 721:15 (*Ad librum . . . Ambrosii Catharini . . . responsio*, 1521), and Chapters One, part 2, and Three, part 2, above.

and sustain faith. The doctrinal element is to be found as soon as justification by faith is proclaimed. The Gospel is at one and the same time a proclamation and a doctrine. "But if a Christian church is to exist and remain, the pure doctrine of Christ and of justification by faith must be upheld." [78] The fact that the Confessions associate themselves with the three ancient creeds and separate themselves from other persuasions also reveals that the question of doctrine was not shunted aside.[79]

According to the Catholic position, which is opposed in AC VII, church unity requires subjection to papal jurisdiction and obedience to the ordinances of the church. The Lutheran confessors replied to this by asserting that only that which gives birth to faith results in the true church and is necessary for unity. Spiritual unity requires unanimity concerning the Word, the Gospel, and the sacraments (cf. Ap VII 31). Unity therefore involves not only the fact *that* the Word is proclaimed and the sacraments are administered, but also *what* is proclaimed and administered. Or, in the words of Nicholas of Lyra: "Therefore the church is made up of those persons in whom there is true knowledge and the confession of faith and truth." [80]

Those theologians who repudiate the doctrinal content of the proclamation and the administration of the sacraments attach great significance to the fact that *docere* and *predigen* are used interchangeably in the Latin and German texts.[81] *Docere* is therefore said to imply proclamation and *doctrina* preaching, without further defining the content of each. But two things are worthy of note. First, that *doctrina* is frequently translated as teaching, and not preaching,[82] and second, that the combination of "preaching and teaching" is very common.[83] This clearly indicates that preaching was thought to have a distinctive doctrinal content—the very thing the Confessions are dealing with— the central point of which is justification by faith. Preaching and teach-

---

[78] 231:17-18 (Ap IV 377, German text).

[79] E. Schlink (1961), pp. 202 and 206. Cf. Chapters Two and Four above.

[80] *Biblia, cum postilis Nicolai de Lyra* (F. Mai, 1485), 36 r: ecclesia consistit in illis personis, in quibus est noticia vera et confessio fidei et veritatis. Cf. 239:5 ff. (Ap VII 22).

[81] A. Nygren in STK (1957), p. 69. Cf. E. Schlink (1961), pp. 198 f.

[82] E.g., 78:23 and 79:1 (AC XX 22). 83, c.7 (Beschluss des ersten Teils, 1). 253:7 and 15-18 (Ap XII 3). 272:39-40 (Ap XII 98).

[83] 671:24 — Predigt, lehret und redet (LC III 40). 716:37-40 (LC V 44). 305:10-45 (Ap XV, 42-44). 258:22 — Was lehren doch solche Prediger und Doctores . . . (Ap XII 34). 239:23 — neben den rechten Predigern werden einschleichen falsche Lehrer und Wölfe (Ap VII 22).

ing are synonymous, and preaching was also the form for the communication of doctrine. Actual differences of opinion concerning the Gospel created divisions (Ap XII 90). By holding to work-righteousness, which is contrary to the Gospel, the opposition cut itself off from Christ and His church (LC II 56). The Confessions summarize their concept of the conditions for church unity thus: "The church cannot be better governed and maintained than by having all of us live under one head, Christ, and by having all the bishops . . . joined together in unity of doctrine, faith, sacraments, prayer, works of love, etc." (SA II IV 9)

The Triune God is the basis for unity. As He is one, so must the church be one. God the Holy Spirit calls the faithful to live together in love under their Head, Christ, "in one faith, mind, and understanding" (LC II 51). Inasmuch as the Word and sacraments are God's work among us, all that does not originate with them is of no significance for the unity of the church. The Confessions include in this category everything that can be referred to as *traditiones humanae,* e. g., worship services and ceremonies which have no support in the Bible.[84] Such things do not create that faith which is the presupposition for the inner spiritual unity of the church. The Confessions therefore resort to the Bible in order to tell the difference between God's work and man's. The teaching of the Gospel is certainly a proclaimed Word, but it has a specific content — which the confessional writers derive from Scripture. *Doctrina evangelii* is the same as *doctrina apostolorum,* "the teaching and clear words of the apostles" (Ap VII 38 German). If a person is in harmony with what the apostles proclaimed and taught, then he has the entire universal church behind him, but if anyone, even the pope, teaches something contrary to Scripture, he has no authority.[85] The church is found among those who proclaim the Gospel of Christ and who avoid teaching their own opinions. The Lutheran confessors formulated their primary accusation against the opposition thus: "They defend human opinions contrary to the Gospel, contrary to the authority of the holy fathers." [86]

---

[84] 241:43 — non esse necessarium similitudinem rituum *humanorum* (Ap VII 31). The Confessions thus do not turn away from all questions of order, but only from those they look upon as human ordinances. For more, see E. Schlink (1961), pp. 205 f.

[85] 265:14-25 (Ap XII 66). 177:30-34 (Ap IV 83). Cf. Chapter One above.

[86] 233:37 — Proinde non perturbent nos iudicia adversariorum, cum humanas opiniones contra evangelium, contra auctoritatem sanctorum patrum, qui in ecclesia scripserunt, contra piarum mentium testimonia defendunt (Ap IV 400).

It is obvious that "the Gospel" in this context cannot refer to a proclamation without doctrinal contours. It must have a distinct content—just as the administration of the sacraments must be associated with a clear idea of where the line between true and false sacraments runs. The Confessions found their norms and criteria in the Scriptures. The words of the Bible give expression to the divine activity which creates the church and preserves it in the true, unifying faith. The Confessions summarize the content of Scripture and provide a vital witness to the Christian faith; at the same time they serve as a source for the unity of the Lutheran Church.

Chapter Eleven:

The Christian Life

1. Faith and Works

If one is a true member of the church, one partakes of the forgiveness of sins and thereby also lives the new life of faith. AC VI, which follows the articles on justification and its means, declares "that this faith is bound to bring forth good fruits and that it is necessary to do the good works commanded by God" (AC VI 1). AC places great emphasis on this obvious truth. It returns to this matter in Article XX and calls attention to it also in other connections. Ap goes into the question in detail in Article XX as well as in the section entitled "Love and the Keeping of the Law" (Ap IV 122 ff.). It is also dealt with in other parts of the confessional writings.

The explanation for this emphasis is to be sought in the Catholic polemic against the Reformation doctrine of justification,[1] which is not a rejection of works as a whole, but only such as are done with justification in view. When the Lutheran confessors opposed meritorious works, the Catholics interpreted this as a repudiation of all works. The emphasis on faith alone seemed to confirm their interpretation, which of course was built on an erroneous view of the doctrine of justification. "The particle 'alone' offends some people, even though Paul says (Rom. 3:28), 'We hold that a man is justified by faith apart from works of law.' . . . If they dislike the exclusive particle 'alone,' let them remove the other exclusive terms from Paul, too, like 'freely,' 'not of works,' 'it is a gift,' etc., for these terms are also exclusive. We exclude the claim of merit, not the Word or the sacraments, as our opponents slanderously claim. . . . Love and good works must also follow faith. So they are not excluded as though they did not follow, but trust in the merit of love or works is excluded from justification." (Ap IV 73-74)

In contrast to the reformers, the Catholic theologians laid great stress on the merit concept, which is nowhere to be found in the New Testament. In the Old Testament it occurs in a few contexts, but it is not central. That it finally gained entrance to scholasticism was

---

[1] Cf. J. Eck., art. 198—202, with superscription *contra opera* (W. Gussmann, II [1930], 127).

due to the fact that it was in part linked with the New Testament reward concept[2] and in part with certain late Jewish ideas and with the concept of penance under the influence of Anselm of Canterbury.[3] However, the merit concept is found already in Augustine, who was compelled by the Pelagians to discuss its implications. The followers of Pelagius declared "that the grace of God is granted to us according to our merits" [4] as opposed to the view of Augustine that salvation is a gift bestowed on us by the Holy Spirit.[5] In his controversy with Pelagianism, Augustine expressed his view: Grace influences our will, causing it to perform good works.[6] No one would have opposed the Pelagians had they seen our prayers and works and faith as gifts from God, which may be called merits but do not constitute the ground for personal credit.[7] "If then your good merits are God's gifts, God does not reward your merits by virtue of your merits but by virtue of His gifts." [8]

The Catholics accepted this proposition in order to defend their merit concept.[9] When God rewards our merits, He crowns His gifts. The Catholics considered themselves unjustly attacked for an alleged

[2] N. Herborn, *Enchiridion*, chap. 5.

[3] *Handbuch theologischer Grundbegriffe*, *II* (1963), 394. P. E. Persson in STK (1963), pp. 92 ff.

[4] *Ep. 214 ad Valentinum* — illi haeretici dicunt, gratiam Dei secundum merita nostra dari. Ibid. — Illi vero haeretici se ipsos a se ipsis iustos fieri putantes, quasi hoc eis non dederit Deus (MPL 44, 875).

[5] *De sp. et litt.*, 13,22 — collegimus non iustificari hominem praeceptis bonae vitae nisi per fidem Iesu Christi, hoc est non lege operum, sed lege fidei, non littera sed spiritu; non factorum meritis, sed gratuita gratia (CSEL 60, 176). Cf. Ap IV 87, where this passage is quoted in part.

[6] *Ep. 214 ad Valentinum* — liberum arbitrium adjuvari fateantur per Dei gratiam (MPL 44, 875). *De sp. et litt.*, 3,5 (CSEL 60, 157). *De gratia et libero arbitrio*, 9, 21 (MPL 44, 893; cf. Ap IV 322).

[7] *De gratia et libero arbitrio* 6, 15 — Si enim merita nostra sic intelligerent, ut etiam ipsa dona Dei esse cognoscerent, non esset reprobanda ista sententia (MPL 44, 890). *Ep. 214 ad Valentinum* — Omne datum optimum, et omne donum perfectum desursum est, descendens a Patre luminum [Jacobi 1, 17]; ne quisquam dicat meritis operum suorum, vel meritis orationum suarum, vel meritis fidei suae, sibi traditam Dei gratiam (MPL 44, 875).

[8] *De gratia et libero arbitrio* 6, 15 — Si ergo dona sunt bona merita tua, non Deus coronat merita tua tanquam merita tua, sed tanquam dona sua (MPL 44, 891).

[9] CR 27, 96 — Unde ait B. Augustinus: Cum Deus remunerat merita nostra, coronat dona sua. Iniuste igitur calumniantur Catholicos, praesertim Monachos, Lutherani, quasi ex propriis viribus aut meritis, absque gratia Dei boni aliquid facere velint aut praesumant, quod vitam promereatur aeternam. Non ista dicunt Catholici, sed Pelagiani (Foreword to Confutation, 1530).

Pelagian heresy, namely that we are able by our own strength and merit to do good and attain eternal life. By ourselves our works are not meritorious, but they become meritorious through the grace of God.[10] Ostensibly, then, the Confutation takes the same position as Augustine; but there are characteristic differences, which cause the emphasis to shift toward the meritorious character of the works. The difference lies in that Augustine argued against the doctrine of works, while the Catholics in the 16th century contended for it. Therefore, alongside of the pure Augustinian statements there are phrases which cannot be interpreted as anything but a pure doctrine of works. Merits are said to contribute to justification and the forgiveness of sins.[11]

In the Lutheran Confessions, on the other hand, we find the one-sided emphasis that they argue exclusively against the full-blown doctrine of works but never discuss the finer distinctions of the Augustinian view, which in the name of clarity should have been of interest even though the reformers could not accept it. The parties simply did not communicate with each other: the reformers argued against an unmitigated doctrine of works, the Catholics against a misconception of the doctrine of justification.[12]

The reformers did not oppose works as such, but the meritorious character of good works. Supported by Scripture and Augustine, they insisted that good works do not bestow justification. Justification is a gift by which we are brought into a new relationship with God and are born again. As good fruits, the works are to grow and develop out of regenerating faith.[13] The notion that justification should not lead to a life of good works was absurd to the reformers.[14] The faith of which they spoke is the work of the Holy Spirit (Ap IV 64) and is kept alive through the struggle against sin by daily repentance.[15] No true

[10] CR 27, 95 — omnes catholici fatentur, opera nostra ex se nullius esse meriti; sed gratia Dei facit, illa digna esse vita aeternam (Confutation, 1530).

[11] CR 27, 121 — de bonis scilicet operibus, quod non mereantur remissionem peccatorum, quod, ut superius reiectam et improbatum est, ita et nunc reiicitur et improbatur (Confutation, 1530). N. Herborn, *Enchiridion,* 33:25—35:6.

[12] CR 27, 96 — Caeterum, quod Lutherus plaerumque docuit, nos sola fide iustificari, et neque baptismus neque bona opera ad iustificationem facere, ingens profecto et nocens error est (Foreword to Confutation, 1530).

[13] 60:2 — fides illa debeat bonos fructus parere (AC VI 1). 262:47-49 (Ap XII 58).

[14] 187:32 — Falso igitur calumniantur nos adversarii, quod nostri non doceant bona opera (Ap IV 136); 316:33-40 (Ap XX 15).

[15] 188:14 — fides illa, de qua loquimur, existit in poenitentia (Ap IV 142); 227:7 (Ap IV 350).

faith exists unless good works follow in its steps (cf. Ap IV 263). The new life is a result of Baptism. If one lives in his baptism, he lives in that repentance whose meaning is daily death unto sin and resurrection with Christ to a new life "in righteousness and purity" (SC IV 12). Thus works are liberated from being a condition for justification; they are performed, not in order that justification may take place but because it already has taken place; [16] and they are the result of the Holy Spirit's activity.

To understand the meaning of this we must again remind ourselves of the extraordinary role which the affections were regarded as playing for the personality, its volitional life and its relationship to God.[17] On account of their strength and irrational unruliness one is unable to control them without the help of the Holy Spirit, who is bestowed in justification. "It is only by faith that forgiveness of sins and grace are apprehended, and because through faith the Holy Spirit is received, hearts are so renewed and endowed with new affections as to be able to bring forth good works." (AC XX 28-29)[18]

The evil affections, with their hostility to God, are superseded by the good impulses which the Holy Spirit awakens in the heart. We then begin to fear and love God, look to Him for help, thank Him even in outward need, and love our neighbor. Since the spiritual impulses are in harmony with the Moral Law, we are enabled by the Spirit's help to fulfill it.[19] The precise boundary between regeneration, which belongs to faith, and the Christian life, which follows faith, is hard to determine. It might be most correct to say that regenerating faith lays hold on the comfort and the nullifying of the judgment of conscience, while the Christian life is the result of God's love having taken the place of divine wrath. The Holy Spirit fits us for fulfilling God's law and for living in spiritual righteousness. After being justified we are

---

[16] 227:4 — Ideo iustificamus, ut iusti bene operari et obedire legi Dei incipiamus. Ideo regeneramur et spiritum sanctum accipimus, ut nova vita habeat nova opera, novos affectus, timorem, dilectionem Dei, odium concupiscentiae etc. (Ap IV 348 f.). Cf. *De sp. et litt.,* 7, 11 — nec quia recti sunt corde, sed etiam ut recti sint corde praetendit iustitiam suam, qua iustificat impium (CSEL 60, 163).

[17] See above, Chapters Five and Six.

[18] 80:16 — Tantum fide apprehenditur remissio peccatorum et gratia. Et quia per fidem accipitur spiritus sanctus, iam corda renovantur et induunt novos affectus, ut parere bona opera possint (AC XX 28 f.).

[19] 185:23 — Quia vero fides affert spiritum sanctum et parit novam vitam in cordibus, necesse est, quod pariat spirituales motus in cordibus. Et qui sint illi motus, ostendit propheta, cum ait: Dabo legem meam in corda eorum (Ap IV 125); 195:30 (Ap IV 175).

able anew to fear and love God[20] and give evidence of "chastity, patience, the fear of God, the love of our neighbor, and the works of love."[21]

Ap forcefully emphasizes that the Law can be fulfilled only when the Holy Spirit has been given to us through faith. This is in harmony with Rom. 3:31: "Do we then overthrow the law by this faith? By no means! On the contrary, we uphold the law" (cf. Ap IV 123).[22] Without the Holy Spirit the Law cannot be fulfilled, but with His help we can at least begin to carry out what God demands of us. The fulfilling of the Law is, however, never perfect, but our works are pleasing to God for the sake of faith (Ap IV 293). When the Christian by faith embraces God's promise, he receives the Holy Spirit, who takes up the struggle against sin, fills his heart with new affections, and makes the fulfilling of the Law possible. The doctrine of faith "brings pure grace and makes us upright and pleasing to God. Through this knowledge we come to love and delight in all the commandments of God because we see that God gives himself completely to us, with all his gifts and his power, to help us keep the Ten Commandments."[23]

This, however, does not take place without a struggle. Keeping the Law becomes possible, thanks to the Holy Spirit; but it is nevertheless always inadequate. The whole Reformation view of the ascendancy of the emotional life precludes any thought of perfection even though one has become a partaker of the Holy Spirit. "In this life we cannot satisfy the law, because our unspiritual nature continually brings forth evil desires, though the Spirit in us resists them."[24] The Holy Spirit creates the prerequisites for our keeping of the Law, but the power of sin is such that the Law is never kept perfectly.[25]

---

[20] 187:11 — Cum autem audito evangelio et remissione peccatorum fide erigimur, concipimus spiritum sanctum, ut iam recte de Deo sentire possimus (Ap IV 135).

[21] 241:52 — effectus Spiritus sancti, sicut castitas, patientia, timor Dei, dilectio proximi et opera dilectionis (Ap VII 31).

[22] 186:34 — non potest lex vere fieri nisi accepto spiritu sancto per fidem (Ap IV 132); 174:8 f. (Ap IV 70); 196:42 f. (Ap IV 184); 258:48 f. (Ap XII 37); 316:35-40 (Ap XX 15); 83:15-23 (AC XX Editio princeps).

[23] 661:34-40 (LC II 68-69). Cf. 435:7-8 (SA III I 10).

[24] 189:14 — Nam in hac vita non possumus legi satisfacere, quia natura carnalis non desinit malos affectus parere, etsi his resistit Spiritus in nobis (Ap IV 146). The *totus homo* view of man is not discussed in the Confessions. See, e. g., A. Gyllenkrok (1952), pp. 78—131.

[25] 195:30 — quod fide renati concipiant spiritum sanctum, et habeant motus consentientes legi Dei, sed multo maxime refert et hoc addere, quod sentire nos oportet, quod procul a perfectione legis absimus (Ap IV 175).

Inasmuch as sin is present, good works in the Holy Spirit involve a constant struggle against it in daily repentance (Ap IV 350, 353). The Spirit "daily cleanses and expels the sins that remain and enables man to become truly pure and holy" (SA III III 40). The new life in the Holy Spirit is viewed less as a progressive sanctification than as a daily struggle against sin. The meaning, however, is that the Law is to be kept. If someone falls into open sin, it is an unfailing sign of the forfeiture of both faith and the Holy Spirit, for "the Holy Spirit does not permit sin to rule and gain the upper hand in such a way that sin is committed, but the Holy Spirit represses and restrains it so that it does not do what it wishes. If sin does what it wishes, the Holy Spirit and faith are not present" (SA III III 44). Here works have ceased to be a prerequisite for justification; they do not stand under the category of merit, *meritum*, but under that of grace,[26] and they are directed towards our fellowmen, for their benefit.

What good works then are to be performed, and what are the criteria of good deeds? This question is essential for all ethics, and it was discussed also at the time of the Reformation. Theoretically, many different possibilities present themselves, from a pure situation ethics, where man, either by virtue of rational deliberation or the Holy Spirit's guidance does what is good, to a legalistic ethics or to casuistry. Man can be thought of as a "channel," an instrument for God's actions, or the ethical activity in practice may be regarded as being carried out by his own reason or his reason enlightened by the Holy Spirit.

If we turn to the Confessions with these questions, we find that the background of all ethical action is justification and the Holy Spirit. Without the aid of the Holy Spirit, God's will can be done only in an outward sense, but no truly good works are done. But what is the relation of good works to the Law? Is the Christian through the Spirit set free in relation to God's law, thus becoming his own sovereign lawmaker, who in a given moment perceives what is God's will? Holl regards the posing of this question to be genuinely in the spirit of the Reformation and finds that Luther saw a tension between the freedom based on relationship to God, and an external Moral Law. The tension was resolved in this way, that the will which is linked to God is free in relation to the Law.[27] Love triumphs over all laws; through the enlightenment of the Spirit the Christian becomes his own lawgiver and establishes new decalogs, which are superior to the Moral

[26] Cf. W. Joest (1951), p. 74; B. Werkstrom (1963), p. 57; Althaus (1962), pp. 213 f.

[27] Karl Holl (1923), pp. 207 and 220 f.

Law of the Bible. Holl indeed emphasizes that only the perfect Christian can create these new decalogs and that there is a fixed will of God which the Christian is able to perceive; but the mark of true morality is nevertheless freedom from the Law.[28] Althaus calls attention to a tension between an indicative and an imperative in the Christian's life. As surely as the sun radiates warmth and the tree bears good fruit the Christian performs good works, but he must nevertheless be exhorted thereto by the Commandments.[29]

The problem was discussed already during the time of the Reformation under the express presupposition that the justified person endeavors to carry out the divine will expressed in the Moral Law and the natural law. By means of different nuances one stressed now spontaneity, now necessity in ethical action. In the first edition of the *Loci* Melanchthon underscores spontaneity: by the aid of the Spirit the Christian does spontaneously what the Law demands; and he is able to do it, since the Holy Spirit is God's living will.[30] In FC there is less confidence in man's spontaneous action. If Christians were perfect, they would do God's will voluntarily and without the compulsion of the Law, just as the sun and the stars move in their cycle according to God's appointed plan. However, since no one possesses this perfection, the admonition of the Law is necessary also for Christians. (SD VI 6 ff.)

The Confessions take a middle position in this question so vital for ethics. The motive power for moral action lies with God the Holy Spirit, but since the power of the affections is never broken, we are not perfect (Ap IV 146) but need God's command – besides the natural law – to obtain enlightenment concerning His will. Since the object of the command is love out of a pure heart and a good conscience,[31] there arises, at least theoretically, no conflict between the two. If we say that "love triumphs over all laws," we proceed from a fundamental

[28] Holl, pp. 223—25. The influence of Holl's interpretation of Luther's ethics is enormous, and would be well worth a special examination. Cf., e. g., Gustaf Wingren, *The Christian's Calling* (1958), pp. 44 f., and L. Haikola, *Usus legis* (1958), p. 150.

[29] Paul Althaus (1931), pp. 27—30, and the same author (1962), pp. 232 ff.

[30] CR 21, 195 — Qui spiritu Christi innovati sunt, ii iam sua sponte, etiam non praeeunte lege, feruntur ad ea, quae lex iubebat. Voluntas dei lex est. Nec aliud spiritus sanctus est, nisi viva dei voluntas, et agitatio, quare ubi spiritu dei, qui viva voluntas dei est, regenerati sumus, iam id ipsum volumus sponte, quod exigebat lex (*Loci,* 1521).

[31] 208:20 — Finis mandati caritas est de corde puro et conscientia bona et fide non ficta (Ap IV 245; quote from 1 Tim. 1:5).

antithesis between the commandment of love and the commandment of God, but overlook the fact that it is the same God who has given both the commandment of love and the other commandments; these quite likely do not contradict the basic commandment of love but rather exemplify it. Theoretically, love, which is the fulfilling of the Law, need not stand in opposition to God's commandment: the Christian ought to "do all such good works as God has commanded, but we should do them for God's sake." [32] Here again [33] we encounter the concept of *mandatum,* command, which is so vital for the Lutheran Confessions and the Reformation theologians. Which good works are commanded by God, and how can one be certain to carry out precisely that which has God's *mandatum* and is the expression of His will?

Apart from God's commands are all the usages, customs, and rules which come under the common designation of human traditions and are set up in the service of work-righteousness. The false works which these regulations brought forth stand under the sign of the merit concept. Before, consciences were tormented by the doctrine of works, declare the Confessions. "Some persons were by their consciences driven into the desert, into monasteries, in the hope that there they might merit grace by monastic life. Others invented works of another kind to merit grace and make satisfaction for sins" (AC XX 20-21). Everything that is contrary to the article on justification is outside of God's command. A negative characteristic of *mandatum,* then, is its incompatibility with work-piety (Ap IV 345). God has not commanded works which are at variance with the fundamental article of justification by faith. None of the works commanded by God are designed to bring about salvation (Ap IV 12). The Confessions arrive at this view of *mandatum* by two premises which are made the basis for a general conclusion: in the first place, the acceptance of the Bible as the supreme authority in all questions relating to faith and life; second, the conviction that the doctrine of justification is in accord with the Scriptures. Since this doctrine is taught in all Scripture, none of the works commanded by God can be contrary to it. (Ap XV 29-30)

A direct or indirect word of Scripture must always constitute the basis for a divine command. The Confessions do not set forth an un-

---

[32] 60:3 — Translated from the German. The Latin reads: [fides] oporteat bona opera mandata a Deo facere propter voluntatem Dei (AC VI 1). P. Althaus (1931), p. 31 — Die Sittlichkeit hat keinen anderen Sinn als den, Gehorsam gegen Gottes Willen zu sein. Althaus does not tell us, however, exactly what he means by "the will of God."

[33] Cf. above, Chapter One, part 1.

critical Biblicism, but in argumentation they often draw conclusions from firm premises drawn from Scripture. These conclusions serve to give pertinent significance to the Biblical phrases.[34] Since work-piety is a phenomenon that lacks Scriptural support, all humanly conceived usages and customs meant to serve God are rejected in principle even if Scripture does not directly contain a pronouncement concerning them in each individual instance. Other customs may be retained under the assumption that they will not be used with a view to justification. A general presupposition for the Christian's life is that only that manner of life is good which finds support in God's command,[35] and this must in some way be capable of being traced back to Scripture, since God's living and ever-actual will is expressed there.[36]

Aside from being Scriptural in the sense just adduced, *mandatum* is also characterized by its active, creative character. Previously, in the section on the Lord's Supper, we have illustrated how this aspect of the command shows itself valid in the words of institution,[37] which create the Presence when spoken by virtue of God's command. Another striking example is found in the Confessions' discussion of marriage. Marriage is grounded on God's command in Gen. 1:28, and its validity is confirmed by the sexes' natural attraction to one another.[38] Since the command is from God, it belongs to the unchangeable natural law which no human law can revoke.[39] The Scriptural commands, then, are to be found in the Bible and are at times active in creation, which is the work of God. Thus there comes into being a natural connection between the words and will of God contained in Scripture and the varied multiplicity and wealth in creation. This can be illustrated by the Confessions' view of vocation and marriage, both of which are vital concepts in Reformation ethics.

---

[34] H. Preuss in ThStK (1908), pp. 62—83. J. M. Headley (1963), p. 43 — In the first place reason has no theological content independent of Scripture. It is a formal method of elucidating logical conclusions from already recognized premises. WA 6, 554:20 ff. (*De captivitate babylonica*, 1520).

[35] 118:30 — Bonum et perfectum vitae genus est, quod habet mandatum Dei (AC XXVII 58). 290:9 — qui sint boni fructus docent mandata (Ap XII 174).

[36] 299:45 — Quomodo de voluntate Dei certos reddet homines, sine mandato et verbo Dei? (Ap XV 14); 300:9-13 (Ap XV 17).

[37] Above, Chapter Seven, part 3.

[38] 334:50 — Genesis (1:28) docet homines conditos esse, ut sint foecundi, et sexus recta ratione sexum appetat. Loquimur enim non de concupiscentia, quae peccatum est, sed de illo appetitu, qui in integra natura futurus erat (Ap XXIII 7).

[39] 335:38 — haec creatio seu ordinatio divina in homine est ius naturale (Ap XXIII 9); 336:7-18 (Ap XXIII 11 f.); 613:44 — 614:6 (LC I 211 f.).

2. Vocation

In opposition to the self-chosen works based on human traditions, *traditiones humanae* (cf. Matt. 15:3), the Lutheran Confessions emphasize the life commanded by God in vocation, *vocatio*. Here we encounter a concept that was extremely important for Reformation theology. The term, which is an interpretation of the New Testament *klesis* (1 Cor. 7:20), is designed to describe where the Christian is to perform good works as a service of love to his neighbor. This use of the German word *Beruf* was introduced by Tauler and German mysticism, but through Luther and Melanchthon it was invested with a new and living content.[1]

The reformers developed their theology of vocation in their controversy with the church of the Middle Ages because of its over-emphasis on the priestly and monastic life. While one cannot by any means overlook the fact that scholasticism had a social order which provided room also for the temporal estate, one is compelled with Holl[2] to acknowledge that the monastic ideal conveyed a different view of the Christian life. One aspect of this development was the antithesis between clergy and laity, so clearly evident during the Middle Ages.[3] According to the Catholic view, Christian perfection (Matt. 19:21) consisted of obedience to the evangelical counsels, which according to their content could be identified with the monastic vows. He who had become a monk was said to possess the true *vocatio*. According to the Lutheran Confessions, however, the monastic estate is not commanded by God, who is to be served "by observing the commands he has given and not by keeping the commands invented by men" (AC XXVII 57). In this connection it is interesting to note the reasoning of the confessional writers. While the Catholics based the monastic system, for example, on Jesus' promise to those who for His sake have forsaken home and family (Matt. 19:21),[4] the reformers expressly hold that the monastic state is a human invention. They arrive at this conclusion through general deductions in which one or more premises are drawn from Scripture. For example, the Bible

---

[1] Karl Holl, III (1928), 189—219. N. Paulus in *Historiches Jahrbuch der Görres-Gesellschaft* (1925), pp. 308—16. F. Lau in RGG I (1957), 1076—81 (Article on "Beruf"). H. Bornkamm (1961), pp. 128 f.

[2] K. Holl, III (1928), 190—99.

[3] F. Arnold in *Universität Tübingen: Reden bei der feierlichen Übergabe des Rektorates* (1954), pp. 28 ff.

[4] CR 27, 172 (Confutation, 1530).

knows of no meritorious works; the monastic life is a meritorious act; consequently it is a human invention without a divine command (Ap XXVII 24-25). Or: According to the Catholic view, perfection consists in observing external precepts; Scripture declares that perfection means growth in the fear of God; accordingly, the monks cannot appeal to Scripture (Ap XXVII 26-27). On the other hand, those who devote their life to the works of their everyday vocation can do this.

In Catholic moral theology a distinction is made between precept and counsel, *praeceptum* and *consilium* (AC XXVII 12; Ap XXVII 24). The precepts, drawn from the Decalog and the legislation of the church, are intended for all; the counsels are for those who would attain a higher degree of perfection.[5] In conscious opposition to the Catholic doctrine, the Lutheran confessors draw a line across counsels; in the matter of precepts they reckon only those God commands in the Decalog, foremost among which are the works of one's vocation.[6] The monastic system, celibacy, and the life of the mendicant friar do not constitute the model for Christian perfection. This consists in "that we fear God honestly with our whole hearts, and yet have sincere confidence, faith, and trust that for Christ's sake we have a gracious, merciful God; that we may and should ask and pray God for those things of which we have need, and confidently expect help from him in every affliction connected with our particular calling and station in life; and that meanwhile we do good works for others and diligently attend to our calling" (AC XXVII 49). Each one in his calling should strive for perfection.[7] We are to observe both tables of the Law, and the observance of the Second Table takes place in one's earthly calling. "What constitutes true good works is taught in the Ten Commandments."[8]

To that which God has commanded in His Word belong the three "estates," but not monasticism.[9] This view is unfolded in LC's ex-

---

[5] F. Lau in RGG II, 785 f. H. Laemmer (1858). J. Mausbach-G. Ermecke, I (1954), 313 f.

[6] 302:17 — Deinde obscurantur praecepta Dei, haec opera arrogant sibi titulum perfectae et spiritualis vitae et longe praeferunter operibus praeceptorum Dei, ut operibus suae cuiusque vocationis . . . (Ap XV 25). For more on this see the entire section of Ap XV 25-28.

[7] 389:2 — Omnes enim homines in quacunque vocatione perfectionem expetere debent (Ap XXVII 37).

[8] 290:9-10 (Ap XII 174 German). Cf. 639:16 — dass ausser den zehen Geboten kein Werk noch Wesen gut und Gott gefällig kann sein (LC I 311).

[9] 310:17-42 (Ap XVI 13). 413:32 — Habemus enim satis mandatorum Dei in ecclesia, in magistratu, in oeconomia, quibus satisfacere numquam possumus

position of the Fourth Commandment. The monks perform only their own self-chosen works. The fact that the monastic ideal has managed to get such a foothold in men's consciousness is due to inadequate instruction as to what God actually commands. But obedience to the Fourth Commandment "is better than the holiness of all the Carthusians, even though they kill themselves with fasting and pray on their knees without ceasing. Hence you have a sure text and a divine testimony that God has commanded this; concerning the other things he has not commanded a word." [10] The entire doctrine of vocation, according to Luther, has its origin in the Fourth Commandment, which, next to the First, is foremost. God has placed the estate of parents foremost and in His stead on earth (LC I 125-126). From the Fourth Commandment Luther deduces not only the vocation of father and mother but also the place of government (LC I 150), and with this commandment as the point of departure he derives the assurance that the daily work of servants is far superior to the holiness and rigorous life of the monks.[11] Also here we find that Luther in his exposition goes beyond what the commandment actually deals with and fashions a kind of social ethics. The reason for this procedure is his method of drawing conclusions from given premises in regard to prevailing social conditions, and his creation faith.

When the reformers in their battle against meritorious, self-chosen works fell back on the divine commands in Scripture, it was because the Author of Scripture is also the Creator of the world. What God has commanded in His Word possesses a corresponding element in the rich multiplicity of the created world. Scripture contains the command, and its accuracy is confirmed in creation. Instead of *mandatum,* the Confessions can speak of God's *creatio et ordinatio,* "creation and institution" (AC XXVII 20). The connection between the command, Scripture, and creation lends a deepened perspective to God's present activity. Because God has commanded certain actions, and because He is continually active as the Preserver of creation, the good works enjoined by the commandments become so important, yes necessary, in

(SA Preface 14). With regard to Luther's teaching of the three estates or ranks, see also WA 50, 652:1-32 (*Von den Konziliis und Kirchen,* 1539), and 26, 504:30 to 505:10 (*Vom Abendmahl Christi Bekenntnis,* 1528).

[10] 591:18-24 (LC I 120). Also see the entire section in LC I 112-126.

[11] 597:42 — Ist's nicht ein trefflicher Ruhm, das zu wissen und sagen: "Wenn Du Dein tägliche Hauserbeit tuest, das besser ist denn aller Monche Heiligkeit und strenges Leben"? (LC I 145). 639:20—640:49 (LC I 311—16). Gustaf Wingren makes a rather different judgment of the role of the Fourth Commandment in the Christian calling (1958), pp. 68 f.

vocation.[12] To stand in one's everyday calling implies pursuing the service to one's neighbor which God thereby has in mind.

All the benefits we receive through men are in reality also gifts from God. Created things are like God's hands; they are "the hands, channels, and means through which God bestows all blessings. For example, he gives to the mother breasts and milk for her infant, and he gives grain and all kinds of fruits from the earth for man's nourishment – things which no creature could produce by himself. No one, therefore, should presume to take or give anything except as God has commanded it" (LC I 26-27). In practice, this implies that one is to remain in the calling one has received from God and live in it according to His will. Everyone has God's command to do good to one's neighbor; everyone ought to display gentleness and patience, live in chastity and be helpful, all according to the injunctions of the Ten Commandments. If this is disregarded and other works without God's command are chosen, they are not pleasing to Him. The everyday duties which the individual person can perform for the benefit of others have God's command and approval. They are best performed in the daily duties of one's calling.[13]

Ever since the investigations of the Swedish theologian Einar Billing into the Lutheran concept of vocation,[14] those who have engaged in Luther research have been keenly alive to the decisive role of vocation in Reformation theology. The principal work is Gustaf Wingren's monogram entitled *Luthers Lehre vom Beruf (The Christian's Calling: Luther on Vocation)*, whose main theses may be summarized in the following points: (1) For Luther, law is not a fixed entity. It cannot then be identified with the Moral Law in the Decalog.[15] (2) The Law emerges in vocation; this is the concrete form

---

[12] 102:9 — mandata Dei iuxta vocationem (AC XXVI 10).

[13] 639:11—640:8 (LC I 311-14). Cf. WA 32, 324:30 — Item so muss auch ein rein werck und hertz heissen, ob gleich ein knecht odder magd im hause ein unfletig, unsauber werck tuet, als mistladen, kinder wasschen und rein machen. Darumb ists ein schendliche verkerung, das man die stende so inn den zehen gebott gefasset sind, so gering achtet und nach andern sonderlichen gleissenden wercken gaffet (*Wochenpredigten über Matt. 5—7*, 1530—32).

[14] Einar Billing, I (1900), 87 f. and 187. The same author, *Our Calling* (1909), trans. Conrad Bergendoff.

[15] Gustaf Wingren, *Luthers Lehre vom Beruf* (1952), trans. Carl C. Rasmussen, *The Christian's Calling: Luther on Vocation* (1958), p. 143 — To Luther the law is not a fixed magnitude that is codified, either in the Bible or in any other book. Wingren completes suggestions initiated by Herbert Olsson, I (1934), pp. 34 ff. Also see Ruben Josefson (1943), pp. 89 ff., and (1953), pp. 178 ff.; plus L. Haikola, *Usus legis* (1958), pp. 99 ff. Cf. this with Althaus (1962), pp. 218 ff.

of the Law; vocation is law.[16] (3) Since the Law is the expression
of God's living will and its essence is love for one's neighbor, its
content is flexible. It "constantly requires something new and un-
expected." [17] (4) The point of unity between the Law as something
static, appearing in vocation, and as something fluid, determined by
the situation, rests with the now-active God.[18] – We are given a picture of God as the one who holds sway over everything created, and
who in this world has established different stations and offices which
each person must serve according to his ability. From the positions in
which men are placed there issues a demand for love of one's neighbor, consideration, and tolerance. By virtue of being placed in these
services all human beings, regardless of whether they profess to be
Christians or not, become "channels" for God's love, "masks" behind
which is concealed the God who never rests.[19]

In his vivid view of creation Wingren obviously follows ideas from
Reformation theology, but in relation to the Confessions there is the
decisive difference that they never identify vocation with the Law.
They hold, rather, that the works of one's vocation are commanded by
God and sanctioned in His commands. The Confessions find the commands chiefly in the Decalog, as it appears as Moral Law in all of
Scripture and receives its confirmation in creation and the natural
law. From the declaration of LC that the Decalog sanctions vocation,
making it possible for man to perform good works in it, Wingren
erroneously concludes that the Law is identical with vocation.[20] The
absolute will of God in the Decalog is pushed aside; while the Confessions deduce from the Bible the command not to abandon the daily
duties for the monastery, Wingren draws forth this command from
vocation.[21]

The Confessions do not identify vocation with the Law, but vocation is an expression of what God has positively commanded in His

---

[16] Wingren, *The Christian's Calling* (1958), p. 28 — Vocation is law and
commandment, a synthesis of God's commands to the person who occupies the
particular place on earth that his offices indicate. P. 123 — Vocation is the concrete form of the law. Cf. p. 149.

[17] Ibid., p. 143.

[18] Ibid., p. 145.

[19] Ibid., p. 126 and pp. 137 ff.

[20] Ibid., p. 69 — Vocation is primarily law.

[21] Ibid., p. 73 — The insight the gospel gives, that no work is to be done
before God for the purpose of conciliating him, can also be mediated to us
through the command to work for the sake of our neighbor, that is, through the
command of our vocation.

Word. There it has its foundation, and its distinctive feature is that it excludes every form of work-righteousness. The good works commanded by God must be done in order that we may "do God's will and glorify him" (AC XX 27). This will, which is found in or is deduced from Scripture, gains its confirmation in creation. "Accordingly, I constantly repeat," declares Luther, "that all our life and work must be guided by God's Word if they are to be God-pleasing or holy" (LC I 92). Whenever this does not occur, what we do is unholy in the sight of God, be it ever so highly esteemed by men, as is the case with a spiritual estate invented by men "who do not know God's Word but seek holiness in their own works." [22] In Wingren one searches in vain for this direct connection with the word of Scripture; with him the command is a general demand for love of one's neighbor, "for to discern that something is required by love to one's neighbor is the same as being commanded by God to do that." [23]

The similarity between Wingren's view and the reformers' view of *mandatum* is very slight. In the Confessions the command is always linked to some specific word of Scripture, which often finds its confirmation also in creation. The frame for the works of vocation is indicated in the Ten Commandments. [24] Within this general frame a rich, varied multiplicity prevails, of which there is abundant intimation in the exposition of the Commandments in LC; as a general rule, however, it is held that the works enjoined by the Decalog "are the true, holy, and divine works" (LC I 198). The Decalog points out "all that God wishes us to do or not to do" (LC II 1); everyone is to observe God's commands in his vocation. (AC XXVII 13)

Against this background it is meaningless to ask whether vocation belongs to the Law or to the Gospel; [25] it belongs to God's *mandatum*. The doctrine of vocation is to such an extent a consequence of justification by faith that all works now are removed from the concept of merit. One is justified before God by faith for the sake of Christ. But as justification is founded upon God's promise expressed in Scripture, so His commands preserved in Scripture have the same power to liberate

[22] 584:3-5 (LC I 93). That "God's Word" here refers to the Bible is made clear by the foregoing, in which Luther speaks of the necessity of preaching, reading, or hearing God's Word (LC I 92).

[23] Wingren, *The Christian's Calling* (1958), pp. 208 f. Cf. p. 203.

[24] This is correctly pointed out by R. Josefson (1953), p. 181.

[25] This is an important point in Wingren's controversy with Einar Billing; Wingren, *The Christian's Calling* (1958), pp. 74 f. For more on the distinction between commandment and law see Chapter Three, part 1.

the conscience from the compulsion to perform works with a view to obtaining justification. In our daily duties we are to attempt only to bear the fruits of faith. He who gave the command is the same God who is the world's Creator and Preserver. As we have repeatedly pointed out, the consequence of this is a connection between the command of Scripture and the rich, varied world of creation.

However, to deduce the content of the commandment from "the temporal order, the station and vocation in which man actually lives," [26] cannot be done from the points of departure the Symbols employ. They do not deduce the content of the commandment from the natural awareness that there is a God who is to be worshiped and a neighbor who is waiting to be loved.[27] The Law is indeed written in the hearts of all men, but most frequently it is poorly observed, and never perfectly. For this reason instruction in the Ten Commandments is necessary. This gives vocation a concrete content in the person whom it succeeds in enlightening as to what the commandment wishes to say in an actual situation.[28] As the will of God takes shape in the different vocations, the result is an openness to life's changing richness. There is never a question as to any rigid uniformity in the ethical. On the contrary, the Symbols realistically reckon with the fact that men behave differently toward what God commands.[29] In a twofold manner one may go beyond the commandment, partly by lacking confidence in God, the Giver of all good gifts, and partly by doing self-invented works and making vows in opposition to the express commandments of God. The prerequisite for proper good works is to be found in one's relationship to God. When this has become new through faith, we are able to perform the works of our vocation in the full assurance that they are in accordance with His commands and good pleasure (AC XX 27 ff.). Therefore the doctrine of vocation stands in close connection with the righteousness of faith and with the Christian life. (Ap XXIII 32)

3. Marriage

Among the things God has commanded is marriage. But at the same time — in apparent contradiction thereto — marriage is said to

---

[26] L. Haikola, *Usus legis* (1958), p. 94, n. 34. The thesis set forth here by Haikola is poorly supported in the passages quoted from *Vorlesung über den Prediger Salomo* (WA 20, 36 ff.).

[27] L. Haikola (1958), p. 95.

[28] H. Ivarsson (1956), pp. 144—63. Cf. G. Wingren (1960), pp. 36 f.

[29] 649:38-41 (LC II 21); 661:5-46 (LC II 66 f.).

be "an external, temporal matter." [1] To understand both of these seemingly contradictory statements we must examine the background and seek to establish why they were made.

The reformers, in their controversy with the Catholic view of marriage, regard marriage as "a worldly estate" (TB 3; LW 53, 112). The Catholic Church considers marriage as the seventh sacrament and regards it, according to Eph. 5:32, as an image of Christ's intimate relationship with His bride, the church. [2] Already in *De captivitate babylonica* Luther opposes the sacramental view of marriage. (1) It has no support in the Word of God. (2) Therefore it does not fulfill the conditions requisite for a sacrament, namely that it is to constitute an outward sign to which is added a divine word of promise. [3] (3) *Sacramentum* in Eph. 5:32, which is a translation of the Greek *mysterion,* meaning mystery, something hidden, does not allude to marriage but to the relationship between Christ and the church. The mystery, *sacramentum,* in the New Testament is Christ. [4] (4) Marriage is an order of creation. Since it has existed from the beginning of the world and continually exists among unbelievers, there is no reason to reserve it for Christians and call it a sacrament. [5]

In the confessional writings we find only a few traces of this direct criticism of the sacramental view of marriage. Eph. 5:32 plays no role in the argumentation; the only instance where it is mentioned indirectly is in a marriage prayer where reference is made to "the sacramental union of thy dear Son, the Lord Jesus Christ, and the church, his bride" (TB 16; LW 53, 115). Even here, then, the mystery is not marriage, but Christ in relation to His bride, the church. On the other hand, TB 12 (LW 53, 114) cites other parts of Ephesians 5, governing the mutual relationship between husband and wife. Also, Ap denies that marriage can be a sacrament. To be sure, it is commanded by God, but it is older than the New Testament and lacks the promise of grace which characterizes the sacraments of the church. (Ap XIII 14-15)

---

[1] WA 30 III, 205:12 (*Von Ehesachen,* 1530).

[2] Denz., 702 — Septimum est sacramentum *Matrimonii,* quod est signum coniunctionis Christi et Ecclesiae, secundum Apostolum docentem: "Sacramentum hoc magnum est: ego autem dico in Christo et in Ecclesia" (Eph. 5:32).

[3] WA 6, 550:21-32 (*De captivitate babylonica,* 1520).

[4] WA 6, 551:6—552:27 (*De captivitate,* 1520). Luther's observations on this, that the *sacramentum* of the New Testament is not identical with the ecclesiastical concept of "sacrament" are very much to the point. See, e. g., P.-Th. Camelot in RThom (1957), pp. 429—49, and J. de Gellinck, I (1924).

[5] WA 6, 550:33—551:5 (*De captivitate babylonica,* 1520).

When Luther calls marriage "a worldly estate," he means, negatively, a repudiation of its sacramental character, without, however, assuming a modern, secularized view. "The temporal surely does not mean 'temporal' in our modern sense, but it has a purely negative connotation, 'not spiritual.' The Reformers were far removed from the thought of surrendering marriage to the profane, that is, to an order detached from God." [6] Marriage belongs to the order of creation and not to the order of salvation.

For their positive view, grounded in God's creative will, the confessional writers adduce several reasons. Marriage, which is one of the three estates,[7] is the oldest and therefore also, in the opinion of the confessors, superior to the others (LC I 209). When God created men and commanded them to be fruitful and replenish the earth, He endowed them with an impulse which draws the man to the woman and the woman to the man. This natural *appetitus*,[8] which must not be confused with "the sinful lust which has attended man since Adam's fall" (Ap XXIII 7 German), builds upon God's plan with His creation and gives to all men a "natural right," *ius naturale* (Ap XXIII 9), which cannot be revoked as long as God has not changed human nature.[9] On the contrary, after the Fall the sexual impulse has received such a renewed vigor that marriage, in addition to its original intention, given in creation, is also an aid to human infirmity, necessary for all whom God has not endowed with the grace of restraint. (AC XXIII 4-6) [10]

Marriage, then, receives its confirmation through our natural knowledge of God's creative will, but it assumes its proper position in that it is supported by God's specific *mandatum*. What is distinctive about marriage, according to the Confessions, is that in contrast to the monastic system it finds support in Scripture and is commanded

---

[6] S. Reicke in GF 6 (1953), 51. Cf. F. K. Schumann in GF 8 (1955), 156, and G. Gloege in *Gedenkschrift für Werner Elert* (1955), p. 351.

[7] 413:33 — ordo ecclesiasticus, politicus and oeconomicus (SA Preface 14). 523:30 ff. (SC Haustafel).

[8] 334:52 — Loquimur enim non de concupiscentia, quae peccatum est, sed de illo appetitu, qui in integra natura futurus erat (Ap XXIII 7); 336:16 (Ap XXIII 12); 614:4 (LC I 212). Cf. STh III, q. 15, a. 2.

[9] 336:9 — coniunctionem maris et feminae esse iuris naturalis. Porro ius naturale vere est ius divinum, quia est ordinatio divinitus impressa naturae. Quia autem hoc ius mutari non potest sine singulari opere Dei, necesse est manere ius contrahendi coniugii (Ap XXIII 12).

[10] 613:44 — Denn wo die Natur gehet, wie sie von Gott eingepflanzt ist, ist es nicht muglich, ausser der Ehe keusch zu bleiben (LC I 211).

there. "For though it is a worldly estate, yet does it have God's Word in its favor and was not invented or instituted by men, as was the estate of the monks and nuns" (TB 3; LW 53, 112). Both the Fourth and Sixth Commandments confirm that marriage "is not only an honorable estate but also a necessary one, and it is solemnly commanded by God . . . ." [11] Ap XIII 14 asserts that marriage has the *mandatum Dei* and rejects the reasons advanced by others for its sacramental character. [12] God's command to cohabitation in marriage is referred to in Ap as well as in the catechisms as the principal argument against the monastic system. The *mandatum* to which Ap no doubt points most frequently is characteristically enough 1 Cor. 7:2: "Because of the temptation to immorality, each man should have his own wife." [13] This commandment, which more likely ought to be regarded as a permission rather than a command, is sometimes referred to in Ap as "the commandment of the Holy Spirit." [14] Other important Scripture passages relating to marriage are Gen. 1:27 f. [15] and 1 Cor. 7:9. [16] Together with the oft-quoted Matt. 19:11 [17] they confirm that marriage is an order of creation which no human being ought to or without special divine help can evade.

The creative word "be fruitful and multiply" (Gen. 1:28) "did not form the nature of men to be fruitful only at the beginning of creation, but it still does as long as this physical nature of ours exists" (Ap XXIII 8). The natural inner attraction for one another which man and woman experience is increased through concupiscence, so that the attraction, without any special divine assistance, is irresistible. Therefore in order that we may avoid the sins of unchastity, God commands us throughout Scripture to contract and live in marriage. [18] It follows from this that marriage is a prerogative of all, and one which

[11] 613:34-36 (LC I 211). See also 612:16 ff. (LC I 206 ff.) and 592:39 ff. (LC I 126).

[12] 294:16 — Habet autem mandatum Dei, habet et promissionem, non quidem proprie ad novum testamentum pertinentes sed magis pertinentes ad vitam corporalem (Ap XIII 14).

[13] 87:12 (AC XXIII 4); 336:35-39 (Ap XXIII 14); 337:9-11 (Ap XXIII 17); 346:23-26 (Ap XXIII 63).

[14] 392:25 — mandatum spiritus sancti (Ap XXVII 51).

[15] 87:14 — Deus creavit hominem ad procreationem, Gen. 1 (AC XXIII 5); 334:50-52 (Ap XXIII 7); 533:33-47 (TB 15).

[16] 87:10 — Melius est nubere, quam uri (AC XXIII 4); 336:48 (Ap XXIII 16).

[17] 87:12 (AC XXIII 5); 336:49 (Ap XXIII 16); 337:25 (Ap XXIII 19).

[18] 336:51 — Quia nunc post peccatum concurrunt haec duo, naturalis ap-

no human laws or monastic vows can set aside.[19] All who do not have the capacity to exercise abstinence, but are filled with lust, ought to marry. Thus our human nature as well as the Word of God gives marriage precedence over every other estate. This double justification, in creation and in God's command, becomes the main premise from which light is shed on the seemingly contradictory statements about marriage as "a worldly estate" which nevertheless has "God's Word in its favor." This premise also becomes a deciding factor in the intricate questions of divorce and remarriage.

Not only the fact that marriage was in use long before the Christian era and exists in all cultural circles, but also the Word of God attests that it is an ordinance instituted in creation. According to the reformers, this logically demands that marriage should be under the jurisdiction of the temporal government and not of the church. In *Von Ehesachen* Luther calls attention to the important distinction between spiritual and temporal government [20] and shows why questions relating to marriage must be removed from the spiritual government. The church's threefold mission of proclaiming the Word, administering the sacraments, and administering the power of the keys (AC XXVIII 5) does not include exercising the external authority required for regulating the affairs of marriage.[21] "Since marriage and the married estate are worldly matters, it behooves us pastors or ministers of the church not to attempt to order or govern anything connected with it, but to permit every city and land to continue its own use and custom in this connection" (TB 1; LW 53, 111). In practice, however, this principle could not be carried out, since many legal procedures in the realm of marriage also include ethical aspects, and the temporal government, according to Reformation theology, is God's mandate which requires the church for guidance. Here the question again arises as to the role of the word of Scripture for the structur-

petitus et concupiscentia, quae inflammat naturalem appetitum, ut iam magis opus sit coniugio, quam in natura integra (Ap XXIII 16).

[19] 87:19 — Nam mandatum Dei et ordinationem Dei nulla lex humana, nullum votum tollere potest (AC XXIII 8). This statement is often repeated: 90:40 ff. (AC XXIII 24); 113:17 ff. (AC XXVII 18); 114:8 ff. (AC XXVII 22 f.); 116:21 ff. (AC XXVII 40); 335:27 ff. (Ap XXIII 8); 337:4 ff. (Ap XXIII 16); 392:19 f. (Ap XXVII 51). WA 6, 555:4-6 (*De captivitate*, 1520).

[20] WA 30 III, 206:6 — Nu weis ja (Gott lob) alle welt wol, mit was vleis und muhe ich daran geerbeitet habe und noch daran erbeite, das die zwey ampt odder regiment, Weltlich und Geistlich unterschieden und von einander gesondert (*Von Ehesachen*, 1530). See also ibid., 243:19 f., and 122:21 ff. (AC XXVIII 12 ff.); plus E. Schlink (1961), pp. 226 ff., and O. Sundby (1959), pp. 25 ff.

[21] WA 30 III, 205:24—206:5 (*Von Ehesachen*, 1530).

ing of marriage. What does it mean that marriage is not only "a worldly estate," but that it also has "God's Word in its favor"?

Sundby, who has written a book on the Lutheran view of marriage, has not ignored the problem, but he accords it a scanty and not particularly enlightening explanation. Sundby's thesis is that marriage as "a temporal matter" is placed under the natural law which all men know through their human reason, and whose content is love for one's neighbor. The Law in this sense functions partly in the order of creation, partly in specific situations, and partly through the action of the temporal government.[22] Since marriage falls under the natural law, its ethics are to be regulated by human reason with the welfare of one's neighbor as its main objective. To employ the Word of Scripture as a norm is to repeat the error of "the fanatics," namely of applying the word of Scripture to questions it is not intended to regulate.[23] Luther's many utterances to the effect that the Word is the basic foundation of marriage allude to "the regulation, the fashioning of that which is given by nature."[24]

One immediately sees that there is a wide gap between this view and that of the Confessions, where "the Word" always refers to Scripture and where *mandatum* always includes a reference to a specific Bible passage. In practice the Bible played a very important role in the formation of the ethics and jurisprudence of marriage. As Reicke correctly points out, the government discharges its duties towards marriage "in accord with the norms of revelation, in practice in collaboration with the theologians and servants of the church."[25] Nor was there any interest in establishing a line of separation, since the natural law and the commandment of Scripture mutually support one another. Scripture confirms that marriage is an order of creation and makes clear God's original intention with it (cf., for example, WA 30 III, 236:9 ff.). Rather than ask whether Scripture has anything to do with marriage, therefore, let us investigate how the ethics of marriage were fashioned on the foundation of the Bible. However, to bring forth detailed rules from the New Testament cannot be done, among other reasons, because it doesn't provide such precepts. Even if the reformers had wished to erect a new legislation entirely upon Scripture — which

[22] O. Sundby (1959), pp. 31 f. and 183.

[23] Ibid., p. 191.

[24] Ibid., pp. 37 f.

[25] S. Reicke in GF 6 (1953), 51. An illustration of this is to be found in Laurentius Petri's "Church Order" of 1571.

they did not—they would have found that Biblical statements very frequently are not to be found.[26] Not infrequently, therefore, the reformers fell back on "the use and custom" of "every city and land" (TB 1). In Scripture they sought the more general and fundamental views of marriage, which were later applied through logical deliberation.[27]

The Bible declares first and foremost that marriage, despite its temporal character, is a "divine estate"[28] in which man and woman enter into such an intimate union as to become "one flesh and blood" (LC I 200). What is essential for marriage is the mutual, public assent of the contracting parties.[29] The Confessions make no demand that the vow shall be given in the presence of a clergyman, but neither do they raise any objection to such a practice—which may appear strange against the background of the division of work between the spiritual and the temporal governments. Fundamentally the church has nothing to do with the contracting of marriage, since this is "a worldly estate"; and yet Luther produced a marriage service which became a model for such rites in all Lutheran lands and churches.[30] The intention was that the ecclesiastical act should be an act of blessing, but it also received a juridical significance. If the officiating pastor was regarded as the representative of the temporal government, it is quite remarkable that the contracting of marriage is confirmed by the ancient church's form "in the name of the Father, and of the Son, and of the Holy Ghost" (TB 9; LW 53, 113). No doubt there is here an ambiguity which would in due time appear and lead to conflicts.[31]

---

26 S. Reicke in GF 6 (1953), 52.

27 Cf. WA 26, 225:20-30 (*Unterricht der Visitatoren,* 1528).

28 529:30 — diesen göttlichen Stand (Taufbüchlein 3; LW 53, 112); 612:24 — einen göttlichen, seligen Stand (LC I 206); 530:33 — zum heiligen Stande der Ehe (TB 6).

29 531:15 — Weil denn Hans N. und Greta N. einander zur Ehe begehren und solchs hie öffentlich für Gott und die Welt bekennen (TB 9). Cf. O. Lähteenmäki (1955), p. 109, and O. Sundby (1959), pp. 46 ff. It is interesting to see how Luther justifies the publicizing of the promise on the basis of the Fourth Commandment: Es [a secret engagement] ist viel mehr widder Gott und sein wort, nemlich widder der eltern gehorsam, welchen Gott offenbarlich geboten hat, und Gott ynn dem selbigen gebot ist und verbeut solche verlöbnis und gar nicht zusamen fugt (*Von Ehesachen,* 1530). On the basis of a given premise he draws conclusions concerning concrete relationships.

30 O. Albrecht in WA 30 III, 70.

31 Concerning this problem in its entirety the reader is referred to O. Albrecht in WA 30 III, 60 ff. O. Lähteenmäki (1955), pp. 110—13. O. Sundby (1959), p. 49. Chapter 25 of Laurentius Petri's "Church Order" (1571) asserts that the

The purpose of marriage is that husband and wife shall "be true to each other, be fruitful, beget children, and support and bring them up to the glory of God" (LC I 207). The Confessions place special stress on unity in marriage. Since the two partners in marriage, according to the language of the Bible, have become one flesh, marriage cannot be dissolved. In the New Testament divorce is forbidden,[32] and experience shows that those who have broken their marriage vow "will not escape punishment. . . . Nothing he does will in the end succeed; everything he may gain by the false oath will slip through his fingers and will never be enjoyed." (LC I 67)

We know, however, that Lutheranism quite early permitted divorce on the ground of adultery and willful desertion, a practice that goes back to Luther himself.[33] This question is not discussed in the Confessions at all, but it is assumed that the innocent party in a divorce has the right to remarry.[34] The confessional writers did not arrive at this conclusion through a discussion of the entire New Testament material, but in the choice between the necessity of marriage and the prohibition of divorce the former took precedence. Since the impulse for marriage is a part of human nature and cannot be resisted without special divine help, one of the most important purposes of marriage is to prevent unchastity (LC I 211 ff.) and serve as a remedy against sin, *remedium peccati*. This applies also to innocent divorced persons, who must have the right to remarry.[35] But thereby one had actually surrendered the indissolubility of marriage and left the possibility of separation open. This point of view is linked with the idea that marriage is a temporal matter. The New Testament's instruction regarding marriage issues in part from other presuppositions — life in the church and communion with Christ through the Holy Spirit. The New Testament also regards harmonious wedded life as one of the fruits of the Christian life.

concerns of the marriage estate belong more properly to the secular than to the spiritual order, but in view of the fact that the church has been in charge for so long, it ought to continue.

[32] 637:37 — Weil im Neuen Testament den Ehelichen verpoten ist, sich vonander zu scheiden (LC I 305).

[33] O. Lähteenmäki (1955), pp. 69 ff. and 75 ff. E. Kinder in *Luther-Mitteilungen der Luthergesellschaft*, 24 (1953), 25—86.

[34] 494 — Iniusti etiam traditio est, quae prohibet coniugium personae innocenti post factum divortium (Tr 78).

[35] Cf. O. Lähteenmäki (1955), pp. 78 ff. and 81. O. Sundby (1959), p. 57.

Chapter Twelve:

Eternal Life

Only in a few brief sections, "The Return of Christ for Judgment" (AC and Ap XVII), do the Confessions discuss the last things, and they do it in terms which aroused no opposition on the part of the Catholics.[1] The reason is that the Lutheran Symbols take the same position as that of the symbols of the ancient church and confess "that at the consummation of the world Christ will appear for judgment and will raise up all the dead. To the godly and elect he will give eternal life and endless joy, but ungodly men and devils will he condemn to be tormented without end." [2]

If the scanty references should lead us to suppose that for the Lutheran Confessions eschatological questions are nonessential and uncontroversial, we would be sadly mistaken. Schlink [3] correctly points out that the subject of eschatology is so essential for them that it pervades the entire presentation, setting its stamp upon all doctrinal statements. Reformation theology was shaped with the eternal things in view, and it has a clear eschatological direction. Melanchthon wrote Ap with the great day of reckoning in view,[4] and in SA Luther fixes his eyes on Christ's return, there to await the solution of the difficulties in which he is involved and of which he can see no end.[5] The reformers are convinced that they live in the last times. The world has aged; the Antichrist has established his domain [6] and brought about abuses such as the worship of saints, new forms of worship, and prohibition

---

[1] CR 27, 117 f. (Confutation, 1530).

[2] 72:3-9 (AC XVII 1 ff.) Cf. WA 26, 509:13 ff. (*Vom Abendmahl Christi Bekenntnis,* 1528).

[3] E. Schlink (1961), pp. 270 f.

[4] 144:39 — Commendabimus itaque causam nostram Christo, qui olim iudicabit has controversias (Ap Foreword 19). 403:7-11 (Ap Conclusion 24 f.)

[5] 414:1-3 (SA Preface 15); 432:17-20 (SA II IV 15).

[6] 89:11-14 (AC XXIII 14); 344:9-11 (Ap XXIII 53). Luther identifies the pope with Antichrist (SA II IV 10). E. Schlink (1961), pp. 279 ff. Concerning the eschatological tendency in reformation thought consult, e. g., P. Althaus (1956) and H. Kraft in RGG 2 (1958), 678 (article on "Eschatology"). Also Asendorf, *Eschatologie bei Luther* (1967).

against marriage.[7] More important than this, however, is the fact that
the Triune God's dealing with men is viewed in the light of eternity.
Through sin death came into the world, through Christ came life and
salvation. Just as the Creed begins with creation and ends with the
resurrection, so is the Christian life embraced between these two
poles.

Therefore everything that has gone before may be summed up as
an arena where God the Holy Spirit is at work through Word and sacraments to lead men from the world of sin and death into His eternal
kingdom. In the world of eternity the image of God will again be fully
restored in man, so that he will live in perfect reliance and confidence
in God.[8] Justification, which through the Gospel regenerates man, is,
as it were, a beginning of eternal life,[9] and gives us not only a reflection
of eternal life but the blessings themselves. "The Gospel brings not
only the shadow of eternal things but the eternal blessings themselves,
the Holy Spirit and the righteousness by which we are righteous before
God." [10] The comfort which the Gospel, the Promise, provides
emerges from these eschatological points of departure in its true right
and becomes not only a psychological happening but involves deliverance from the powers hostile to God (Ap IV 314) and participation in
the divine life which belongs to the eternal world; in us it is brought
into effect in faith. "It is eternal things, the Word of God and the Holy
Spirit, that work eternal life in the heart" (Ap XXVIII 10). The Gospel, in all the shapes in which it appears — whether as proclaimed Word,
absolution, Baptism, or the Lord's Supper — bestows on us eternal life,
"for where there is forgiveness of sins, there are also life and salvation"
(SC VI 6). Thus Baptism is seen as an event that stretches over one's
entire life on earth and prepares the baptized person for eternal life
with God.[11] In the same way the Lord's Supper frees us from sin and

---

[7] See, e. g., 424:11 — Anrufung der Heiligen ist auch der endchristlichen
Missbräuche (SA II II 25); 300:50-52 (Ap XV 19); 459:24 ff. (SA III XI 1).

[8] 227:15 — regeneramur, ut ait Paulus, ad agnitionem Dei, et intuentes gloriam Domini transformamur in eandem imaginem, id est concipimus veram notitiam Dei, ut vere timeamus eum, vere confidamus nos respici, nos exaudiri (Ap
IV 351). Cf. Chapter Five above.

[9] 227:18 — Haec regeneratio est quasi inchoatio aeternae vitae (Ap IV 352).

[10] 237:17-21 (Ap VII 15). 237:6 — At evangelium affert non umbram
aeternarum rerum, sed ipsas res aeternas, spiritum sanctum et iustitiam, qua coram
Deo iusti sumus (Ap VII 15). Cf. Chapter Six above.

[11] 707:14 — Also siehet man, wie ein hoch trefflich Ding es ist ümb die
Täufe, so uns dem Teufel aus dem Hals reisset, Gott zu eigen macht, die Sünd
dämpft und wegnimmpt, darnach täglich den neuen Menschen stärket und immer

death (LC V 22). From this eschatological outlook light is shed on the never-ceasing work of the Holy Spirit to gather the church through Word and sacrament and prepare her for eternal life.[12] As a consequence, eternal life is viewed both as a now and as a then. The Kingdom means God's dominion over sin and death through Christ (LC III 51), and it "comes to us in two ways: first, it comes here, in time, through the Word and faith, and secondly, in eternity, it comes through the final revelation" at Christ's second coming (LC III 53). Through faith in the promises of the Gospel we become partakers already here in time of the life which belongs completely to the world of eternity. Through justification eternal life becomes not only a "future," but is already a "present perfect." [13]

The connection between eternal life here and in eternity appears also in the important and continually controversial question regarding men's faith and works, their justification and sanctification, and it sheds light on their lot in the world to come. Actually, there is an apparent parallelism, so that what conditions men's salvation here in time also becomes decisive for their lot at the last judgment.

Whether justification is described as regeneration, the forgiveness of sins, victory over the powers of evil, or comfort for the troubled conscience, it is understood as a righteousness imputed to men and bestowed through Christ. It is received in the faith which embraces the promises, and this faith alone justifies men. Justification is complete and perfect; through faith in Christ God accounts us "altogether righteous and holy" (SA III XIII 1). We possess perfection, which involves participation in eternal life, despite the imperfection of our works. Faith, which signifies that the heart has been born again unto the fear of God and spiritual life, does not exclude good works. On the contrary, they too, as the fruits of faith, are wrought by God.[14] The faith we are dealing with here is not mere theoretical knowledge,

---

gehet und bleibt, bis wir aus diesem Elend zur ewigen Herrligkeit kommen (LC IV 83). Cf. 53:8-11 (AC II 2), and Chapter Seven, part 2, above.

[12] 658:25 — Darümb ist alles in der Christenheit dazu geordnet, dass man da täglich eitel Vergebung der Sunden durch Wort und Zeichen hole, unser Gewissen zu trösten und aufrichten, solang wir hie leben (LC II 54). Cf. Chapters Four and Ten.

[13] P. Althaus in RGG 2 (1958), 681. See also P. Althaus (1956), M. Schmaus (1948), and E. Brunner (1953).

[14] 657:46 — dadurch er die Heiligung machet und mehret, dass sie täglich zunehme und stark werden im Glauben und seinen Früchten, *so er schaffet* (LC II 53). Cf. Chapter Eleven.

but a matter of the will, and it has its existence in repentance.[15] Its basis is in the Reformation dialectic between Law and Gospel.[16]

Works, however, do not justify, but they are accepted by God for the sake of faith.[17] The keeping of the Law in faith is always imperfect; sanctification signifies growth in faith, in good works, and in mortifying the flesh in order that the new man of faith may in eternity appear pure, no longer burdened by sin. "Since holiness has begun and is growing daily, we await the time when our flesh will be put to death, will be buried with all its uncleanness, and will come forth gloriously and arise to complete and perfect holiness in a new, eternal life." (LC II 57)

Since the baptized and believing person thus already by faith is a partaker of eternal life [18] and through the putting to death of sin in repentance and sanctification reaches out toward the eternal world, it also follows that eternal life is bestowed on him as a divine gift by grace. The Symbols clearly point out the connection between eternal life now in faith and there in perfection: "Even as the forgiveness of sins and righteousness are imputed to us, not for the sake of our works or the law, so also righteousness together with eternal life are offered us, not for the sake of our works nor for the sake of the law, but for the sake of Christ." [19]

This faith can be confessed in harmony with Scripture and "the whole church." [20] Here, however, was a problem which required further clarification. It could be pointed out that the Athanasian Creed, with which the Lutheran Symbols were in agreement, declares that men on the last day shall render an account of their works, so that those who have done good will receive eternal life but those who have done

---

[15] 227:7 — Haec fides, de qua loquimur, existit in poenitentis (Ap IV 350).

[16] Chapters Three and Eight above.

[17] 192:37 — tamen nunc multo clarius perspici poterit, quod illa inchoata legis impletio non iustificet, quia tantum est accepta propter fidem (Ap IV 161); 229:60 ff. (Ap IV 368); 460:13—461:6 (SA III XIII 2 ff.). Cf. Chapter Six above.

[18] 227:25 — Sicut autem iustificatio ad fidem pertinet, ita pertinet ad fidem vita aeternam (Ap IV 354).

[19] 223:40-44 (Ap IV 333 German). 221:53 — certo statuere debemus, quod propter Christum donetur nobis iustitia et vita aeterna (Ap IV 320).

[20] 222:10 — Tota ecclesia confitetur, quod vita aeterna per misericordiam contingat (Ap IV 322). 226:10 — cum tota ecclesia docemus, quod per misericordiam salvemur (Ap IV 338). 226:37 (Ap IV 344). In Ap quotations are taken from Augustine, *De gratia et lib. arb.*, 6, 15 and 9, 21 (MPL 44, 890) (Ap IV 356), and 893 (Ap IV 322), plus Cyprian, *De oratione dominica*, 22 (MPL 4, 534 c) (Ap IV 322). Cf. Chaps. Two and Eleven above.

evil will be condemned to the eternal fire.[21] Furthermore, it could also be said that Scripture clearly teaches that men's lot in eternity will be determined not according to their faith but according to their works. Ap recognizes these objections against eternal life as a gift for the sake of justifying faith: "Our opponents argue that good works properly merit eternal life, since Paul says (Rom. 2:6), 'He will render to every man according to his works.' . . . John 5:29, 'Those who have done good will come forth to the resurrection of life'; Matt. 25:35, 'I was hungry and you gave me food.'" [22]

The reply to these objections is analogous to the defense of righteousness by faith, which means that eschatology too, in the proper sense, receives its rightful illumination from the dialectic between Law and Gospel. As we recall from Chapter One, the Lutheran Confessions and the Reformation theologians hold that the doctrine of justification, which is drawn from Scripture, becomes intelligible if a distinction is made between the Law and the promises, between Law and Gospel (Ap IV 183-188). If we keep this distinction in mind, we can accord works their proper place in the Christian life and understand what Scripture says about them. When Scripture praises works, it is always as the fruits of faith (Ap IV 277 f.). In other words, when Scripture speaks of good works, it presupposes faith as self-evident, just as it maintains that spiritual righteousness always produces good fruits.[23] The same applies to the manner in which Scripture speaks about eternal life at the end of time. Since Christ has said that "apart from Me you can do nothing" (John 15:5), all truly good works are performed only by those who are already justified (Ap IV 372). Here, under the perspective of eternity, we have another illustration of the method of Scripture interpretation the Confessions employ. John 15:5 becomes a *canon,* a *regula,* which determines the interpretation of all the utterances of Scripture concerning good works. The Confessions adopt the two premises that no one apart from Christ (John 15:5) or without faith (Heb. 11:6)

[21] 30:20-25 (Athanasian Creed 38 f.). 414:24-26 (SA I 4). In SA, Luther bypasses this problem, saying nothing about it.

[22] 230:10 — Verum urgent adversarii, quod proprie mereantur vitam aeternam bona opera, quia Paulus dicit Rom. 2: Reddet unicuique secundum opera eius. Item: Gloria, honor et pax omni operanti bonum. John 5: Qui bona fecerunt, in resurrectionem vitae. Matth. 25: Esurivi et dedistis mihi manducare etc. (Ap IV 370).

[23] 229:15 — Et sicut scriptura saepe mentione bonorum operum fidem complectitur, vult enim complecti iustitiam cordis cum fructibus (Ap IV 365). P. Brunner in KuD 4 (1961), 272—83.

can please God, and that Scripture praises works. The conclusion of the matter is not that Scripture is contradictory, but that the good works which are praised are such as are performed in faith by those who already are justified.[24] All the Scripture passages that praise works must be understood only according to the rule "that works apart from Christ are not pleasing to God, and that one must in no wise exclude Christ the Mediator. Therefore, when the text says that eternal life will be given to those who have done good, it wishes thereby to show that it will be given to those who by faith in Christ already are justified." (Ap IV 371-372 German)

In support of this viewpoint there is also a motive concerned with the cure of souls. If we were required to merit eternal life by our works, we could never be certain of our salvation, but would live in fear and anxiety and in our hour of death be easily beset by doubt.[25] Yet, there is no danger that the Reformation view of eternal life would lead to moral laxity,[26] since the faith involved here has as its background the proclamation of the Law and grows and develops out of the promises of the Gospel. It has its existence in penitence. (Ap IV 353)

The intimate relationship between justification and eternal life is bound to have an effect on the shaping of eschatology in the proper sense. Eschatology receives its distinctive characteristic from premises grounded in Scripture, from which the confessional writers argue. Although the restrained tone of the statements is apparent, there are clear lines of demarcation on the right as well as on the left. As to the soul's destiny after death, there is no explicit information. In eternity the forgiveness of sins will no longer be necessary, since in that life we shall be "perfectly pure and holy people, full of goodness and righteousness . . . living in new, immortal, and glorified bodies." [27] The Confessions have nothing to say about an intermediary state between death and resurrection, but their view is that the Holy Spirit, who has created our faith and wrought our sanctification, will complete

---

[24] See, e. g., the section 210:16-45 (Ap IV 254 ff.); 213:40-50 (Ap IV 266); 220:39-41 (Ap IV 315); 230:27 — sine me nihil potestis facere. Ex hoc canone diximus supra iudicari posse omnes locos de operibus (Ap IV 372). Cf. Chapters One and Three above.

[25] 226:52 — Si spes niteretur operibus, tunc vero esset incerta, quia opera non possunt pacare conscientiam (Ap IV 346). Cf. 223:10-14 (Ap IV).

[26] 227:1-2 (Ap IV 348). Cf. 224:11 — Hie werden sie aber sagen: So wir durch lauter Barmherzigkeit sollen selig werden, was ist denn für ein Unterschied unter denen, die da selig werden, und die da nicht selig werden? (Ap IV).

[27] 659:10-16 (LC II 58); 674:27 f. (LC III 54).

His work and will consummate in an instant what He has begun, forever making us partakers of eternal life.[28] In practice this means
a repudiation of all notions of a millennium as well as a purgatory.

Origen's idea of the restoration of all things and the hints in the
Book of Revelation regarding a millennium had gained acceptance
within baptismal movements during the Reformation period.[29] That
AC [30] positively rejects the idea of a millennium is linked with a concern for accentuating the difference between the Lutheran Reformation and the radical reformatory tendencies. Nevertheless, its position
was deeply anchored in the Reformation view.[31]

The rejection of the doctrine of purgatory is a consequence both
of the interpretation of Scripture and of the doctrine of justification.
Since the teaching about purgatory is not found in Scripture (SA II
II 12 ff.) and is inconsistent with justification by faith, it must be
rejected as an expression of the doctrine of works. We find here
another illustration of the connection between Scripture, justification,
and a specific doctrine. The point of departure in the argumentation
is Scripture; the accuracy of the interpretation presented is proved
by the consistency among the different statements of doctrine.

According to the Confessions the doctrine of purgatory is intimately connected with work-righteousness and the idea of merit.
They argue that the satisfactions which, according to Catholic doctrine, must accompany penance are designed to lessen or bring deliverance from the punishments which the soul would otherwise
endure in purgatory.[32] This teaching is, however, without support

28 659:21 — Wenn wir aber verwesen, wird er's ganz auf einem Augenblick
vollführen und ewig dabei erhalten durch die letzten zwei (dass heisst, Auferste-
hung des Fleisches und das ewige Leben) (LC II 59).

29 On this see W. E. Nagel (1930), pp. 130—34; F. Blanke (1955), pp. 68 ff.;
P. Kawerau (1954); T. Bergsten (1961), pp. 467—71.

30 72:10 — Damnant Anabaptistas, qui sentiunt hominibus damnatis ac diabolis finem poenarum futurum esse. Damnant et alios, qui nunc spargunt iudaicas
opiniones, quod ante resurrectionem mortuorum pii regnum mundi occupaturi sint.
ubique oppressis impiis (AC XVII 4 f.).

31 See 72:26 — Hie werden verworfen die Nachfolger Origenis und die Wie-
dertaufer, so lehren, dass zuletzt auch die Verdambten und Teufel aus der Pein
erlöst werden, desgleichen die, so uf judische Meinung sagen, die Verheissung
von Eroberung des gelobten Lands müssen leiblich verstanden werden, und dass
vor der Urständ und jungsten Gericht werden die Gottlosen allenthalben von den
Heiligen untergedruckt und sie das zeitlich Regiment unter sich bringen (NA 16).
W. E. Nagel (1930).

32 276:34 — satisfactiones tantum esse poenas redimentes purgatorium (Ap
XII 118); 256:29-33 (Ap XII 24). According to N. Herborn, *Enchiridion*, pp.
160—64, where the doctrine of purgatory is set forth, purgatory is an expression

in Scripture and in the ancient fathers,[33] who instead teach that the forgiveness of sins delivers us from the guilt as well as the punishment of sin. Good works in the form of satisfactions, which ought to accompany penance, had no purpose other than to promote church discipline and external order (Ap XII 120). In opposition to the Catholic interpretation that the satisfactions should compensate for the punishment which follows sin,[34] the Lutheran Symbols point out that God alone inflicts punishment in the remorse of penance and a stricken conscience.[35] Through justification by faith these punishments are removed, while the sufferings and visitations that befall all men exist for the Christians in order to exercise their faith and to put to death the sin which still clings to them (Ap XII 151 f.). In agreement with the New Testament the Symbols sever the connection between suffering and punishment (Ap XII 158 ff.). The sufferings are an expression of God's alien work through the Law.[36]

On the basis of the witness of Scripture concerning justification by faith the Confessions reject purgatory and the custom of offering Masses for the dead.[37] On the other hand, Ap, in conformity with the practice of the ancient church, permits prayer for the dead.[38] However, it is here on earth that men determine their position in the warfare between God and the hostile powers of the devil by accepting in faith the promised salvation and carrying it out in daily repentance and in the works of their calling. In this way all of one's earthly life, from birth until death, is placed under the perspective of eternity, where one's eyes are fixed on the final consummation.

The strength of the Reformation proclamation lies, not in negative aberrations but in the joyful, Scriptural assurance of salvation through

of God's justice as well as of His mercy: Iam si negligas ipse in te vindicare, quod admisisti, facinus, Deus non modo quia iustus est, sed etiam quia misericors sit et praestabilis super malitia . . . certum locum expiandis animabus designavit (ibid., 161:6-9). Cf. A. Winklhofer in *Handbuch theol. Grundbegr.* (1962), pp. 330 f.

[33] 276:40 — Haec tota res est commentitia, recens conficta sine auctoritate scripturae et veterum scriptorum ecclesiasticorum (Ap XII 119).

[34] N. Herborn, *Enchiridion,* 160:30 — Puniuntur autem vel poenis a Deo inflictis vel ab homine spontaneis castigationibus.

[35] 285:11 — Verius igitur contritio poena est, quam satisfactio (Ap XII 150); 286:6-9 (Ap XII 156); 284:33-36 (Ap XII 148). Cf. Chapter Eight above.

[36] 286:44-48 (Ap XII 158). Cf. Chapter Three, part 1, above.

[37] 373:35 ff. (De missa pro defunctis; Ap XXIV 89 ff.). 420:1-12 (SA II II 12).

[38] 375:45 — scimus veteres loqui de oratione pro mortuis, quam nos non prohibemus (Ap XXIV 94).

faith in Jesus Christ. Although this theology certainly contains a good deal of doctrinal explosive, its penetrating power is explained by the consistency with which it was able to make vivid the ancient church's confession that Jesus Christ is Lord (Phil. 2:11; LC II 26). For this reason it is properly understood only when it is interpreted as a song of praise to the Lord, who has overcome the power of the devil and of death in order to bring us into His eternal kingdom.

Bibliography

Aalen, L. *Den unge Zinzendorfs teologi.* Oslo, 1952.

Aland, K. *Kirchengeschichtliche Entwürfe.* Alte Kirche, Reformation und Luthertum, Pietismus und Erweckungsbewegung. Gütersloh, 1960.

Albrecht, O. Introduction to *Ein Traubüchlein für die einfältigen Pfarrherr 1529,* in WA 30 III. Weimar, 1910.

Algermissen, K. *Konfessionskunde.* Paderborn, 1957.

Althaus, P. *Der Geist der lutherischen Ethik im Augsburgischen Bekenntnis.* Munich, 1931.

————. *Gebot und Gesetz: Zum Thema "Gesetz und Evangelium."* Gütersloh, 1952.

————. Review of W. Joest, *Gesetz und Freiheit,* 1951, in ThLZ 80 (1955).

————. *Die letzten Dinge.* Gütersloh, 6th ed., 1956.

————. The article "Eschatologie" in RGG, II. Tübingen, 1958.

Andrén, A. *Högmässa och nattvardsgång i reformationstidens svenska kyrkoliv.* Lund, 1954.

Arnold, F. *Kirche und Laientum. Universität Tübingen: Reden bei der feierlichen Übergabe das Rektorates zu Beginn des Sommersemesters am 7. Mai 1954.* Tübingen, 1954.

Askmark, R. *Ämbetet i Svenska kyrkan i reformationens, ortodoxiens och pietismens tänkande och praxis.* Lund, 1949.

Augustine, A. See J. P. Migne, *Patrologiae cursus completus . . . series latina.* Paris, 1844 ff.

————. See *Corpus scriptorum ecclesiasticorum latinorum,* I ff. Vienna, 1866 ff.

Aulén, G. *Till belysning af den lutherska kyrkoidén: Dess historia och dess värde.* Uppsala, 1912.

————. *Den kristna försoningstanken.* Lund, 1930.

————. *För eder utgiven: En bok om nattvardens offermotiv.* Stockholm, 1956.

Die Bekenntnisschriften der evangelisch-lutherischen Kirche. Göttingen, 5th ed. 1963.

Benz, E. *Wittenberg und Byzanz: Zur Begegnung und Auseinandersetzung der Reformation und der östlich orthodoxen Kirche.* Marburg, 1949.

————. *Die Ostkirche im Lichte der protestantischen Geschichtsschreibung von der Reformation bis zur Gegenwart.* Munich, 1952.

Bergstenn, T. *Balthasar Hubmaier: Seine Stellung zu Reformation und Täufertum 1521—1528.* Kassel, 1961.

Biel, G. *Collectorium circa libros sententiarum I—II.* Basel, 1501.

————. *Expositio canonis missae.* Basel, 1510.

Billing, E. *Luthers lära om staten,* I. Uppsala 1900.

————. *Vår kallelse.* Uppsala, 1909. *Our Calling,* trans. Conrad Bergendoff.

Billing, G. "Vilken uppfattning af traditionen är utmärkande för det lutherska reformationsverket?" in *Bihang till Linköpings Stiftstidningar,* 8—9 (1871).

————. *Lutherska kyrkans bekännelse.* Lund, 1876—78.

Bizer, E. *Fides ex auditu: Eine Untersuchung über die Entdeckung der Gerechtigkeit Gottes durch Martin Luther.* Neukirchen, 1961.

Blanke, F. *Brüder in Christo: Die Geschichte der ältesten Taüfergemeinde.* Zurich, 1955.

Bornkamm, H. "Luthers Bericht über seine Entdeckung der iustitia dei," in ARG 37 (1940).

————. "Iustitia dei in der Scholastik und bei Luther," in ARG 39 (1942).

————. *Das Jahrhundert der Reformation.* Göttingen, 1961.

Boyer, Ch. "Le péché originel," in *Théologie du Péché.* Tournai, Belgium, 1960.

Bracht, H. *Die mündliche Überlieferung.* Munich, 1957.

Brandenburg, A. *Gericht und Evangelium: Zur Worttheologie in Luthers erster Psalmenvorlesung.* Paderborn, 1960.

Bring, R. *Dualismen hos Luther.* Lund, 1929.

————. *Gesetz und Evangelium und der dritte Gebrauch des Gesetzes in der lutherischen Theologie.* Publications of the Luther-Agricola Society in Finland, No. 4, 1943.

————. "Luthersk bibelsyn," in *En bok om bibeln.* Lund, 1947.

————. *Bibelns auktoritet och bibelns bruk.* Lund, 1958.

————. *Att lyda bibeln.* Stockholm, 1961.

Brinkel, K. *Die Lehre Luthers von der fides infantium bei der Kindertaufe.* Berlin, 1958.

Brinktrine, J. *Die Lehre von den heiligen Sakramenten der katholischen Kirche,* I—II. Paderborn, 1961—62.

Brunner, E. *Das Ewige als Zukunft und Gegenwart.* Zurich, 1953.

Brunner, P. "Vom Amt des Bischofs," in *Schriften des Theol. Konvents Augsburgischen Bekenntnisses,* 9. Berlin, 1955.

————. "Die Notwendigkeit des neuen Gehorsams nach dem Augsburgischen Bekenntnis," in KuD 7 (1961).

Brunotte, W. *Das geistliche Amt bei Luther.* Berlin, 1959.

Brunstäd, F. *Theologie der lutherischen Bekenntnisschriften.* Gütersloh, 1951.

Ein, Buch . . . von der Kirche, ed. G. Aulén et al. Leipzig, 1951.

Camelot, P.-Th. "Sacramentum: Notes de théologie sacramentaire augustienne," in RThom 57 (1957).

Carpzov, J. B. *Isagoge in libros ecclesiarum lutheranarum symbolicos.* Leipzig, 1675.

Christenheit, Die evangelische . . . in Deutschland, Stuttgart, 1958.

Clark, F., *Eucharistic Sacrifice and the Reformation.* London, 1960.

Confutation of the Augsburg Confession, in CR 27. Brunswick, 1859.

Congar, Y., "Jalons pour une théologie du laïcat." *Unam Sanctam,* 23. Paris, 2d ed. 1954.

Corpus iuris canonici, I. *Decretum Magistri Gratiani,* ed. A. Friedberg. Leipzig, 1879.

Corpus reformatorum. Philippi Melanchthonis opera quae supersunt omnia, I ff. Halle and Brunswick, 1834 ff.

Corpus scriptorum ecclesiasticorum latinorum, I ff. Vienna, 1866 ff.

Cyprian. See J. P. Migne, *Patrologiae cursus completus . . . series latina.* Paris, 1844 ff.

Delitzsch, F., *Vier Bücher von der Kirche: Seitenstück zu Löhes drei Büchern von der Kirche.* Dresden, 1847.

Denifle, H., *Die abendländischen Schriftausleger bis Luther über Iustitia Dei (Röm. 1, 17) und Iustificatio.* Mainz, 1905.

————. *Luther und Luthertum in der ersten Entwicklung. Quellenmäßig dargestellt,* I, 2. Mainz, 2d ed. 1906.

Denzinger, H., and J. B. Umberg, *Enchiridion Symbolorum definitionum et declarationum de rebus fidei et morum.* Freiburg,. 25th ed. 1943.

Dettloff, W. *Die Lehre von der acceptatio divina bei Johannes Duns Scotus mit besonderer Berücksichtigung der Rechtfertigungslehre.* Were, Westphalia, 1954.

————. *Die Entwicklung der Akzeptations- und Verdienstlehre von Duns Scotus bis Luther mit besonderer Berücksichtigung der Franziskanertheologie.* Munich, 1963.

Dibelius, M. "Die alttestamentlichen Motive in der Leidensgeschichte des Petrus- und des Johannes-Evangeliums," in *Zeitschr. für die alttest. Wissenschaft. Beih.* 33 (1918).

Diekamp, F. *Katholische Dogmatik nach den Grundsätzen des heiligen Thomas. Zum Gebrauch bei Vorlesungen und zum Selbstunterricht,* III. Münster, 1937.

Diestelmann, J. *Konsekration: Luthers Abendmahlsglaube in dogmatisch-liturgischer Sicht an Hand von Quellenauszügen dargestellt.* Berlin, 1960.

Dinkler, E. *Die Anthropologie Augustins.* Stuttgart, 1934.

Ebeling, G. *Evangelische Evangelienauslegung: Eine Untersuchung zu Luthers Hermeneutik.* Munich, 1942.

————. "Zur Lehre von triplex usus legis in der reformatorischen Theologie," in ThLZ 75 (1950).

————. "Die Anfänge von Luthers Hermeneutik," in ZTK 48 (1951).

Ebneter, A. "Luther und das Konzil," in ZKT 84 (1962).

Eck, J. "Vierhundertvier Artikel zum Reichstag von Augsburg 1530," in W. Gussmann, *Quellen und Forschungen zur Geschichte des Augsburgischen Glaubensbekenntnisses.* Kassel, 1930.

Elert, W. *Morphologie des Luthertums,* I—II. Munich, 1931. *The Structure of Lutheranism,* I, trans. Walter A. Hansen. St. Louis: Concordia Publishing House, 1962.

————. "Eine theologische Fälschung zur Lehre vom tertius usus legis," in ZRG 1 (1948).

Engelland, H. *Melanchthon: Glauben und Handeln.* Munich, 1931.

Engeström, S. von. *Luthers trosbegrepp.* Uppsala, 1933.

Die evangelischen Kirchenordnungen . . . des 16. Jahrhunderts, I, ed. E. Sehling. Leipzig, 1902.

Evangelisches Kirchenlexikon: Kirchlich-theologisches Handwörterbuch, ed. H. Brunotte and O. Weber, I—IV. Göttingen, 1956 g.

Fagerberg, H. *Bekenntnis, Kirche und Amt in der deutschen konfessionellen Theologie des 19. Jahrhunderts.* Uppsala, 1952.

————. "Gottfrid Billing och den kyrkliga bekännelsen," in STK 29 (1953).

————. "Anders Nohrborgs teologi: Några synpunkter," in STK 31 (1955).

Feckes, C. "Die Rechtfertigungslehre des Gabriel Biel und ihre Stellung innerhalb der nominalistischen Schule," in *Münsterische Beiträge zur Theologie,* 7. Münster, 1925.

Feuerlin, J. G. *Bibliotheca symbolica evangelica lutherana,* ed. J. B. Riederer. Nuremberg, 1968.

Finkenzeller, J. "Erbsünde und Konkupiszenz nach der Lehre des Johannes Duns Skotus," in *Theologie in Geschichte und Gegenwart: Festschr. für M. Schmaus.* Munich, 1957.

Fraenkel, P. "Revelation and Tradition," in ST 13 (1959).

————. "Ten questions concerning Melanchthon, the Fathers, and the Eucharist," in *Luther and Melanchthon in the History and Theology of the Reformation: Essays and Reports of the Second International Congress for Luther Studies, Münster, Aug. 8—13, 1960,* ed. V. Vajta. Philadelphia, 1961.

————. *Testimonia patrum: The Function of the Patristic Argument in the Theology of Philip Melanchthon.* Geneva, 1961.

Die fränkischen bekenntnisse: Eine Vorstufe der Augsburgischen Konfession, ed. W. F. Schmidt and K. Schornbaum. Munich, 1930.

Fresenius, J. F. *Utförlig afhandling om en arm syndares rättfärdiggörelse inför Gud.* Stockholm, 1763.

Fries, H. "J. H. Newmans Beitrag zum Verständnis der Tradition," in H. Bracht, *Die mündliche Überlieferung*. Munich, 1957.

Geiselmann, J. R. "Das Konzil von Trient über das Verhältnis der Heiligen Schrift und der nicht geschriebenen Traditionen," in H. Bracht, *Die mündliche Überlieferung*. Munich, 1957.

———. *Die Heilige Schrift und die Tradition. Quaestiones disputatae*, 18. Freiburg, 1962.

———. See J. A. Möhler, *Die Einheit in der Kirche*, 1956.

Gennrich, P.-W. *Die Christologie Luthers im Abendmahlsstreit 1524 to 1529*. Königsberg, 1929.

Gensichen, H. W. *Damnamus: Die Verwerfung von Irrlehre bei Luther und im Luthertum des 16. Jahrhunderts. Arbeiten zur Geschichte und Theologie des Luthertums*, 1. Berlin, 1955. *We Condemn: How Luther and 16th-Century Lutheranism Condemned False Doctrine*, trans. Herbert J. A. Bouman. St. Louis, 1967.

Ghellink, J. de. *Pour l'histoir du mot "sacramentum,"* I. Louvain and Paris, 1924.

Gloege, G. "Vom Ethos der Ehescheidung," in *Gedenkschrift für Werner Elert*. Berlin, 1955.

Gollwitzer, H. "Die Abendmahlsfrage als Aufgabe kirchlicher Lehre," in *Theologische Aufsätze für Karl Barth zum 50. Geburtstag*. Munich, 1936.

Grane, L. *Confessio Augustana*. Copenhagen, 1959.

Grass, H. *Die Abendmahlslehre bei Luther und Calvin: Eine kritische Untersuchung. Beiträge zur Förderung christlicher Theologie*, 2. Reihe, 47. Band. Gütersloh, 1954.

Gratian. *Decretum Divi Gratiani universi iuris canonici . . . una cum glossis et thematibus prudentum*. Lyons, 1554.

Gussmann, W. *Quellen und Forschungen zur Geschichte des Augsburgischen Glaubensbekenntnisses*, II. Kassel, 1930.

Gyllenkrok, A. *Rechtfertigung und Heiligung in der frühen evangelischen Theologie Luthers*. AUU (1952), 2. Uppsala, 1952.

———. "Några Synpunkter på lag och evangelium i Luthers teologi," in NKT 22 (1953).

Hägglund, B. *De homine: Människouppfattningen i äldre luthersk tradition. Studia theologica lundensia*, 18. Lund, 1959.

Haendler, K. Review of J. Diestelmann, *Konsekration*, in ThLZ 86 (1961).

Hahn, A. *Bibliothek der Symbole und Glaubensregeln der alten Kirche*. Breslau, 3d ed. 1897.

Hahn, F. "Luthers Auslegungsgrundsätze und ihre theologischen Voraussetzungen," in ZST 12 (1934—35).

Haikola, L. *Gesetz und Evangelium bei Matthias Flacius Illyricus: Eine*

Untersuchung zur lutherischen Theologie vor der Konkordienformel. Lund, 1952.

―――. *Studien zu Luther und zum Luthertum.* AUU (1958), 2. Uppsala, 1958.

―――. *Usus legis.* AUU (1958), 3. Uppsala, 1958.

―――. "Rättfärdiggörelsen i Apologin och Konkordieformeln," in *Studier tillägnade Hj. Lindroth.* Motala, 1958.

Hamel, A. *Der junge Luther und Augustin: Ihre Beziehungen in der Rechtfertigungslehre nach Luthers ersten Vorlesungen 1509—1518 untersucht,* I—II. Gütersloh, 1934—35.

Handbuch theologischer Grundbegriffe, I—II, ed. H. Fries. Würzburg, 1962 to 1963.

Hase, *Handbuch der protestantischen Polemik gegen die römisch-katholische Kirche.* Leipzig, 4th ed. 1878.

Headley, J. M. *Luther's View of Church History.* New Haven, 1963.

Heckel, J. *Initia iuris ecclesiastici protestantium.* Munich, 1950.

―――. *Lex charitatis: Eine juristische Untersuchung über das Recht in der Theologie Martin Luthers.* Abhandl. d. Bayer. Akad. d. Wissenschaften, Phil.-hist. Kl. NF. 36. Munich, 1953.

Herborn, N. *Locorum communium adversus huius temporis haereses enchiridion. Corpus catholicorum,* 12. Münster, 1927.

Hermann, R. *Zum Streit um die Überwindung des Gesetzes: Erörterungen zu Luthers Antinomerthesen.* Weimar, 1958.

Heubach, J. *Die Ordination zum Amt der Kirche.* Berlin, 1956.

Hirsch, E. "Initium theologiae Lutheri," in *Festgabe für Julius Kaftan.* Tübingen, 1920.

―――. *Geschichte der neuern evangelischen Theologie im Zusammenhang mit den allgemeinen Bewegungen des europäischen Denkens,* V. Gütersloh, 1954.

Höfling, J. W. F. *Grundsätze evangelisch-lutherischer Kirchenverfassung.* Erlangen, 3d ed. 1853.

Hök, G. *Herrnhutisk teologi i svensk gestalt.* AUU (1949), 8. Uppsala, 1950.

―――. "Luthers lära om kyrkans ämbete," *En bok om kyrkans ämbete.* Uppsala, 1951.

Hoffmann, G. "Zur Entstehungsgeschichte der Augustana: Der Unterricht der Visitatoren als Vorlage des Bekenntnisses," in ZST 15 (1938).

Hofmann, F. *Der Kirchenbegriff des hl. Augustinus in seinen Grundlagen und in seiner Entwicklung.* Munich, 1933.

Holl, K. *Gesammelte Aufsätze zur Kirchengeschichte,* I—III. Tübingen, 3d ed. 1923—28.

Holte, R. "Skrift och tradition," in *Kyrka, folk, auktoritet.* Stockholm, 1960.

Hus, J. *Tractatus de ecclesia. Historia et monumenta.* Nuremberg, 1558.

Ingebrand, S. *Olavus Petris reformatoriska åskådning.* AUU. *Studia doctrinae christianae upsaliensia,* 1. Uppsala, 1964.

Iserloh, E. *Die Eucharistie in der Darstellung des Johannes Eck: Ein Beitrag zur vortridentinischen Kontroverstheologie über das Messopfer.* Münster, 1950.

―――. *Der Kampf um die Messe in den ersten Jahren der Auseinandersetzung mit Luther. Katholisches Leben und Kämpfen im Zeitalter der Glaubensspaltung,* 10. Münster, 1952.

―――. See P. Meinhold, *Abendmahl und Opfer.* Stuttgart, 1960.

Ivarsson, H. *Predikans uppgift.* Lund, 1956.

Jerome. See J. P. Migne, *Patrologiae cursus completus . . . series latina.* Paris, 1844 ff.

Jervell, J. *Imago Dei. Forsch. z. Rel. u. Lit. d. A. u. N. T. N. F.,* 58. Göttingen, 1960.

Joest W. *Gesetz und Freiheit: Das Problem des tertius usus legis bei Luther und die neutestamentliche Parainese.* Göttingen, 1951.

Josefson, R. *Den naturliga teologins problem hos Luther.* AUU (1943), 4. Uppsala, 1943.

―――. *Luthers lära om dopet.* Stockholm, 1944.

―――. "Det andliga ämbetet i Svenska Kyrkans bekännelseskrifter," in *En bok om kyrkans ämbete.* Uppsala, 1951.

―――. *Bibelns auktoritet.* Uppsala, 1953.

―――. "Christus und die Heilige Schrift," in *Lutherforschung heute.* Berlin, 1958.

―――. "Kyrkosyn och kyrkorätt: Kommentar till bekännelseskrifternas teologi." *Forum theologicum,* 17 (1960).

Kähler, E. *Karlstadt und Augustin: Der Kommentar des Andreas Bodenstein von Karlstadt zu Augustins Schrift De spiritu et litera.* Einführung und Text. *Hallische Monographien,* 19. Halle, 1952.

Kahl, W. "Der Rechtsinhalt des Konkordienbuches," in *Festgabe d. Berliner Jurist. Fakultät f. O. Gierke,* I. Breslau, 1910.

Kamlah, W. *Christentum und Geschichtlichkeit: Untersuchungen zur Entstehung des Christentums und zu Augustins "Bürgerschaft Gottes."* Stuttgart, 2d ed. 1951.

Kantzenbach, F. W. *Das Ringen um die Einheit der Kirche im Jahrhundert der Reformation.* Stuttgart, 1957.

Kattenbusch, F. *Das apostolische Symbol: Seine Entstehung, sein geschichtlicher Sinn, seine ursprüngliche Stellung im Kultus und in der Theologie der Kirche. Ein Beitrag zur Symbolik und Dogmengeschichte,* I—II. Leipzig, 1894—1900.

Kawerau, P. *Melchior Hoffman als religiöser Denker.* Haarlem, 1954.

Kelly, J. N. D. *Early Christian Creeds.* Beccles, England, 1950.

Kinder, E. "Beichte und Absolution nach den lutherischen Bekenntnisschriften," in ThLZ 77 (1952).

————. *Allgemeines Priestertum im Neuen Testament. Schriften des Theol. Konvents Augsb. Bekenntnisses*, 5 (1953).

————. "Luthers Stellung zur Ehescheidung," in *Luther-Mitteilungen der Luthergesellschaft*, 24 (1953).

————. "Der Gebrauch des Begriffs 'ökumenisch' im älteren Luthertum," in KuD 1 (1955).

————. The article "Busse," in EKL, I. Göttingen, 1956.

————. *Der evangelische Glaube und die Kirche*. Berlin, 1958.

————. The article "Rechtfertigung," in RGG, V. Tübingen, 1961.

Kittel, G. *Theologisches Wörterbuch zum Neuen Testament*, III. Stuttgart, 1938.

Klein, L. *Evangelisch-lutherische Beichte. Konfessionskundliche und kontrovers-theologische Studien*, 5. Paderborn, 1961.

Klieforth, Th. *Acht Bücher von der Kirche*, I. Schwerin and Rostock, 1854.

Köhler, W. *Luther und die Kirchengeschichte nach seinen Schriften, zunächst bis 1521*, I, 1. Erlangen, 1900.

Köllner, E. *Symbolik aller christlichen Konfessionen*, I. Hamburg, 1837.

Köstlin, J. *Luthers Theologie in ihrer geschichtlichen Entwicklung und ihrem inneren Zusammenhang*, I—II. Stuttgart, 2d ed. 1901.

Koopmans, J. *Des altkirchliche Dogma in der Reformation*. Munich, 1955.

Kraft, H. The article "Echatologie," in RGG, II. Tübingen, 1958.

Kraus, H. J. *Psalmen*, I—II. Neukirchen, 1958—60.

Lähteenmäki, O. *Sexus und Ehe bei Luther. Schriften der Luther-Agricola-Gesellschaft*, 10. Turku, 1955.

Laemmer, H. *Die vortridentinische katholische Theologie*, 1858.

Larsson, E. *Christus als Vorbild*. Uppsala, 1962.

Lau, F. The article "Beruf," in RGG, I. Tübingen, 1957.

————. The article "Evangelische Räte," in RGG, II. Tübingen, 1958.

————. "Theologie der Schöpfung gleich Theologie überhaupt? Zur Auseinandersetzung mit Löfgrens Luther-Buch," in *Luther-Jahrbuch*, 29 (1962).

Lialine, C. "Ordo och jurisdictio: Prästerlig och konungslig ämbetsmakt enligt romersk-katolsk åskådning," in *En bok om kyrkans ämbete*. Uppsala, 1951.

Lieberg, H. *Amt und Ordination bei Luther und Melanchthon*. Göttingen, 1962.

Lindroth, Hj. *Försoningen: En dogmhistorisk och systematisk undersökning*. AUU (1935), 8. Uppsala, 1935.

————. The article "Rättfärdiggörelse," in NTU, III, 1957.

Lindström, H. *Skapelse och frälsning i Melanchthons teologi*. Stockholm, 1944.

Ljunggren, G. *Synd och skuld i Luthers teologi*. Stockholm, 1928.

Löfgren, D. *Die Theologie der Schöpfung bei Luther. Forschungen zur Kirchen- und Dogmengeschichte*, 10. Göttingen, 1960.

Loewenich, W. von. *Von Augustin zu Luther. Beiträge zur Kirchengeschichte.* Witten, 1959.

Lohse, B. Review of D. Löfgren, *Die Theologie der Schöpfung bei Luther*, 1960, in ThLZ 86 (1961).

Loofs, Fr. "Die Bedeutung der Rechtfertigungslehre der Apologie für die Symbolik der luth. Kirchen," in ThStK (1884).

Luther, M. *D. Martin Luthers Werke.* Kritische Gesamtausgabe. Weimar, 1883 ff.

Lyttkens, H. "Luthers syn på ämbete och allmänt prästadöme," in NKT 27 (1958).

McDonough, Th. M. *The Law and the Gospel in Luther: A Study of Martin Luther's Confessional Writings.* London, 1963.

Marheinecke, Ph. *Christliche Symbolik oder historisch-kritische und dogmatisch-komparative Darstellung der katholischen, lutherischen, reformirten und socinianischen Lehrbegriffe*, I—III. Heidelberg, 1810—13, 2d ed., 1897.

Maurer, W. *Pfarrerrecht und Bekenntnis: Über die bekenntnismässige Grundlage eines Pfarrerrechtes in der evangelisch-lutherischen Kirche.* Berlin, 1957.

Mausbach, J. *Die Ethik des heiligen Augustinus*, I—II. Freiburg, 1909.

Mausbach, J., and G. Ermecke. *Katholische Moraltheologie*, I. Münster, 9th ed. 1959.

Meinhold, P., and E. Iserloh. *Abendmahl und Opfer.* Stuttgart, 1960.

———. *Konzile der Kirche in evangelischer Sicht.* Stuttgart, 1962.

Melanchthon, Ph. *Corpus reformatorum: Philippi Melanchthonis opera quae supersunt omnia*, I ff. Halle and Brunswick, 1834 ff.

Meyer, J. *Grosser Katechismus. Quellenschriften zur Geschichte des Protestantismus*, 12 (1914).

———. "Luthers Dekalogerklärung 1528 unter dem Einfluss der "sächsischen Kirchenvisitation," in *Neue kirchliche Zeitschrift*, 26 (1915).

———. *Historischer Kommentar zu Luthers Kleinem Katechismus.* Gütersloh, 1929.

Migne, J. P. *Patrologiae cursus completus . . . series latina.* Paris, 1844 ff.

Mirbt, C. *Quellen zur Geschichte des Papsttums und des römischen Katholizismus.* Tübingen, 4th ed. 1924.

Modalsli, O. *Das Gericht nach den Werken: Beitrag zu Luthers Gesetzbegriff.* Gottingen, 1963.

Möhler, J. A. *Symbolik oder Darstellung der dogmatischen Gegensätze der Katholiken und Protestanten, nach ihren öffentlichen Bekenntnisschriften.* Mainz, 4th ed., 1835.

———. *Die Einheit in der Kirche oder das Prinzip des Katholizismus dar-*

gestellt im Geiste der Kirchenväter der drei ersten Jahrhunderte, ed., with introduction and commentary, by J. R. Geiselmann. Cologne and Olten, 1956.

Mohrmann, Christine. "Sacramentum dans les plus anciens textes chrétiens," in *The Harvard Theological Review,* 47 (1954).

Murphy J. L. *The Notion of Tradition in John Driedo.* Milwaukee, 1959.

Nagel, W. E. *Luthers Anteil an der Confessio Augustana: Eine historische Untersuchung. Beiträge zur Förderung christlicher Theologie,* 34. Gütersloh, 1930.

Nicolaus von Lyra. *Biblia cum postillis Nicolai de Lyra et expositionibus Guillelmi Britonis in omnes prologos S. Hieronymi et additionibus Pauli Burgensis replicisque Matthiae Doering.* Nuremberg: Anton Koberger, 7 Mai 1485. GW 4288 — Hain 3166.

Nohrborg, A. *Den fallna människans salighetsordning föreställd uti betraktelser öfwer de årliga sön- och högtidsdagars evangelier.* Stockholm, 1771.

Nygren, A. *Eros und Agape: Gestaltwandlungen der christlichen Liebe,* II. 1937.

————. "Simul justus et peccator hos Augustinus och Luther," in *Filosofi och motivforskning.* Lund, 1940.

————. The article "Evangelium," in NTU, I (1952).

————. "Kyrkans enhet: Till frågan om kyrko- och nattvardsgemenskap," in STK 33 (1957).

Oberman, H. A. *The Harvest of Medieval Theology: Gabriel Biel and Late Medieval Nominalism.* Cambridge, Mass., 1963.

Olsson, H. *Grundproblemet i Luthers socialetik,* I. Lund, 1934.

————. "Förhållandet mellan Melanchthons teologi och Luthers," in STK 20 (1944).

————. "Den naturliga gudskunskapens problem enlight den senmedeltida nominalismen," in STK 26 (1950).

Ott, L. *Grundriss der katholischen Dogmatik.* Freiburg, 2d ed. 1957.

Paulus, N. "Zur Geschichte des Wortes Beruf," in *Historisches Jahrbuch der Gorres-Gesellschaft,* 45 (1925).

Pedersen, E. Th. *Luther som skriftfortolker,* I. *En studie i Luthers skriftsyn, hermeneutik och exegese.* Copenhagen, 1959.

————. "Troen og sakramentet: Non sacramentum, sed fides sacramenti iustificat," in *Festschr. für K. E. Skydsgaard.* Copenhagen, 1962.

Persson, P. E. *Kyrkans ämbete som Kristusrepresentation. Studia theologica lundensia,* 20. Lund, 1961.

————. "Öst och väst i teologien," in STK 39 (1963).

Peters, A. *Glaube und Werk: Luthers Rechtfertigungslehre im Lichte der Heiligen Schrift.* Berlin, 1962.

————. *Realpräsenz: Luthers Zeugnis von Christi Gegenwart im Abendmahl.* Berlin, 1960.

Petri L. *Laurentius Petris Kyrkoordning av år 1571.* Uppsala, 1932.

Pinomaa, L. *Sieg des Glaubens: Grundlinien der Theologie Luthers.* Göttingen, 1964.

Planck, G. J. *Abriss einer historischen und vergleichenden Darstellung der dogmatischen Systeme unserer verschiedenen christlichen Hauptparteien nach ihren Grundbegriffen, ihren daraus abgeleiteten Unterscheidungslehren und ihren praktischen Folgen.* Göttingen, 4th ed. 1804.

Pleijel, H. *De lutherska bekännelseskrifterna.* Lund, 1936.

————. *Vår kyrkas bekännelse.* Malmö, 1941.

————. "Die schwedische Kirche und das Bekenntnis während des letzten halben Jahrhunderts," in *Ein Buch von der Kirche.* Leipzig, 1951.

Plitt, G. *Einleitung in die Augustana,* I—II. Erlangen, 1867—68.

Polman, P. *L'élément historique dans la controverse religieuse du XVI siècle.* Gembloux, 1932.

Poschmann, B. *Poenitentia secunda.* Bonn, 1940.

Prenter, R. *Spiritus Creator.* Copenhagen, 2d ed. 1946. German ed.: Munich, 1954.

————. "A Lutheran Contribution," in *Biblical Authority for Today.* London, 1951.

————. "Das Augsburgische Bekenntnis und die römische Messopferlehre," in KuD (1955).

————. "Luthers Lehre von der Heiligung," in *Luthersforschung heute.* Berlin, 1958.

————. *Embedets guddommelige indstiftelse og det almindelige praestedomme hos Luther.* AUU (1960), 12. Uppsala, 1961.

————. *Der barmherzige Richter: Iustitia dei passiva in Luthers Dictata super Psalterium 1513—1515.* Copenhagen, 1961.

————. "Die göttliche Einsetzung des Predigamtes und das allgemeine Priestertum bei Luther," in ThLZ 86 (1961).

Preuss, H. "Was bedeutet die Formel 'Convictus testimoniis scripturarum aut ratione evidente' in Luthers ungehörnter Antwort zu Worms?" in ThStK 81 (1908).

Rad, G. von. *Theologie des Alten Testaments. Einführung in die evangelische Theologie,* I. Munich, 1957.

Rahner, H. "Antenna crucis VI: Der Schiffbruch und die Planke des Heils," in ZKT 79 (1957).

Ratzinger, J. *Volk und Haus Gottes in Augustins Lehre von der Kirche. Münchener Theologische Studien,* II, 7. Munich, 1954.

Reicke, S. "Geschichtliche Grundlagen des Deutschen Eheschliessungsrechts," in GF 6. Gelsenkirchen, 1953.

Die Religion in Geschichte und Gegenwart: Handwörterbuch für Theologie und Religionswissenschaft, I—VI, ed. K. Galling. Tübingen, 1957 ff.

Rietschel, G. *Luther und die Ordination.* Wittenberg, 2d ed. 1889.

Ritschl, A. *Die christliche Lehre von der Rechtfertigung und Versöhnung*, I. Bonn, 2d. ed. 1882.

Ritschl, O. *Dogmengeschichte des Protestantismus*, I. Leipzig, 1908

————. "Der doppelte Rechtfertigungsbegriff in der Apologie der Augsburgischen Konfession," in ZThK 20 (1910).

Roth E. *Die Privatbeichte und die Schlüsselgewalt in der Theologie der Reformation*. Gütersloh, 1952.

Rückert, H. "Die Weimarer Lutherausgabe: Stand, Aufgaben und Probleme," in *Lutherforschung heute*. Berlin, 1958.

Runestam, A. *Viljans frihet och den kristliga friheten: En undersökning i Luthers teologi*. Uppsala, 1921.

Sägmüller, J. B. *Lehrbuch des katholischen Kirchenrechts*, I, 1—2. Freiburg, 1925—26.

Sasse, H. *This Is My Body. Luther's Contention for the Real Presence of the Sacrament of the Altar*. Minneapolis, 1959.

Scheel, O. *Martin Luther. Vom Katholizismus zur Reformation*, II. Im Kloster. Tübingen, 4th ed. 1930.

Schlink, E. *Theologie der Lutherischen Bekenntnisschriften*. Munich, 3d ed. 1948. *Theology of the Lutheran Confessions*, trans. Paul F. Koehneke and Herbert J. A. Bouman. Philadelphia, 1961.

————. "Das theologische Problem des Naturrechts," in *Viva vox evangelii: Festschr. für H. Meiser*. Munich, 1951.

————. "Gesetz und Paraklese: Antwort." *Festschrift für Karl Barth*. Zürich, 1956.

Schmaus, M. *Von den Letzten Dingen*. Münster, 1948.

Schmid, H. *Die Dogmatik der evangelisch-lutherischen Kirche dargestellt und aus den Quellen belegt*. Erlangen, 1843.

Schmidt, F. W. See *Die fränkischen Bekenntnisse*. Munich, 1930.

Schneckenburger, H. *Vergleichende Darstellung des lutherischen und reformierten Lehrbegriffs*, I—II. Stuttgart, 1855.

Schumann, F. K. *Um Kirche und Lehre: Gesammelte Aufsätze und Vorträge*. Stuttgart, 1936.

————. "Zur systematischen Erwägung der Fragen des Eheschliessungsrechts," in GF 8. Essen, 1955.

————. "Die Kirchen der Reformation," in *Die evangelische Christenheit in Deutschland*. Stuttgart, 1958.

Seeberg, R. *Lehrbuch der Dogmengeschichte*, III and IV, 2. Leipzig, 1930 and 1920.

Siebeck, H. *Geschichte der Psychologie*, I, 2. Gotha, 1884.

Siirala, A. *Gottes Gebot bei Martin Luther*. Helsinki, 1956.

Silén, S. *Den kristna människouppfattningen intill Schleiermacher*. Uppsala, 1938.

Skydsgaard, K. E. "Kristus, traditionens Herre," in *Kristen gemenskap* 25 (1952).

———. "Schrift und Tradition," in KuD 1 (1955).

Sohm, R. *Kirchenrecht*, I. Leipzig, 1892.

Sperl, A. "Zur Geschichte des Begriffes 'Tradition' in der evangelischen Theologie," in *Das Wort Gottes in Geschichte und Gegenwart: Theologische Aufsätze* . . . , ed. W. Andersen. Munich, 1957.

Stahl, F. J. *Die Kirchenverfassung nach Lehre und Recht der Protestanten.* Erlangen, 2d ed. 1862.

Sundby, O. *Luthersk äktenskapsuppfattning.* Lund, 1959.

Tappert, Th., et al., ed. and trans. *The Book of Concord: The Confessions of the Evangelical Lutheran Church.* Philadelphia, 1959.

Thielicke, H. "Jus divinum und jus humanum," in *Ecclesia und Res Publica. Festschr. für K. D. Schmidt.* Göttingen, 1961.

Thomas of Aquinas. *Sancti Thomae Aquinitatis opera omnia iussu impensaque Leonis XIII*, IV ff. Rome, 1888 ff.

———. *Die deutsche Thomas-Ausgabe: Vollständige, ungekürzte deutschlateinische Ausgabe der Summa Theologica*, I ff., 1933 ff.

Thomasius, G. *Die Dogmengeschichte als Entwicklungsgeschichte des kirchlichen Lehrbegriffs*, I—II. Erlangen, 1874—76.

Tottie, H. W. *Evangelistik.* Uppsala, 1892.

Troeltsch, E. "Protestantisches Christentum und Kirche in der Neuzeit," in *Die Kultur der Gegenwart*, I, 1., Abt. IV, 1. Berlin and Leipzig, 1909.

Trusen, W. *Um die Reform und Einheit der Kirche: Zum Leben und Werk Georg Witzels.* Münster, 1957.

Tschackert, P. *Die Entstehung der lutherischen und reformierten Kirchenlehre samt ihren innerprotestantischen Gegensätzen.* Göttingen, 1910.

Vajta, V. *Die Theologie des Gottesdienstes bei Luther.* Lund, 1952. *Luther on Worship*, trans. and condensed by U. S. Leupold. Philadelphia, 1958.

———. "Den kristna friheten och kyrkans enhet," in STK 33 (1957).

Vilmar, A. F. C. *Die Lehre vom geistlichen Amt.* Marburg and Leipzig, 1870.

———. *Kirche und Welt oder die Aufgaben des geistlichen Amts in unserer Zeit. Zur Signatur der Gegenwart und Zukunft*, I. Gütersloh, 1872.

———. *Dogmatik*, I—II. Ed. K. W. Piderit. Gütersloh, 1874.

Vogelsang, E. *Die Anfänge von Luthers Christologie nach der ersten Psalmenvorlesung. Arbeiten zur Kirchengeschichte*, 15. Berlin and Leipzig, 1929.

Volk, H. "Die Lehre von der Rechtfertigung nach den Bekenntnisschriften der evangelisch-lutherischen Kirche," in *Pro veritate: Ein theologischer Dialog. Festgabe für L. Jaeger und W. Stählin.* Münster, 1963.

Weber, H. E. *Reformation, Orthodoxie und Rationalismus,* I, 1. *Beiträge zur Förderung christlicher Theologie,* 2. Reihe, Band 35 (1937).

Werkström, B. "Bekännelse och avlösning," in *Studia theologica lundensia,* 24. Lund, 1963.

Winer, G. B. *Comparative Darstellung des Lehrbegriffs der verschiedenen Christlichen Kirchenparteien.* Leipzig, 2d. ed. 1882.

Wingren, G. *Luthers Lehre von Beruf. Forschungen zur Geschichte und Lehre des Protestantismus,* 10. Reihe, Band 3. Munich, 1952. *The Christian's Calling: Luther on Vocation,* trans. Carl C. Rasmussen. Edinburgh and London, 1958.

———. *Die Predigt.* Göttingen, 1955.

———. *Kyrkans ämbete.* Malmö, 1958.

———. *Evangelium und Kirche.* Göttingen, 1963. *Gospel and Church,* trans. Ross Mackenzie. Philadelphia, 1964.

Winklhofer, A. The article "Eschatologie," in *Handbuch theologischer Grundbegriffe.* Stuttgart, 1962.

Wittram, H. *Die Kirche bei Theodosius Harnack. Ekklesiologie und prakt. Theologie. Arbeiten zur Pastoraltheologie,* 2. Göttingen, 1963.

Zahn, Th. *Das apostolische Symbolum.* Erlangen and Leipzig, 1893.

	DATE DUE	
JAN 26 1988	OCT 17 2005	
DEC 16 1992	DEC 19 2005	
NOV 19 1994	JAN 02 2013	
DEC 3 1994		
DEC 16 1994		
OCT 22 1996		
DEC 18 1997		
DEC 07 1999		
DEC 18 1999		
NOV 21 2000		
DEC 01 2003		